## WERTHEIM PUBLICATIONS IN INDUSTRIAL RELATIONS

Established in 1923 by the family of the late Jacob Wertheim "for the support of original research in the field of industrial cooperation. . . ."

R. E. Livernash      Samuel A. Stouffer
B. M. Selekman    John T. Dunlop, *Chairman*

# Wertheim Publications in Industrial Relations

J. D. Houser, *What the Employer Thinks,* 1927

*Wertheim Lectures on Industrial Relations,* 1929

William Haber, *Industrial Relations in the Building Industry,* 1930

Johnson O'Connor, *Psychometrics,* 1934

Paul H. Norgren, *The Swedish Collective Bargaining System,* 1941

Leo C. Brown, S.J., *Union Policies in the Leather Industry,* 1947

Walter Galenson, *Labor in Norway,* 1949

Dorothea de Schweinitz, *Labor and Management in a Common Enterprise,* 1949

Ralph Altman, *Availability for Work: A Study in Unemployment Compensation,* 1950

John T. Dunlop and Arthur D. Hill, *The Wage Adjustment Board: Wartime Stabilization in the Building and Construction Industry,* 1950

Walter Galenson, *The Danish System of Labor Relations: A Study in Industrial Peace,* 1952

Lloyd H. Fisher, *The Harvest Labor Market in California,* 1953

Theodore V. Purcell, S.J., *The Worker Speaks His Mind on Company and Union,* 1953

Donald J. White, *The New England Fishing Industry,* 1954

Val R. Lorwin, *The French Labor Movement,* 1954

Philip Taft, *The Structure and Government of Labor Unions,* 1954

George B. Baldwin, *Beyond Nationalization: The Labor Problems of British Coal,* 1955

Kenneth F. Walker, *Industrial Relations in Australia,* 1956

Charles A. Myers, *Labor Problems in the Industrialization of India,* 1958

Herbert J. Spiro, *The Politics of German Codetermination,* 1958

Mark W. Leiserson, *Wages and Economic Control in Norway, 1945–1947,* 1959

J. Pen, *The Wage Rate under Collective Bargaining,* 1959

Jack Stieber, *The Steel Industry Wage Structure,* 1959

Theodore V. Purcell, S.J., *Blue Collar Man: Patterns of Dual Allegiance in Industry,* 1960

STUDIES IN LABOR–MANAGEMENT HISTORY

Lloyd Ulman, *The Rise of the National Trade Union: The Development and Significance of Its Structure, Governing Institutions, and Economic Policies,* 1955

Joseph P. Goldberg, *The Maritime Story: A Study in Labor-Management Relations,* 1957, 1958

Walter Galenson, *The CIO Challenge to the AFL: A History of the American Labor Movement, 1935–1941,* 1960

Morris A. Horowitz, *The New York Hotel Industry: A Labor Relations Study,* 1960.

# BLUE COLLAR MAN

*Patterns of Dual Allegiance in Industry*

## Theodore V. Purcell

HARVARD UNIVERSITY PRESS
Cambridge, Massachusetts    1960

HD
8039
P152
U57

© 1960 by the President and Fellows of Harvard College

All rights reserved

Distributed in Great Britain by Oxford University Press, London

Library of Congress Catalog Card Number 60-10041

Printed in the United States of America

*To The*
*Packinghouse Workers of America*
*Unionists and Employees*

To The

Washington Workers of Industry

Laborer and Employer

# Foreword by Ross Stagner

The impressive economic accomplishments of Western civilization have been made possible by bringing large numbers of workers into a productive relationship with a complex technology. The significance of this development, as regards the individual caught up in this system of mass production, has largely been ignored by scholars. It has been rather easy to focus attention on our remarkable advances in productive machinery, or to concentrate on management and union as organizations, or to write of human relations problems in terms of an armchair conception of worker psychology.

Fortunately, this situation is changing. It has become apparent that, if we wish to understand the human foundations of our industrial civilization, research must be done on the people at the bottom of this pyramid — the workers in the mass-production industries. This is a tedious job. Mass-production factories have masses of employees. Big unions have great numbers of members. To get to these men and women, to induce them to reveal their feelings about the complex environment within which they function, and to search this vast haystack of data for the needle of interpretive significance, is a task calling for patience, intelligence, and ingenuity.

Scholars concerned with the behavior of human beings in a social setting are therefore deeply indebted to Father Purcell for his painstaking investigations of the packing-house workers, as reported first in *The Worker Speaks His Mind* and now in *Blue Collar Man*. In both instances he has listened carefully and sensitively to hundreds of men and women, who have described to the best of their abilities the work environment as each experiences it. He has then sifted these reports methodically to find those uniformities in perception and evaluation which provide the basis for scientific analysis.

The theme of both books has been that the worker in general develops dual allegiance, that is, he approves of and supports both his company and his union. That dual allegiance in the mass-production industries is the rule rather than the exception seems adequately proven, not only by Father Purcell's own data, but also by numerous other investigators. That conflict situations may prevent such dual allegiance is clear in his material, as it is in some other studies.

The concept of dual allegiance is distasteful to some scholars in this area. Their rejection seems based largely on a tendency to rely on logic rather than on psychology, or to use any exception as a basis for discarding the major tendency in the data. Partisans of either management or union may assert that it is illogical for workers to prefer a state of dual allegiance; but in his innocence of logic, the worker reveals a profound psychological truth. Living within a social organization, each man must come to terms with the institutions which make up that organization. Different institutions have different functions: the family, the school, the church, and industry are examples. On occasion the demands of one's family may come into conflict with the demands of the church; the individual must now choose one or the other, whereas normally his preference is to maintain loyalty to both.

In modern industry the worker must relate himself to two major institutions: the management and the union. He perceives them as existing within the same environmental context; often he experiences them as parts of an integrated whole. He receives need-satisfactions from both. In the normal course of events he probably will be frustrated by or unhappy with some aspects of each organization.

The armchair theorist would have it that the worker must choose one organization and reject the other. Either he should try to maximize personal advantage by rising within the company, or he should follow group interest and identify with the union. As long as no one bothered to ask the worker, it was easy to assume that he behaved in accordance with these neat, logical principles. Studies of the union-management relationship which went no deeper than corporation executives and union officials could ignore the realities of worker psychology. But as soon as investigators began to explore the problem at its proper level — in the rank and file of the mass-production factory — it became clear that the theory of unilateral loyalty had to be replaced by a more complex formulation taking account of the phenomena of overlapping membership and multiple allegiances.

We need not conclude, however, that there is a fundamental conflict between the facts uncovered by Father Purcell's interviews and those recorded in earlier studies of union and management leaders. Father Purcell's data indicate a relatively high proportion of unilateral loyalty among persons occupying official roles within either organization. It seems safe to assume that, at higher levels than those covered in his research, unilateral allegiance would be the rule, with few exceptions indeed. Such an assumption would account for the widespread belief, among top union and management executives, that dual allegiance is impossible.

The world as experienced by the worker is, of course, subject also to the laws of economics, sociology, and technology. Father Purcell does surprisingly well at playing the roles of sociologist and economist along with his work as psychologist.

# FOREWORD

The significant contribution of this book will be found in the penetrating insights into the thought and feeling of the mass-production worker. Employers and union leaders alike have often been baffled by the failure of the worker to behave as predicted. They have not understood that the worker behaves in accordance with reality *as he experiences it* — not as defined by the logic of Karl Marx or Adam Smith. Once we become familiar with the world in which the worker lives, we find that his actions are perfectly reasonable.

Father Purcell apparently takes the stand adopted by most of the people he interviewed, that both employer and union are necessary parts of industrial reality. I think, too, that he has no illusions about the complete abolition of union-management conflict. His research, however, represents a major step toward minimizing the more savage aspects of such conflicts. Improved understanding of the psychological realities here portrayed must precede laws and other efforts to bring about industrial peace.

# Foreword by Peter F. Drucker

Were I in charge of industrial relations in an American company — unionized or not — I would want my management associates to read this book. They would learn more about the worker, his world, and his union than in any other book I could find, and even the managers who themselves came out of the shop would be reminded what it is to be a "blue collar man." Above all, reading this book would clear away many misconceptions.

The production workers are revealed by Father Purcell as human beings instead of the statistical abstractions that most management men and many sociologists and industrial relations people see in their mind's eye when they say "worker." Further, our readers will find that workers are human beings who do not ever "like" everything, nor do they completely "dislike" everything. They discriminate. They are never "satisfied" but also seldom totally "dissatisfied." They judge.

What they like and dislike, what satisfies them and what alienates them, are exactly the conditions, actions, and experiences that please or displease other Americans, including executives. By and large, the conditions in the plant about which Father Purcell's blue collar workers complain are exactly the things management people themselves know to be wrong; the conditions that please them, exactly the things an intelligent management strives for.

The second idea I would expect my associates to get out of this book is the realization that the blue collar man knows a great deal: about the plant and its people, the industry, its products and problems, the community and society in which he lives. But he values different aspects of the same reality.

That the company has to make money to stay in business, he knows; and he need not be told that making a profit is not automatic. But this is to him a restraint, a necessary, imposed limitation; it is not something desirable or good in itself. He knows that his job depends on the firm's remaining competitive. But he does not see its success as a benefit to him, although its failure is a threat. The blue collar man (and I suspect that to be true for most white collar workers, too) is not, in other words, economically illiterate. And all the "economic education programs" which, a few short years ago, were the vogue miss the mark. He is a fairly knowledgeable adult who, for instance, does not have to be shown the value of a dollar. But his relationship to the economy is different from that of the executive or economist. And rather than try the dubious job of "educating" him politically or economically, managers might be well advised to try to educate themselves: what are the values, what is the *Gestalt* of the employee's economy and society? It is not only that these determine his behavior. It is also that they are more nearly the values of the great majority — and perhaps even more real and relevant.

My management associates could learn from this book what a union really is, what union leaders are and how they think, work, and become effective — all things as alien to most managers as life in a Tibetan monastery. I would also hope that the more perceptive among our readers will realize that their own life, work, and rationale, the "common sense" of the manager, must be mysterious to union leaders (especially local leaders) and to workers. It is not, I believe, an accident that in all the hundreds of talks with workers and foremen Father Purcell records, not one referred to higher management except occasionally as a mysterious "they" who act no one knows how or why.

Finally, I would expect my management associates to put down this book with a very disquieting question: are we in management about to create a new and infinitely worse race problem? Father Purcell has chosen as his field the meat packing industry, one with the largest proportion of colored workers. His study, though not focused this way, thus becomes a report on the Negro in industrial America and in the plant community. It shows clearly that we face a major problem: the denial of opportunities for advancement to the educated Negro.

Increasingly our unskilled and semiskilled workers in this country will be members of minority races — Negro or Puerto Rican — over the next ten years. Increasingly they will be young and highly educated people — educated not only way above their predecessors with their two or three years of grade school, but far beyond any demands of the job. In the factory we therefore face in this country the great challenge of the rising tide of expectations of the world's underprivileged and underdeveloped peoples.

Here is a major challenge to American managers and a major opportunity: to give the Negro the first-class citizenship in the plant which he is now slowly gaining in the eyes of the law. Enlightened self-interest alone should make management work toward this goal even harder than the Negro leaders do: otherwise the "dual allegiance" to management and union, which is the theme of this book, will turn into vindictive and demagogic unionism as the intelligent and educated among the Negro workers are forced to find in the union the chance to be effective that is denied to them in the plant.

I said that I would want my associates in management to read this book.

For this book not only reports on one of the most careful and best defined research efforts in the social sciences, but it does so in a language rarely written by the social scientist, made even more readable by the vivid personality, the unmistakable aliveness of Father Purcell's "characters," the men and women in the three meat packing plants he studied, young and old, intelligent and slow-witted, gay or bitter — all real people despite their anonymity, all speaking in the language of this country, its aspirations, its experiences, and its shared destiny. Father Purcell — a Ph.D., a professor, and a very learned man — will probably not think it a compliment; nor, I am afraid, will the learned members of the Wertheim Committee. But to me and to most management readers, it is very great praise that his book, which is as relevant as any factual report, is also as readable as a Balzac novel.

## Contents

| | |
|---|---|
| Foreword by Ross Stagner | vii |
| Foreword by Peter F. Drucker | x |
| Author's Preface | xvii |

### PART ONE. HIS DUAL WORLD

| | |
|---|---|
| Chapter I. Workers' Tale of Three Cities — A Comparison | 3 |
| Chapter II. Plants and Unions | 11 |
| Chapter III. Neighborhoods and Packinghouse Workers | 41 |

### PART TWO. HIS ROLE AS EMPLOYEE

| | |
|---|---|
| Chapter IV. The Worker Looks at His Company | 59 |
| Chapter V. Foreman and Worker | 81 |
| Chapter VI. Five Aspects of the Job | 98 |
| Chapter VII. The Chance to Get Ahead | 119 |
| Chapter VIII. Problems of Wage Incentives | 137 |
| Chapter IX. Aspirations for His Children | 153 |

### PART THREE. HIS ROLE AS UNIONIST

| | |
|---|---|
| Chapter X. The Worker Looks at His Union | 167 |
| Chapter XI. Union Member and Union Leader | 185 |
| Chapter XII. Grievances | 200 |
| Chapter XIII. Patterns of Rank-and-File Union Participation | 210 |

### PART FOUR. HIS ACTIONS AND REACTIONS

| | |
|---|---|
| Chapter XIV. Strikes and Allegiance | 221 |
| Chapter XV. Three Patterns of Dual Allegiance | 248 |
| Appendixes | |
| I. Statistical Tables | 265 |
| II. The Nonparametric Statistics and the Joint-Median Test Used in This Research | 276 |
| III. Intercomparisons of Company and Union Allegiance and of All Other Attitudes | 278 |
| Notes | 283 |
| Index | 289 |

## Tables

1. Key characteristics of the three plants: Chicago, Kansas City, East St. Louis. — 15
2. Trend in Local 28 membership, 1946–1959. — 18
3. UPWA raids on Local 12, 1943–1959. — 21
4. Trend in Local 12 membership, 1953–1958. — 22
5. Trend in Local 78 membership, 1953–1958. — 25
6. Key characteristics of the three local unions. — 27
7. Neighborhoods of East St. Louis workers. — 45
8. Workers' comparative service profile. — 48
9. Workers' comparative education. — 49
10. Workers' comparative ages. — 50
11. Workers' comparative skills. — 50
12. Comparative geographic origin of male, colored workers in Chicago, Kansas City, East St. Louis. — 51
13. Workers' comparative turnover. — 52
14. Workers' estimated comparative absenteeism. — 53
15. Comparative wage assignments of workers in Chicago, 1949–50; East St. Louis, 1953. — 54
16. Summary of company-related attitudes. — 61
17. Percentages of Kansas City packinghouse workers favoring the UPWA–CIO. — 65
18. Employees with company disallegiance, Swift Kansas City, 1953. — 71
19. Workers who leave Swift, 1953. — 73
20. The company allegiance of 11 CIO leaders, Swift Kansas City, 1953. — 75
21. Three-plant company allegiances of the foremen. — 78
22. Foremen background data. — 86
23. Foremen's attitudes toward their gangs. — 91
24. Comparison of white foremen's attitudes to colored and white workers. — 93
25. Foremen's merit ratings of their interviewed workers. — 94
26. Estimated average annual gross income, 1952 (Chicago, 1949). — 110
27. Departmental comparison relating output with other variables in five major departments in Kansas City Swift plant, 1953. — 146
28. Departmental comparison relating output with other variables in eleven major departments in East St. Louis Swift plant, 1953–1954. — 147

# TABLES

| | |
|---|---|
| 29. Ten company-related attitudes : a three-plant ranking. | 163 |
| 30. Summary of union-related attitudes. | 168 |
| 31. What the union means to the East St. Louis Swift-Local 78 workers, 1953–1954. | 174 |
| 32. The foremen's union endorsement. | 177 |
| 33. Third-step grievances, 1954. | 206 |
| 34. Comparative steps of grievance adjustment. | 208 |
| 35. Percentage of workers unionized, 1950–1958. | 213 |
| 36. Percentage of membership voting in annual or biennial elections of officers, 1947–1958. | 214 |
| 37. Nine union-related attitudes: a three-local ranking. | 216 |
| 38. Dual allegiance (I). | 253 |
| 39. Dual allegiance (II). | 257 |

## Appendix Tables

| | |
|---|---|
| I. Attitudes toward the company. | 265 |
| II. Attitudes toward the foremen. | 266 |
| III. Attitudes toward the job. | 267 |
| IV. Attitudes toward the gang. | 267 |
| V. Attitudes toward pay. | 268 |
| VI. Attitudes toward working conditions. | 268 |
| VII. Attitudes toward the suggestion system. | 269 |
| VIII. Attitudes toward advancement. | 269 |
| IX. Attitudes toward equal opportunity. | 270 |
| X. Attitudes toward the Standards System. | 270 |
| XI. Percentages of workers on various types of standards application. | 271 |
| XII. Attitudes toward having their children work at the packinghouse. | 271 |
| XIII. Attitudes of union allegiance. | 272 |
| XIV. Attitudes toward Employee Representation Plan. | 272 |
| XV. Attitudes toward the union shop. | 273 |
| XVI. Attitudes toward union leaders. | 273 |
| XVII. Attitudes toward the UPWA–CIO. | 274 |
| XVIII. Attitudes toward grievance handling. | 274 |
| XIX. Attitudes toward the stewards. | 275 |
| XX. Packinghouse workers' union participation. | 275 |
| XXI. Relative attitude comparisons: percentage levels of significance for median test between pairs of attitudes, 1. Chicago; 2. Kansas City; 3. East St. Louis. | 279 |

# Illustrations

(following page 238)

Father Purcell and four workers.

The Chicago Armour plant.

The Wilson, N. C., Swift plant.

Automation in the meat packing industry.

Electric cutter on the hog dressing line.

Automatic hide removing machine.

Beef branders.

The 1956 packinghouse workers' strike.

The 1959 strike.

The 1959 strike.

Swift and UPWA-Amalgamated teams in 1959 negotiations.

Rank-and-file packinghouse workers.

# Author's Preface

On the banks of the Kaw River before it sweeps into the Missouri, rises a jumble of factory buildings, the Kansas City plant of Swift & Company, the meat packer. Here also is Local 12 of the National Brotherhood of Packinghouse Workers' Union. Miles to the east, across the wide Mississippi from St. Louis, the National Stockyards Swift plant juts out of the marshy prairie. Here Local 78 of the Amalgamated Meat Cutters Union represents the workers. To the north, on Chicago's southwest side, in mile-square Packingtown, stands the Chicago Swift plant and Local 28 of the United Packinghouse Workers. The men and women working in these three plants and belonging to these three unions are, I would like to think, the ultimate tellers of this story.

The typical American factory worker belongs to two partly overlapping work societies, his company plant and his local union. Because these two organizations have different goals, there is built-in conflict within the local plant itself. In spite of this conflict, we found, in *The Worker Speaks His Mind on Company and Union*, that the Chicago packinghouse workers wanted both company and union to live and let live. We found that they had "dual allegiance" to their company and their union. They did not feel that their allegiance or approval was like a cake, that company and union divide, so that one side's gain would mean the other side's loss.

This dual allegiance finding, along with similar findings of other research, has attracted some attention. People came to see that American factory workers, although mostly unionized, were not necessarily antimanagement. Others were interested to learn that workers might sincerely support the union movement though not always participating actively in it. A small number felt that the finding of dual allegiance was flatly obvious, scarcely meaningful, or even completely false.

Certainly the concept of dual allegiance needed clarification, especially regarding strike behavior and other company and union attitudes. I shall attempt this clarification especially in the four chapters on company allegiance, union allegiance, strikes, and finally on dual allegiance. This book explores the packinghouse workers' many company-related and union-related attitudes and feelings, but our unifying theme is the workers' dual allegiance or, as some call it, their dual loyalty.

I thank those whose grants made possible this rather expensive type of research: the Rockefeller Foundation, Swift & Company, the Amalgamated Meat Cutters and Butcher Workmen, the Loyola University Press, at whose Jesuit House of Writers as a Canisius Fellow I spent a pleasant year writing this book, and The Wertheim Foundation which assisted with publication.

The generous cooperation and trust of the Amalgamated Meat Cutters, the National Brotherhood of Packinghouse Workers and the United Packinghouse Workers of America, together with that of Swift & Company, made a bilateral, union-management research project like this possible.

To my many friends, some of more than ten years' standing, in the three unions and in the company, I express my gratitude for their help toward my achieving greater objectivity in the controversy-staked area of industrial relations.

My colleagues, too, have furthered this book with their challenging but friendly criticisms, especially Peter F. Drucker, Ross Stagner, Gordon W. Allport, John T. Dunlop, Bernard Karsh, Joel Seidman, and Dale Yoder. Of course none of the institutions or people I mention is responsible for my findings. To the staff of our Research Group on Human Relations in the Meat Packing Industry, and to my Research Associate, Francis X. Paone, I owe a debt for imaginative and stimulating analysis of a great mass of data.

Finally I must mention the rank-and-file packinghouse workers of Chicago, Kansas City, and East St. Louis, of whom I can quote but a fraction in this book. I thank these men and women for their confidence and their willingness to tell through me the interesting story of their work life.

Chicago
June 1960

Theodore V. Purcell

PART ONE

His Dual World

CHAPTER I

*Workers' Tale of Three Cities — A Comparison*

This book cuts across space — three midwestern cities; and time — ten years. By this comparative approach over the course of time we hope to get a better understanding of the American blue collar worker.

The difficulty with industrial relations case studies is that each one is unique, and uniqueness precludes repetition. But we can approach duplication if we keep the research design and the key variables as uniform as possible. The research reported in this book adds two subsequent case studies from Kansas City and East St. Louis to the Chicago study of 1953.

Along with this rough duplication, goes a marked change of certain variables. We compare the influences of three different cities, plants, workforces, local managements, and unions, hoping to assess their impact on worker attitudes and behavior. As one discerning observer comments on American industrial relations research: "A greater use of the comparative method can be expected to yield more fruitful results." [1]

We are holding constant the industry, meat packing, and the company, Swift. The same general policies affect the Chicago, Kansas City, and East St. Louis plants, though of course the local plant managers and executives vary in each case.

In all three studies, the author was the interviewer. Since interviewers differ so much and might therefore get different attitudes from the workers, there is an advantage in keeping such variation to a minimum. No single interviewer is perfectly consistent in his manner of listening to hundreds of people. For one thing he will surely grow in skill as he proceeds. But most of his personal mannerisms and faults can be kept reasonably constant.

We used the same research design throughout, with random sampling and stratification of the hourly-paid employees by sex, race, and service. We investigated the same attitudes, though certain additions and refinements were added in the two later studies.

Among the changing variables, the three different international unions and the three locals comprised the biggest variation. The meat packing industry is unusual in that three competing industrial unions represent the operating employees of the industry: the CIO United Packinghouse Workers, the AFL Amalgamated Meat Cutters, and the independent union, the National Brotherhood of Packinghouse Workers.[2] The UPWA and the Amalgamated represent about equally most of the estimated two-hundred thousand workers in the meat packing industry, with the UPWA having a larger representation among the bigger packers, such as Armour, Swift, Wilson, Morrell, Cudahy, and Hygrade, and the Amalgamated with a larger representation among the smaller so-called "independents," such as Oscar Mayer. The National Brotherhood is very small, but it has a strategic position in the Swift chain.

These unions differ greatly in age, strategy, leadership, and policies. The fact that the United Packinghouse Workers and the Amalgamated Meat Cutters have repeatedly, though barely, failed in their merger efforts lends relevance to our comparative approach, as also does the fact that the independent National Brotherhood is a prize each of the other unions would like to win.

The local unions differ greatly. We chose Chicago Local 28 as a key local in the home plant of Swift & Company, and as one of the pioneer locals of the United Packinghouse Workers. Local 12 and Local 78 were chosen because they are large and important locals of their respective internationals. Of course, none of the locals is entirely typical of the other locals in its own international. The leadership and policies of the three locals differ. This is an important difference, and more influential than the differences in the three managements.

The workers also vary in the three studies in such matters as age, turnover, racial proportions, length of service, and so forth. Finally, the three cities differ in no small degree. We added Kansas City and East St. Louis to the Chicago study as middle-sized cities, still in the midwest, but border communities between the north and the south. The customs, neighborhoods, and especially the size of these two cities set them quite apart from Chicago, introducing some interesting new variables.

The comparative method also applies to changes over time. We have studied Chicago Local 28 for ten years, from 1949 to 1959. We have observed Local 12 and Local 78 for six years, 1953 to 1959. Of course the main interviews of the hourly-paid employees were obtained at one time. But in addition to these, we have conducted second interviews with the Local 28 rightwing leaders, done six years after the original study. Conversations with key people in management and the unions have been conducted periodically over the six or ten year period, along with observations of general behavior, and the gathering of membership, voting, and other statistics.

By doing this research in a small area but over a period of time, we overcome, to some extent, the pitfalls of the "one-shot" study. Many important events have happened since we began, which should give us sharper and more accurate insights. While this was a period of prosperity, it was equally a period of rising prices, wages, and dividends. During this time, Swift cut back sharply its operations in the Chicago plant, and in 1956 and 1959, the Amalgamated and the United Packinghouse workers teamed up for the seventh and eighth strikes in the history of the industry, though they failed to merge in October 1956.

This book focuses on local union-management relations. With the growth of large companies and large unions, it is important to study the small units of both. A better understanding of these local units may help to keep them strong. Indeed some local union-management research is now appearing.[3] However, we are well aware that the local management and union are parts of larger and more influential governments which affect them greatly. We shall try to show that influence as we go along.

METHODS OF RESEARCH

Most of this book is based on the author's personal interviews with hundreds of people in the meat packing industry and our research staff's detailed analysis of those interviews. The rest is based on observation of work, union meetings, employment, company, union statistics, published sources, and so forth.

To get the story of these working people the interviewer lived for a year and a half, from 1949 to 1951, near the Chicago plant in Negro Bronzeville and in Back-of-the-Yards. During the summer of 1953, he lived in the Mexican part of Armourdale and on Strawberry Hill with the Croatians, not far from the Kansas City Swift plant. During the fall of 1953 and the winter of 1953–54, he lived in Goose Hill in the heart of East St. Louis, near the National Stockyards plant.

Aside from countless informal conversations over morning coffee or after work at night or on the telephone, the author shared in nearly eight hundred interviews, of an hour or more in length, with the packinghouse workers, foremen, union stewards and leaders, and a few neighborhood leaders, over a period from 1949 to 1959.

>   Approximate number of interviews:
>   Chicago, 1949–51; 1956      400
>   Kansas City, 1953           190
>   East St. Louis, 1953–54     200
>                               ———
>                               790

For the Kansas City and East St. Louis studies, recordings were made of the interviews, with the workers' permission, and the typed transcripts were analyzed by three research assistants working independently with both the recording and the transcript.

About twenty attitudes were isolated from each interview and graded on a scale from 1.0 meaning very favorable (ranging through 1.5, 2.0, 2.5, 3.0, 3.5, 4.0, 4.5) to 5.0 meaning very unfavorable. A high degree of reliability among the interview analysts was achieved. We have as a result a considerable mass of statistical data. This book takes a quantitative as well as a qualitative approach to the packinghouse workers' attitudes.

We may rightly challenge social science research with the sometimes devastating question: Is it really valid? For example, does the packinghouse worker really know his own attitudes? If he knows them, can he put them into words? If he can tell his attitudes, will he? Even if he does tell them, will these attitudes relate to his behavior?

Judging from the language used by the packinghouse worker, his mannerisms and the ease or hesitancy of his conversation, especially his consistency or inconsistency of expression through an hour's interview, we think that most of the workers involved in our three studies were well aware of their real attitudes about most aspects of their work life.

Work attitudes are often partly caused by deeply embedded traits and personality dynamics. It is true that not all workers had insight into such root influences, but most were aware of the attitudes that resulted. It was not our purpose to make a prolonged clinical diagnosis of the personality structure and dynamics of each worker, but such areas were frequently exposed in the interview, as for example, the insecurity and feelings of persecution of a certain skilled craftsman who was highly sensitive about his work and very critical of most aspects of both union and company.

The ability to verbalize attitudes certainly varied, from the taciturn worker to the talkative one, and from the introvert to the extrovert. In each case we had sufficient verbal and external gesture data so we could give the man's attitude numerical values, even if it would not make an interesting quotation. Often the workers expressed their attitude with remarkable ease in the fresh language of people who like their words to project lively pictures.

As an example, Walter Cobb, a Negro old-timer and a union politician, says this about his boss:

*Cobb:* Well I'd rate my foreman as okay. A little "fractious." But they all "fractious." They is so many of 'em. He's nothin' outa the ordinary. Only at times. And that's when *they* burn him out. Naturally *he* got ta burn down there.

*Interviewer:* He's got a boss, too.

*Cobb:* That's right. And when they pour it on him, he got to pour it on somebody. That's right. And that's the only time he get outa line is when they pour it on him out here. . . . On the whole he's okay, fine, one of the best. Now he's got a fella under him there. . . . He believes in dischargin' because he'll get mad at 'em; 'If I get mad at you today, an' you one of the best men I got, I think you should be fired!' But Bill don't have that attitude. That's his last resort. He'd rather do anything in the world than discharge a man. I like that about him.[4]

Even if the worker knows and can express his views, will he do so to an interviewer? The interviewer's dual role as psychologist and priest, member of neither company nor union, investigating not religious but work attitudes, apparently helped to get the confidence of these packinghouse workers. In most cases, the employees and union leaders seemed quite glad to be interviewed and to speak their minds freely. We think that the interviews quoted in this book will have the ring of sincerity.

Finally, assuming you have the worker's attitudes, what has this to do with his work behavior? The data show dependable relationships. In the Chicago Swift-UPWA study, we find a remarkable correlation between the packinghouse worker's attitudes toward the local union leadership in 1950 and his (independently verified) behavior of joining the union. Knowing these people, we conclude that the decision of whether or not to rejoin Local 28 in 1950, shortly after Taft-Hartley and the 1948 meat strike, was greatly influenced by their over-all attitudes toward the UPWA and Local 28. In the East St. Louis study, a definite relationship appears between the department foremen's attitude toward the wage-incentive system and the departmental output of those foremen as independently measured. There are other examples. But attitudes are very complex. The pattern of dual allegiance, for instance, will not by itself perfectly predict the workers' "dual behavior" during a strike. Yet dual allegiance has its own behavioral importance and influence as one attitude.

Since this book is the worker's story and since we quote so many men and women at length, seeking their very personal and private thoughts and feelings about their work, we shall further pursue this matter of their openness of speech. Did they consciously or unconsciously distort, or hold back their true attitudes and feelings?

Among the influences affecting a person's openness of speech is the role of the interviewer. One study of antisemitism in New York, for example, found that people may express quite different views about Jews when the interviewer has a Jewish-sounding name and a so-called Jewish appearance, as opposed to an interviewer with a non-Jewish name and appearance.[5]

The interviewer's role of priest–psychologist, as he went about the packinghouses and union halls, may be considered from the five points of view of race, religion, sex, university background, and personality.[6] Being white, he might be expected to elicit less confidence from the Negro workers. His role of priest helped to make up for this racial obstacle. He had been investigating attitudes toward religion, his priest role surely would have inhibited some free responses. But since the workers knew he sought their views about company and union, industrial relations matters, this priest role was a kind of guarantee to them that he was not a member of management or union.

In one department of the Swift East St. Louis plant, a few employees were concerned that a Baptist minister was not also invited to conduct similar research. But in studying the interviews from that department we do not find evidence of distortion due to such comments. One woman employee, an ex-Catholic, told her dressing-room matron, "I'm not going down and tell him much!" She didn't. Her comments were quite terse. This was a rather unsatisfactory interview, yet we find the essential attitudes even of this employee, at least regarding her work, the company, and the union.

Would the worker talking to a clergyman tend to play down attitudes of conflict or criticism? As we shall see, in practically every interview some conflict and criticism was shown. The worker's language was about the only thing modified.

The fact that the interviewer was a man might have affected the openness of the women employees, but as far as we could tell, once the interview was under way, the women were as much at ease as the men.

The university professor role was an obstacle to overcome, since there is a gap in language, interests, and so forth between a university person and the average packinghouse worker. The author's experience in Chicago taught him the jargon and slang connected with packinghouse work, and this helped in the Kansas City and East St. Louis phases of the study. Also the role of priest helped here.

The personality traits of the interviewer are a very important aspect of his role. His frowning coldness or his naive eagerness, may offend the worker. Here we shall have to be content with letting the interviews themselves reveal the author.

Finally, the interviewer's sincere belief in the dignity and importance of each worker is probably more important than any aspect of his role as such. This conviction will affect the interviewer's mannerisms in many subtle ways, and the packinghouse workers will be quick to notice its presence or absence.

In trying to determine empirically whether or not the packinghouse workers spoke freely, we may consider seven criteria: the worker's explicit statements about the interview situation; his signs of ease or nervousness manifested; speech mannerisms; willingness to criticize certain aspects of either company or union; willingness to be interviewed; comparisons of reinterviews in different times or places; comparisons of attitudes with behavior.

A fair minority of workers made explicit comments about their own openness: "It's good to be here." "You get a load off your mind." "I'm gonna tell you just how I feel about it." "Now in *my* opinion. . . ." "Speaking man to man. . . ." "Now that's how *I* feel, I don't know about others." Almost none made explicit statements to the contrary, but one foreman did, saying: "I guess that's what Swift's would want me to say." Statements like these are a partial clue to the openness of most of the workers.

Secondly, signs of emotion shown during the interview give us a further clue. Laughter is generally a sign of being at ease. Hesitations in speech or drumming on the table may indicate nervousness. Immediately after every interview the author noted down any of these signs he had observed. Also many of these can be heard in the recorded interviews.

Various speech mannerisms or choice of words are further indications. For example, does the worker refine or correct his opinion, or perhaps contradict himself?

Fourthly, willingness to criticize shows at least a lack of fear of the interviewer. A man might hesitate to criticize the company before his foreman, or the union before his local president. In practically every interview, the workers had at least a few points of criticism — understandably enough. One might think that the short-service Negro workers were the least secure and therefore people who would be cautious in the interview, showing approval of everything. But in some plants these people are the most critical of management. At Kansas City, they are the most critical of the local union leaders.

Our fifth criterion is the willingness of the workers to be interviewed. The interviews were, of course, quite voluntary. Only about two people in each of the plants preferred not to be interviewed. And one of these, a Mexican-American woman employee of the Kansas City plant, misunderstood the nature of the research. Since she lived near the author's residence in the Mexican Armourdale neighborhood, he made a brief visit to her home and explained the research. She then agreed to be interviewed and seemed to be quite frank and at ease in the subsequent interview at the plant.

Reinterviewing gives another clue to the genuineness of the worker's comments. Some of the employees, especially the union leaders or foremen were interviewed twice, in some cases both at the plant and at their homes. There was no discernable difference in the openness of these people. A sample of the Chicago packinghouse workers was interviewed six years after the original study. These workers tended to repeat their same attitudes. Some actually used the same phrases to express these attitudes.

Comparing the attitudes expressed, with the workers' actual behavior can give us a final clue to the validity of our observation and measurement of those attitudes. For instance, the attitude of the Kansas City packinghouse workers toward the raiding UPWA coincides quite closely with their independently verified voting behavior toward the UPWA in the NLRB elections. The degree of union allegiance among the Chicago packinghouse workers of 1950 closely resembled the pattern of their behavior in rejoining the union after the Taft-Hartley act required new membership cards. Regarding the company attitudes, we find several attitudes about the wage-incentive system correlated with the independently given output-record of the workers.

Putting together all these seven criteria, we can honestly say that a remarkable majority of the workers spoke their minds freely and openly. A small minority did not.

By comparing groups of workers under three very different conditions, by listening carefully to them, by trying to be as exact as possible in measuring their attitudes yet never forgetting that they are people and not statistics, we hope to throw new light on their thoughts and feelings about union, job, and company.

CHAPTER II

## Plants and Unions

To understand why the packinghouse workers think and act the way they do, we shall want to see what kind of plants they work in and what sort of unions they belong to. Our major interest is to see how the three plants and unions differ.

History of the Three Plants

The detailed story of how the three Swift plants developed is not vital to our understanding of the present-day workers. But a few events are important. The Kansas City Swift plant was the first to be built after the mother plant in Chicago.

The ferment of America's 1890's was about to begin when the following article appeared in frontier Kansas City's *The Star* of December 2, 1887:

The machinery at the new Swift packinghouse was started at an early hour yesterday morning, and at seven o'clock several hundred men entered the building and at once began work. About 200 beeves were killed and dressed, and the number will be increased day by day. Many things about the plant are not yet completed, but everything will be in first-class order by the first of January, at which time the company expects to employ about 1000 men.

Today, over seventy years later, the Kansas City Swift plant can process 150 cattle in one hour instead of 200 in one day. The plant has grown greatly, of course, sloughing off some old buildings and erecting some new ones. The rectangular, many-sized buildings rise on the shore of the Kaw river, and the plant is called one of Swift's "river plants." Cattle come to it by bridge from the Kansas City stockyards on the river's east bank.

Three times, the friendly river became a deadly enemy, flooding the plant in 1903, again in 1908 and finally on Friday, the 13th of July, 1951. This last flood was disastrous. A collapsing embankment caught everyone by surprise, putting the plant and nearby Armourdale thirty feet under water. At the plant, five million dollars worth of meat and equipment were ruined.

It was an important managerial decision to reopen the plant at great cost in 1951. Across the street, the Cudahy plant was closed down for good. A few blocks away, Wilson closed down, later to reopen only a small plant across the river. Great courage and cooperation of management, union, workers, and neighbors finally accomplished the back-breaking cleanup job. Today Kansas City Swift is a moderately efficient plant. It still needs rebuilding and modernization, but improvements have been added, such as a new loading dock and assembly packing cooler.

In the 1880's the refrigerator car transformed the whole food industry. Swift was plunging all his savings into rapid expansion. Just five years after his move to Kansas City, Swift followed Nelson Morris into East St. Louis in 1892, and built the National Stockyards plant there on the flat prairies by the Mississippi.

The plant is now one of the leading Swift plants, while the East St. Louis stockyards (not owned by Swift) developed into the largest hog market in the world. Like the Kansas City plant, National Stockyards, or East St. Louis, as we shall call it, is a mixture of the old and the new, and appears to the stranger as a confusing mass of buildings and ramps rather haphazardly put together. This plant, too, is moderately efficient.

Two social groups developed over the years at Swift East St. Louis, unlike anything at either Kansas City or Chicago. These are two clubs, the "Arrow-S" for whites and the "Booster Club" for Negroes, run by the employees with the approval and some assistance from the company. Together they operate an employees' canteen or snack bar in the utility building, an employee gathering-place where the employment office is also located. Arrow-S also runs a pleasant picnic grounds where members may bring their families. Among the major projects of the two clubs are their Christmas parties for children of members. The foremen, hourly-paid employees, and Local 78 leaders all cooperated in running these parties. This cooperation is a good example of friendly Swift-Local 78 relations. Employee clubs are not common in the Swift chain. No doubt these two clubs at East St. Louis have contributed their share to the good morale of which we shall later see evidence.

An important change occurred in 1957 and 1958, affecting both the Kansas City and the East St. Louis plants, as well as the entire industry. The national shortage of cattle marketed in those years seriously reduced the plants' supply of raw material. The result was a major cutback in beef operations with the consequent layoff of many workers. In Kansas City, the workforce was cut back 25 per cent by 1958. East St. Louis suffered a 17 per cent cutback. Some foremen were retired or transferred into such departments as Standards. Workers, even of several years' seniority, were out of work. Undoubtedly the 1957-1958 cutback affected employee morale.

*The Chicago Cutback.* The history of the Chicago Swift plant was told in *The Worker Speaks His Mind,* but there is one extremely important event that has happened since 1954: the sharp cutback in Chicago plant operations. For years, the whole Chicago stockyards had been declining in its worldwide importance because of the decentralization of the meat packing industry, the sprouting of southern plants, and the trend from railroad shipping to trucking. The Chicago Swift plant was gradually getting smaller. Shortly before 1950, the beef and sheep operations were halved, the cheese factory was transferred to Wisconsin, and the glue and fertilizer factories, along with the ancient wool house, were moved elsewhere. In 1952, the spectacular hog-kill department was closed after seventy-five years of operation. Pork slaughtered in outlying plants was shipped to Chicago in refrigerated cars and trucks to be fabricated in the Chicago plant.

In 1955 Wilson and Company stopped its entire Chicago meat packing operations, practically closing down an entire plant employing about two thousand people. Finally, in January 1957, Swift's Chicago plant manager wrote this letter to all Chicago employees:

Our experience has shown that it isn't economically sound to continue. . . . Therefore, it has been decided to discontinue pork operations on the Chicago plant. . . . This was not an easy decision to make. We fully appreciate the effect it will have on the employment situation of many of our people. . . . Just as soon as we are able to work out more specific details, those of you who are affected will be fully informed. . . .

In April, the fresh pork operations in Chicago Swift were discontinued and at least four hundred packinghouse workers lost their jobs. Swift tried to place the older workers on other jobs throughout the plant. Thanks to plant-wide seniority, the older workers could retain their jobs, though sometimes at reduced pay. Others chose to take their separation allowance and leave. Some older people were eligible to take a "premature pension." As for the younger workers, Swift made some efforts to place them in other employment.

Hundreds of disputed cases arose, with the UPWA claiming that employees did not receive the severance pay to which they were entitled, or did not get a sufficient amount of severance pay.

The drastic reduction of operations and workforce, the biggest Swift has ever made, was not as drastic as the Wilson closing. Naturally, the workers feared further reductions. In January 1958, sheep operations were stopped, cutting out four more departments. In June 1958, sausage and canned meats production were largely discontinued, cutting out three or four hundred more jobs. Swift stated that this would "complete the adjustments which must be made at this time." But Local 28's *Flash* asked: "Does this mean that the employees now working can quit worrying about losing their jobs?" Finally in June 1959, all beef operations were discontinued, cutting out about three hundred more jobs. In all, about three thousand jobs were lost in the seven-year period from 1952 to 1959.

In 1959 plans called for continuing the following operations at the Chicago plant: dry sausage, oil and lard refinery, margarine, dog food, soap, animal feeds, and adhesives. Also the research laboratories were to be continued there. The general offices were to be moved to a Loop office building in 1961.

Morale among workers and foremen has undoubtedly suffered in the recent years of the Chicago plant. Had our allegiance findings been based on these years, we might have found substantially less company allegiance than we found in 1950.

Naturally, the United Packinghouse Workers protested the move. The Back of the Yards Council, representatives from Mayor Daley, and others inquired about the cutback. But Swift management felt that the company could no longer stand the losses of its old-fashioned and outmoded Chicago plant. It was a hard decision to have to make and many older workers found themselves in the difficult situation of being out of the only work they knew how to do.

Swift's primary motive was economic. One might speculate that Swift's poor industrial relations with Local 28, the local's constant criticism, anti-company tactics, and the 1956 strike along with the fact that the Chicago workforce was less productive and more troublemaking than the workforces of many other plants, might have influenced Swift's decision. One packinghouse worker in 1950 feared that the union might "kill the goose that lays the golden egg." However, as far as can be determined, the matter of poor labor relations in Chicago did not enter into the discussions of the cutback.

Continuing the meat packing decentralization trend from old, high cost, multi-storied plants to modern, smaller, mechanized plants, Armour, in the summer of 1959, closed six butchering plants in Chicago, East St. Louis, Tifton, Ga., West Fargo, N.D., Atlanta, and Columbus, Ohio. Five were UPWA plants, and one with the Amalgamated. Armour gave several reasons for the closing: obsolescent plants, some fifty years old; sectional shifts in livestock production; declining receipts of livestock at certain locations; overproduction in the meat packing industry. The big Chicago Armour plant shut-down cost the jobs of two thousand people.

*Minor Differences.* Table 1 gives us a quick summary of the main differences and similarities among the three plants.

Table 1. *Key characteristics of the three plants: Chicago, Kansas City, East St. Louis.* (1950–1953)

|  | Chicago | Kansas City | East St. Louis |
|---|---|---|---|
| Year | 1877 | 1887 | 1892 |
| Size | 4000 workforce (1950) | 2000 | 2000 |
|  | 1350 (1958) | 1350 (1958) | 1675 (1958) |
| Local plant management | Close to Chicago gen. office top management | Farther removed from general office top management | |
| Foremen | About 175 | About 70 | About 70 |
| Average education | 10 years | 10.5 | 10 |
| Average service | 26 years | 25.5 | 20.5 |
| Served as foreman | 20 years | 9 | 9 |
| Average age | 50.5 | 47.9 | 41 |
| Average number of dependents | 1.9 | 2.7 | 2.4 |
| Gang experience | 80% | 72% | 92% |
| Maximum number of employees per dept. foreman affecting foreman-worker contacts | Beef dressing 100 | 97 | 90 |
|  | Sliced bacon 123 | 85 | 79 |
|  | (A few departments are larger in Chicago than in KC or ESL, but many have about the same gang sizes. Where there is a significantly larger department (Chicago), the foreman will usually have one or more assistant foreman.) | | |
| Foremen-superintendent contacts | (More difficult in Chicago because of larger number of foremen. About the same in the other two plants.) | | |
| Worker-plant superintendent contacts | (Some differences in the possibility of such contacts, considering the larger number of employees in Chicago.) | | |

There is no great difference in the age of the three plants, their working conditions, type of operations, type of location, or job requirements. The main difference is in size, with Chicago as large (in 1950) as the other two plants combined. Greater size makes frequent contacts more difficult between top management and foremen, between the foremen themselves, and between workers and foremen. We did not count such contacts, in any precise way, as one interesting study did in an automobile assembly plant.[1] However, our impression is that such contacts were actually less frequent in the Chicago plant, with not much difference between the other two plants.

One final difference in Table 1 needs to be noted: The East St. Louis foremen are significantly younger; and more of them have had gang experience than the foremen in either of the other two plants. Later on we shall relate this difference to some of the attitude differences we observed.

In a word, we do not find much difference among the three plants either in their physical makeup or in the personalities of their management and supervisors. There are small differences, and these do have some effect.

## History of the Three Unions

The history of the three local unions (unlike the history of the three plants) involved in this book is important because the local unions differ so much, and exert such varied influences on their rank-and-file membership. We want to know, briefly, how they "got this way."

*Local 28, UPWA-CIO, Chicago.* Local 28 had a turbulent background from its certification in January 1942, with its campaign against the International UPWA in 1948 and 1949, its left-right struggles of the early 1950's and the rightwinger's unusual victory of 1953.

In the elections of January 1954, however, the pendulum swung back, and the rightwingers were defeated once more by the leftwing group, with evident District One support. The influence of the Communist Party was again being felt in Local 28 leadership through a very few party members and a larger number of fellow travelers. For the next six years through 1960, the leftwingers were able to hold their control over Local 28, with only one serious challenge in 1955.

*The Secession Movement in Local 28.* The "Real Unity Committee," a rank-and-file group led by Ralph Gantt, one of the founders of Local 28 and a former rightwing officer of the local, protested the 1955 local elections as rigged, with District One support.

Some of their grievances presented to the International UPWA are as follows:

(1) We think that the Local Union meetings should be held in the vicinity of the Packing Plant.
(2) Stop interference from elements outside the Local Union.
(3) The Election Committee should draft the election rules and present them to the membership for approval.

(4) The District Director and his staff should be forbidden to hold factional meetings at the District Hall.
(5) The use of our District's material and printing facilities for aiding factional groups should be stopped.
(6) The ballot box should remain in the Union Hall and in full view throughout the election.
(7) Ballots before given to a voter should be signed by a member of each faction.
(8) In the conduct of the election the Election Committee should be required to be governed by the Local Constitution and the accepted election rules.

To the election protest of the Real Unity Committee, UPWA President Ralph Helstein wrote the following reply on July 8, 1955 (in a letter to local unionist Robert Brothers):

We have examined carefully the questions raised by the protest against the Local 28 election of this year. Officers of the International Union have conferred at length with the individuals involved. We could wish, of course, that details in the election procedure in all locals could be handled in a manner that would give rise to no possibility of any argument or question. This ideal is not always possible, both because minor technical errors may always occur and because, human nature being what it is, defeated candidates may raise questions. In the present situation it is our considered conclusion that no defect appeared which affected the basic fairness of the election or which can be said to have adversely affected the rights of any candidate.

The Real Unity Committee had requested a formal hearing on its grievance before the International Executive Board of the United Packinghouse Workers. This hearing was not granted, and President Helstein's letter reporting the July decision of the closed meeting of the board ended the matter. The Real Unity Committee felt that it had now been rebuffed by the International UPWA as well as by the District One Group. Believing that they could no longer work against the leftwingers from within Local 28, Gantt and the Real Unity Committee withdrew their membership from the UPWA. About four or five hundred men followed their example. But not all the rightwing groups agreed with this move. Some stayed in Local 28, and one or two were later elected to minor offices in the local.

The leftwingers charged that anyone opposing them was thereby a "company stooge":

LOCAL 28 FLASH

UPWA-CIO

Vol. 3 No. 48                                    Friday, August 12, 1955

DOING A JOB FOR THE COMPANY

Ralph Gantt and his anti-International clique has vowed to deliver two thousand of Local #28 members to Swift & Co. by signing them out of the union. Swift & Company is behind this move to wreck our Local. . . . The question is where will the Gantt clique lead us . . . to the AFL? No! The AFL Meatcutters has a no-raiding pact with the United Packinghouse Workers of America-CIO. The AFL Meatcutters respects that agreement, and they will not jeopardize the chances of merging with UPWA.

Then where can we go? *The answer is company unionism,* of course.

This was an old cry against the Gantt group. But the Gantt group was militant enough, and certainly no agent of Swift. For instance, they supported the UPWA picket lines in the 1956 strike, a strike they personally opposed.

Since its beginning in 1937 or 1942, Local 28 has endured continual political turmoil with its own factions and particularly with UPWA District One, and the UPWA International. It is interesting to see the trend of membership over these divided years.

Table 2. *Trend in Local 28 membership, 1946–1959.*

| Year | | Eligible in CIO bargaining unit | Number in local | Percentage of unit in local |
|---|---|---|---|---|
| (December) | 1946 | 5522 | 4638 | 84 (strike) |
| | 1947 | 5706 | 4735 | 83 |
| | 1948 | 5954 | 5118 | 86 (strike) |
| | 1949 | 5518 | 2483 | 45 (Taft-Hartley required resigning members) |
| | 1950 | 5455 | 3763 | 69 |
| | 1951 | 4971 | 3877 | 78 |
| | 1952 | 4240 | 3554 | 84 |
| | 1953 | 4043 | 3457 | 86 |
| | 1954 | 3886 | 3339 | 86 |
| | 1955 | 3594 | 2757 | 77 (Real unity committee withdrawal) |
| | 1956 | 3422 | 2767 | 81 (strike) |
| (June) | 1957 | 2456 | 1937 | 79 |
| (January) | 1958 | 1900 | 1356 | 71 |
| (July) | 1959 | 950 (about) | 700 | 73 |

Table 2 shows us a local that has just managed to maintain its membership. The UPWA-Swift contract provides for dues deductions for union members during the life of the contract, but not for any type of union shop or closed shop agreement. In 1949, when the Taft-Hartley law became effective, deductions of union dues by management could be made only if the employees signed written authorizations. Local 28 promptly began to have its members sign such authorization cards. But there was a temporary drop in membership until this could be accomplished. The Real Unity Committee withdrawal of 1955 also caused a drop. This drop is additionally significant because it involves a number of white unionists and also some good potential leadership material for the local. Another point is important: the local is getting constantly smaller because of the Chicago plant cutbacks.

In sum, we see in Local 28 the picture of an aggressive but insecure local union. This militancy and insecurity are some of the main reasons for the big differences we shall see in the attitudes and behavior of the packinghouse workers.

*Local 12, NBPW-Independent, Kansas City.* After the declaration of the constitutionality of the Wagner Act in 1937, a hectic period of union organizing began in the meat packing industry. The failure of the Amalgamated Meat Cutters to gain a strong representation in the industry was due to several reasons,[2] mainly the worker's memories of the disastrous strike of 1921 and the distrust of many Negroes for the AFL. The incipient UPWA, then called the Packinghouse Workers' Organizing Committee, was much more successful, but not uniformly so, especially in the Swift chain of plants.

Swift, in 1937, disbanded the Employees Representation Plan in order to conform to the new labor law. Many ERP leaders then formed local groups called the Security League, or Swift Employees Associations. These people distrusted the PWOC as either leftwing or at least too radical. Moreover, Swift & Company obviously favored these local independent unions.

The PWOC naturally tried to win over the leaders and members of the independents. Competing leaflets, meetings, and raids were common in those Swift plants where the independents were strong. Naturally, the leaders of the various independent local unions began to write and visit one another to secure mutual support. During organizational raids by the PWOC or the AFL, one independent would help another through exchange of leaflets, information, trained men, and sometimes through financial assistance. Periodic meetings were held, still on an informal basis.

In 1938 the Fair Labor Standards Act took effect. The major packers took the position that they were exempted under the provisions of the act. The Wage and Hour Administration disagreed, and in February 1940, brought suit against Swift & Company. The PWOC and the Independent Unions also filed suits. In 1941 the court decided against Swift. After that, Swift decided to bring all its employees under the benefits of the act, thus going beyond the requirements of the act and the court. But both unions counted this as their victory and each used it to strengthen its position with the workers it was trying to organize. The independents claimed that the Fair Labor Standards Act decision helped them to bring about the formation of a national organization.

The first organizational meeting of the independents was held in East St. Louis, Illinois in 1939.[3] Later in 1939, a constitutional convention was held in Chicago, Illinois. This was the first concerted effort by the independents to form a national organization. Two sections were formed; the Independent Brotherhood of Packinghouse Workers and the International Brotherhood of Swift Employees. These nominal divisions were dropped in 1944, and the title, National Brotherhood of Packinghouse Workers was adopted.

In 1942, the National Brotherhood secured its first master agreement with Swift. The UPWA and the Amalgamated also won their own master agreements at the same time. At that time the NBPW had nine locals in the Swift chain, in Chicago, the Swift Omaha Packing Company (subsequently closed down), South St. Paul, Winona, Cleveland, Marshalltown, Harrisburg, Fort Worth, St. Louis, and St. Joseph. The NBPW has managed to retain most of these locals. It lost St. Paul, Cleveland, and Winona to the UPWA. It gained Kansas City, Wichita, San Antonio, and the truck drivers at Lake Charles, Louisiana.

Meanwhile, in Kansas City, the UPWA-minded and the Independent-minded leaders contested for the support of the Swift Kansas City packinghouse workers. On April 10, 1942, the Independent Packinghouse Workers' Union (IPHWU) was organized. In June of that year a membership meeting was held, with eight hundred men and women attending. Executive officers were elected.

The political battle between the IPHWU and the UPWA-CIO waxed strong. Sharply-worded leaflets were passed from hand to hand throughout the plant. Finally, a year later, July 1, 1943, during the middle of World War II, a certification election was conducted by the National Labor Relations Board. The IPHWU won by a large majority and was legally certified on July 8, 1943, and became Local 12 of the National Brotherhood.

After World War II ended and price controls were lifted, the UPWA put its newfound power to its first test. Along with the Amalgamated, the UPWA struck for a wage increase in 1946. The NBPW also considered the situation serious and took a strike vote. But its membership voted overwhelmingly to instruct the NBPW negotiators to continue negotiations. The NBPW did not strike.

In Kansas City the UPWA men from the Cudahy and Wilson plants across the street from Swift, and the UPWA men from the Armour plant across the river, picketed the nonstriking Swift plant. Some violence occurred and the Swift plant was partly closed for a very short time, oddly enough by other than its own employees. That same year, after the strike, the UPWA again challenged the Independent Union in another NLRB election. Again the UPWA lost by a wide margin. The pattern of raids on Local 12 by the UPWA was beginning. Table 3 brings this out.

Table 3. *UPWA raids on Local 12, 1943–1959 (in per cent).*

| Year | NBPW vote | UPWA vote | No-union vote |
|---|---|---|---|
| 1943–(certification) | Large majority | ? | ? |
| 1946 | Large majority | ? | ? |
| 1948 | Large majority | ? | ? |
| 1952 | 67 | 31 | 2 |
| 1954 | 66 | 33 | 1 |
| 1957 | 54 | 46 | 0 |
| 1959 | 59 | 40 | 1 |

Meanwhile the 1948 strike was called by the UPWA. This time the Amalgamated refused to go along. Again the NBPW did not strike. Finally the joint Amalgamated-UPWA strikes of 1956 and 1959 against Swift were called. Again the NBPW refused to strike.

During these years, the UPWA raids against the NBPW continued with success in some cities. For example, Swift St. Paul went from the Brotherhood over to the UPWA. The UPWA spent heavy efforts to win Local 12 in Kansas City. One UPWA leader stated that in the eighteen-month period of 1952 and 1953, for example, the United Packinghouse Workers spent $38,000 to capture Local 12.

For its raiding strategy, the UPWA made many claims: Local 12 is just a company union. Local 12 does not take an aggressive stand on grievances. Local 12 does not fight for Negro rights. (This was an important part of the UPWA's approach.) The National Brotherhood does not really bargain effectively; it just goes in after the other two unions have fought the struggle and gets the same terms. Local 12 never had a strike, and this fact proves it is too company-minded.

Local 12, for its part, made counterclaims: The UPWA strikes too much, loses money and time for its people. The UPWA is leftwing. (It is true that some leftist organizers from Chicago took part in the UPWA 1954 raid efforts in Kansas City.) The UPWA's contract terms are not as good as the Independent's. Local 12's dues are lower than those of the UPWA.

In the raiding campaigns, the UPWA has had the big advantage of much more money and expert advice, along with experienced organizers and pamphleteers. The UPWA for years has maintained a regular union office located conveniently just outside the Swift plant gate. CIO-minded people often came there for strategy talks or just to talk and eat lunch.

Local 12 held the allegiance of its members quite consistently until 1957, at which time it barely won the NLRB election. The abandoned merger of the UPWA and the Amalgamated may strengthen Local 12's position. But since 1957 the local has been and remains rather insecure though it gained during the 1959 NLRB election. As Table 4 shows, Local 12 has a good majority of the packinghouse workers consistently staying on its membership roles.

Table 4. *Trend in Local 12 membership, 1953–1958.*

| Year (December) | Eligible in NBPW bargaining unit | Number in Local 12 | Percentage of unit in local |
|---|---|---|---|
| 1953 | 2087 | 1749 | 83 |
| 1954 | 2026 | 1708 | 84 |
| 1955 | 1926 | 1620 | 84 |
| 1956 | 1861 | 1580 | 85 |
| 1957 | 1550 | 1478 | 95 |
| 1958 | 1325 | 1286 | 97 |

Nevertheless, not all the Kansas City Swift workers support the NBPW. The effects of the UPWA raiding and of the union rivalry upon the thinking of the employees will become quickly apparent to the reader of the following chapters, especially those describing union attitudes.

*Local 78, Amalgamated Meat Cutters, East St. Louis.* Local 78 is the largest and most important local union in the Amalgamated's share of the meat packing industry. Although equal to the UPWA in the meat packing industry, the Amalgamated failed in the late 1930's to win many plants of the biggest producers such as Swift and Armour. Therefore, its success in gaining the workers of Swift's East St. Louis plant is noteworthy.

Since there were some key PWOC-CIO leaders in the East St. Louis Swift plant, and especially in the Armour plant immediately next door, we may ask first: Why did the PWOC not also win Swift East St. Louis as it did so many other Swift plants? Three Local 78 leaders give some reasons:

*Tom Hubert:* Well I'll tell you one thing, Father, you know after the CIO looked as though they were losing their foothold, the boys in the plant who belonged to the CIO joined the AFL. And they were some of our best men....

*Cleveland Anderson:* The handwritin' was on the wall. The Company seen it. They knew that the SEA. [the Swift Employees' Association] was goin' out the window. And naturally rather to have the CIO, they kinda give credit to the AFL. 'Course a lotta boys on the killin' floor, after they found out that the Company would agree to the AFL rather than the CIO, naturally the boys got to organizing for the AFL.

*Sam Agnew:* Speakin' of the CIO, why didn't they go ahead with that [NLRB] election during the period that they had this plant on their side. I think they just wasn't thinking. They didn't have men in there to try and organize and just *thoughtful* enough what to do. And we were fortunate enough to have a man [John Powderly] in there who was just a little smarter, thinkin' to try an' organize *our* forces, see?

From those remarks we would think that the UPWA at one time had a fair chance to win Swift East St. Louis. The fact that the Swift Employees' Association was so strong, as we shall see, coupled with the fact that the Amalgamated leader's were politically alert, are the main reasons why the UPWA failed.

The Amalgamated had no easy time of it. People remembered the AFL's ill-fated strike of 1921. The Negroes were skeptical. As Cleveland Anderson puts it:

Them people that got stuck with the old '21 union, they were kinda skeptical of the unions. We had a problem there selling that thing to some of these people. I'm gonna be honest about it, I mean in *all* the nationalities. [He means among Negroes, too.] They said they got stuck here in '21. And I said: Well, it's different now. This is a new day. The same fellas that was in office in them days is gone. We don't have nothin' to do with 'em.

Moreover, the leaders of the old SEA were campaigning to form an independent union. We recall that the first organizational meeting of the incipient NBPW was held in East St. Louis in 1939. The time for a test of strength was clearly approaching by the summer of 1940. In 1941, three NLRB elections were held.[4] In the first election, the "no-union" part of the ballot was eliminated. In the second election, the UPWA was clearly defeated. The duel now remained between the Amalgamated and the Independent Brotherhood. In the final election, the Amalgamated squeezed out victory by the very narrow margin of 33 votes out of over 1000. The Amalgamated received 556 votes and the Independent had 523.

Local 78 leaders claim that Swift favored the Independent Union, giving it such advantages as the right to hold meetings in the company cafeteria, permitting its circulars to be run off in the plant, restricting the circulation of AFL handbills and so forth. For instance, the fire chief of National City declared that the AFL handbills scattered about the stockyards area were a fire hazard and so he banned them.

On the other hand, one AFL leader admits that his own group used strong-arm methods:

> We were confronted with the SEA. . . . And they held some meetings outside of the plant. And I remember pretty well that a group of the CIO and some of the boys that were in the AFL attended that meeting and they busted it up. It was over at 13th and St. Louis Avenue, upstairs. . . . They threw a guy down the steps and somebody got hurt and they called the police and finally got things straightened out. And some guy adjourned the meeting. And that was all there was to it. But later on they held them at the Community House because they were more or less protected there than they were out on 13th Street. . . . They tried to break up the company union, you know what I mean.

The great strength of the Independent Union which evolved out of the old Swift Employees' Association, sometimes called the Employees' Protective Association, surely demonstrates the satisfaction many employees had with SEA. We shall come back to this point in a later chapter. Across the Mississippi River, the National Brotherhood won the Swift St. Louis plant.

While the UPWA had strength in 1939 at Swift East St. Louis, it was never a challenge in 1940 or 1941. But at the National City Armour plant, the UPWA won out. Hence, within the St. Louis metropolitan area we have the triple unionism of the meat packing industry demonstrated rather dramatically: Armour with the UPWA; East St. Louis Swift with the Amalgamated; St. Louis Swift with the NBPW. The Amalgamated won two small packing plants in East St. Louis: Hunter and Circle.

After Local 78 was certified as bargaining agent in 1941, it joined the other Amalgamated locals from small Swift plants in Watertown, Montgomery, Nashville, Portland, San Francisco, and Baltimore in seeking a country-wide agreement. The first collective bargaining contract was finally negotiated and took effect on August 20, 1942.

With a good contract in its pocket, Local 78 began to grow. The second World War brought peak business to the Swift plant, along with a diminished supply of ablebodied labor. Local 78 had to win the new workers coming to the union movement. Membership grew. After the war, Local 78 participated in the nation-wide meat strike. But in spite of the strike, relations were good between Local 78 and Swift. The Amalgamated refused to join the CIO Packinghouse Workers in the 1948 strike, though Local 78 offered strike relief to the UPWA Armour local next door. The help was refused. The 1956 strike, a crucial one for Local 78, will be treated later in greater detail and in relation to dual allegiance.

As Local 78 prospered, President John Powderly made this report to the membership meeting of January 19, 1951, in Polish Hall:

It's with pride that with nine years behind us, tonight we can look at a financial report such as ours, assets of practically $31,000, accumulated since 1946 when, after the strike, we were about broke. Now with a building fund of $25,000, we are in a good position to really look forward to a building in the not too far distant future.

That same year Local 78 bought and redecorated a handsome hall on North Ninth Street.

One proof of the solid growth of Local 78 is obvious from the figures in Table 5.

Table 5. *Trend in Local 78 membership, 1953–1958.*

| Year (December) | Eligible in AWC & BW bargaining unit | Number in Local 78 | Percentage of unit in local |
|---|---|---|---|
| 1953 | 2067 | 1937 | 94 |
| 1954 | 2045 | 1982 | 97 |
| 1955 | 1870 | 1822 | 97 |
| 1956 | 1979 | 1920 | 97 |
| 1957 | 2077 | 2025 | 97 |
| 1958 | 1619 | 1586 | 98 |

Eleven years of growth did not bring monolithic political structure to Local 78, however. In 1952, after a severe factional struggle, based mostly on personalities, the local's founding president John Powderly was defeated and a new political group gained control of the local executive board under the presidency of Tony Kleine. Mr. Powderly later joined the staff of the International Union as industrial engineer. In the 1954 and 1956 local elections, strong rivalry persisted. In these elections there were no great political issues regarding the conduct of the local. Yet 85 per cent of the membership voted. Local 78 has been a democratically run union, though a cash payoff to certain factions probably occurred in at least one election campaign. One might think that with such democracy, and the recent turnover in local officers, Local 78 might be unstable. Such is far from the case, however. The local has become quite strong and secure, celebrating its fifteenth anniversary as a highlight of the big Labor Day celebration of labor-minded East St. Louis in 1957.

*Major Differences.* Unlike the three Swift managements, the three local unions differ widely, not so much in their structure, but in a half dozen matters of policy and action.

First, the locals differ in the type of international union with which they are affiliated. The old conservative and secure Amalgamated Meat Cutters, with its aggressive but cooperative attitude toward management, certainly differs from the relatively new, more radical and faction-ridden UPWA, with its militant aggressiveness toward management. Both these internationals differ in turn from the much smaller, less centrally organized, less aggressive, financially poorer National Brotherhood of Packinghouse Workers, independent. While we are concerned in this book primarily with the local unions, we shall see that the policies and philosophies of their internationals have a profound effect upon them. Table 6 compares briefly the main similarities and differences of our three locals.

As to master agreements, under which all three locals live — there is not a very great difference. Advantages which one union secures quickly tend to be incorporated into the contacts of the others. But in security and stability, the three locals differ greatly, with Local 28 being least secure, and Local 78 being most secure. Such security or its absence is partly related to the degree of turnover among the local officers. The various factions and rivals of Chicago's UPWA Local 28 have rendered its turnover of officers excessive, to the resulting harm of the local. The other two locals have had a rather healthy turnover, indicating a degree of democracy in their organizations. The decline of meat packing in the Chicago area has also affected the security of Local 28 and indeed the security of District One of the UPWA.

Election activity for local officers is an important variable among these three locals. Local 28 has the least active electoral membership, Local 78 the most active. Presumably, this activity of Local 78 should mean a more democratic, more responsive-to-the-membership leadership. We shall examine this possibility later.

In number of stewards and in number of grievances, there is a considerable difference between the locals, with Local 28 having the most stewards and the most grievances. There is not necessarily a connection between these two facts. The main reason for the larger number of grievances in Chicago is the greater dissatisfaction of the Local 28 officers and their greater aggressiveness. There is not necessarily an equal difference among the workforces themselves in satisfaction with their work. We shall find, for instance, that the Chicago packinghouse workers have as much company allegiance as the others, and are about as well satisfied with their foremen.

In the matter of racial integration, there is also a great difference among the policies of the three locals, with Local 28 being by far the most aggressive, and Local 78 the least aggressive. Such policies reflect in part the policies of the two different international unions to which these locals belong, but

Table 6. *Key characteristics of the three local unions: 28, 12, and 78.*

| | Local 28, UPWA-CIO, Chicago | Local 12, NPBW-Independent, Kansas City | Local 78, AMC & BW-AFL, East St. Louis |
|---|---|---|---|
| Certification | January 1942 | July 1943 | January 1941 |
| Master agreements | No great difference among these three agreements. | | |
| International unions | These three differ greatly in their philosophy, international political structure, activity, and so on. This makes a very different impact on the three locals. | | |
| Local security | Severe internal factional trouble. Also occasional poor relations with International. Very insecure local. | No severe factional problems, but local is perennially raided by UPWA-CIO. Somewhat insecure local. | No factions or raids. Very secure local. |
| | None is either "closed shop" or "union shop." | | |
| Local leaders | Dominated by left wing. Mostly Negro. Very aggressive and hostile to company. Somewhat unpopular with many members. President is part-time union job. | White-dominated. Very cooperative with management. Rather popular with workforce. President is part-time union job. | White-dominated. Very cooperative with management. Popular with workforce. President-business agent is full-time union job. |
| Turnover of leaders | High turnover in last 15 years. | Little turnover of white officers. Some of Negro. | Little turnover of Negroes. Some of white officers in 1951, 1953, 1956. |
| Local hall | Fair meeting hall. Distant for Negro workers. Many meetings at District One hall in Negro neighborhood. | Small hall, near plant gate. | Excellent hall, some distance from plant in white neighborhood. |
| Communications | Weekly newssheet, *The Flash.* | Newssheet, *The Truth Teller,* comes out sporadically, especially at elections. | Monthly newssheet, *Local 78 News,* began about 1956. |

Table 6. *Continued*

| | | | |
|---|---|---|---|
| Committees | 8. Grievance committee most important, up to 12 members. | 3. No grievance committee. | Temporary committees. Grievance committee has 3–7 members. |
| Meetings | All three locals have the usual monthly meetings with no vastly differing amount of participation. Participation will be treated later. | | |
| | Many social meetings attended mostly by Negroes making for virtual, but by no means official, segregation. | Very few socials. Tacit social segregation. | Very few socials. Tacit social segregation. |
| Elections | 40 to 60% at annual election. (Least electoral participation.) | 80 to 90% | 90% (Greatest electoral participation.) |
| Dues | $4.00 (plus later assessments). | $1.00 (lowest by far in 1953. $2.00 by 1958). | $4.00 |
| Stewards | Several stewards per department. (170) Most stewards. | Average of one steward per department. (55) | One steward takes several departments. (15) Least stewards. |
| Grievance procedure | Most grievances. 1.35 grievances per 100 employees, 1954. | .77 grievances per 100 employees, 1954. Most settled at first step. | Least grievances. .67 grievances per 100 employees, 1954. Least settled at first step. |
| Racial Integration | There is full racial integration in all three locals in union business and officers. They differ, however, in their plant policies as follows: | | |
| | Most aggressive | Moderately aggressive | Least aggressive |
| Strikes | Four strikes: 1946; 1948; 1956; 1959. Frequent stoppages. | Never any strikes or stoppages. | Three strikes: 1946; 1956; 1959. Rare stoppages. |
| Contact—members and union leaders | 10 leaders per 4000 members. Leaders go about plant. | 10 leaders per 2000 members. President and others go about plant for credit union. | 10 per 2000 members. President in employee lobby anytime. |
| Contact—members and union stewards | Much contact. Yet factionalism makes for some confusion. | Least contact. | Contact is sometimes difficult. (Steward is in different department.) |

also, in part, they reflect the particular local and district union leadership's attitudes and policies.

A very important difference in policies of the locals and especially, of their respective internationals, is their behavior regarding strikes. Local 28 (though it opposed the 1948 strike) has engaged in four strikes against Swift in 1946, 1948, 1956, and 1959. Local 78 engaged in three; Local 12 in none. Without a doubt, the decision to strike or not is a significant indication of union-management policy, and philosophy on the part of the union officers and members.

To sum up some of these differences: We find in Local 28 an insecure, unstable, aggressive local, very antimanagement. In Local 78, we find a secure, conservative local, promanagement, though also aggressively pro-union. In Local 12, we find a local challenged rather strongly by the UPWA, concerned that it retain its affiliation with the independent National Brotherhood of Packinghouse Workers, definitely promanagement, but less secure than Local 78 because of its somewhat threatened position, and its less affluent or aggressive international.

THE STALLED MERGER

The story of the two major meat packing unions' on-again, off-again efforts to merge emphasizes the differences between the UPWA and the Amalgamated.[5]

From the early organizing days after the Wagner Act, the two unions were opposed. This was brought out by the Amalgamated's yielding of power among the Big Four meat packers to the UPWA, and the UPWA's lesser share of the smaller independents. During the National War Labor Board days, and also during the short 1946 strike, there was some cooperation between the rival unions. But sharp opposition erupted between them during the 1948 strike, when the Amalgamated settled for a nine-cent raise while the UPWA chose to take a losing and disastrous ten-week strike. At that time the Amalgamated leaders asserted that the UPWA was too radical, leftwing, aggressive and prone to "trigger unionism." The UPWA, for its part, charged that the Amalgamated "sold us down the river." Costly raiding between the two unions began.

However, during the subsequent contract negotiations there was some exchange of information, and minorities in both unions were talking about the need for a merger. The Amalgamated could see more and more meat being processed in meat packing plants rather than in the retail stores, with the consequent decline of its block butchers. The UPWA needed members. Both felt that by unity they could gain in organizational savings, in bargaining, and in striking strength. Closer cooperation in bargaining followed. A no-raiding agreement was signed in 1953.

Merger was in the air, of course, throughout the entire American labor movement. The famous AFL-CIO merger convention of December 1955, gave the final incentive to the merger efforts of the two meat unions. From this convention, the unions sent a joint telegram to President George Meany asserting that they would plan one of the first major mergers. This was given much publicity.

In March 1956, the executive boards of both unions ratified a merger agreement, and a joint convention was planned for June of that year. But the Amalgamated was not satisfied with the structure of the new union and requested more seats on the new executive board. The UPWA agreed to this, but it was too late to have the merger convention as planned. Instead, each union had its own convention in Cincinnati during adjacent weeks in June. Both ratified their merger agreement.

This period marked the highpoint of good feeling between the two unions. The UPWA's *Packinghouse Worker*, July 1956, describes the UPWA convention as follows:

The huge hall was a mass of exuberant confusion as delegates shouted themselves hoarse, threw confetti and paraded the vast arena with Helstein and other union officers on their shoulders. Exploding firecrackers only served to punctuate the general din. Amalgamated Secretary-Treasurer Patrick E. Gorman told cheering UPWA delegates that he believed the new constitution could be ready within eight weeks. The move will form a united labor organization in the meat and related food industries numbering 450,000 members. Both Helstein and Gorman predicted an immediate organizing campaign aimed particularly at low wage non-union plants in southern states.

A final joint merger convention was planned for October 1956. Meanwhile, for the first time in history, the UPWA and the Amalgamated bargained as one with the meat packing companies, arriving at identically worded, though separately printed contracts. The 1956 and 1959 strikes against Swift were conducted by both unions, incidentally showing the strength to be found in unity.

But things were not going well between the unions in their working out of some important constitutional amendments and interpretations, especially regarding salaries for officials, and regarding union department heads as vice presidents not subject to the new union's executive officers. After a particularly stormy session, just a few days before the final merger convention, the Amalgamated, instead of attending further sessions, sent a telegram to the UPWA calling off the merger. In half-page ads in all the Chicago papers the Amalgamated said that "labor unity in meat packing" was "postponed."

The UPWA held its October convention anyway and ratified both the merger and the new proposed constitution, subject to agreement on the controverted issues. But for the Amalgamated, the merger now seemed out of the question.

In March 1957, there was some talk of a "mutual aid" pact possibly leading to a merger between the UPWA and the Retail Clerks International Association, though nothing came of it. But the move indicated the UPWA's need for a broader-based membership.

The UPWA still continued to hope for a merger with the Amalgamated. The UPWA Merger Committee on June 28, 1957, in a mimeographed memorandum, made the following statements to all UPWA representatives:

We state now that these problems [raised by the Amalgamated in calling off the merger] could have been resolved by the Joint Unity Committee. . . . While we recede to the jungle of division, the industry is undergoing profound changes. New distribution processes have appeared. New labor-saving devices are being daily installed. Markets are shifting. There is great flux in this country's economy, and all of these changes operate to reduce the number of jobs available, and the conditions under which these jobs are performed. The statistics almost shout danger. . . . A reasonable time has gone by; tempers should have cooled. Both parties have had an opportunity to reflect. The UPWA feels that the time has come when the dream of the leaders and members of both organizations should be realized.

A minority in the Amalgamated felt the same way. John Jurkanin, for instance, president of Amalgamated Local 500 in Cleveland, and organizer and chairman of the "National Retail and Packinghouse Committee to Save the Merger," asked the Amalgamated International officers for the privilege of appearing before the International Executive Board "in order to support position for merger with UPWA." He was granted the privilege. But there was no further mention of the merger in the public meetings or publications of the Amalgamated.

The UPWA, losing members through plant shutdowns, passed a resolution at its 1958 Convention in New York:

Whereas, the reasons for the failure to complete the merger appear to be vague and unimportant to the rank and file . . . and whereas, the problems . . . still plague both unions, and many more staggering political economic and financial problems have risen since 1956 to tax our strength,

Therefore, Be it resolved,

1. That we recognize that there are today many more compelling reasons for the merger than there were at the time of the last UPWA, AFL-CIO International Union Convention.
2. That we call upon the officers of both unions to arrange a meeting of the merger committees for the purpose of resolving the differences which prevented the completion of the merger.[6]

For the Amalgamated, however, the merger was a dead issue, at least for the near future. In the spring of 1959, with contract negotiations coming up again after a three-year interval, the leadership of the two unions met to discuss bargaining plans. Just at this time, however, the UPWA became the target of an investigation by the House Un-American Activities Committee. In some publicity the UPWA indirectly but clearly blamed the Amalgamated for this investigation. In a letter to the House Committee read at the hearings, President Helstein stated:

It is an unfortunate fact, however, that your Committee's decision to conduct these hearings happens to coincide in time with certain other developments.

A rejected and disgruntled former officeholder [A. T. Stephens] has been engaged in an effort to revive the long dead Communist issue, as it affects our union, in what appears to us to be a frantic effort, unquestionably doomed to failure, to foist himself back on to a membership which has rejected him. There is also some evidence which suggests that he is acting for another union which is suspected of having hopes of gobbling up the membership of our organization.

Angered, the Amalgamated retorted: "As far as we are concerned, we shall approach a new agreement as though most of the leadership of the UPWA were not in existence at all."[7] During the 1959 contract negotiations, however, the two unions did cooperate by mutual exchange of information and finally, by joint bargaining leading to a joint strike. But prospects for a merger remain very remote.

It is important to understand the main reasons for the failure of the merger in meat packing. First, there were some basic differences between the two unions. They differed in size and types of membership, the Amalgamated being twice as large as the UPWA, strong in meat packing, but also firmly based in many allied industries, while the UPWA's main strength was in meat packing alone. In addition, the Amalgamated was in a stronger financial position.

Very different approaches to the race question mark both unions. Both are liberal and have opposed racial discrimination, but the UPWA has been more militant. It has accomplished much.[8] But the Amalgamated leadership thinks the UPWA has sought too much publicity in its efforts, as though mere publicity were the same as solid accomplishment toward integration. Some UPWA leaders think that the Amalgamated is conservative and has not sufficiently fostered the rise of Negro leaders in its ranks.

Different philosophies of collective bargaining distinguish the unions. The Amalgamated is aggressive, but dislikes strikes, especially slowdowns or wildcats. It often talks about cooperation with management. For example in the controversial area of wage incentives, the UPWA had often strongly opposed incentives, in some statements calling the whole system mere "speedup." The Amalgamated was critical, but of the operation of the system rather than of its existence. The Amalgamated was the first to set up its own explicit industrial engineering department to iron out inequities in wage-incentive planning. The UPWA has been quicker to strike, more marked by slowdowns, and in its publications, such as the *Packinghouse Worker,* at times quite antimanagement. To the UPWA, the Amalgamated has been too quick to compromise with management thus failing to get "the last penny in the pot." To the Amalgamated, the UPWA has often been guilty of "trigger unionism" and "idiotic militancy" unrelated to economic reality.

There are considerable differences in the structures of the two unions and in their internal government and social relations, especially between the internationals and the locals. The Amalgamated's locals are generally much stronger and more autonomous than the locals in the UPWA. Yet in certain decisions, financial and political, the UPWA constitution puts more limitations on the power of the International officers than does the Amalgamated.

In their philosophy of dealing with communism, the two unions have shown marked differences. The UPWA had a deliberate policy of handling its leftwingers with kid gloves. The Amalgamated had been more openly anti-Communist though less consistent. Paradoxically, in 1954 the Amalgamated asked approval from the AFL to merge with the Fur and Leather Workers' union that had been expelled from the CIO for leftwing activities.

National AFL officers were seriously concerned. President Meany wrote Gorman that Ben Gold and the Fur and Leather leadership "have never failed . . . to follow the Communist propaganda line through all its twists and turns." [9] But the Amalgamated made serious efforts to get rid of the Communist influence in Fur and Leather. Certain people were dropped; all officers now signed the non-Communist affidavits; the Fur and Leather newspaper and camp were closed and the union funds transferred to Amalgamated control. Finally, a year later, in October 1955, the Executive Council of the AFL approved the merger. Since this time the Amalgamated has stiffened its anti-Communist position. Its Fur and Leather Division and the UPWA have retained friendly mutual interests.

The more specific reasons for the failure of the merger in October, 1956, were stated in newspaper ads[10] by the Amalgamated:

(1) The Amalgamated did not want its Education Department to become the "errand boy" of the vaguely structured Program Department of the UPWA.
(2) The relatively new Engineering Department would be consolidated with the Industrial Union Department and the Amalgamated felt this would limit the engineers' servicing the nonmeat-packing locals.
(3) The UPWA proposal to head all departments by vice presidents would have lessened the influence of the Amalgamated's present department heads.
(4) The major concern of the Amalgamated was that none of the departments or districts of the merged union should be under the control or supervision of the Executive Officers of the merged organization.

After the breakdown of the merger, the UPWA claimed that salaries were an issue and that the Amalgamated had insisted on wage cuts for certain UPWA staff members. In its newspaper ad, the Amalgamated explicitly denied this, saying that salaries were not the issue.

Behind these stated grievances, however, there were deeper unstated issues. Not only was there the question as to who would, or would not, get the union staff jobs, but one big question remained: who would lead the merged organization in the future? Gorman of the Amalgamated was sixty-three, but Helstein of the UPWA was only forty-seven. No single man in the Amalgamated seemed at the time in a position to succeed Gorman. Another question was, what might happen to the relatively autonomous retail butchers if they were now outnumbered, or if the Meat Packing Division and the Fur and Leather Division were to form a coalition against them?

Even these unstated differences might have been surmounted, but there was a still deeper problem: President Gorman and other Amalgamated leaders no longer trusted the motives and good faith of the UPWA leadership. This was only partly due to the Communist question. Almost alone among Amalgamated leaders President Gorman was pushing for the merger because he felt it was good trade unionism. Now his International Executive Board brought strong pressures to bear and the merger idea was abandoned.

The final position of the Amalgamated at the time of the 1956 break-up was made in the November-December 1956 *Butcher Workman:*

The UPWA, in its fifteen years of existence, was in its period of adolescence and growing pains. It believed in militancy and more militancy to accomplish its ends. Concerning our own organization . . . because of its bitter past experience in struggles and strikes, we laid less emphasis upon *force* and more emphasis upon *reason* to accomplish a fair contract for the membership. We believe that both philosophies can be merged into one, out of which would come "sensible militancy." . . . We are still going to keep a very open mind on the matter of the merger, but we are going to make sure that others do not throw trash into it.

President Helstein stated his views at the October 1956 UPWA convention:

We will just have to endure these disappointments and pocket our pride as many times as it takes to get the job done. . . . We support the position taken by our representatives on the Joint Unity Committee that such a merger must reflect an honorable joiner of the two unions, not the absorption of one by the other. . . . The Draft Constitution, prepared by the Joint Unity Committee . . . must contain the best possible adjustment and balance of the traditions and background of the two organizations. . . . We feel that the Draft Constitution represents such a balance and adjustment, and should make possible the kind of structure and administration which will properly serve the interests of the members of both unions.

So the merger of the two meat packing unions was definitely off for the immediately foreseeable future. Because of the contracting and sectional shifting of the meat packing industry, pressures toward the merger may come more strongly from the UPWA. But until there is an attitude of greater trust, the constitutional problems of merger will probably not be surmounted.

THE COMMUNIST ISSUE

The Communist issue has long beset the United Packinghouse Workers, but in recent years it has become more publicized and hence deserves treatment here. It is common knowledge that when John L. Lewis formed the CIO, he was willing to take in Communists, as they were often good union organizers. Lewis felt he could control them. The Packinghouse Worker's Organizing Committee was in turn infiltrated by some Communists. Apparently the party felt that the meat packing industry, as a basic food industry with important chemical by-products, was a crucial industry, along with the electrical industry and others.

After the UPWA was formed, the leftwingers had power in certain districts and locals, especially in Chicago and New York. But the Communists never completely controlled the UPWA. The historic CIO purge of its Communist unions at the 1949 Cleveland convention left the UPWA unchallenged. After this, the party renewed its efforts to capture the American Negro. Since the UPWA had so many Negro members, the party intensified its efforts among the UPWA members.[11]

At the 1950 Minneapolis convention of the UPWA, CIO President Philip Murray spoke out strongly against the Communists' efforts to use the trade union movement for their own ends and said he had confidence that the UPWA would take a forthright stand against the Communist conspiracy.

But the leftwingers in the UPWA continued vocal. In 1952, the House Un-American Activities Committee held hearings in Chicago, exposing a number of Communists in key positions of UPWA District One. In 1953, the CIO appointed a committee to investigate alleged communism in the UPWA. The committee, chaired by UAW officer Emil Mazey had as its purpose (1) to see if the UPWA was Communist-dominated; and (2) to see if the UPWA was going to be absorbed by the Amalgamated Meat Cutters. (The two unions had just completed a no-raiding, mutual assistance pact in the summer of 1953.) Mazey's findings in October 1953, were that there was no truth in either charge. He declared that the UPWA was not Communist-dominated and would not be absorbed by the Amalgamated. However, not all top CIO officers were satisfied with the Mazey report and some felt that it was a whitewash.

At any rate, about two weeks after the Mazey report was sent to the UPWA, Walter Reuther sent a covering letter to President Helstein amending the Mazey Report and saying that he hoped that the UPWA "would take affirmative action in dealing with Communist influence at the local and district levels" . . . "would remove from its staff and from the staff of all subordinate bodies . . . all Communists and other persons who, although their Communist Party membership cannot be proved, consistently follow the Communist Party programs and policies."

But the UPWA did very little "removing." District One Communist Herb March left the UPWA on a leave of absence and went to California. A few others left. But most of those who were alleged to the leftwingers remained, and still remain, in the UPWA. According to labor observer, David Saposs:

"An even more flagrant case of continuing Communist influence in a strong CIO union is that of the United Packinghouse Workers of America. This union has yet to take any action that is critical of the Soviet Union; [before Helstein's 1959 statements] its literature does not contain any derogatory references toward Communism or Soviet Russia; its anti-Communist leaders have not been able to attain elective leadership.[12]

In 1958 came the episode at the UPWA New York convention referred to above. President Helstein said that either he or Vice President A. T. Stephens would have to go. Political support went to Helstein, and Stephens, realizing his position, did not run for reelection. Stephens then brought public charges of communism against the UPWA. Helstein denied all Stephens' charges. Stephens, on the other hand, admitted that in his previous union days he had been duped by the Communists, but stated that his fight against Communists began at least one year before his election defeat. Stephens claimed that he had tried to persuade President Helstein "to take affirmative action in eliminating Communist Party influence in the affairs of our Union." [13] He claimed that these efforts were "futile."

President Meany held a private hearing for top UPWA officials and also with A. T. Stephens. Although the UPWA leaders wanted to set up their own investigative committee, Meany decided to see to the investigation himself. At the AFL-CIO Executive Council meeting in Puerto Rico in February 1959, the UPWA Communist issue was further discussed.

In May 1959, the House Un-American Activities Committee again held hearings in Chicago about Communist activities among the UPWA members. Two ex-packinghouse workers testified to Communist activities among several key District One and International staff members. District One Director Charles Hayes was especially singled out. Before the hearings, the CIO Cook County Industrial Union Council supported the UPWA. After the hearings, President Reuben Soderstrom of the State AFL-CIO demanded the resignation of Charles Hayes from the state organization. Hayes refused to resign.

During the hearings, all the alleged Communists denied that they were presently members of the Communist Party. When asked if they had once been members of the party, or had quit the party simply for convenience, or when asked if they would help expose the others and thus cooperate with the government, they took the Fifth Amendment. Helstein denied that his associates had used the Fifth Amendment against the AFL-CIO Ethical Practices Committee policy. He stated in the May *Packinghouse Worker:*

Persons who might have no reluctance to testify with respect to themselves and yet do not wish to be cast in the role of informer upon former friends and associates, may choose to invoke their own privilege against self-incrimination . . . for one who waives the privilege with respect to himself will find that refusal to name others may lead to contempt proceedings.

Meanwhile, George Meany refused the UPWA request to shelve any further the Communist investigations. Instead of referring the charges to the AFL-CIO Ethical Practices Committee, Meany set up a two-man subcommittee to study the UPWA situation and to report back to the AFL-CIO Executive Council. Walter Reuther, president of the United Auto Workers and George M. Harrison, president of the Brotherhood of Railway Clerks constituted the subcommittee.

The attitude of the UPWA toward the 1959 HUAC hearings was stated in a pamphlet entitled *Democratic Unionism:*

Many observers and many participants failed to understand what we were doing. They were angry or perplexed because our union often did not conform to more typical patterns of Communists and anti-Communists. We declined to be pushed by the McCarthys and others who demanded a conformity of word and stance in fighting totalitarianism. . . .

To the extent that there were those of Communist persuasion in the UPWA, the influence of the philosophy declined — perhaps too slowly for the tastes of some, but none the less steadily. That decline was the result of debate and analysis of each issue as it arose — as part of our exercise of free speech and free discussion. . . .

In a letter to the House Un-American Activities Committee, dated May 1, 1959, President Helstein stated:

Our union was born in the midst of the distress and disillusion of the depression and post-depression years of the 1930's and 1940's. In the light of the background of the industry, the economic and social tensions of the times and the bitter opposition of the packing companies to our efforts at organization and improvement of conditions, it would have been strange indeed if among the packinghouse workers there were none who turned to one or another of the utopian panaceas held out from various sources to the disillusioned: communism, socialism, technocracy, single-tax programs and all the rest.

Before our union was very old, therefore, it was faced with a fundamental choice of procedure. It could have embarked upon a program that might have led to bitter internal conflict, diverting energies urgently needed for the task of providing economic improvements for the packinghouse workers. Our membership developed a different program, one which we believe to be in the best traditions of our nation. There was never the slightest question or possibility of yielding control to a Communist group or any other ideology. But we felt that the challenge of communism could best be met not by a civil war certain to blunt the union's collective bargaining effectiveness, but by demonstrating that a positive and democratic brand of unionism would produce results, thereby defeating the attractions of communism by undercutting its ground. [The International UPWA did not hesitate, however, to wage a quasi "civil war" against the anti-Communists in 1948-9 and again in 1953.] We believe our program was right for the packinghouse workers. We know that it worked. . . .

No member of the Communist Party is or will be permitted to hold elective or appointive position in our union. . . . We do not feel that we serve any useful purpose by seeking to dredge up the muck of a dead past. If there are in our ranks persons with a Communist past, their present adherence to the democratic principles of our union represents a symbol of the victory of democratic totalitarianism, and we see no purpose in placing them in the public pillory . . .

Soon after the 1959 Hearings were concluded, a controversial article appeared on May 14, in the *Washington Post and Times Herald* to the effect that the House Committee was unknowingly "used" by corrupt unionists when it investigated communism in the UPWA. The article stated that the UPWA and the expelled Hoffa Teamsters were competing to organize the Puerto Rican sugar workers and that the committee's investigation would help Hoffa. Also the story asserted that the hearings helped the UPWA's rival union, The Amalgamated, which had been investigated by the Senate Rackets Committee. (Only a few Amalgamated New York locals had been investigated and Amalgamated's officer Max Block had resigned from the union.)

Representative Morgan Moulder, a Democrat with a prolabor record, had conducted some of the Chicago hearings. Angered by the charges of the Washington paper, he stated that he knew nothing of the two conditions cited but that the committee was simply doing its job of pursuing Communists wherever they may be. He pointed out that it had been a Communist technique for the last ten years for members to disassociate themselves from the party so they might sign the non-Communist affidavits and continue in the party underground.

He went on to say:

Not only did reliable, competent witnesses testify that the United Packinghouse Workers was saturated with Communists, but that the persons who had been identified as Communists invoked Constitutional privileges in response to questions as to whether their technical resignation from the Communist Party was a ruse. Mr. Speaker, in 1952, the Committee on Un-American Activities held hearings in Chicago, at which time a number of Communists were then found to be in key positions in the United Packinghouse Workers of America. Immediately the United Packinghouse Workers let loose a barrage against the Committee of Un-American Activities, but did not rid its ranks of Communists.[14]

President Lloyd and Secretary-Treasurer Gorman of the Amalgamated got into the fray with an editorial in the June 1959 *Butcher Workman:*

In all good faith, just a short time ago, our officers met with the leadership of the UPWA. We discussed plans on how best to approach the packers in the hope of consummating a good agreement in the interests of packinghouse workers generally. However, when the Un-American Activities Committee blasted their findings concerning the UPWA leadership on the front pages of all Chicago newspapers, President Helstein, as usual, tried to put the blame for the investigation upon the Amalgamated.

Lloyd and Gorman then cited Representative Moulder's statement before Congress and continued:

It will be difficult to restore confidence after the brazen attempt of Mr. Helstein to smear the Amalgamated when the garments of his own organization were terribly soiled in the smog of deceit and mistrust. The vast majority of UPWA membership are good, strong trade unionists. They deserve better leadership, and one day, as sure as the sun rises, they shall have it.

Meanwhile the Reuther-Harrison subcommittee held a hearing with the UPWA officers (though not with Stephens) who stated that they approved the AFL-CIO Ethical Practices Codes, intended to observe them, and would set up their own UPWA subcommittee to investigate A. T. Stephens' charges. They further stated that they would set up a Public Advisory Review Commission (doubtless modeled after the UAW Public Review Board) of five nationally known citizens to "review any and all actions by the Executive Board . . . as they relate to compliance with the Ethical Practices Codes." Reuther and Harrison reported to Meany that:

Your subcommittee believes that the steps taken and the procedures outlined by the Executive Board of the United Packinghouse Workers of America represent sound and acceptable procedures for dealing with the allegations, and we have advised the United Packinghouse Workers of America to proceed on this basis.[15]

The scope and fact-finding initiative of this public commission were to be further clarified at later meetings, deferred because of the prolonged UPWA 1959 contract negotiations and strikes. Thus, whether the long-standing Communist issue in the UPWA remains, or is whitewashed, or is finally laid to rest, will depend largely on the fact-finding effectiveness of the Public Advisory Review Commission.

It would be a mistake to assume that the Communist issue was the only reason for the distrust and difference between the Amalgamated and the UPWA. But it was a major factor as the events of 1958 and 1959 brought out. The Amalgamated's officers clearly distrusted the UPWA's neutralism toward communism.

In summary, we have seen the similar company background, but very different union backgrounds, both local and international, of the three groups of packinghouse workers. We shall now take a brief look at their neighborhoods, and individual racial, and occupational characteristics.

CHAPTER III

# Neighborhoods and Packinghouse Workers

A worker's city and neighborhood inevitably affect his attitudes and behavior both in his industrial plant and in his local union. We shall take a look at the neighborhoods in the three cities where the packinghouse people live, and we shall place side by side some general statistical facts about the three groups of workers, such as their service, turnover, age, and so forth. These two sets of facts will complete the stage setting, as it were, before which the packinghouse workers will speak in the following chapters.

In Chicago the famous packinghouse neighborhood, Back-of-the-Yards, has not changed very much in recent years. The other main neighborhood, Negro Bronzeville, has changed in that it is much larger. Other Chicago Negro neighborhoods have rapidly developed on the near north and the west sides of the city. These Chicago neighborhoods, with their social problems greatly affecting the attitudes of the packinghouse workers, have been described elsewhere.[1]

## KANSAS CITY

Winding northeast through the plains of Kansas, the Kaw or Kansas River pushes into a loop of the Missouri River to form a natural crossroads, the present-day thriving Kansas City. A line dropped from the confluence of the two rivers divides Kansas and Missouri, so that Greater Kansas City sits on the land of two states and two municipalities. About 60 per cent of the Swift packinghouse workers live in Kansas City, Kansas, and about 40 per cent in Kansas City, Missouri. Most of the office workers live in Missouri.

Greater Kansas City has a population around a million. Among the earliest immigrants to the city and to the Swift plant were Germans, Swedes, and Irish. In the early nineties came the Poles, then the southern Slavs, the

Croatians, Slovenians, and a few Serbs. After the turn of the century, a few Russians, Lithuanians, and Greeks came. Also the Italians entered the city, but they mostly avoided the packinghouses, as they did in Chicago. Later came the Mexicans, also Belgians, and other Europeans. The Negroes arrived too, especially during the two World Wars.

*The Mexicans.* Kansas City has many Mexican-Americans who work for railroads, like the Santa Fe, or in the packinghouses. Over 10 per cent of the Kansas City Swift workers are Mexicans. The Mexicans live in modest homes on Guadalupe Hill or along the low banks of the Kansas River in Armourdale, Argentine, and Rosedale. On the whole, they have made steady advancement in Kansas City. There is some discrimination affecting them, especially if they are dark-skinned, and they resent this. But their problems are not those of the Negro.

*The Negroes.* Negro-Americans constitute about 12 per cent of Greater Kansas City, mostly living on the Missouri side in a large square neighborhood extending southward from the Missouri River. The housing varies from a few sections of shacks and shanties around 12th and 18th streets to modest homes or a few fine residences along such avenues as Brooklyn and Benton. The tall tenements of Chicago's Bronzeville are not to be found here. Even in the few shanty sections remaining, we at least see light, air, and room.

To understand the position of the Negro people in the two Kansas Cities, we must remember that Missouri was once a slave state, and therefore a "southern state." More accurately, we would call it a "border state," but it is fast losing such a characterization. The half-defined racial patterns of border states make interracial relations more complex and unpredictable than the clearer patterns of either northern or southern states. Kansas, on the other hand, was never a slave state. Thus Kansas is slightly ahead of Missouri in civil rights practice. For example, Kansas passed an antibias law in March, 1959, making it a state offense to discriminate in schools, hotels, theatres, and restaurants. While the public schools in both Kansas Cities were still segregated in 1953, since that time the schools and most of the restaurants and hotels in both cities have been desegregated. Incidentally, it was estimated in 1950 that discrimination cost Kansas City about $37,500,000 annually.[2]

Some of the key organizations of the Negro people are their many churches (overwhelmingly Baptist), many clubs, the NAACP, the Urban League, and so forth. Their newspaper, *The Call* circulates throughout the southwest.

Where do the Negro people work? Throughout the many industries of the area, including the Swift and Armour packinghouses, Remington Arms at Lake City, the Pullman Company, and others. The colored are mostly found in unskilled and semiskilled jobs or in government jobs at the post office, tax department, and so forth. Very few industrial establishments hire Negro skilled machinists. And of such men there is not yet a large supply. Negroes are hardly accepted as office workers. A few major plants in the Kansas City area now employ Negro women in clerical jobs.

Both Missouri and Kansas have, in past years, defeated FEPC legislation. The chambers of commerce of the Kansas City area have not actively promoted integration in employment. In general, however, Negroes are active in organized labor in Kansas City. Negroes have achieved equal status in most of the unions except some of the AFL craft unions, such as the plumbers, electricians, and typographers.

The Negro people of Kansas City are not by any means as aggressive as the Negroes of Chicago, New York, and Detroit. They are more conservative, more depressed. They do not have the considerable professional and leadership groups, such as we find in Chicago's Bronzeville. Then, too, the rather Southern mentality of Missouri has only recently been changing. In Kansas City, the Negro is definitely a second-class citizen though he is making great progress. Conditions are changing, and so is the thinking of the Negro people, especially of the younger men. In Kansas City, Kansas, Negroes held the positions of Wyandotte County Commissioner and Municipal Judge in 1953, and in Jackson County, Missouri, a Negro judge was elected for the first time in 1957.

*Strawberry Hill.* The Slavic peoples who work at Swift mostly live on Strawberry Hill in Kansas City, Kansas, overlooking the Kaw River and the Missouri, with the skyscrapers of Kansas City, Missouri, in the background; with the stockyards and the big Armour and Swift plants and a new throughway in the foreground. Here is the large Croatian community, also Poles, Slovenians, Lithuanians. Their homes are neat and comfortable. A number of these people have now risen to supervisory positions in the packinghouses. Their children, however, have less tendency to work in the packinghouses than their fathers did.

EAST ST. LOUIS

East St. Louis is a river town. It stretches its factories and homes and railroads along the flat Illinois banks of the Mississippi River across from the metropolis of St. Louis. East St. Louis is the home of the Swift National

Stockyards packinghouse workers. Approaching the city by one of the three high bridges over the Mississippi, one sees a sprawling industrial and business center, rather ugly but powerful.

About a hundred thousand people live in East St. Louis. There are packinghouse workers, aluminum workers, chemical workers, truck drivers, railroad engineers and brakemen, construction workers. More than one-third of them are Negroes, living in the "South End." Most of the white people were born in America, some still keeping traditions from their "old country" such as the Poles and Lithuanians. Many nationalities are represented: Czech, Greek, German, Irish, Italian. About 40 per cent are Protestant and about 40 per cent are Catholic. By 1960, the city was becoming more and more colored.

There are several striking facts about East St. Louis. Most of its business firms are absentee-owned. Only five of the twenty-three major firms are owned by local families. Also there is an absence of attractive residential areas. Most of the higher management people and the better-paid or younger workers live outside the city. Finally, the city definitely is not attracting new industry. Of its eighteen manufacturing establishments employing over 125 employees, all but two originated before 1930.

In view of these facts it will be revealing to see where the packinghouse workers of the Swift National City plant live.

Most of the Swift Negro workers live in East St. Louis. The balance of Negro workers live in St. Louis itself. These are mostly the longer service men. Among the whites, most of the younger men live in the smaller, newer towns of Illinois, located in suburban, rural, or coal mining areas. Some of these workers drive as much as one hundred miles a day to and from the Swift plant. Most of the older workers live in East St. Louis; surprisingly enough, most of the foremen live there also.

The Swift plant is not actually located in East St. Louis proper, but in National City, Illinois. This is a curious town, separately incorporated, carved out of the top of East St. Louis, with a corridor over to the Mississippi. National City comprises the great stockyards, with the smaller packinghouses, Hunter (now bought out by Morrell) and Circle (actually in East St. Louis itself), and the great Armour and Swift plants dominating the scene. The town was set up separately to avoid the high East St. Louis taxes. It is owned by the Stockyards Company, Armour and Swift. It has its own mayor and miniature fire and police departments. There are a few rather plain, company-owned workers' houses in National City, where some packinghouse workers live. To the southwest of East St. Louis, on the banks of the Mississippi, there is another large tract, separately incorporated,

Table 7. Neighborhoods of East St. Louis workers.

Random, stratified, and weighted sample of 152 hourly-paid employees and 25 foremen, 1953–1954 (in per cent).

| White men | East St. Louis | Belleville | Collinsville | Other[a] | St. Louis |
|---|---|---|---|---|---|
| Under two years' service | 21.5 | 0 | 21.5 | 57 | 0 |
| Short service, 2 through 6 yrs. | 50 | 7 | 7 | 36 | 0 |
| Middle service, 7 through 15 yrs. | 36 | 21 | 0 | 43 | 0 |
| Long service, over 16 yrs. | 79 | 0 | 14 | 7 | 0 |
| *Negro men* | | | | | |
| Under two years' service | 72 | 0 | 0 | 14 | 14 |
| Short service, 2 through 6 yrs. | 79 | 0 | 0 | 14 | 7 |
| Middle service, 7 through 15 yrs. | 72 | 0 | 0 | 7 | 21 |
| Long service, over 16 yrs. | 57 | 0 | 0 | 7 | 36 |
| *White women* | | | | | |
| Under two years' service | 30 | 10 | 10 | 50 | 0 |
| Short service, 2 through 6 yrs. | 40 | 10 | 10 | 40 | 0 |
| Middle service, 7 through 15 yrs. | 70 | 10 | 0 | 20 | 0 |
| Long service, over 16 yrs. | 80 | 10 | 0 | 10 | 0 |
| *Foremen* | 72 | 8 | 4 | 12 | 4 |
| Weighted percentage of all white women who live in East St. Louis | | | | | 49 |
| Weighted percentage of all white men who live in East St. Louis | | | | | 47 |
| Weighted percentage of all Negro men who live in East St. Louis | | | | | 71 |

[a] These are mostly small towns in Illinois, such as Edwardsville, Breese, Granite City, Madison, Caseyville, Venice.

called Monsanto, Illinois, and primarily dedicated to the large Monsanto Chemical Company plant there.

Going about East St. Louis, one gets the impression of a city in a state of arrested growth. Frequently the sidewalks are not built, and the zoning appears inadequate. Walking through an attractive neighborhood suddenly one comes to a vacant lot next to a big tank or factory. Everywhere are railroads with their gradecrossings. This is a city of railroads, and Diesel engines with the throaty blast of horns, and the rumbling of freight cars. Trucks abound, along with gas stations, snack bars, and coffee shanties.

The old Valley District, the red light and gambling district not far from the entrance road to the stockyards, has been evacuated in recent years. Politics in East St. Louis is undoubtedly better than it used to be, with much improvement still needed. Still, one gets the impression of a city in a state of social stress, with poor community spirit, and grave social problems. Crime and vice are commonplace. One constantly reads in the single newspaper, the *East St. Louis Journal* (now called the *Evening Journal*), of gas stations being held up, and of tavern fights. Probably most of the gangsters of earlier days have been forced to move out of town. But the smaller operators continue. The fact that East St. Louis is just across the river and the state line from the metropolis of St. Louis makes for some of its problems.

The leaders in East St. Louis have tried with some success to clean up the city. The manager of the Chamber of Commerce, Charles Spilker, felt that East St. Louis was unfairly maligned:

I still hear about the Valley and its lights outside houses of prostitution, the wide-open gambling, and bookmakers on every corner. Surely since 1946 the word should have seeped out that the gambling hells are closed, that the dealers have other jobs, that the bookies have given up except on a sneak basis, the Valley for years has been a highway. . . .[3]

Yet he admitted that: "there must be engendered a civic spirit, a spiritual awakening. . . ." While East St. Louis is sensitive about its lurid reputation, it appears at least to this observer (who has not made a thorough sociological study of the city) that much still remains to be done to weld East St. Louis into a true community and to solve its social and economic problems.

In view of the failure of new industry to come into East St. Louis, a University of Illinois study of the problem comes to these conclusions:

In general the author is inclined to believe that the crux of the industrial development problem lies outside of labor relations. The long-time reputation of a community for violence, crime, vice, and corruption is likely to have an adverse effect long after the original causes of the reputation have been reduced or eliminated. Any new occurrence tends to have a disproportionate impact because of this past history. Furthermore, most people probably do not separate East St. Louis from the rest of "Southern Illinois" in their thinking. The fact that the construction anti-racketeering cases of 1954, for example, were heard in federal district court in East St. Louis undoubtedly left a black mark on East St. Louis although only one local man was involved.

The reputation of the city as a place in which to work but not to live also may be a discouraging factor to new industry. Even a superficial examination indicates the need for improvement along many lines, including housing, smoke control, slum clearance, etc. One of the difficulties in attacking this problem apparently has been the relative lack of interest on the part of business owners and industrial executives who live outside of the communities. The recent efforts of community business, labor, and professional people to improve community conditions are most important in this connection.[4]

Actually, East St. Louis has been losing industry. In recent years the Alcoa plant, employing around two thousand employees, reduced itself to mere maintenance level with five hundred employees. In August 1959, the big Armour plant closed, putting fourteen hundred packinghouse workers out of jobs. Since the neighboring Swift plant is just about as old, it is a question as to whether Swift will remain in National Stockyards, especially since the company has its St. Louis Independent plant across the river. Some possibility of consolidating the two greater St. Louis plants is likely. Anxiety about the future of their jobs is surely present among the East St. Louis Swift workers in 1960.

Negroes in East St. Louis live in the "South End." Some of this is low land near the Mississippi River. Here you see frame shanties with dark patched-up shacks in the back yard. Yards are littered with junk, tin cans, and waste. It is a depressing slum of wooden firetraps. There are several fire casualties among them nearly every year. Southeast are the better homes and apartments. There is no wealthy Negro district, such as one finds in part of Chicago's Bronzeville. The poorest shacks are at the edge of town near the Illinois Central tracks.

South End has its clubs and churches, and one small newspaper, *The Crusader*. There are some Negro leaders in the community, mostly lawyers. But South End must also look for leadership across the river to the larger and more prosperous Negro community of St. Louis, with its two newspapers, the *St. Louis Argus* and the *St. Louis American*.

South End has its own serious social problems. Many of its citizens were born in the south and are finding difficult the adjustment to northern, urban, industrial life. The family suffers most. Various welfare agencies, institutions, and community leaders are making an attempt to solve these problems.

East St. Louis probably took many of its interracial patterns from the former slave state of Missouri across the river. The city was largely Jim Crow until recent years. Now the schools have been nominally integrated together with the downtown movie theatres and a few restaurants. But there is less free intermingling between Negro and whites than there is in a city like Chicago, for instance. The pattern in East St. Louis is quite similar to that in Kansas City. We have, in both cases "border" cities, neither fully northern, nor fully southern.

CHICAGO

Now we should ask: How do these cities differ from each other and especially from Chicago, and how might these variables affect our results?

Probably the biggest difference in Chicago, Kansas City and East St. Louis is size. Chicago with nearly five million people is five times as large as the metropolitan areas of each of the other two cities, taking East St. Louis as a part of the St. Louis area. Size can mean many things, such as distance from work, greater neighborhood anonymity, more competing job opportunities, and so forth. One would expect it to be harder, for instance, to induce union members to come to local meetings in Chicago, than in Kansas City or East St. Louis. Housing in Chicago is more crowded, expensive, and difficult to find. There appears to be no great difference between East St. Louis and Kansas City, though, as to the effects of metropolitan area size.

Chicago, unlike the other two cities, has, in a certain sense, less "rural-mindedness." For instance, a number of the packinghouse workers in East St. Louis and Kansas City have come from farms, or they now live on small or large farms. This is less likely to be the case in Chicago. Since Chicago is so much larger, more urban, more industrialized, its working people are more urban-minded than they are farm-minded. In Kansas City and East St. Louis there is more "sympathy" among the working people toward such a farm-related industry as meat packing than there is in Chicago. In Chicago many workers attach a stigma to "working in the stockyards." This stigma is much less pronounced in the other two cities.

As for differing patterns of race relations, Chicago is the most liberal and advanced. Kansas City and East St. Louis, both "border" cities, are similar to each other, but quite different from Chicago. These variables influence racial differences, as we shall see.

Table 8. *Workers' comparative service profile.*
Chicago, Kansas City, East St. Louis (in per cent of the respective workforces, excluding people under two years' service).

|  | Men |  |  |  |  |  | Women |  |  |  |  |  |
|---|---|---|---|---|---|---|---|---|---|---|---|---|
|  | Colored |  |  | White |  |  | Colored |  |  | White |  |  |
| Service | Chgo. | K.C. | E.S.L. | Chgo. | K.C. | E.S.L. | Chgo. | K.C. | E.S.L. | Chgo. | K.C. | E.S.L. |
| Short | 26 | 19 | 14 | 2 | 21 | 9 | 7 | 0.6 | 0 | 2 | 9 | 10 |
| Middle | 13.5 | 9 | 17 | 11.5 | 16 | 19 | 1.5 | 0.4 | 0 | 3 | 2 | 5 |
| Long | 11 | 9 | 10 | 20 | 12 | 14 | 0.5 | 0 | 0 | 2 | 2 | 2 |

|  | Chicago | Kansas City | East St. Louis |
|---|---|---|---|
| Men | 85 | 86 | 84 |
| Negro | 55 | 38 | 44 |

## The Packinghouse Workers

A very interesting aspect of our three-plant research is to see how the packinghouse workers, as three groups, differ from each other demographically. Later we shall try to relate these differences to the attitudes we find.

First, consider the length of time the packinghouse workers have been with the company, also their race, and their sex, as shown in Table 8.

Among both the men and the women, Chicago has the most marked trend toward a greater number of Negro workers. Among the short-service workers, both men and women, Chicago has the smallest number of white workers. Kansas City seems to be maintaining its white proportion, while in East St. Louis the Negro proportion is mounting.

All three plants use about the same proportion of women workers. These women are mostly Negro in Chicago. In Kansas City they are mostly white. In East St. Louis they are all white. This lack of racial comparability should be considered when we later compare the men's views with the women's.

As for the old-timers (an important part of any workforce), the Chicago plant has by far the biggest proportion of long-service white men — 20 per cent the workforce of our Chicago sample.

The differing formal education of these packinghouse workers, Table 9, makes for interesting comparisons.

Table 9. *Workers' comparative education.*
Chicago, Kansas City, East St. Louis
(years of schooling).

|  | Men | | | | | | Women | | | | | |
| --- | --- | --- | --- | --- | --- | --- | --- | --- | --- | --- | --- | --- |
|  | Colored | | | White | | | Colored | | | White | | |
| Service | Chgo. | K.C. | E.S.L. | Chgo. | K.C. | E.S.L. | Chgo. | K.C. | E.S.L. | Chgo. | K.C. | E.S.L. |
| Short | 8.1 | 8.6 | 7.8 | 7.1 | 8.5 | 7.6 | 10.8 | 10.6 | — | 7.9 | 8.9 | 8.6 |
| Middle | 6.9 | 9.3 | 6.3 | 8.3 | 8.8 | 9.1 | 9.3 | 10.3 | — | 9.0 | 9.4 | 8.5 |
| Long | 5.1 | 7.4 | 5.8 | 6.6 | 5.2 | 7.9 | 7.5 | — | — | 7.4 | 5.5 | 8.2 |

The familiar pattern of the younger workers having more education repeats itself. These differences are noteworthy: the colored men of Kansas City have more education than the colored men of either of the two other plants. The colored women of Kansas City continue the Chicago pattern of having more schooling than the white women. The Negroes of the East St. Louis plant have somewhat less education than those of either Chicago or Kansas City. We recall that a high percentage of these people are southern-born.

Educational differences would seem to constitute at least a minor variable.

Let us now see how the workers differ in age. Table 10 shows that differences between the plants are not startling. Kansas City's white men and women have a wider age span; that is, the short-service workers are

Table 10. *Workers' comparative ages.*
Chicago, Kansas City, East St. Louis
(for workers of two years' service and over).

|  | Men | | | | | | Women | | | | | |
|---|---|---|---|---|---|---|---|---|---|---|---|---|
|  | Colored | | | White | | | Colored | | | White | | |
| Service | Chgo. | K.C. | E.S.L. | Chgo. | K.C. | E.S.L. | Chgo. | K.C. | E.S.L. | Chgo. | K.C. | E.S.L. |
| Short | 34 | 36 | 35 | 37 | 32 | 34 | 33 | 31 | — | 38 | 33 | 39 |
| Middle | 44 | 41 | 44 | 41 | 44 | 38 | 35 | 49 | — | 34 | 43 | 39 |
| Long | 52 | 56 | 56 | 51 | 57 | 46 | 51 | — | — | 43 | 57 | 48 |

Weighted average, Chicago 41.3
Weighted average, Kansas City 41.5
Weighted average, East St. Louis 41.5

younger than in the other two plants, and the long-service workers are older. The Negro men follow a most regular pattern. The Negro women are not really comparable. The average ages for workers of two years' service and over are remarkably similar.

How the workforces are divided as to job skills gives us a further clue for comparison.

Table 11. *Workers' comparative skills.*
Chicago, Kansas City, East St. Louis
(in per cent grouped by race, sex, and service).

|  | Men | | | | | | Women | | | | | |
|---|---|---|---|---|---|---|---|---|---|---|---|---|
|  | Colored | | | White | | | Colored | | | White | | |
| Service | Chgo. | K.C. | E.S.L. | Chgo. | K.C. | E.S.L. | Chgo. | K.C. | E.S.L. | Chgo. | K.C. | E.S.L. |
| *Short* | | | | | | | | | | | | |
| Skilled | 8 | 0 | 7 | 29 | 36 | 21 | 0 | 0 | — | 0 | 0 | 0 |
| Semiskilled | 46 | 93 | 86 | 54 | 64 | 79 | 38 | 86 | — | 63 | 75 | 90 |
| Unskilled | 46 | 7 | 7 | 17 | 0 | 0 | 62 | 14 | — | 37 | 25 | 10 |
| *Middle* | | | | | | | | | | | | |
| Skilled | 8 | 7 | 21 | 52 | 37 | 50 | 0 | 0 | — | 0 | 0 | 0 |
| Semiskilled | 59 | 93 | 50 | 44 | 43 | 50 | 75 | 100 | — | 25 | 100 | 100 |
| Unskilled | 33 | 0 | 29 | 4 | 0 | 0 | 25 | 0 | — | 75 | 0 | 0 |
| *Long* | | | | | | | | | | | | |
| Skilled | 26 | 14 | 14 | 38 | 29 | 64 | 0 | — | — | 0 | 0 | 0 |
| Semiskilled | 69 | 56 | 72 | 45 | 71 | 36 | 25 | — | — | 77 | 100 | 100 |
| Unskilled | 5 | 0 | 14 | 17 | 0 | 0 | 75 | — | — | 33 | 0 | 0 |

NEIGHBORHOODS AND WORKERS

One obvious difference in Table 11 is the larger percentage in Chicago of unskilled workers for all service levels except the colored old-timers.

Among the white men of long service, we note that East St. Louis men are much more skilled. Negro men seem to have both more skilled jobs and more unskilled jobs in East St. Louis than they do in Kansas City.

While there are a number of differences in the variation of skills by length of service, race, and sex, it is hard to find in Table 11 a distinctive pattern that will be useful later in explaining some of the attitude differences. The total proportion of skilled workers is about the same in each of the plants: 25 per cent.

Table 12. *Comparative geographic origin of male colored workers in Chicago, Kansas City, East St. Louis (in per cent).*

|  | Northern born | | | Southern born | | |
|---|---|---|---|---|---|---|
| Service | Chgo. | K.C. | E.S.L. | Chgo. | K.C. | E.S.L. |
| Short | — | 36 | 21 | — | 64 | 79 |
| Middle | — | 50 | 21 | — | 50 | 79 |
| Long | — | 50 | 21 | — | 50 | 79 |
| Weighted totals | — | 43 | 27 | — | 57 | 73 |

The geographic origin of the colored workers in the plants shows a significant difference between East St. Louis and Kansas City. Nearly three quarters of the former Negro workers are southern-born, as opposed to a little more than half of the Kansas City workers. (We have no Chicago data.) Since Negroes from the South have tended in the past to have less education than northern Negroes, and since they have problems of adjustment to northern life, the fact that nearly three-fourths of the National Stockyards Negro workers are southern-born is important. These Negroes are more satisfied with work at Swift than the Kansas City Negroes. They are less aggressive and militant in seeking their advancement. This difference in percentage of southern-born is surely one explanation.

Three behavioral characteristics of the packinghouse workers: turnover, absenteeism, and wage assignments, show revealing differences.

*Turnover.* The main fact evident in Table 13 is the lower turnover in Chicago. Since the Chicago plant is in a stage of contraction, we might expect the workers to be more conservative about quitting and about giving cause for discharge. During a depression, for example, there tends to be less turnover. A declining plant has similar conditions. Yet Chicago also has

Table 13. *Workers' comparative turnover. Chicago, Kansas City, East St. Louis (hourly-paid workers only in percentages of average workforce).*

|  | 1951 | | | 1952 | | | 1953 | | | 1954 | | |
|---|---|---|---|---|---|---|---|---|---|---|---|---|
|  | Chgo. | K.C. | E.S.L. | Chgo. | K.C. | E.S.L. | Chgo. | K.C. | E.S.L. | Chgo. | K.C. | E.S.L. |
| Quits | 14.2 | 42.9 | 22.9 | 8.4 | 28.2 | 34.2 | 15.0 | 14.8 | 28.6 | 4.6 | 7.1 | 7.4 |
| Discharges | 7.2 | 3.9 | 4.2 | 12.4 | 23.2 | 5.6 | 2.9 | 11.5 | 4.4 | 2.3 | 6.5 | 2.1 |
| Layoffs | 35.2 | 69.8 | 66.1 | 35.6 | 53.9 | 47.9 | 26.0 | 14.3 | 39.3 | 23.0 | 51.1 | 50.2 |
| Retirements and deaths | 3.4 | 1.9 | 2.7 | 3.8 | 1.6 | 1.9 | 3.4 | 2.9 | 1.3 | 3.1 | 1.2 | 1.0 |
| Average size of workforce | 4789 | 2436 | 2622 | 4589 | 2072 | 1971 | 3978 | 2204 | 2090 | 3762 | 2017 | 2075 |
| Turnover | 60.0 | 118.5 | 95.9 | 60.2 | 106.9 | 89.6 | 47.3 | 43.5 | 73.5 | 53.0 | 65.9 | 60.7 |

Four-year average

|  | Chicago | Kansas City | E. St. Louis |
|---|---|---|---|
| Quits | 10.5 | 23.3 | 23.8 |
| Discharges | 5.2 | 11.3 | 4.1 |
| Layoffs | 30.0 | 47.3 | 51.0 |
| Retirements and deaths | 3.4 | 1.9 | 1.7 |
| Turnover | 49.2 | 83.7 | 79.9 |

less layoffs. In part, this might be due to the greater diversity of plant operations in Chicago, allowing management to transfer employees rather than to lay them off. This more favorable layoff record means that the Chicago packinghouse workers had more job stability. Steady work is important to the packinghouse workers. Of course the major cutback in the Chicago plant, starting in 1956, has changed all this.

We must be cautious in arguing from the "quit" figures. Quits do not necessarily indicate dissatisfaction with work. Sometimes they merely indicate the farmers or students who only intend to work in the packinghouse temporarily. Chicago has definitely less of such labor, and this is probably the main reason for its better quit record. There are no differences between Kansas City and East St. Louis regarding quits.

Competing job opportunities are about the same in the three communities, with some advantage to Chicago as a larger city with more diversified businesses. Packinghouse wages and fringes compare very favorably to nearby industries in the three cities. But packinghouse working conditions necessarily are not as comparatively attractive.

Discharges-for-cause give a partial clue to troublemakers or unsatisfactory employees. The main difference here is in Kansas City, where there is a significantly greater number of such workers. One reason for this was the number of UPWA-minded, rather dissatisfied, anticompany workers hired in 1952, some from the closed-down Cudahy plant across the street. On the other hand, the greater militancy and aggressiveness of Local 28's leftwing leadership may prevent discharges that would otherwise occur.

It is difficult to draw a single and simple conclusion out of Table 13. Probably the main point is that Chicago is a different kind of plant — declining, with less farmers, students, casual, and temporary labor, and with the lowest turnover rate. Rather significantly the lowest discharge rate is in East St. Louis with the highest in Kansas City.

*Absenteeism* is a behavioral characteristic that clearly differentiates the workforces. Being absent from work makes problems for a man's foreman, especially on a production-line job. It also indicates something of the stability of the employee and of his attitude toward work.

Table 14. *Workers' estimated comparative absenteeism. Chicago, 1950; Kansas City, 1952; East St. Louis, 1952*
(Percentages by race, sex and service of employees who worked less than 52 weeks in the given year).

|  | Men | | | | | | Women | | | | | |
|---|---|---|---|---|---|---|---|---|---|---|---|---|
|  | Colored | | | White | | | Colored | | | White | | |
| Service | Chgo. | K.C. | E.S.L. | Chgo. | K.C. | E.S.L. | Chgo. | K.C. | E.S.L. | Chgo. | K.C. | E.S.L. |
| Short | 28 | 21 | 17 | 25 | 7 | 7 | 58 | 44 | — | 25 | 0 | 0 |
| Middle | 35 | 7 | 8 | 17 | 29 | 7 | 100 | 0 | — | 33 | 25 | 0 |
| Long | 20 | 43 | 7 | 20 | 8 | 0 | 43 | — | — | 25 | 13 | 10 |
| Weighted totals | 26 | 27 | 11 | 19 | 14 | 5 | 63 | 29 | — | 28 | 7 | 1 |

Table 14 shows us some sharp differences between the three workforces. We must recall that these are only estimated figures, so that the smaller percentage differences must be regarded with caution. Also the fact that the years are different suggests caution. Among the colored men, there is not much difference between Chicago and Kansas City. But the East St. Louis Negroes, proportionately more southern-born and of rural extraction, are distinctly less likely to be absent from work than the more northern-born Negroes of Kansas City and Chicago. Chicago has more trouble with absenteeism than the other plants, while East St. Louis has the least. These figures suggest a more restless, less satisfied workforce in Chicago, with the most satisfied packinghouse workers in East St. Louis.

*Wage assignments,* finally, are a minor statistic perhaps, yet revealing. Since Kansas law does not provide for such assignments, we can compare only the Chicago and East St. Louis workers. Wage assignments are often an indication of imprudent installment-buying and of living beyond one's means. They also show the marginal savings of so many workers who are living from weekly paycheck to paycheck. The number of wage assignments tends to go up in the summer time, and during holidays such as Christmas. Most of the assignments come from firms dealing in clothing, jewelry, loans, and automobiles. Not a little blame for causing workers to live beyond their means must fall upon the advertising, high pressure selling, and credit policies of these companies. Table 15 gives us the findings.

Table 15. *Comparative wage assignments of workers in Chicago, 1949-50; East St. Louis, 1953.*

|  | Chicago | E. St. Louis |
|---|---|---|
| Total | 6240 | 1013 |
|  | 120 per week | 19 per week |
| Percentage of all assigned employees who have already had previous wage assignments | 90 | 57 |
| Percentage of all assigned employees assigned for first time | 10 | 43 |
| Per cent of assignments affecting whites | 5 | 12 |
| Per cent of assignments affecting Negroes | 95 | 88 |
| Number of workers getting assignments | 1000-1500 (about 20% of workforce) | 339 (16% of workforce) |
| Average number of assignments per assignee | 5 | 2.98 |
| Maximum number of assignments per assignee | 22 | 34 |

In comparing our East St. Louis findings with those in Chicago, we find that the East St. Louis workers are less affected by wage assignments. Here it is only 16 per cent of the workforce, as opposed to 20 per cent in Chicago. Only 57 per cent of the assignees are repeaters, as opposed to the 90 per cent in Chicago. Differences in the percentages of colored and white having assignments are not great between the two plants. We may conclude that the East St. Louis workers are more provident than the Chicago workers. Also there may be less social competition among them and a greater carryover of rural values. Along with lesser absenteeism, this greater financial stability of the East St. Louis workers clearly sets them apart from the Chicago packinghouse workers.

Of the three cities in this study, Chicago differs from the other two in a way that will affect our findings. In looking at the service, race, and sex composition of the three workforces, we find this difference: an increasingly higher proportion of Negroes in Chicago, and a slight trend in

East St. Louis toward such an increase. The East St. Louis Negroes are more southern-born than those in Kansas City. There is not much difference in age, education, or skill of the workers in the three plants.

Three differences in behavior are present. Turnover is lowest in Chicago, but this is primarily because of the fewer layoffs there. The lower quit-rate in Chicago might seem to indicate greater work satisfaction, but it is really due to the more numerous student and farmer workers in the other two plants, who quit after their temporary employment. We cannot clearly relate turnover or quitting to worker attitudes, so far as Chicago is concerned.

But absenteeism and wage assignments are clearer behavioral facts. Chicago leads in both. These two findings, Chicago's marked differences in the service, sex, and racial composition of its workforce, along with the problems of Chicago's Bronzeville, at least suggest that among the very different attitudes of the packinghouse workers, the Chicago workers may be the least satisfied.

PART TWO

His Role as Employee

CHAPTER IV

# The Worker Looks at His Company

## The Meaning of Company Allegiance

The recently developed concepts of dual allegiance,[1] and of company and union allegiance have aroused numerous comments and some criticisms. Recognizing the justice of some of these criticisms, we shall try to clarify the rather difficult attitude or concept that we call "company allegiance."

Company allegiance, as we are using the abstraction in this book, is partly the worker's attitudes about his total work situation, and partly his attitudes toward the "company," or "Swift & Company," as an institution.

Company allegiance is partly a summation of the worker's attitudes toward job, pay, standards, gang, foreman, and so forth, for two reasons. The interviewer frequently brought up the topic of company allegiance by saying: "Putting it all together, John, what would you say about Swift as a place to work?" This question evidently suggests to the worker that he put together, or add up, his attitudes about his work. Secondly, the topic of company allegiance tended to come up near the middle of the interview, when most of the worker's attitudes toward his job, pay and so forth had already been expressed. To some extent the worker would look at this topic as a summation.

But company allegiance is not merely a summation; it also involves the worker's attitude toward the company, as he perceives the company. It means the worker's degree of approval of the company as an institution.

Obviously the "company" is not seen by every worker in exactly the same way. Looking at "Swift & Company" through different workers' eyes we see: "the little red [butcher's] wagon"; "the Swift boys"; "Swift policy"; "pensions"; "good consideration and pay"; "steady work"; "a place where you have a clean job." It would be interesting to give a sentence-completion test to a sample of employees and ask them to write the first thing that comes to their mind when you say: "Swift & Company." We would get very different answers, because each worker and his perceptions are unique. Yet these answers are comparable and indeed measurable as the workers' common interpretation of the same physical or objective event: Swift & Company.

To express these ideas, allegiance seems to be a more suitable word than esteem, endorsement, attraction, acceptance, approbation, approval, loyalty, dedication, identification, concern, interest, and so forth. Obviously no single word can sum up the thinking of working people. Perhaps loyalty is the closest approach to allegiance, but loyalty implies more intensity and emotional depth than we want. Many packinghouse workers with allegiance will also have loyalty, but not all.

Company allegiance does not mean that the worker must be happy with everything about his job. Nor does company allegiance mean a deep pride in one's work or creative self-expression in it. Some workers had these. More did not. Yet the workers were generally satisfied with Swift and with most aspects of their jobs. This satisfaction is an important finding in itself. Deeper, creative self-fulfillment in work is often absent. This is another matter, very important, but not detracting from the importance of company allegiance.

Admittedly, company allegiance is a complex attitude, but one need only go to the interviews themselves to see that it is a meaningful abstraction.

It will be interesting now to see the relationship between a worker's attitude of company allegiance, to his other company-related attitudes. Table 16 gives a summary of this.

We see in Table 16 some relationship between company allegiance and the other attitudes, but not a perfect correlation. The packinghouse workers in East St. Louis (at least the men) have the most company allegiance, and we can see that most of the other company-related attitudes of the East St. Louis workers are also more favorable.

Three attitudes are mostly unfavorable for the hourly-paid workers: attitudes toward advancement opportunities, toward wage incentives, and toward having one's children come to Swift to work. A worker's unfavorable or neutral attitude in these areas is not effectively inconsistent with a general attitude of company allegiance.

No packinghouse worker shows company allegiance and at the same time dissatisfaction with most company-related attitudes. Of course, he might be dissatisfied with a few things, for example, his foreman, or the working conditions. People who fail to have company allegiance are generally dissatisfied people. But not all. A man might be satisfied with practically every aspect of his job except his racially limited advancement opportunities. This alone might cause his company disallegiance.

Table 16. *Summary of company-related attitudes.*
Chicago, 1950 — Kansas City, 1953 — East St. Louis, 1953-4.

| Attitude | Chicago | | | Kansas City | | | East St. Louis | | |
|---|---|---|---|---|---|---|---|---|---|
| | Hourly-paid | Union ldrs. | Foremen | Hourly-paid | Union ldrs. | Foremen | Hourly-paid | Union ldrs. | Foremen |
| Company allegiance | 1.6 | 2.3 (rt. wing) (1.6) | 1.6 | 1.9 | 1.4 (CIO) (3.1) | 1.4 | 1.5 | 1.3 | 1.3 |
| 1. Toward the foreman | 1.8 | 2.3 (rt. wing) (1.6) | | 2.0 | 2.0 (CIO) (3.5) | | 1.8 | 1.6 | |
| 2. Toward the job | 1.8 | 2.3 (rt. wing) (1.8) | 1.9 | 1.9 | 1.6 (CIO) (2.9) | 2.0 | 1.6 | 1.6 | 1.8 |
| 3. Toward the gang | | | 2.4 | 1.9 | 1.6 | 1.7 | 1.9 | 1.4 | 1.7 |
| 4. Toward pay | | | | 2.1 77%[a] | 1.8 90% | 2.0 74% | 1.9 87% | 1.7 100% | 2.0 88% |
| 5. Toward working conditions | | | | 2.1 73% | 63% | | 1.8 81% | 33% | |
| 6. Toward the suggestion system | | | | 2.9 49% | 3.0 | 1.3 | 2.4 74% | 3.4 | 2.6 |
| 7. Toward (a) advancement and (b) equal opportunity | 43% | | 52% | 44% 20% | 50% (CIO) (10%) | 72% | 56% 28% | 57% | 88% |
| 8. Toward standards | 25% | 14% | | 47% | 44% (CIO) (0%) | 67% | 66% | 14% | 74% |
| 9. Toward children following | 18% | | 33% | 25% | 17% | 36% | 47% | 50% | 32% |

Scale: 1.0 Very favorable; 2.0 Favorable; 3.0 Neutral; 4.0 Unfavorable; 5.0 Very unfavorable.

[a] Percentages mean per cent favorable. For some attitudes we have both the numerical scale and the per cent favorable. For other attitudes we present only one measure.

Since company allegiance represents the worker's views about the company as an institution, and also his approximate summation of his other company-related attitudes, this company allegiance attitude plays a more important role in our analysis than the attitudes of the worker toward his pay, gang, the standards system, the foreman, and so forth.

For scientific and logical reasons, we can cut off a man's company allegiance from his other attitudes. But for a full understanding of the attitudes and motivations of one employee or of any group of employees, we must put together again all the company-related attitudes which we have separated. Our concept of company allegiance needs to be related to the nine other company-related attitudes.

East St. Louis Workers

In spite of the differences in cities, plants, and local managements, a main finding of this research is that the Swift hourly-paid packinghouse workers in our three plants differ very little in their company allegiance. We find a definitely favorable degree of company allegiance in Chicago, Kansas City, and East St. Louis. Appendix Table I gives the range of findings wherein we see that Swift East St. Louis leads slightly, with a mean weighted score for "all workers" of 1.5, or between favorable and very favorable.

While the scores for "all workers" shown in Appendix Table I appear different, tests of significance[2] among the scores of the three plants show no significant differences between the three workforces taken as a whole. That is, differences between the mean scores (1.5 for East St. Louis, 1.6 for Chicago, and 1.9 for Kansas City) could have happened by chance.

The male packinghouse workers, however, are by far the most important group, representing 85 per cent of the employees in each plant. Statistical tests show the East St. Louis men to be significantly more favorable than the Chicago men. Comparing the East St. Louis and Kansas City men, we find a slight edge favoring East St. Louis. Comparing Chicago and Kansas City men, we find no significant difference because the white and colored cancel each other out. The Kansas City white men are more favorable than the Chicago white men, but the Kansas City Negroes are less favorable than the Chicago Negroes.

As for the women workers, both the Chicago and the Kansas City women are significantly more favorable to Swift than the East St. Louis women. But since the women represent a small minority, we can fairly discount their views here and say that East St. Louis has a slight lead in company allegiance.

## WORKER LOOKS AT HIS COMPANY

To put flesh and blood on these statistics, let us hear why some of the East St. Louis men workers are so company-minded.

Machine operator, Hall Moore, forty-eight years old, has been with Swift-East St. Louis about ten years and has strong company allegiance. Things that come first to his mind are various facilities afforded the employees. Mr. Moore is not satisfied with everything. He thinks his job should have a higher rate, and he thinks Negroes should be treated more equitably. But his company allegiance is clear, though his reasons for it are not necessarily typical:

*Interviewer:* How do you feel about Swift as a place to work when you put them all together, Hall? Think it's a good place, or not so good? Or in between? How would you rate this place if you were telling somebody about Swift —

*Moore:* Well, the company is, — I don't think you could work for a better company.

*Interviewer:* Why would you say that? What is there that makes you feel that way about it?

*Moore:* Well, they got — places where you can have your lunch, places where you can buy cigarettes, places you can sit down, and places you can go an' take your bath, there's towels, showers, and towels and soap, all furnished free. *And I don't think, they ain't very many companies would do that.* And then they don't — they have the market, you might not get cut-rate on your prices but you can always rest assured you gets a pound when you buy a pound. And there is outside stores where it's different, they throw your piece of meat up there on the scales and before it stops wavin' they take it off and charge you a dollar for it while it ain't but fifty cents' worth of meat. But at Swift you can rest assured. If you get bad meat, somethin' like that, bring it back and they'll exchange it or give you your money back. *And I think the company is mighty swell.*

Old-timer Joe Hetzel is a skilled craftsman who likes neither his job nor his foreman. But he clearly distinguishes between supervision, and Swift & Company. He definitely has company allegiance. With Swift since he was seventeen, he is forty-one, tall and lean; he speaks frankly:

Well, they got so many things that are good for the employees, see. When we're off sick we get half time or quarter time; we don't have to fight to get it and sometimes you're allowed so much for each year you been here, two weeks half time, see for sickness. And sometimes these fellows' time runs out see. 'Course, they can drop them off the list but they write Chicago and Chicago writes back to keep them on, payin' 'em, see?

Well, that's a gift, there. They really don't have that a'comin', see. *And Swift's policies are great. You won't find 'em any better, I don't believe.* You take our union contract and raises, you probably read through it. Holiday pay, vacation pay. We got vacations from Swift & Company years ago when they didn't know what a vacation was! You take back, well, when I started here in '29, they worked four years and got a week's vacation. [This is an error. In 1929 Swift employees waited five years before getting one week's vacation.] Well, you take outside industry, you take Borden and them places there, why, they were just starting to give vacations, and some of 'em didn't. The railroads never did know what a vacation was.

Ex-farmer and skilled machine operator, Herman Gleffe, repeats the same idea of "Swift's policy." It was a frequent reason for the high East St. Louis Company allegiance:

Oh, it's A Number One. . . . Oh year, sure they're the best. . . . *Steady work and the Swift Policy.* Some man will do this thing or that thing, and they will say that's not Swift's policy, see? It's just kind of generally understood that Swift's policy is just A Number One, up and above board. You know, there's nothin' to worry about as far as their policy's concerned. They're going to give you a square deal. That's always been the idea around the company.

Finally we come to another long-service employee, Charles Harwood. Harwood started with Swift right after the first World War. Then he quit and later came back. He is now a skilled craftsman, with real loyalty to Swift, due in no small part to the treatment he was given when he was in a health crisis:

Well, I like them because I think they're loyal to their employees. . . . They have been with me. I can tell you, Father, one occasion that I had an accident in St. Louis . . . I got this shoulder knocked down to here. I was ruint. The doctors at the hospital said, you're ruint. When they pulled it back, it pulled all these ligaments loose, and my arm was bound to my body . . . and I came back here and talked to Dr. _____ about it . . . and Dr. _____ said: Charlie, you're ruint. I hate to say that to you. And I said: No, doc, don't say that: I'm not ruint, I'm a young man yet.

And he said: Yeah, you're ruint. I said: Well, couldn't I pull them loose, them ligaments, that are set? And he said: Yeah, but you won't. And I said: Doc, will you let me go to work: And he said: You work? I said: Yes, if I don't work, I am ruint, because a man that's settin' around, he will—

And he said: Hey you, get out of here. Any man that's got that much guts, I'm goin' to let him work. He called my boss and told him to get a man to help me. . . . If a man's got that much will power about him, he says, we're goin' to stick by him. And I went a year, close to a year, with my arm in a sling, I got full pay. . . .

There's a man went with me, I showed him what to do . . . most of it, I done what I could. . . . And the company stuck to me on that. Well, they won't stick to me more than they will to any man, because, listen, if he does what's right. . . . Now that's the confidence I have in the Company.

Another reason for the company allegiance of these East St. Louis packinghouse workers included the local union itself. Because Local 78 appeared to some workers as a sensible and cooperative union, they gave

## WORKER LOOKS AT HIS COMPANY

this as one reason why they liked the company. This is not necessarily illogical, for company policy has something to do with the kind of local union the company gets, though obviously many other factors enter in. Then too some workers perceive the work situation as a whole, and do not really discriminate among its components, the company and the union.

To summarize a fair cross-section of the workers' comments, here is what we find: Swift is better than other packers; good treatment; good pay; my fellow workers are friendly; good benefits, pension, medical, etc.; good union; good working conditions; no strikes; steady work; good worker-foreman relations.

Appendix Table I shows the Kansas City packinghouse workers as having less company allegiance (1.9) than the people from Chicago (1.6) or East St. Louis (1.5). These average attitude scores can be deceiving because they can be pulled down, or up, by the very unfavorable or favorable scores of a few individuals. That is why, in our nonparametric statistical comparisons, we used the median scores rather than the mean. A closer look at the scores of the various Kansas City groups shows that most of the workers are high in company allegiance, but they are brought down by three groups: the colored men of short service and of middle service, and the white men of short service. These three groups definitely have the least company allegiance of any equivalent groups in our entire study. Also they are least favorable to their foremen and jobs.

Table 17. *Percentages of Kansas City packinghouse workers favoring the UPWA-CIO (121 hourly-paid employees).*

| Men | | Women | |
|---|---|---|---|
| Negro | White | Negro | White |
| 36 | 23 | 25 | 0 |
| 36 | 15 | 40 | 0 |
| 21 | 7 | — | (20)[a] |

[a] This figure is unreliable because of insufficient response.

One reason for this is that the two Negro men groups are the best educated of all the Negro men in our study, with 8.6 and 9.2 years of schooling. Education is only one clue. A more important clue becomes evident in Table 17.

We see that the three groups with the lowest company allegiance are the most CIO-minded men in the Kansas City plant. This UPWA-CIO-mindedness is partly a cause and partly a symptom of lower allegiance to

Swift. The UPWA-CIO, which has been trying actively for some years to raid this plant and take it away from the National Brotherhood of Packinghouse Workers, incites its supporters against the company. This is evident from its election-time leaflets and from conversations with UPWA-CIO leaders in the Kansas City plant. Also men who are angry with the company tend to listen to the UPWA. Yet some of the CIO supporters in our sample do have clear company allegiance.

Then too, this UPWA-mindedness is also a symptom of more fundamental discontents. Two of the white men of short service who are unfavorable to Swift are Mexican-Americans. These men think that they do not get fair treatment in the Kansas City plant. On the other hand, a third Mexican in this group who is against the company for the same reasons is also against the UPWA-CIO. Such variations in attitudes are not surprising and they bid us to be cautious in explaining the causes of the attitudes and behavior of the packinghouse workers.

Among the colored men of short service, almost all the anticompany workers are UPWA-minded. Some of these men came to the plant from other Kansas City plants, such as the Cudahy plant where the UPWA had bargaining rights. This partly explains their lack of company allegiance. With time, these men may change their views about Swift.

The question might be raised: Why should UPWA-mindedness mean less company allegiance in Kansas City than in Chicago, where all the employees who are in the union belonged to the UPWA-CIO? The answer is this: The UPWA men in the Kansas City plant were more aggressive, and therefore more anticompany, because they had not achieved their objectives; namely, to win bargaining rights in the Kansas City Swift plant. They have been defeated repeatedly in NLRB elections by the incumbent independent union. In Chicago the UPWA was at least fairly secure. It is true that in Chicago many Swift men dropped out of Local 28, yet there was no attempt to have an NLRB election in order to certify another union. If the Kansas City UPWA-CIO men eventually win the plant, they might well develop at least as much company allegiance as the UPWA-CIO people in the Chicago plant.

But we must not oversimplify. The influence of the UPWA-CIO is not the only factor. Among the colored men of middle service, for example, two men are quite dissatisfied with their jobs. They want to be mechanics, one, an auto mechanic. For such reasons, and not because of the UPWA, these two men have little company allegiance.

As for the colored old-timers, Table 17 demonstrates to us that 21 per cent of them favor the UPWA-CIO. Yet they tend to have high company allegiance. Perhaps this is because they are old-timers. We have constantly seen how greater length of service means greater company allegiance. One man says:

Eventually this union will go CIO. The CIO is the most broadminded union in America. [He is thinking about Negro rights here.] The CIO would be more active for the people. [Yet he goes on to say:] The company is pretty nice, pretty fair.

*Company allegiance differences by sex.* Following the research design of the original Chicago study, the packinghouse workers of the subsequent studies were compared by three key variables influencing their attitudes: sex, race, and length of company service. Analyzing the workers' attitudes according to these three variables will give us a better understanding of why the workers think as they do about their company and union.

The women packinghouse workers have a high degree of company allegiance. This is true in all three plants. The Kansas City women are among the most favorable to the company. This is in spite of the less favorable colored women there. Since the latter are such a small proportion of the plant, their attitudes have little influence on the total score of the women workers.

In Chicago, there was a significant difference between the men and the women in their allegiance to Swift as a company, with the women definitely being more favorable. This pattern tends to repeat itself in Kansas City. There is no significant difference between men and women in East St. Louis.

The high company allegiance of these women factory workers, so often higher than that of the men, is due to the following reasons:

(1) Comparative pay advantages (over neighboring companies' jobs for women, especially office jobs).
(2) Less desire of women for advancement, with less likelihood of possible frustration.
(3) Early quitting time (more important for a woman than a man).
(4) Less difficult jobs, with better working conditions.
(5) Perhaps more respectful treatment by supervision.

As for differences among the three plants, the women workers are not a major factor since they are a small minority in each plant. Interplant comparisons just for the women workers show that the Kansas City women have the most company allegiance and the East St. Louis women have the least, though all the women are generally favorable to the company.

Listening to some of the Kansas City women will show why the women workers have such definite company allegiance. For example, cafeteria worker Marian Brunswick is impressed with Swift's various employee benefits, among other things:

It's a good place to work, I like it very much. My husband put up thirty-six years here. . . . I worked at Armour's for three years when I was quite young . . . and when I come here we get better benefits in *every* respect. . . . *Now you take the Pension. . . . I know a fellow that lives two doors from us, worked at Armour's for 47 years* and . . . he was only getting $7 a week. . . .

My husband worked here thirty-six years and came out. He gets $53.10 a month and then his insurance is taken out and that's what's left every month. . . . I guess in all packing houses they're overworked . . . But I think that we've got a few people around here that don't do very much of nothin'!

Myra Spreckels, a stout and affable lady who is a grader, gives pay and working conditions as reasons for her allegiance:

Well, if I had my choice I believe I'd still pick Swift. . . . I've worked at Cudahy's and I've worked at Wilson's . . . and I would think I'd rather work at Swift's. . . . *They pay more.* They've always paid more. And seems like *working conditions are so much better.*

Semi-skilled meat worker, Alta Foster has had one year of college. She returns to the theme of pay:

Well, considering the other places I have worked and some places that I've heard about, I think it's a pretty nice place to work, since I have to work. *For one thing, I make more money.*

On the other hand, independent steward Anna Larson, has hardly any company allegiance. She came to Swift during the depression because her father died and their farm was in a precarious position. She would not want her children to work either in the Swift plant or office. She says: "When I leave this place, I forgit, in fact I don't mention it to my husband." Yet for herself, she thinks Swift is a pretty good place to work:

I think it's nice. I think they're nice. . . . I worked at Wilson's when I first came up here. I didn't like it. I was just a kid. First job I'd ever had and scared to death. Cried everyday if anybody looked at me. But it wasn't as nice.
*Interviewer:* You think Swift is better?
Yes, definitely.
*Interviewer:* How do they compare with Armour, I wonder?
Oh Armour's is dirty too. From what I hear. I've never been there, but I've been told that by people that worked there. It's just terrible. And besides C.I.O. is in there. I don't think it's good for anybody. C.I.O. is good for some people. But not here for us. . . . It's a pretty good place [Swift], if you hafta work.

*Company allegiance differences by race.* Important as the racial variable is in a few attitudes, especially regarding union leaders, it is of only minor importance regarding company allegiance. In no one of the three plants, do the colored workers differ greatly from the white workers in their general attitude of company allegiance, though they tend to be less favorable. The only real exception is the Kansas City white women, who are significantly more favorable than the colored women there.

It follows that racial differences do not much affect the interplant differences. As for the comparative company allegiance of Kansas City and Chicago, for instance, the races cancel out what might otherwise be a significant difference. The Negro workers definitely feel that they do not have the opportunities for advancement that white workers have. Naturally, such feelings affect the Negroes' attitudes. The surprising thing is that the Negroes are not more affected and that they still manage to have definite company allegiance.

Here is one example of a Kansas City Negro packinghouse worker whose dissatisfaction about his opportunities affects his allegiance to Swift. Husky young Ronnie Johnson wants to be a machinist or a mechanic for which he has had training. He says that anybody can do the work he is doing — loading. He wants to get out and take up a trade or buy himself a dump truck, since he believes he has no opportunity at Swift. All this destroys his company allegiance. While Johnson is not exactly typical, he illustrates the lesser company allegiance of some of the Negro workers, especially the younger men:

*Interviewer:* Well, if you put it all together, Ronnie, what would you say about Swift as a place to work — good, bad, or in-between. How would you rate this place, I wonder, compared with other places?
*Johnson:* Well, I would rate Swift third-class.
*Interviewer:* Would you? Comparing it with some other place what would you rate it?
*Johnson:* As far as I know, I mean speaking for myself, I haven't worked in any other packing house but Swift's so much. I've worked in Cudahy's about two months. That was where I was workin' before the flood. But, I don't even know how the *best* packing house is run. But to my estimation I would rank Swift around third-class.
*Interviewer:* I wonder how it would compare with Cudahy, would you say?
*Johnson:* When I was workin' there at that time? Oh, they would be approximately the same.
*Interviewer:* About the same? What would you rate as first-class? Any special other place that you'd rate better?
*Johnson:* Well, I think I would rate General Motors around second-class. [He has applied there several times and had not gotten a job.]

*Interviewer:* Yes, that's considering opportunity in jobs, and future and everything?

*Johnson:* Yes. And Ford Plant about second-plus. *Because I think they have [colored] machinists out there.*

*Company allegiance differences by service.* The number of years a packinghouse worker works for Swift affects his attitudes toward the company. It is interesting to see that the Chicago pattern is repeated in Kansas City and East St. Louis. The old-timers in every case are more favorable to the company. A few variations are notable: The women workers in both Kansas City and East St. Louis do not manifest this service difference. The newer women workers are about as favorable as the older ones. There is an exception even to this, though, at East St. Louis. We deliberately included an extra group in our East St. Louis sample: the workers under two years' service to see if they would differ much from the older workers. Among the women in this plant, these very new workers do have somewhat less company allegiance than the others. Such a finding is rather what we would expect. But if we allow for minor variations, the pattern of the more company-minded older worker is a continuing finding. What are the reasons for this?

(1) The old-timer has had a longer opportunity to study the policies of the company and to compare them with those of other companies. He has had more opportunity to experience Swift's generally fair treatment.
(2) The disgruntled and dissatisfied employees have mostly left the company by the time they reach long service.
(3) The old timers' greater age, conservatism, maturity, less formal education, and perhaps less ambition, and their frequent foreign or southern origin — these factors tend to make them less critical and more apt to be content with the company.

It is probable that the patterns we have found in these three Swift plants are quite common in American industry.

*Company disallegiance.* The idea of company allegiance will become clearer if we listen to the packinghouse workers who fail to have it, who have actual "disallegiance." Since there are few of them we shall not quote them at length.

In Chicago, we found varied reasons for dissatisfaction with the company: lack of future advancement; an accident blamed on the company; bad working conditions; "overeducation"; and so forth.

In Kansas City Table 18 shows 7 per cent of the workforce quite dissatisfied.

Table 18. *Employees with company disallegiance, Swift-Kansas City, 1953.*
*(About 7 per cent of the workforce)*

|  | Per cent |
|---|---|
| Colored men, short service | 2.47 |
| Colored men, middle service | 1.65 |
| Colored women, middle service | .82 |
| White men, short service (Mexican) | 1.65 |
| White men, middle service | .82 |

These people, as can be seen, are mostly colored, short-service, and Mexican. There is only one noncolored or non-Mexican in the group. These facts in themselves may partly explain the disallegiance of these people.

Otto Nagler is the one white man in the group. He is thirty-two years old, a semi-skilled butcher, a big, rather affable person. He is a generally dissatisfied man, unhappy with his job, pay, standards, working conditions, boss, and so forth. His main complaint is that he was not given the chance he thought he deserved to learn a higher-paying, more skilled job in his department. "It's making the skill, or improving your way, is what I wanted to do. And then the B's [wage-incentive units of output] would come along with the experience. But they don't seem to understand that." He actually did try the job he mentions, but his hands swelled up and he was sent back to his former job. He thinks the foreman did not give him adequate training. "Lotta times, the company won't recognize the ability of a fella. They'll just say: 'You go work there,' and no other spot." The Standards System (Swift's wage-incentive system) is also very irksome to him.

It is interesting to notice the foreman, Louis Baron's opinion of Nagler:

He is not at all satisfactory as far as I'm concerned. I wouldn't recommend him on anything. . . . I can go a little bit, probably in his favor, a little. I could make a statement in this respect: If he wanted to, he could make one of the best operators there is in the business. There are times that he takes flashes and he just works, I'm tellin' you, he can do two men's work. . . . But he doesn't have those times often, though. I don't expect two men's work out of him. . . . He's a problem.

He could develop into a problem if you'd let him. His work, now, the work that he does, you can't complain of. I mean as far as the quality's concerned. Far as making his cuts is concerned, he's very good. But he's just the sorta type of fellow that always finds excuses to get off the job some way other. Five or ten minutes, or something. I think he's one of the poorer quality people we have out there. . . . He doesn't like to take orders. He's dependable as far as absenteeism is concerned.

*Interviewer:* What kind of a disposition does he have?

*Baron:* I would say it's under par. . . . Well, he's one of these, — what we think — yet probably will get it in the course of conversation — we call them sympathizers. That is, outside sympathizers.

*Interviewer:* With the CIO, right?

*Baron:* Uh huh.

As for the two young Mexicans in this group, they feel strongly that there is discrimination against Mexicans. Julio Contreras, for instance, came to Swift three years before, from Wilson. About Swift he says:

It's a good place to work . . . for people [he laughs] other than me! No, Father, I wish I could tell you that it's — we just haven't got no choice. We just have to work. . . . It's — a place to work. . . . Well, if you want my opinion — me now — If I work here fifteen, twenty years, I'd feel that I should have an opportunity at least to have some job where I make better money. *Have a little more standup. You know — something to work for!* I lack education. [He had two years of high school.] But I don't think that after twenty years that I couldn't learn certainly enough of the plant that I could run certain parts. . . .

Well, pardon the expression, it's just that the white man has always stuck together. . . . [Here he opposes Mexicans to whites.] 'Course now, in twenty years from now, I would like to see that where *I* could have a chance to say — well — I'm a foreman. I have so many men I'm running — *someplace*. 'Course I couldn't get a foreman, even if I want to. . . . I talk to a lot of my people . . . been here for thirty, forty years. They say: "See that man? I was here ten, twenty years before he come in. . . . I know more about this job than he does." . . . So, my people don't get a chance. Not just my people, the colored people, the same.

The Negro workers who have disallegiance almost all have the same basic reason: their belief that they do not get fair opportunities in the plant. For most Negroes this belief does not destroy their company allegiance. For this minority, it does.

*Why workers leave.* More light can be thrown on company disallegiance by studying the workers who leave the company. While we do not have general exit-interview data for all three plants, we do have some interesting facts about the East St. Louis workers who quit. Table 19 gives the picture.

We see in Table 19 that a rather large number of people, nearly six hundred, or 28 per cent of the workforce, left the East St. Louis plant within a given year — 1953. The "average man" who left the plant that year was twenty-six years old, had two years of high school, nine months of service, was likely to be married, and to have one or two children. This is revealing, for such a mythical "average man" is not a mere high school boy experimenting with his first job. This "average man" is a man who has acquired responsibilities, but may not have accepted them. (Of those who

Table 19. *Workers who leave Swift, 1953.*
(*Swift East St. Louis-Local 78 AMC & BW plant community*)

| | | | | |
|---|---|---|---|---|
| Workers who quit (giving some reason) | | | 359 | 60% |
|   Workers who are dissatisfied | 139 | 39% | | |
|   Workers going back to school | 86 | 24% | | |
|   Workers going to military service | 26 | 7% | | |
|   Workers quitting for miscellaneous reasons | 108 | 30% | | |
| Workers who were "dropped" (who simply failed to appear for work, giving no reason) | | | 160 | 27% |
| Workers discharged | | | 79 | 13% |
| Total leaving, excluding retirements and deaths | | | 598 | 100% |
| Average size workforce | | | 2090 | |
| The total number leaving as a per cent of average workforce | | | | 28% |

left, 41 per cent were single, 57 per cent married, and 2 per cent divorced. 94 per cent were men.)

Thirty-nine per cent of the men and women left because they were dissatisfied with work at the plant. This is about 7 per cent of the entire workforce. By "dissatisfied," we mean that the worker's reason for quitting was that he disliked some phase of his work with Swift, or, that he had another job elsewhere which he preferred. Of course, some of the people who give "miscellaneous" reasons for quitting might be said to be dissatisfied at Swift. Also some of the people "dropped" were probably not satisfied. On the other hand, preferring a former job does not always mean active dissatisfaction with the present one. Here are some of the meanings of "dissatisfied": another job; work too hard; too damp; too cold outside; don't like job; account of health; to old job; refused transfer; to farm; to go in business; to railroad; not enough money; to play ball; to be schoolteacher; can't work nights.

These findings of 7 per cent dissatisfied workers are similar to our attitude findings of disallegiance. Such workers tend to be just a few months with the company. At Swift East St. Louis we sampled at random the workers under two years' service. In these groups, especially among the colored, we also find about 7 per cent who fail to have company allegiance.

As for those who quit for military service or going back to school — these are self evident and do not involve company allegiance. Here are some "miscellaneous" reasons given for quitting, along with reasons for discharge:

*Miscellaneous reasons for quitting:* going home; leaving town; sore back; wife sick; child sick; bad leg; death in family; financial trouble; back to Tennessee; back to Arkansas; to California; to Europe; to Chattanooga; to Arizona; family trouble.

*Reasons for discharge:* pilfering; absenteeism; insubordination; wage assignments; unsatisfactory worker; not up to standard; intoxicated; falsifying birth; wasting product.

The workers who left the Swift East St. Louis plant manifest the mobility and restlessness of many American workers. Also they show the dissatisfaction of a minority about work in the Swift packinghouse. The dissatisfied workers are nearly always the younger workers. We pointed out that one reason why the older workers are higher in company allegiance is because the dissatisfied younger workers have simply quit. These statistics bear out our statement. Also, when a man is new with the company, he has not had time enough to come to like his job or to understand his company and develop allegiance to it. As a matter of fact, some of these new workers do not have much union allegiance either.

## UPWA Union Leaders

Because local union leaders can greatly influence public opinion in a plant, it is important to see what these leaders think about their company. Are union leaders necessarily anticompany? Not according to our findings:

*Local union leaders' company allegiance*

| | |
|---|---|
| UPWA Kansas City raiders | 3.1 |
| UPWA Local 28, Chicago (leftwing) | 2.3 |
| UPWA Local 28, Chicago (rightwing) | 1.6 |
| NBPW Local 12, Kansas City | 1.4 |
| AMC&BW Local 78, East St. Louis | 1.3 |

The East St. Louis unionists lead in clear company allegiance. The Chicago Local 28 leaders are significantly less favorable to Swift than the others. Considering that the Chicago leaders were mostly leftwingers, this lesser company allegiance is to be expected. If we look at the company allegiance of the rightwingers in Chicago (men who have not been consistently in power in Local 28 from 1949 to 1960), we find a score quite in line with the other locals: 1.6. This score is somewhat less favorable than the others but not greatly so.

But if we look at the attitudes of the UPWA-CIO raiding leaders in Kansas City (men who have no official position in the plant community), we find the least favorable score of all our samples: 3.1. Many of these men are quite anticompany, even more than the leftwingers in Chicago. The reason for this difference is probably the fact that the Chicago leaders were secure in power, while the Kansas City CIO men were still struggling, trying to bring the Kansas City packinghouse workers over to the UPWA-CIO. This struggle is marked by an anti-Swift campaign, as anyone can see by reading their election-time handbills. Union organizers often show more antagonism toward their company when they are organizing than they do once they have achieved recognition and security. The UPWA-minded leaders at Kansas City are no exception. They think that the best way to win the workers over to their cause is to attack Swift. Their lack of company allegiance is a reflection of such strategy.

Table 20 shows two-thirds of the Kansas City UPWA men to lack company allegiance:

Table 20. *The company allegiance of 11 CIO leaders, Swift Kansas City, 1953.*

| | | |
|---|---|---|
| Very favorable | 1.0 | 18% |
| | 1.5 | 18% |
| Favorable | 2.0 | |
| | 2.5 | |
| Neutral | 3.0 | 9% |
| | 3.5 | 18% |
| Unfavorable | 4.0 | 9% |
| | 4.5 | 18% |
| Very unfavorable | 5.0 | 10% |

In interviews with two key UPWA-CIO men in Kansas City, George McComb and Theodore Stillman (one interview was conducted in Stillman's house), we come upon a clearer understanding of the mixed views of some UPWA-CIO leaders. Both these men are veterans with Swift, one starting just after the first World War, the other during the depression. They are dissatisfied with many things, but their lack of company allegiance is not extreme. Mr. McComb explains his views with revealing comments on Swift's personnel policies:

*Interviewer:* Then coming to the company as a whole, putting it all together from the company's side, how would you rate the company, George? Have you ever been at other places, like Armour or Cudahy, Wilson?

*McComb:* No, I haven't. But I have a pretty good idea, or knowledge, of the company's policies, operations. . . . You take the Swift plant, what I have learned of it, within the Swift chain, the general sentiment with all, more or less the biggest majority of the Swift workers that work for Swift and Company, is that they're workin' at the best plant. Or the best plants.

*Interviewer:* Best packinghouse, you mean?

*McComb:* Yeah. Because of the policy that Swift & Company uses. Pretty elaborate thing, as far as the personnel that they employ, know how to press the employees to a point of speed without causing a reversal in their attitude towards working, you know what I mean. They're pressing almost to the breaking point, you know, and yet and still they're still pattin' them on the back, and sayin' this and that and the other, and then offerin' them little incentive plans, I mean incentives, and all the other concessions, you know. And fixin' up the dressin' rooms a little better than in Armour's or Cudahy's or Wilson's plant where those plants, Armour is pretty firm, with its employees, along with Cudahy's and Wilson's. Swift's has a more diplomatic policy in handling its employees. But on the whole, and on the up and up, Swift is exactin' more work per man out of the employees, through this policy that they use, than they are in Armour's or Wilson's or Cudahy's.

Now the people, in relation to that, are pretty much pacified and consoled, see, under these existing conditions; and they're not so easily to erupt as they are in Wilson's or Cudahy's or Armour's plants. And that is the reason, one of the reasons, that the strikes more or less occur within the Armour's and the Wilson's rather than in the Swift's plant. [Not true in 1956 and 1959, however.] Because of the untactful way that Armour's handles its employees, you know. But Swift is more tactful with its employees, if that might answer the question in a sense you know. But the job loads are greater. That is, in plants where they don't have stronger unions, you know. . . .

*Interviewer:* You wouldn't necessarily rate them over the others?

*McComb:* Oh-no-no. No. They're no better in a sense, to the employee, that is, of course they use the, well it's hard to explain, for me — in other words, if I can just get the gist of the thing, where Armour's would say: "You do this and you do that," and that's all it is to it, you know, Swift would come along and use a different tack you know. They might come along and use a little different tack, or pat the guy on the back, or offer him a little concession, or say we're all one big happy family and we all live together, and we all work together, and we're just lovely, and all those things, you know. So that's the tactful way that they get away with that.

The interviews show that Stillman differs from McComb in some things, but here he agrees, and ends with a not entirely uncommon distinction between Swift's policies and their practice:

*Interviewer:* How would you feel about that, Ted? About how would you rate the company as a whole, putting it all together?

*Stillman:* Well, in a general sense, my opinion would be about the same as George's on that. As he stated, they do have more diplomatic procedure in handling their employees. If they want to have you do something they would not come right out and say "Now you do so-and-so," They'd prob'ly say; "Well how *about* you doin' so-and-so." That's the term that my foreman uses all the time — "How about you doin' this," or "would you like to work this place," or "would you like to do this."

And in the meantime, if you don' do as he asked you, then he's gonna come out and say "Well, I want you to work this." See, it's just a general procedure that they have. But if you backfire, then that's when you get into the ruckus with him, see. You get below the surface. And then they will just tell you; He'll tell you in a minute; "Well, I'm runnin' this gang and you're gonna do what I say, or you're not gonna work in here, that's all." "If you can't do what I say, you go home and stay until you think you can do it, and then you can come back to work." See? Such as that, he would tell you that in a minute, see?

And he is backed up by that Mr. _____, his supervisor-superior, and all the way down to the office. They'll tell you, you go down there and talk to them about something. They'll say "What did your foreman tell you to do?" "Do as your foreman tells you to do. Don't take the bull by the horn, if you think you have a grievance or something, you go on ahead and do what he tells you to do, then come to us about it, see?" Well, all the time a fella just don't feel like he's being treated right, he feels like he's not gonna do it. But the company as a whole, they have a good policy, I believe, for the employees, if we could get everything that's in that policy for our benefit. [We recall foreman Hugh Driscoll also saying that.] The whole proposition is, as fer as the Kansas City, Kansas plant is concerned, I *do* know about that, because I've worked there, you don't get everything out of Swift's policy that's *due* ya. That's my answer on that.

As for the Local 12 Independent union leaders, they are generally quite favorable to Swift. For instance, independent leader George Sandberg thinks that Swift gives good treatment to its people, on the whole. He has allegiance and puts it this way:

I've been here twenty-three years. . . . I think it's above average. . . . I do think they're fair. Sometimes I think they're a little more than fair. I think sometimes they kinda bend over backwards. We've had people here that I know if *I* had hired 'em, I wouldn't have them. *But [Swift], they'll give 'em one chance after another.* 'Course sometimes seems like they get kinda unfair with people. But as I said before, it's jist human beings. We make those mistakes. . . .

The Local 78 Amalgamated leaders also have very definite company allegiance. For instance, Roger Duro, one of their older Negro leaders, says:

Well, on the whole, I think Swift is one of the best places to work, *'cause checkin' on other companies, why, the employees don't have the breaks* . . . like leavin' your job when you want to and come down and get your coffee, an' smoke, an' loiter around on some jobs . . . You won't find the opportunity in other industries, *pensions and vacations and so on* — which is just about what the average company does. Some companies don't. So I think it's a good place to come to work.

In conclusion, if we consider the rightwing leaders in Chicago, who are out of office, and the elected local leaders of Local 12 and Local 78, we find that these unionists not only have definite company allegiance, but they have the same amount of company allegiance in their respective plants as the foremen in those plants: 1.6, 1.4, and 1.3 for Chicago, Kansas City, and East St. Louis. We might expect the role of union leader to pull a man away from the company to some degree. In some cases this is true, especially with the UPWA-CIO men. But it is not true regarding the Independent and AFL union men, for they have high company and dual allegiance.

### Differences Among the Foremen

We would expect the foremen, more than the plant production workers, to have company allegiance. But there is not much difference.

Table 21. *Three-plant company allegiances of the foremen. Chicago (32 men), 1950; Kansas City (19 men), 1953; East St. Louis (25 men), 1953–54.*
*(per cent favorable)*

|  |  | Chicago | Kansas City | East St. Louis |
|---|---|---|---|---|
| Very favorable | 1.0 | 44 | 53 | 76 |
|  | 1.5 | 22 | 26 | 8 |
| Favorable | 2.0 | 25 | 16 | 12 |
|  | 2.5 | 3 | 5 |  |
| Neutral | 3.0 |  |  | 4 |
|  | 3.5 |  |  |  |
| Unfavorable | 4.0 | 6 |  |  |
|  | 4.5 |  |  |  |
| Very unfavorable | 5.0 |  |  |  |
| Mean score |  | 1.6 | 1.4 | 1.3 |

The main finding in Table 21 is that almost all these foremen have a high degree of allegiance to Swift as an institution. There is not very much difference between Kansas City and East St. Louis foremen. The company allegiance of the Chicago foreman is somewhat lower, and is brought down by a minority who do not have company allegiance at all.

Why do the Chicago foremen have less company allegiance? Their attitudes toward the job, and toward having their children come to work at Swift hardly differ from the other two plants. But their attitude toward advancement opportunities is definitely less favorable. Also they are more critical of their workforce, especially regarding the work qualifications of the Negro employee. They are much less satisfied with the idea of having a union in the plant, and with the local union leaders. Then too, in Chicago, the "Stockyards" has less comparative prestige than in the other cities. In other words, some Chicago foremen find many things dissatisfying about their work in the Chicago Swift plant. This dissatisfaction affects their company allegiance.

We also see in Table 21 that East St. Louis has a slight lead in the company allegiance of its foremen. The East St. Louis foremen give a variety of foundations for their allegiance to Swift: Swift's policy, peaceful union-management relations; pensions; good treatment; and so forth. One of them, Kile Ritchie, says:

I think their *over-all policy* of dealing with supervision and the hourly-paid employee is good. I think they have a good system. I think their policies have been carried out well enough that their relations have been very much on a peaceable scale compared with other industries. *I have always been proud of the fact that I am connected with Swift for that one reason,* you can look down the street, to cite one of our competitors, the unusual amount of trouble that they had down there. . . . *It makes me proud of the fact that we do carry on our business on a much more peaceable level.*

Mr. Ritchie's comments are fairly typical.

Our main conclusion is that the attitude of company allegiance exists and in a rather high degree, for a wide variety of workers, under different conditions.

Secondly, in spite of different plants, plant managements, cities, neighborhoods, foremen, unions, and local union leaders, there is no vast difference among the workers in their views about working with Swift. The major exception to this is the UPWA-CIO local union leaders. In both Chicago and Kansas City, we find these men quite critical, because of the special crisis situations of Local 28 and the Local 12 raiders. We could surely find some Swift UPWA local unions (especially among the more conservative Canadian locals) where the local leaders had definite company allegiance. But the local situation, added to the anticompany philosophy of the international UPWA, lead the local UPWA leaders in this study to small enthusiasm for Swift.

A third conclusion is that while the differences between plants are small, Swift East St. Louis does maintain a slight lead, as the plant with the highest company allegiance. At least one behavioral fact supports this. We saw in the absenteeism figures presented in the previous chapter, that East St. Louis has far less absenteeism than either of the other two plants. While absenteeism tells us more about the living conditions and habits of the workers than about their company attitudes, this low absenteeism does give us one additional clue to the high company allegiance we find at East St. Louis. One study has shown, for instance, a high correlation between absenteeism in an auto assembly plant and the implicit degree of job satisfaction on a conveyor-paced job.[3]

Finally we have learned something of what the company and work mean to employees. The next five chapters will support this in greater detail, by tapping the workers' attitudes about specific aspects of their work with the company. Better understanding of their hopes and aspirations should gradually emerge.

CHAPTER V

## Foreman and Worker

We come now to an important company-related attitude: the ideas and feelings of the worker and the foreman toward each other. Certainly the foreman is a key person in influencing the various company attitudes of workers. While our original Chicago research found that the packinghouse workers clearly distinguished between their company and their foremen, we also found how much the foreman can influence the morale of his employees. Also, the kind of gang the foreman thinks he has will influence his attitudes toward his own job and his company.

EAST ST. LOUIS WORKERS AND FOREMEN

If we compare the attitude scores of both the men and the women toward their foremen in the three plants, we find no significant differences between them. But if we take the men only, then we see, as in Appendix Table II, that East St. Louis leads with a score of 1.7.

The East St. Louis workers are, on the whole, the most satisfied with their foremen. Differences between Kansas City and Chicago are not great, but the Chicago men seem to be the least favorable of the three plants. The Kansas City average is brought down by the white men of short service and the colored men of short service and middle service, the same groups that were low in company allegiance. However, in all three plants, the foremen are generally well liked.

These findings are similar to our company allegiance findings, in which East St. Louis had a slight lead. There is surely some mutual influence at work here between the workers' attitudes toward the company and toward their foremen.

Why are the East St. Louis men generally so favorable to their foremen? Here is a sample of their comments:

—He's pretty *fair*, he's trying to be anyway. You know you can't please everybody . . . it's a big job, an awfully big job.

—He's above average. *Doesn't holler* at you much. He comes in in the morning and tells us what to do and that's it.

—It's amazing the *consideration* that you have today [from the foremen] that you didn't have before the union came in.

—We got a good boss, *good natured and good hearted. He don't holler*, that's what I mean.

—My bosses in the willwright gang have been *pretty nice* to me.

—I'd say he was *fair*.

—As far as I'm concerned he *doesn't bother me at all*. He ain't as bad as he used to be. Outside of the plant I think he's a nice man.

—*He doesn't bother me*. He tells us what he's goin' to do and we go ahead and do it. I can't complain about any boss I ever had. They all seem to be pretty nice fellows.

—*Those bosses raise cain with you* but *you laugh it off* and forget it and don't pay any attention to them.

—He's never bothered me. He's a regular *gentleman* with me.

—Fine! Fine! Ever since I knowed him. I been glad I went there.

—He's about as *fair* as a fellow can be, I believe.

—I think he's a pretty nice fella. I never have no trouble myself 'cause me and the foreman get along. *He generally* listens to me, comes *to me* lots of times and *asks my advice.*

—Sort of bad in a way. *Talks bad.* A man wants to be treated as a man.

—He do fairly well. He never do *give me no trouble*. He just come out sometime and ask me how I'm getting along.

—He's an old fellow. He has it made and he's a pretty nice fellow. *He doesn't have much to say.* The gang leader really runs the gang.

—The whole gang looks like they turned against him. *I don't like the way he treats the other men.*

—I think he's a pretty nice guy. Treats 'em all about the same.

—*He could be better.* 'Course I know some things that he won't do that he could do, could see about for you, but you know he won't take the time to do it.

Among these East St. Louis workers, we come to Charles Renault, a skilled craftsman, age thirty-one. Renault speaks as a very intelligent man. His foreman thinks he will be a supervisor some day. Here are Renault's comments about his own boss, and about good foremen in general:

My bosses in the _____ gang have been pretty nice to me. They've helped me pretty good. I realize their position, of course, that helps a lot, too. *The plant has to run, and in order to make money, they have to, for us to make money and to keep us workin', they have to be efficient and they have to get so much out, too.*

And a lot a people have the wrong idea of the deal, you know, I mean, they figure they should, oh, the plant owes 'em a livin', you know. Well, actually, if you got so much money invested in a deal, you want to make it pay for yourself.

And a, and sometimes, a, well maybe they will go over a little, you know, maybe a little overbearing, you know, they want too much out of ya.

Well, years ago they used to really press you, they claim. But I believe if a man works his eight hours and gives 'em pretty close to that much work, they should be actually satisfied, because if an individual isn't happy, he spends the time down here, if he's depressed in his work, gets disgusted, he doesn't do the plant a bit a good, you know. And you have to have harmony in the gang, you know that as well as I do.

*Interviewer:* If you want to get a good job done.

*Renault:* That's right.

*Interviewer:* Well, on the whole, then, you'd rate them pretty high, then, the bosses, huh?

*Renault:* They've been pretty nice to me.

*Interviewer:* That's good.

*Renault:* I think, though, that there's other departments that — I mean I wouldn't say they're angels, none of 'em, you know. I think they have to get a certain amount of work, but there have been certain departments that wanted a certain boss or something — that maybe he hasn't been feelin' well or something that causes it, you know. An' then, after a while, why he might straighten up an' make the best boss there is, you know. An' you have to look at all them things, I think, you know.

*Interviewer:* Sure you do. Well, what do you think makes a good boss, Charles, you've had different bosses, and I mean in service you had officers. What would make a good foreman, do you think? I mean, you might be one yourself, you know.

*Renault:* Yeah. Well, a my opinion on a good foreman, *first, he has to know his work well, you know.*

*Interviewer:* Know his job, huh?

*Renault:* He has to know his job, I think. *And he has to know how to, to handle people.* I mean, a, he has to know how to handle his men, I mean, now a young man, it seems like, you, if you always give 'em a job and tell 'em what to do, why he'll work efficient that way. Another man, when you try to tell him something, well, he balks on you, you know. And you have to know psychology, I mean, how to handle people, and you know that better than I do.

*Interviewer:* They're all different.

*Renault:* That's right, and in your position you know that.

*Interviewer:* Sure.

*Renault:* And a, and you have to, a lot of times you have to sit back and figger how you'd feel if an individual'd confront you with a problem, you know. And just how much a man can actually do. Now there's one individual that's strong as a mule. He can do a little more than the other one. Not sayin' the other one shouldn't do as much as him, but maybe he can't to make his health run along good, you know, and get so much out of him. If they could place 'em in a position where he wouldn't work as hard, you know, I mean all them things come into consideration.

*Interviewer:* People are really different.

*Renault:* Oh, I mean, they're just like night and day.

Semiskilled leader, Kurt Wolf, is a short-service man with Swift. He really likes his bosses. A good foreman, according to Wolf, is a man who understands the problems of his men because he experienced those same problems himself:

I originally worked in the freezer. I liked it and we had awfully good bosses.
*Interviewer:* Yeah, I was going to ask you about your foreman.
*Wolf:* Some of them are kind of nervous, but still, you know, after you get used to it, you overlook that. The boss — he's got his orders to carry out, the same as we have.
*Interviewer:* That's right. So you'd rate your boss — would he be good, bad, or in-between?
*Wolf:* I — I think they're awful good, you know.
*Interviewer:* What do you think makes for a good boss? You've had a lot of 'em around here in your experience. What do you like to see most?
*Wolf: Well, I like to see a guy that's started at the bottom of the ladder and built up, myself.*
*Interviewer:* That knows the work?
*Wolf:* That's right. I don't like to see a guy jump in there and — take it more or less like being in Service. You come right out of school and go right into — an easy position. 'Course, they're not easy, 'cause you have to keep on the ball to keep things rollin', theirselves.

They have an awful lot of headaches. Sometimes they spill a few thousand pounds of that lard and they got to explain why it was, an' all that. The original boss — the one that started here — Oscar Wheeling, why — he was awful good, 'cause he, you might say, spent his life down here. *He really knew what the situation was and he understood your problems, the same as he did the company too, see.* He was really good to you. He's out on pension, now.

Middle-service worker, Roger Holmquist makes a distinction about his supervisor. He doesn't like the foreman's occasional partiality. He does like the foreman's understanding at a time of crisis:

Well, personally, I think John Davey, he's one of the best foremen that this plant has got, but then, he's got a couple of fellas he shows a little bit of partiality to. I mean, I imagine you'll find that in every gang, and I don't imagine I'll be the only one to tell ya. In fact, I imagine some of the _____ men might'a told you the same thing this mornin'. But he has a couple he shows partiality to.
*Interviewer:* Uh-huh. You'd rate him pretty high, though, huh?
*Holmquist:* As far as bein' a foreman that's pretty decent toward the men, I'd rate John pretty high, because if something comes up an' happens, well, John never stops you. I mean, just like the day my wife had to go to the hospital, I mean, our baby, it was a baby that had to be taken, it was a Caesarian and it was early.
*Interviewer:* Whose wife?
*Holmquist:* My wife. Well, I mean, she just called up an' she said, you better

come on home, the doctor says you gotta take me to the hospital. So John didn't stand in my way. Now he was busy . . . and I mean, we was workin' out here! But that man never tried to stop me or nothin'. He said go right ahead, he said, come back whenever you want to. *He's always pretty decent, whenever something happens.* Just like the fella out here one day, his wife called up an' some pipe in their bathroom was busted an' floodin' the house, stuff like that, I mean, a lot a guys might, a lot of foremen might think you was just givin' 'em a line to get off'a here, an' might object. I mean, he never questions you too much. You take a guy that's got a habit a layin' off, well, that's different. I guess he could get rough if he wants to.

*Interviewer:* What would you think makes a good foreman, Roger, what qualities?

*Holmquist:* Well, just like, the same thing that makes a good officer, you have 'em gettin' along with his men, leading of his men, understanding, all them characters combined, an' you'll find a good foreman. And, but I still, I don't think a foreman should have a little partiality, I don't think so.

Quite a number of the East St. Louis workers said they liked their foreman because he "does not stand over you." For instance a Negro worker, Tommie Croden, age thirty-eight, says he likes his foreman because he tells you to do something and then leaves you alone to do it. But this foreman is not equally favorable to Croden. He says that Tommie doesn't take orders, is sluggish, and has to be pushed. Also he is absent from work too often.

Leonard Browning, a white employee, repeats the same theme as Croden about his foreman. Browning is unusual for he has worked in fourteen different departments in the last six years! He appears to be rather an isolationist regarding people:

Well, I've had no trouble with him. I've never had any. Only thing that he does, *it seems to me he thinks he's a little superior to the* — workin' person. Usually tries to have a smart answer. A lot of guys tell me — I have never — had any trouble with him.

*Interviewer:* You've had different bosses, I suppose, since you've been here, Leonard. What do you think makes a good boss?

*Browning:* Well, I've been told — right now I prefer something like I have; *one that doesn't bother me as long as I do my job.*

*Interviewer:* He leaves you alone, huh?

*Browning:* He never bothers me. I do my job and he doesn't bother me. I don't want anyone lookin' down my neck or always under me, and he doesn't. He never bothers me.

Finally we come to old-timer William Lang. Mr. Lang is a skilled worker, with strong company and union allegiance. He gives some of the strongest praise we found for the Swift East St. Louis foremen. Clearly his comments show how much the foremen at Swift help build up company allegiance. Lang thinks Swift is the best company he ever worked for — because of good treatment:

*Lang:* Well, I think we have one of the best bunch of foremens that I ever worked for on public works. [He presumably means "industry" by "public works."]
*Interviewer:* Well, that's fine.
*Lang:* Now, I would put them on tops with anything. . . . They're all agreeable; they don't stand over you and look down your — your neck.
*Interviewer:* Yeah, nobody seems to like that much.
*Lang:* They give you a job — they — they — if you don't understand just what it's all about, *they'll explain it to you* or they'll even — my boss even goes with me a lot of times on jobs. And I think we have the tops as far as that's concerned, to work for.
*Interviewer:* Well, it makes it a pleasure to come to work?
*Lang:* It does; it really does. It makes a difference. And our foremens when they go through the plant or somewhere or out on the street somewhere and you run into one of our foremen, even the mechanical men and they've always got a — a good work for you. *They don't high-hat you.* They're all just very common people.

It will be interesting now to show some comparative background data for the foremen of all three plants, as in Table 22.

Table 22. *Foremen background data.*

|  | Chicago (32) | Kansas City (19) | East St. Louis (25) |
|---|---|---|---|
| Average education | 10 years | 10.5 years | 10 years |
| Average service with company | 26 years | 25.5 years | 20.5 years |
| Average service as foreman | 20 years | 9 years | 9 years |
| Service as assistant foreman and foreman | ? | 11.6 years | 9.7 years |
| Average age | 50.5 | 47.9 | 41 |
| Average no. of dependents | 1.9 | 2.7 | 2.4 |
| Gang experience | 80% | 72% | 92% |

Two facts in the table give us a clue as to why the East St. Louis foremen are more successful: They are definitely younger; they have had more experience working in the gang themselves. We heard several workers mention this last point as something they appreciated in a good supervisor. Other factors, of course, would have to be explored to explain the difference. One factor might be the training of the foremen. We did not investigate this. Another factor is the difference between the workforces themselves. We find the people at East St. Louis more satisfied in many ways; no doubt this affects their views about their foremen. Finally, the slightly more favorable opinion of the East St. Louis foremen toward their employees (see below) surely affects the workers' reciprocal views about their own foremen.

INFLUENCES OF SEX, RACE, AND SERVICE

We found in Chicago that women were more favorable toward their foremen than men. This pattern is further borne out in our Kansas City findings, but not in East St. Louis, where the middle-service group of women are critical and pull down the scores of the other groups. The Chicago and Kansas City women are more favorable, for about the same reasons we cited for their greater company-mindedness.

Race and service do not make a patterned difference in the attitudes of the workers to their supervision, though we might well expect these variables to make a difference. However, the Kansas City old-timers are indeed more favorable and quite loyal to their foremen.

Since the Kansas City women packinghouse workers are the most favorable group in the three plants, we shall listen to two of them. First of all, a packer, Noreen Anderson. Mrs. Anderson is a Mexican woman, thirty-five years of age. She has definite allegiance to both company and union, and she likes her work and her foreman:

I like my job an' as I started workin' here. I like the foreman, he's a pretty nice man. . . . He's awfully nice. . . . Doesn't holler at you. . . . About the best foreman I ever had. . . . *He just talks to you nice, an' he understands . . . people.* The other foremen stand up to you an' tell you — you have to. He say — would you like to, an' then you think you *can* do it. . . . He treats everybody equal, he don't favor — *no favors to nobody.* . . .

May Ronson is a large and pleasant woman, also definitely in favor of her company and her foreman. She has been nine years with Swift. She has high union allegiance and is against the UPWA, following the pattern of most of the employees. In regard to her foreman, she remarks:

Well, I think [he's a good boss]. *I have a foreman that I can go in there now and I tell him the situation and . . . if we have difficulty . . . he seems to be glad to agree with us and tell us what he'd like to have done.* . . . As far as I am concerned now, I've never had any difficulty at all. . . . 'Course I happen to be on this on nights, and then when I took sick he came to me and he tol' me, he said: "May, you've been off sick, and I feel like if I can put you on nights, which you are the youngest girl and it's your place to go, but he said that nevertheless I feel you need your morning's rest. And that will give you a rest and also the work isn't quite as hard on nights, and I think it'll make out better for me and you too. Because," he said, *"I want someone on there that I can depend on,"* and he said, *"I can depend on you 100 per cent to go ahead with the work and all."* And I felt that he really meant that he did it for my benefit. . . . [*He's one*] *that you can feel like going in there and telling him your troubles.*

A minority of the packinghouse workers are strongly critical of supervision. For example, medium-built Porter Jackson is a good-looking young colored worker. He has had four years of high school, experience in the army, and he has ambitions to go on to higher studies. He definitely has company disallegiance. He thinks he has to work too hard. But probably his major problem is that he thinks this job is beneath him, that he has no future with Swift. Jackson does not think highly of his foreman:

Well, I tell ya the truth: *In general they jus' strictly comp'ny men.* They want ta git the meat out. *They don' care anything 'bout the men.* Git the cattle out, you know. Ya cut your hand, okay, jus' anything, they don' care.
*Interviewer:* They don't care too much about the men, huh? Do they get on your tail or anything like that?
*Jackson: Aw, alla time.*

Gerald Culpepper is another young employee who throughout his interview is definitely against supervision. He is a CIO man and doesn't believe that the present union is active enough. He was discharged once, for walking off the job. He is a complainer. His principal complaint is that his foreman is always nagging him.

Yeah, in our department it's pretty good, it's always cool . . . but working conditions is, you know, *it's the nag-*[*ging*], *when the boss is always a'hollering an' a'rippin' and a'runnin'.* Ya know it sounds like he's kinda got it in his head like [it was] slavery. Well, ya see, people have not — they're getting weaker and wiser — and people are not gonna like what they useta do. You can't take that old-time and follow it back the way they useta do business *because the people are not gonna do that nowadays.* See, they gonna, *if you try ta force that on them now, they'll walk out.* They won't do it. People won't do that.
*Interviewer:* The boss is kind of nagging?
*Culpepper:* Hollerin', and he'll want you to rip 'n run 'n all that. . . . He's got that, kinda got that in him. . . . He thinks, in a way of speakin', *he thinks if you make a man mad you get more work outa him. But he's just got it backwards. If you make a man mad, the less work you get outa him.*

For southern-born worker Alan G. Doneldson, a slight, neat, colored employee, eight years with Swift, the foreman is also a central problem:

Well, we have a very cruel foreman. Can't hardly do nothin' to suit him no way. . . . *He messes up on the B's.* . . .[1] *We got on the foreman about the bonus yesterday, but he put it on the superintendent.* He says he knows the bonus was wrong, but he had a boss, he had to do what his boss said. . . . We got a very mean boss. . . . I dunno what gets the matter with him. Acts like he have some kind of spells or somethin'.

Sometimes he's pretty good an' then again, you can't do *nothin'* to satisfy him. 'Course everybody around here know an' everybody ken tell you about him! [laughs] . . . He can't git him no men that wants to work under him. . . . I'se see 'em went home rather than work down here. . . . *Yeh, he holler at yuh. He jest argue with yuh all's the time.*

'Course he don't worry us very much, cause y'see our job take keer of itself, see? . . . I just, you know, just go ahead along and don' say nothin' to him. . . . He gets to arguin' with 'em. He ain't — now he's not quick about firin' nobody — I ain't never seed him fire a 'body, but he just raise sand and argue. [laughs]. . . . Yes. He raise a lotta sand, but if you understand him you can get along with him. Man, but he's just mean about the arguin'. . . .

UNION LEADERS AND THEIR FOREMEN

We might expect the local union leaders to be critical of the company foremen. But just as we found the unionists to have company allegiance, we also find them mostly content with supervision. The local leaders, including the UPWA Chicago rightwingers, feel about as favorable toward their foremen as the rank-and-file workers. Sometimes they are even more favorable. The main exception (causing the unionists to differ among themselves more than the rank and file), is the UPWA leadership group, especially in Kansas City. Here the leaders are unfavorable to their foremen, with a score of 3.5. In Chicago the UPWA leftwing leaders of 1950 and 1951 were, on the average, slightly favorable, though definitely less favorable than the rightwingers.

We shall try to explain why the union leaders range from very unfavorable to very favorable in their views of the foremen. For example, we come to George McComb, a veteran CIO leader, active in organizational work in the Kansas City plant. McComb has strong union allegiance, of course. He is an intense person and apparently a keen observer. While he dislikes his foreman's prejudice, he finds many good qualities in his boss:

*I rate my foreman, my general-foreman, as a man who follows a pattern that is set.* And, course, he has certain convictions of his own heart and his own soul, and I think pretty much he is pretty much prejudiced . . . pretty prejudiced toward Negro and Mexican people. And he follows the general pattern that is set in the plant, without any, effort to — he falls more or less right in line with the way he thinks, you know. *And of course, he's a pretty evasive fellow, and he's pretty sly in what he does, you know, and things of that sort.*

He's pretty smooth, about handl'ng men. . . . If he has to reprimand you about something or something like that, *he just won't walk right up to the gang, you know, and pick ya out,* but he will stand there, a little off from you, and call you to him, then he'll walk off a piece, and if there's any loud voice being raised, you will do it, because he won't do it, see. He'll keep his voice down, and he'll tell ya: 'now let's stay down on the ground, let's keep our feet on the ground,' see? He wants to keep it low, you know.

*That's one thing that I've give a little credit because I know a lotta boys would just blast you right in the gang.* . . . I rate him, in that particular instance, better than the majority of the foremen on the plant, because, as I say, he won't just jump right on you. . . . *And another thin', he won't come out and hardly say anything to you, he usually stays in the office. Now that's something else that the majority of the foremen don't do on the plant. They don't just sit in their office. They're with the gangs all the time.* But he will stay right there in the office, and he will put pressure on his subordinates to take care of their job out there, you know what I mean.

On the other hand, we find this UPWA leader in the Chicago plant, Edward Hassett, more satisfied with his boss:

Well, as fur as I'm concerned, about my foreman personally, he's a nice fella. . . . Well he's the kind of fella you can sit down an' discuss your problems with him and talk with him. 'Course he's just like anybody else. Sometimes comes down in the mornin' an' doesn't feel good. Just like me or anybody else. Might raise his voice, that's another thing. . . . But if he gets outa line, he's man enough to come back an' say: I'm sorry, I had so much on my mind I didn't intend to holler at you!' Well, that means a lot! We have a pretty good guy.

Why do these union leaders differ? The UPWA men, especially in Kansas City, are more aggressive and more insecure about the company. We saw their lower company allegiance. We are not surprised to find them also more critical of supervision. The Chicago leftwingers are also aggressive, but more secure, being in power in Local 28. They are critical, but less critical than the Kansas City UPWA men. The different philosophy of the UPWA, its generally more aggressive position, undoubtedly affects the thinking of these local leaders about Swift supervision, though, in the long run, their thinking also affects that philosophy. But the other two groups of union leaders, Amalgamated and Independent, under more company-cooperative union philosophies, are apparently not affected at all by their role as unionists. They are just as favorable to foremen as any other workers. It is significant to note that a man's role as local union leader does not necessarily make him antisupervision.

CHICAGO FOREMEN AND THEIR EMPLOYEES

Turning the coin to the other side, we shall now hear what the foremen of the three plants have to say about their employees. The packinghouse foremen have a difficult enough job, and that job is mainly dealing with people.[2] Their different views about their workforces will give us important new evidence in the three-way comparison we are making, as well as showing some of the problems of being a foreman.

In the foreman interviews, each man was asked to say in general what he thought of the people working for him in his department, his "gang." Table 23 shows the results.

Table 23. *Foremen's attitudes toward their gangs (in per cent).*

|  | Chicago | Kansas City | East St. Louis |
|---|---|---|---|
| Favorable | 71 | 88 | 88 |
| Neutral | 10 | 6 | 12 |
| Unfavorable | 19 | 6 | 0 |
| Mean score | 2.4 | 1.7 | 1.7 |

Evidently, the Chicago foremen are more critical of the people who work for them than the foremen of Kansas City and East St. Louis, though on the average, the Chicago foreman are favorable. There is no real difference between the other two plants. Here are the East St. Louis foremen talking about their gangs:

"My only problem is an occasional absentee that I've got to call in." Keith Kinnamon.

"Well, they're working, but the times have changed, you know. They don't really lie down, but it seems just like the men can't do the work that we used to do." Harry Bouk.

"My absenteeism isn't too large, and the gang as a whole — their output, their production is pretty good. They seem like they're happy in their work." Henry Godow.

"They're a pretty good bunch of boys. . . . I'd say the nucleus of both gangs, you know, is very good with the exception of maybe one. . . . It's the people that you seem to bring in during the rush season. . . . That is where the problems are." Patrick Keane.

"On the whole they're pretty good. . . . It seems like the younger ones that we are getting now are a little bit . . . seems smarter than the older ones. The older ones are more cooperative and they work better an' everything than the younger ones. The younger ones now, why, they don't seem like they wanta cooperate as well. . . . They don't seem as ambitious." Andy Helinski.

"About average. After all, you're just as good as your gangs are." Jack Frigo.

"I would say better than good . . . one thing about my over-all gang picture that has always impressed me is the wonderful spirit that prevails." Kile Ritchie.

"I would say I have a pretty good gang." Phyllis Debs.

"I'd say that I have the best gang, and all of them getting along with each other and also with me. . . . We spend a lot of hours out here together and we can have fun and do our job, as well as we can come out and *fight* with each other. And that's the thing that I don't want to do. I spend forty-eight hours a week here and I want to have a little pleasure with it." John Heid.

"I've got some awful good men. As a gang, as a whole, I would say it's just about tops." Harold DeCamp.

"I would say they are fair." Ed Grelle.

"These guys are showin' more interest in their work now . . . and they're more dependable. I can depend on them more. They're not layin' off. But that problem I think every foreman has." Frank Letto.

Those comments certainly mean rather high praise and satisfied foremen. Such satisfaction is one reason why the East St. Louis foremen have the high company allegiance we saw in the last chapter.

Frank Burke, a Kansas City Swift foreman in charge of a canning production operation, is also quite proud of his men. He thinks that they are sincerely loyal to the company:

*Yeah, we got a good bunch. There are a lot of them trustworthy.* We have some of them on shifts that are very dependable and interested in their job, and it's important that they be dependable. . . . If they see something that's coming up that needs a repair, that maybe we don't catch in the daytime, catch it before they do, why they give us a note on it, and stuff like that. That shows their attitude.

*I think most all the boys workin' over there figure on staying up here with the company.* Most of them, a big per cent, have been there a number of years, and of course, it's to their interest that the thing goes along with the company. . . . *We have a group of about forty and we have about six colored people.* And they've been with us, most of them, quite a while. *They're good loyal fellows.* There's a couple of them been there about thirty-five years working over there and they're as good operators as we've got in the place. *Very loyal and dependable.* And they've got a pretty good head to figure out things.

*Minority Groups.* Since Negroes, and sometimes Mexicans, make up a large proportion of the workers in many meat packing plants, we shall get additional information about the foreman's attitude toward his gang, by pinpointing his attitudes toward the Negroes and Mexicans in it. A good foreman can observe the work qualifications of his people.[3] We want to know how the foremen of the three plants differ in their rating of their Negro employees as identifiable groups. Of course, we must remember that white foremen are speaking, and that prejudice can influence their ratings. Table 24 shows us some remarkable differences among the foremen.

Taking the category, "Colored workers equal to white," we find a regular progression, the Chicago foremen being the least favorable to colored workers, and the East St. Louis foremen being the most favorable. Since

Table 24. *Comparison of white foremen's attitudes to colored and white workers (percentage of foremen).*

|  | Chicago | Kansas City | East St. Louis |
|---|---|---|---|
| Colored workers preferred to white | 4 | 9 | 5 |
| Colored workers equal to white | 15 | 27 | 42 |
| White workers preferred to colored | 77 | 33 | 53 |
| No clear comparative comment | 4 | 31 | 0 |

the Negroes in the Chicago plant were actually a slight majority, and in some departments, such as the beef kill, they constituted practically the entire group, and since the Chicago Negroes were much more aggressive, particularly in their union activities, the critical views of the Chicago foremen are not surprising.

While it is true that more East St. Louis foremen than Kansas City foremen said they preferred white workers to colored, if we could further probe the views of the Kansas City foremen expressing "no clear comparative comment," we would find the Kansas City supervisors about the same as the East St. Louis supervisors. Incidentally, the Kansas City foremen preferred Mexican workers to Negroes. Taking Table 24 as a whole, the East St. Louis foremen seem to be the most satisfied with the Negro minorities in their plant.

It is almost impossible to sum up the varied views of the East St. Louis foremen, but foreman Otto Roehe's comments are fairly representative:

*Roehe:* Well, Father, I've got, let's see — one, two, three, four — I've got five colored people in my gang. They're all very good. . . . Thy measure up — plenty good. I couldn't say nothin' about them. They do their work and they tend to their own business. They don't try to associate with the rest of the people in the union too much; they keep themselves pretty well to themselves. I have a very good bunch up there.

*Interviewer:* They come up to the whites, do they?

*Roehe:* Well, yes; as far as workin' an' studyin'. *I've got three or four up there I'd say are just as good as any white man I got any way you look at it, barrin' he's a colored man.* I never did — you know, was too crazy about the colored people — there's a lot of us that are that a-way — but I always believe in giving them a square deal. So long as they're doin' their work they should be treated like everybody else. I always treat 'em that way.

Foreman Roehe may not sound exactly enthusiastically pro-Negro, but his views are very different from many Chicago foremen, such as Hugh Moriarity, for instance:

My workforce? It's terrible. . . . It's the type of people — mostly colored. Now the old-time colored, they're wonderful, but the wartime jitterbugs — they're the majority now — they're terrible!

*Employee Merit Ratings.* An important feature of our research was to ask the foreman to give a kind of "merit rating" or thumbnail sketch of the work habits and personality of each man in his gang who was interviewed. In this way we can check on the worker's opinion by consulting the views of his foreman, and vice versa. The foreman can greatly assist us in understanding the worker providing we sift the foreman's comments. In addition, the foreman's evaluation of individual members of his gang can also tell us much about the foreman. Since his ability to understand his men will be partly manifested by the breadth and depth of his "merit ratings" of them. But this aspect of our research must lie unexplored at the present time.

We can see in Table 25 that there is very little difference between the merit ratings of the Kansas City and the East St. Louis supervisors, but East St. Louis is again in a slight lead with a score of 2.2. This lead is one more argument in favor of the more satisfactory conditions found in the East St. Louis plant.

Table 25. *Foremen's merit ratings of their interviewed workers.*

Random, stratified sample of 121 hourly-paid employees, Kansas City-Swift; and 138 hourly-paid workers, East St. Louis-Swift, 1953–1954.

|   | Men |   |   |   |   | Women |   |   |   |
|---|---|---|---|---|---|---|---|---|---|
|   | Negro |   | White |   |   | Negro |   | White |   |
| K.C. | E.S.L. | K.C. | E.S.L. |   | K.C. | E.S.L. | K.C. | E.S.L. |
| 2.5 | 2.6 | 2.5 | 2.0 | Short service | 2.5 | — | 2.8 | 2.3 |
| 2.2 | 2.3 | 2.5 | 2.6 | Middle service | 1.7 | — | 1.9 | 1.7 |
| 2.0 | 2.0 | 2.2 | 2.1 | Long service | — | — | 1.8 | 1.3 |

|   | K.C. | E.S.L. |   | K.C. | E.S.L. |
|---|---|---|---|---|---|
| Men | 2.4 | 2.3 | Short | 2.5 | 2.4 |
| Women | 2.5 | 2.0 | Middle | 2.4 | 2.4 |
| Negro | 2.3 | 2.4 | Long | 2.1 | 2.0 |
| White | 2.4 | 2.2 | Mexican | 2.8 | (unweighted) |

Kansas City — All workers — 2.4
East St. Louis — All workers — 2.2

Scale: 1.0, very favorable, to 5.0, very unfavorable. Totals are weighted in proportion to population.

There are not any very significant differences by sex or race among the foremen's merit ratings. But as for service, the old-timers are consistently rated higher. Looking in the opposite direction, however, we did not find greater satisfaction among the old-timers with their foremen, except in Kansas City.

We might wonder that the individual merit ratings (for example in East St. Louis) are less favorable (2.2) than the foremen's evaluation of the gang in general (1.7). The reason for this is not entirely clear, but it is probably as follows: when the interviewer sought employee merit ratings, asking the foremen to think specifically in terms of productivity, tardiness, absenteeism, cooperation, and so forth, the foremen gave somewhat more critical answers. When the interviewer asked the foremen about their gang as a whole, this was not directive in any way. As a result, the foremen probably had different criteria for their judgment. It is quite possible that the sum of a foreman's individual ratings of his gang would not be the same as his rating of the gang, as a whole.

Here are two merit ratings from East St. Louis foreman Kile Ritchie. Mr. Ritchie is thirty-seven years old and has been with Swift since he was twenty. He is a high school graduate. He appears to be a satisfied foreman. His employees are mostly women. Here he discusses his worst and then his best employees:

*Interviewer:* Then we have Merle Evans.

*Ritchie:* Merle — I'd say up to the last three months — had a good attendance record. Something in her personal life or perhaps — the fact that she received some compensation for being off may have had an effect on it, I'm not willing to say — but her attendance has slipped and she misses now about one day out of every two weeks — for various reasons, mostly illness. It may be very justifiable, I don't know. I can't say. But I will say that her attendance record has slipped from better than average to lower than average.

*Interviewer:* Lateness?

*Ritchie:* Very seldom late.

*Interviewer:* How about work?

*Ritchie:* There — she's a little below average — in quality and quantity.

*Interviewer:* And personality?

*Ritchie:* Myrtle, I would say — has an inadequate personality.

*Interviewer:* She's a troublemaker, kind of?

*Ritchie:* No — not necessarily a troublemaker. She's a little bit eccentric — and the girls have the opinion — and of course, I'm not judging her from what the girls think of her — but I think it's worthwhile to mention that they do think she's a little queer — odd. [He laughs.]

*Interviewer:* And then we have Stella Bowski.

*Ritchie:* I'm sure glad you interviewed her, because — I — her attendance record is beyond reproach. I mean, it could be set up as an example for anyone to look at, as an example to the other employees. She hasn't missed a day since I've been here in _____ Department. She was late one morning when we had about a foot of snow, last November 6th, a year ago. She's never late. Her quantity of work is well above average — exceptional, I would say. And the quality of her work is just unbelievable to go along with that exceptional speed. It's so good that whenever I have any special packages — say we're going to put up a display of anything — I go and tell this particular operator that I want so many pounds of _____ and so many pounds of _____ and I can rest assured that those packages will be up to snuff; they will be perfect! She is really an exceptional operator.

*Interviewer:* She'd be one of your top operators?

*Ritchie:* She — if I had to say it, I would say she *is* the top operator.

*Interviewer:* That's remarkable; I'm glad I got her. Her personality?

*Ritchie:* I would say — quiet, tends to her own business. When she does present any kind of argument or grievance, it's well justified, well based or grounded. There have been a few cases where she has felt that she has been dealt with unjustly or some mistake made on her behalf, and I feel that she — she had a legitimate gripe each time.

*Interviewer:* But she's reasonable and — ?

*Ritchie:* Yes. Easy to deal with.

*Interviewer:* An all around top operator?

*Ritchie:* Neat, adept, exceptionally fast. I just couldn't rate her anything other than good — very good.

*Interviewer:* You'd like to have more like her?

*Ritchie:* Yes. Yes, I would. I could run my department by remote control if all the operators were like her!

In these merit ratings, Mr. Ritchie is not one of the most perceptive foremen. For instance, he does not know much about why Merle Evans is eccentric and a poor employee, but at least he is aware of the external good points and bad points of the women employees in his department. Both of these employees, in their turn, rate Mr. Ritchie paradoxically: Merle Evans is favorable to him, Stella Bowski is critical. Mrs. Evans, who is divorced, lives alone in a rooming house, and appears nervous and flighty, says:

Well, I like him all right. Some of 'em don't. But he's always treated me nice. . . . If I got aggravated or somethin', if somethin' happened that I would really get sore, I just would go in and tell him. I went right to him, no one else. And you know he's always treated me right.

Miss Bowski says this:

Well, I don't know how to rate him, Father. I think he's pretty good at times and then again he tries — If he thinks he can get away with it, with something, he'd try it. . . . In fact I think he would try to do some dirty work if he could. 'Cause it's been done. . . . Oh, he speaks pretty good, pretty nice. But there are times when I don't know, he sorta has a different opinion about himself and then if you should tell *him* your view of it, why he has a sort of a way of expressing himself that he knows more than you do. Well maybe he does, in a way. But what I mean is he could give you a chance, or address you in a way that he would [like] himself. . . . Not always now, Father, — I don't mean that about him — but there are certain times that he don't give you a chance to really explain things. . . . He has that impression that he's the boss and you gotta. . . . Now that is the impression that I get. But I don't know, when he first came in here I thought he was real nice. But there are times when he gets that feeling that he's kinda above you. People don't like that.

Incidentally, the union steward in this department makes the same comment about Mr. Ritchie's talking down to the employees. The opposite directions of Ritchie's ratings of his employees, and their rating of him, show how we must not oversimplify by ascribing single causes to many employee attitudes. At any rate, Mr. Ritchie's praise of Stella Bowski as his outstanding worker is an example of how the East St. Louis foremen rate their employees.

We have explored in this chapter many interesting and complex human relations between foremen and workers. We found the East St. Louis foremen to be the most popular, as a whole, and the Chicago foremen the least. There are many reasons for these differences between the three plants, especially the other company-related attitudes. One of the most important reasons is brought out by the second part of the chapter: The East St. Louis foremen are themselves the most satisfied with their gangs taken as a group, with their employees, taken as individuals, and with the Negro minorities in their plant. The Chicago foremen are the least satisfied. The greater mutual satisfaction between foremen and worker is one key to the superiority of East St. Louis.

CHAPTER VI

## Five Aspects of the Job

We are grouping together here, the packinghouse worker's attitudes toward five different aspects of his job with Swift: the job itself; the gang; pay; working conditions, and the suggestion system. These five attitudes are combined in one chapter because the worker is mostly favorable to these aspects of his job, and because the attitudes do not dramatically differentiate the three plants. Though these attitudes are interrelated, they can be sufficiently isolated in the interviews for separate discussion and measurement. They are not all of equal importance. But they all should throw more light on the worker's thoughts about his whole job situation, the company, and his company allegiance.

EAST ST. LOUIS WORKERS AND THEIR JOBS

What does the packinghouse worker think about his job? This subject was introduced into the interview with questions such as: "How do you like your job?" "Do you enjoy the work you are doing, or is it just a job, or what would you say about it?" The replies, varying from a few terse sentences to eloquent ten-minute discussions, were graded on an attitude scale ranging from very favorable to very unfavorable. We are measuring the worker's attitude toward his job, that is, whether he is satisfied or dissatisfied with his job — whatever the word "job" may mean to him. Peter Drucker has questioned whether a worker's satisfaction with his job means anything: "Satisfaction as such is a measureless and meaningless word."[1] But Drucker is referring to written questionnaires asking the simple question, "Are you satisfied with your job?" Our interview method on the other hand permits an interchange between the worker and interviewer until the worker's concept of satisfaction, and the degree of satisfaction he feels toward his job are clarified. This clarification leads to meaningful measurement.

Of course the "job" means different things to different workers. Clearly, it includes such factors as pay, supervisors, coworkers. These findings about the job need to be interpreted in the light of the other attitudes toward, "Their gang," "Do they want their children to be Swift Packinghouse workers?" and so forth. Furthermore, "liking one's job," is not to be equated with pride of work, or love of the job.

It is informative to note what the workers mentioned when discussing their job, especially the first thing that they thought of. Of all the elements involved in a job, the degree of physical difficulty was most often mentioned first: "It's hard"; "That's heavy work"; or, "It's not a hard job"; "It's not heavy work." Next most frequently mentioned was the physical environment: "It's cold"; "A nice, dry place to work"; "It's always wet"; "It's not cold." Next in order of frequency came mention of the monotony or variety involved in the job. Often mentioned was the fact that the job was tiring or not tiring, and that the place of work was dirty or clean. For the Swift workers, "job" and "working conditions" are closely related.

Making definite limitations on what we mean by "attitudes toward the job," our three-plant findings are (see Appendix Table III) that all three workforces express moderate job satisfaction. There is a slight edge of greater approval to be found in East St. Louis, with a mean score of 1.6 among the hourly-paid employees, 92 per cent favorable.

The average scores in the table can be somewhat deceptive unless they are properly interpreted, because the extreme scores of a few people tend to bring down the average. For example, in Kansas City the colored men of short and middle service are the least satisfied of any groups in the three plants, outside of the UPWA local leaders. We saw before that these colored men tend to be quite sympathetic to the UPWA and that they are generally more critical of Swift than other workers.

If we use the median rather than the mean, we find the East St. Louis men significantly more satisfied than the Chicago men, and slightly ahead of Kansas City. Differences between the three plants are small, but I think we can again give East St. Louis the benefit of a slight advantage.

As for differences in job attitudes by race, sex, or length of service, there are no consistent patterns. In Chicago, the women are distinctly more satisfied than the men. In East St. Louis we find the opposite. Similar reversals can be found with racial and service differences.

The foremen, interestingly enough, have about the same attitudes as their employees. The biggest differences in Appendix Table III are among some union leaders, with the continuing pattern of much less satisfaction among the UPWA unionists in Chicago (2.3), and especially in Kansas City (2.9).

Freedom from constant supervision, and freedom to set one's own pace are qualities which make a job pleasing to the worker. Marvin Oliver, a steward, says: "I love my job because I don't have no boss down there to tell me what to do." Medium-service janitor, Tom Clark, is very favorable toward his job. He says: "I don't have no boss over me all the time telling me what to do. Sometimes I see my boss about two or three times a week. I work when I feel like it, and sit down when I want to. And I don't have no boss always tellin' me to hurry up and go — that's the reason I like that job." One of the reasons Evelyn Kowalski gives for liking her job is a very basic freedom of motion, which many packinghouse workers do not enjoy: "I like that job. You can sit down or stand up."

Freedom from having to keep pace with the disassembly line chain is mentioned by quite a few workers as a reason for liking their jobs. Long-service worker, Jim Udell, states his views clearly: "Well, I don't see no other way we could kill hogs, but I can tell you one thing: *any job you can get that is off that chain is better than working on that chain*. They really got you, when you work on it. You can't get a drink unless somebody stops the chain. . . . It ain't like a man who got his work laying in a pile, who can hit and run, and catch up and leave. He can walk around for two, three minutes, come back and catch up again. We can't do that, you see." Long-service colored worker, Charles Martin, says: "I would rather be on my job than on the chain. I tell them, 'No.' " Steward Niles Korbet, agrees: "I like my job better than any other job. Even if I wasn't makin' B's — 'cause I'm off the chain." The regularity of the chain is directly related to the workers' complaints of monotony and tiring work; but the chain's regularity is also related to the high bonus which the workers make. Pace may be unattractive but high pay is very attractive. Thus the workers' preference for the elements of a job may be in opposite directions. Job evaluation systems often take account of this.

*Pride of Work*. In talking about the packinghouse workers' attitudes toward their jobs, we should mention an important auxiliary topic not fully explored in this book: their pride of work. Our impression is that while the packinghouse workers certainly have pride in themselves, many of them do not have pride in the craftsmanship of the work they do with their hands.

Pride of work is not easy to define or discuss. But some workers, especially the skilled craftsmen showed pride of work in their interview. One type of pride of work is pride in the *skill required to do a job*. This skill is the reason, often enough, for the esteem in which the worker, and the job he is doing, are held by coworkers and observers. Walter Riley, for example, regards his ability as a boner the equal of any skilled craftsman's:

*Riley:* Well, I'm a — beef-boner.
*Interviewer:* That's a skilled job, eh?
*Riley:* Well, beef-boning as a whole, I think it is. It takes years of experience. I think a beef-boner is just as much skilled as any brick-layer or carpenter; that's if you're a good beef-boner, because it takes years of experience to learn how to use your knife.... And you use different edges on knives on different jobs.
*Interviewer:* You do, eh?
*Riley:* That's right, and it takes — you don't learn it in one year or two years or three years.... It takes, well, I've been doin' it for a period of twelve years now, an' this has been my best year, that's for sure.... But beef-boners don't, very seldom, get to go any higher because they are so important to the company, as much as I gather, the company can't afford to leave 'em move out. And they try to hold their men, and to keep their men satisfied, that's one thing they do especially.

Another type of pride in work is that which results from doing a job that the worker feels is *important to the success of the company*. Leroy Jefferson, a colored old-timer, expresses this idea perfectly:

They call me the janitor, the clean-up man, but — you couldn't term it just that. Because I haveta handle all machinery, operate them, and everything, and clean 'em and run 'em and I'm responsible for the tanks and everything bein' closed off, steam closed off — lines closed, 'n everything like that, every night. I have a very responsible job, my job is jus' as important as the head man's, but the difference between my job and his is I jus' don' get the pay like he does.
*Interviewer:* That's a responsible job, isn't it?
*Jefferson:* Mine's just as responsible as his.
*Interviewer:* Because if you leave some of those valves open, or if something goes wrong?
*Jefferson:* On the tanks — why, there you've got thousands of dollars down the sewer the next mo'ning.
*Interviewer:* That's right. So you have to be responsible there, don't you?
*Jefferson:* I *am*. Even if they forget and go home and leave steam on in them tanks and it's on there all night, why the next mornin' — they get that lard and carry it to the laboratory — and it won't pass the inspection on accounta bein' brown. It hasn't got the color, neither the flavor, that it would have.... And not only that — I like to see the place in order. Every day. That's my purpose to work and leave it just like that before I go home in the evenin'. And I just hope the Lord'll bless me ta have health and strength — so that I can leave that place in order — the *last* day I leave.... Yeah. I b'lieve that I oughta do my duty — just the same the last day as I did the first I started. Because I believe I owe that honesty to the company. They are payin' me — I'm puttin' my labor an' life on exchange for their pay. And when I do a fair job of it, and get out in the evening, why then *I* feel all right.

Leroy Jefferson gives the impression that pride in work is almost a state of mind. Whatever job Jefferson is given, as long as he sees the purpose for it, he will try to do well. In his make-up appears an uncommon appreciation of the value of work.

The packinghouse workers who have pride in their work will speak about the job at length, eagerly and spontaneously in the interview. A not-so-surprising sidelight on such interest is that several workers who displayed it were convinced that their job was so important that they thought they deserved more money for doing it. Leroy Jefferson was one of these men. As a result, he cannot be said to have a *very* favorable attitude toward his job, because he is not completely satisfied with his pay. Pride of work need not be exactly proportional to satisfaction with one's job. Our final impression remains: Pride of work is the exception.

*Attitude of foremen.* Among the most impressive results of our interviews is the difference between hourly-paid workers and foremen in their outlook toward their jobs. One reason for this difference in outlook is the difference in job content. The hourly-paid worker is rarely required to do work-planning, to keep other workers satisfied, to act as an administrator. Such work takes up much of the foreman's time. Most Swift foremen show a keen appreciation of the importance of their job. "Responsibility" and "worry" are words which the foremen used frequently in talking about their jobs. Most hourly-paid workers never mentioned these words. One foreman, Phil Blanchard, brings out clearly his feelings after his promotion from an hourly-paid job to supervision. He speaks of the differences between the two jobs, and of his worries:

> I used to do _____. And I got away from that. I knew that. You know, it's just like gettin' away from home, getting in someone else's backyard, well, you're not familiar with it, and I didn't know whether I liked it or not. I was disgusted at times, you know. *You didn't do any work any more, it's just thinking.* If something happened, why, you had to get to the bottom of it and correct it. What caused your trouble, you correct it and you finally work out of your trouble.
>
> Although it took me a while to get onto that. I wanted to work; when I saw trouble, I wanted to run over and help. When you get in foremen work, why, you got to figure the way out, and figure in advance — what work you should line up so the men have work constantly. And that was a little rough to get used to. I knew how to _____, and I'd _____, and the next one come, I — all I had to do is do my job over. And — if the chain stopped I'd wait until it started again.
>
> *Interviewer:* A foreman's job calls for a lot more than that?
>
> *Blanchard:* It does. It — calls for a whole lot. You gotta — I study all my employees, when I go up to 'em. One of my good employees — they do some-

thing wrong. I know that the employee did that for some reason. . . . It's on my part to find out why that man did wrong. Something caused that man to do wrong. There's times — maybe a man was up all night, or maybe his wife was sick all night and he didn't get much sleep. He didn't get the proper rest, that would cause him to be . . . out of line. . . .

*Interviewer:* That's a big job, dealing with people. Do you like that work pretty well?

*Blanchard:* Well, at times it worries me. . . .

*Interviewer:* It bothers you sometimes?

*Blanchard:* Oh, it bothers you. You get up durin' the night, and — and go to the bathroom, like I did Sunday even — Monday morning, and get a drink of water and it took me a long time to go back to sleep. I just lay there and think about — I know I'm gonna be snowed and how to get out of it. Where my weak spots are gonna be the next day. . . .

Mr. Blanchard is not typical in his home-anxiety about his foreman's job. But he is typical in his insistence on the responsibility of the job. And most of the foremen, we recall, are satisfied with their jobs. Responsibility seems to be something many workers want in their jobs, at least to a limited degree. And responsibility is often missing there.

To sum up, when we take job satisfaction in the very limited sense used in this book, we find the majority of the packinghouse workers and their supervisors satisfied with their jobs. Job satisfaction does not much differentiate the three workforces.

Satisfaction with Fellow Workers

What a worker thinks about his fellow workers is another important indicator of his general work-satisfaction. A frankfurt packer was once asked if she found her work monotonous. She replied: "No. It's a nice bunch of girls to work with." While she did not answer the question about the actual work of her hands, she did show the importance to her of her "gang," the department workforce.

The importance of fellow workers in work satisfaction would surely be less acute for people who work more in isolation, such as truckdrivers, newspaper reporters, salesmen, and so forth. But almost all the packinghouse workers work in groups, or in pairs or at least in frequent contact with fellow workers in their departments. For them their gang is an important factor in their work-life.

The packinghouse workers' attitudes toward their gang — and also the three following attitudes to be discussed in this chapter — are available in precise, quantitative form only at Kansas City and East St. Louis. For Chicago we have qualitative observations only; but these should give us some basis for comparison.

A general view of the workers' attitudes toward their fellow workers is presented in Appendix Table IV where we see very little difference between the Kansas City and East St. Louis packinghouse workers in their attitudes about their fellow workers. Both are favorable, with an attitude score of 1.9. If we look to our interviews, we find the reasons: The workers help one another, especially if one member of the department is sick. They kid and joke, and so the time passes pleasantly. However, a minority in both plants, and also in Chicago for that matter, dislike their fellow workers, finding their gang argumentative and complaining. Rivalry about standards, especially for workers on group incentives, is a major cause of dissension for such employees.

As for the Chicago plant, the mutual attitudes of the workers were also rather favorable. Considering the definitely larger percentage of Negroes (in a few departments over 90 per cent) harmony between the races in Chicago was fairly good. The Negro worker had few complaints about the whites. But the white workers were often critical of their Negro coworkers. This was more true among the white men than among the white women. Such complaints of white workers about Negro workers were much less frequent in the other two plants. Especially was this true regarding the local union leadership, which only in Chicago has been largely Negro. Because of such criticisms, there was somewhat less "satisfaction with the gang" in Chicago than in the other two plants.

At East St. Louis, there is little variation among the workers, with one exception: the Local 78 leaders. These people have the most favorable attitude of any group in either plant toward their gangs. Why is this? Let us listen to excerpts from their comments: "Pretty nice gang: the relationships are good." "They all cooperate." "I keep 'em all alive!" "They're always a-ridin' each other, and carrying on that way, but otherwise they're all right." "That's a bunch of good workers!" "They're always looking out for each other."

The comment of one leader, "I keep 'em all alive!" is revealing. Being a leader, he takes pride in the good morale and lively conversation of his own work gang. No doubt this is one reason for his very favorable attitude toward the gang. Similar thoughts may well influence the views of the other Local 78 leaders.

At Kansas City, we do find some variations by sex and race. There is no clear trend involving length of service. Among the white women there is some bickering of the young against the old. The colored women are apparently more favorable to their gangs than the white women. This might be because the colored women are a small minority and anxious to get along well. Curiously, the white women of long service are least favorable toward their fellow workers, with a score of 2.4. Some of their comments: "There's an extremely lot of jealousy." "There's always a disagreement in some way or other among some of the gang." "I don't think too much of them. They're too rough . . . makes you ashamed of being a woman!" "Some are smart-alecks who think they own the place."

The packinghouse workers like to have fun-makers in their gang. Their comments indirectly show that the work itself often does not engross their attention or interest. Here are three employees who talk about the department wags. First old-timer, George Kasten:

*Interviewer:* Does it get tiresome doing the same thing over and over again all day, or monotonous?
*Kasten:* Well, in a way, yeah, because you get tired of standin' up. *As far as the work, it's not so tiresome. . . . We talk, we laugh, we have fun. Well, we entertain ourselves to keep from thinkin' about the work to make the work much lighter.* You go in ten hours, if you're goin' to worry over, you'd be in pretty bad shape by half-past five or six o'clock. . . . The men always got somethin' up; well, we'll start maybe jokin' one fella and we all get on him, and maybe someone will bring up somethin' on another one and we get on him. . . . It holds the morale up and makes it fine.
*Interviewer:* The day goes pretty fast that way?
*Kasten:* Sure, the days go fast and you enjoy bein' with the men.

Here is another old-timer, a white man, Frank Elstad:

*Elstad:* A good gang.
*Interviewer:* Have you?
*Elstad:* They'll kid one another, yeah. I was kiddin' a couple of 'em, before I come down here. *I said, I'm goin' to tell Father about all you sinners up here; I'm goin' to tell him, give him your check number! They just kid all the time.* One said if he does, when I go down, I'm goin' to tell him about you holdin' out on your wife, too. [laughs] Well, that's what makes the time go by, if we kid like that, you know, if you kid like that. You take a couple of our guys up there, they make everybody else feel miserable. Where if you got a bunch that's all jolly and cuttin' up, why time goes by and everybody's happy.
*Interviewer:* Well, you have a pretty good crowd. I noticed that.
*Elstad:* Yeah, the colored and the white.

Probably the most important virtue that a worker wants to find in his gang is cooperativeness, readiness to help one another. Working in a gang whose members help one another makes a world of difference in their work-satisfaction. Group incentives are a factor in this. Curtin Neace, for instance, says:

Well, the gang, we all co-operates mighty well, I think real well. We have no disagreement with each other; we see it and we just get together and see it, and that's the way we can see it. *Somebody gettin' overworked, we just all get together and see he needs help,* why — we tell Charley that it's too much work for one man and he'll go over and get somebody else to help him. That's the way we gets along.

Leroy Jefferson, a religious-minded old-timer also thinks much of his gang because they help each other. He has worked with some of his fellows for a quarter of a century:

*Jefferson:* Oh, the gang is swell. Jus' like *one* family. You can't beat it. There's a lotta churches don't come up to the standard of love that that gang has. That's right.
*Interviewer:* They really get along, and help each other?
*Jefferson:* They git along fine. *And if anybody dies, they take him up a respect of flowers.* Anybody gets sick why the boys and girls throws in and cheers 'em up, or sends him a nice letter or a card, and some finance with it. Can't beat that, can ya!

Of course not all the employees think like Leroy Jefferson. Some are definitely not happy about their fellow workers. In some departments feuds and bickering do exist. This seems to be more common among women workers. One reason for such friction among this minority is arguing about the wage-incentive system. For instance short-service worker, Jane Tebbel says this:

*Interviewer:* What kind of a gang have you got there? How do they get along, on the whole?
*Jane Tebbel:* Well, they're women. All they think about is fussin' and fightin'. [laughs]
*Interviewer:* They have a lot of arguments, do they?
*Jane Tebbel:* Well, where I work, there's another girl and I that works at a table all to ourself, and across the room is three belts, and they all work there, and they're fussin' back 'n forth all day. They'll stay mad all day at one another, and won't speak the next day.
*Interviewer:* The older ones, do they take it out on the younger girls like you?
*Jane Tebbel:* We only have 'bout two — no, 'bout three of 'em in there that do that. And they think the boss's lettin' the younger girls get by with stuff. And they're awful bad about, they're the worst to talk, you know. *Holler 'bout B's.* The ones that don't need the money as bad as some of the rest of us.

In sum, we find good social relations among most of the packinghouse workers in all three plants. The workers tend to "stick together." There is little racial friction, though in Chicago we found some whites rather critical of the colored workers. Some women workers tend to be argumentative, especially about incentives. While many attitudes differentiate our three plants, significantly the workers' mutual attitudes do not.

## WAGE SATISFACTION

When we talk about attitudes toward pay, we are talking, of course, about the workers' "realistic," not "idealistic" views about pay. By this distinction we mean that few American workers are completely (idealistically) satisfied with their income. They would all like to get "more" as Samuel Gompers put it. But workers also have a "realistic" attitude, in that they compare their pay with what other people are making, and with what they conceive the so-called American Standard of Living to be for the kind of work they are doing. This latter (realistic) attitude is what we are presenting here.

For the Chicago plant we have no specific attitude scores. The subject of pay came up in a number of interviews, of course, usually crediting the union for getting pay raises. Most of the Chicago packinghouse workers were probably satisfied with their pay. Often they mentioned, especially the colored, that they could not save. The greater amount of wage assignments in Chicago, as opposed to East St. Louis, would seem to bear out the fact that the Chicago workers were spending more freely.

Appendix Table V gives up the findings for Kansas City and East St. Louis. The main finding in Appendix Table V is the fact that the workers in both plants are satisfied with their pay, with a slight margin of greater satisfaction at East St. Louis, where the hourly-paid employees have an attitude score of 1.9. In terms of percentages, 87 per cent of the East St. Louis workers are satisfied, as opposed to 77 per cent at Kansas City.

At Kansas City, too, the old-timers and whites appear to be more favorable. But the women are significantly more favorable than the men and also more than the East St. Louis women. Differences by service, race, and sex at East St. Louis are less marked. We would expect these groups to be more favorable; the old-timers, because they frequently have worked up to higher paying jobs and actually do make more money; the women, because compared to women in office jobs and in not a few other factory jobs, they are making more at Swift; the whites, because they tend to have the more skilled, and therefore higher paying jobs. But our findings show little statistical difference according to the three variables.

As for the local union leaders, if anything, they are slightly more satisfied with their pay than the rest of the hourly-paid workforce. It is quite significant that, in spite of the union leadership role of these people, they do not take a "party-line" role of being dissatisfied with their pay. But the UPWA-CIO leaders in Kansas City do this. They are hardly satisfied (37 per cent) with their pay (3.0). There would seem to be really very few aspects of their work at Swift which they are willing to admit they like.

We might expect to find the East St. Louis foremen somewhat more favorable to their pay than the foremen at Kansas City, in view of the poor morale we found among some of the latter foremen. This would also be expected because one factor in the Kansas City morale problem was insufficient pay differential between the foreman and the gang. Yet we find no difference between the two groups of foremen. Other factors also contributed to the morale problem we found at Kansas City. And, indeed, some foremen at East St. Louis also mentioned the pay-differential problem.

The women workers in Appendix Table V are the most favorable toward pay. Some reasons for this are that women workers often bring home supplementary income and are not always their own sole support. Proportionately more of the women are on individual standards and are therefore more satisfied with their premium earnings. Especially, there is a sharper contrast between the high pay of these factory women and "white collar" women, than there is in the equivalent comparison between factory men and men doing clerical work at least in offices.[2] These women are well aware that they are making more than office girls.

Myrtle Miller, for example, compares her pay very favorably with women who work in stores, laundries, and even in other factories:

*Interviewer:* How about the pay, how do you feel about that?
*Miller:* Oh, I think we make above average pay, I would say in factories. I *know* we do. . . . I make $1.59 an hour (1953). I draw about $60 after. . . . of course, we usually make B's, you know, and then I usually draw around $60 or better, you know. Very seldom I draw anything under $60. . . . I think it's good pay, because I — *I know women that work in a lot of other places like in stores and in laundries and other factories, and there's very few of them that make as high rate of pay as I do.* And then besides we make a bonus.

Pearl Halliday, is also extremely well satisfied:

*We git better pay here than I've ever had in another job offered* me anywhere. We get $1.52 an hour besides our B's . . . Office jobs are a lot cheaper than on the outside. But of course I mean it's nicer as far as an office job and all. But as far as your pay rate and everything, if you put your time out *why not put it where you're gonna get the best?*

When the interviewer asked the worker "How do you feel about your pay?" they would often relate their pay to their premium earnings, working conditions, the skill required for their job, and the pay that others received for similar work.

The workers relate pay to standards earnings: "The pay is okay, we get good B's." Or, "If they'd raise the B's, why we'd make a good check." Or, "if they wouldn't have that B System here, I believe that we'd be so underpaid, that it would be pitiful."

Pay is related to working conditions in that the work is hard or nor hard: "I'm satisfied [with the pay]. It's not hard work on the elevator." Or, "Well, considerin' our job and the conditions there, I think we're underpaid just a little."

Some workers relate pay to skill: "I make $1.60 an hour. Well, compared to labor [unskilled] any place in this area, that's about right you know." Or, "We're not paid accordin' to our ability."

Finally a big factor in wage satisfaction is the worker's easy way of comparing his check with those of his friends: "It's all right compared to most other places." Or, "On our job, we're paid fairly well, I think. Comparin' to the other mechanics in plants. An' then you compare on your outside men, if they have bad weather an' stuff, our pay is equal to theirs." Incidentally, this remark is quite typical. While Swift craftsmen often make less an hour than outside craftsmen, when you consider their steady work and fringe benefits, they do about as well as building and other trades craftsmen.

Against the background of the comparative attitudes we have just seen, it is interesting to see how a sample of the actual earnings in the plants varies. We cannot accurately compare Chicago with the others because of the difference in years, but the Chicago figures can give us race, sex, and service differentials comparable to the others.

The figures of Table 26 must be used with caution, since they are estimates covering only one year during which business variations between the plants might well occur. Also they do not include valuable fringe benefits. But the surprising thing about these figures is that they partly reverse the trend that puts East St. Louis out in front in many attitudes. The Kansas City colored men and white women at least made more money in 1952 than their counterparts at East St. Louis. There is no difference among the white men. There is another interesting difference: At the East St. Louis plant we find the expected differences between the white and colored workers in annual income. Since the whites tend to be employed on the more skilled jobs, they naturally have higher earnings. In Chicago, we see the same general pattern. But at Kansas City, there is very little difference between the white and colored workers: In fact the colored old-timers there made practically as much ($4515) as the middle-service white men ($4578), and these latter have most of the choice mechanical jobs.

We would expect the white women and colored men in Kansas City to

Table 26. *Estimated average annual gross income, 1952 (Chicago, 1949).*
*(in dollars)*

### Men

#### Colored

| Chicago | | Kansas City | | East St. Louis | | |
|---|---|---|---|---|---|---|
| 2900. | (37) | 3846. | (11) | 3516. | (10) | Short |
| 2988. | (17) | 4139. | (13) | 3953. | (12) | Middle |
| 3234. | (16) | 4515. | ( 8) | 3935. | (13) | Long |

#### White

| Chicago | | Kansas City | | East St. Louis | | |
|---|---|---|---|---|---|---|
| 3220. | (25) | 3895. | (13) | 3882. | (13) | Short |
| 3526. | (20) | 4578. | (10) | 4294. | (13) | Middle |
| 3271. | (34) | 4289. | (12) | 4381. | (14) | Long |

### Women

#### Colored

| Chicago | | Kansas City | | East St. Louis | | |
|---|---|---|---|---|---|---|
| 2479. | ( 5) | 3024. | ( 5) | | | Short |
| 2409. | ( 5) | 2965. | ( 5) | | | Middle |
| 2500. | ( 5) | | | | | Long |

#### White

| Chicago | | Kansas City | | East St. Louis | | |
|---|---|---|---|---|---|---|
| 2515. | ( 5) | 3497. | ( 8) | 3194. | ( 9) | Short |
| 2537. | ( 4) | 3485. | ( 6) | 3420. | ( 8) | Middle |
| 3198. | ( 5) | 3904. | ( 7) | 3790. | ( 9) | Long |

(The parentheses indicate the number of persons in each group.)

be more favorable toward their pay than the East St. Louis workers. The women are more favorable, as we can see in Appendix Table V. But the Kansas City colored men are not. Very likely the complex of their other attitudes, in which they are less favorable, influences them here, in spite of the actual pay advantage which they enjoyed. Also a few extremists bring down their score.

To sum up, we have seen that the packinghouse workers are generally satisfied with their pay. Also we have seen the East St. Louis workers maintain their slight edge of greater satisfaction in spite of the fact that their women and colored workers actually made somewhat less on the average than their counterparts in Kansas City.

Working Conditions

The phrase "working conditions" has become fairly common parlance among workers and industrial relations people. An employee will talk with another about "working conditions" and management will be interested in what workers think of "working conditions." By working conditions we mean: (1) Comfortable environment (condition of floors and workrooms, dressing rooms and cafeteria; temperature and humidity, cleanliness and comfort). (2) Safety (floors, tools, and so forth). (3) Efficiency (steady product flow; adequate trucks and help).

Most employees will mean one or another of these. Naturally each worker will have his own unique emphasis when he perceives working conditions, just as all his work attitudes are somewhat personal. In rare cases, some employees might mean mostly "the foreman," or "the job" or "pay," by working conditions.

Another point that needs clarification: What do we mean by "favorable" to working conditions? It means an attitude of general satisfaction. It does not preclude the employee's making some suggestions for improving conditions.

We should ask: Is the employee greatly and emotionally concerned about working conditions? Or, only slightly concerned? In any organization there will be some "griping," for example in the army about the food. Some students of human relations have said that a certain amount of griping can be a healthy thing.

For the packinghouse workers, plant working conditions are not a greatly important issue. Neither, on the other hand, are working conditions of negligible importance. These workers like prestige. We recall some saying that when they get their street clothes on and go home at night, they are glad that they look like anybody else. Dirty work clothes are a source of embarrassment to them. So, also, are working conditions. *The prestige value of working conditions should not be underestimated.* There is some relationship, too, between the packinghouse workers' attitudes toward working conditions and their desire not to have their children come to the plant to work.

As for the Chicago packinghouse workers' views on working conditions, we can only give general impressions. Most seemed to be moderately well satisfied with conditions in the Chicago plant. Some complaints were made about the cold and damp of certain departments. Few comments were made about the heat. Sometimes the danger arising from use of knives or from the elevators was mentioned. Complaints about locker rooms were occasionally made. Some of the old-timers were quite impressed with the great improvements that Swift had made over the years. The white men of short service were one of the most critical groups. The women were the most satisfied.

We have more precise data about the other two plants, as shown in Appendix Table VI, showing 73 per cent of the Kansas City hourly-paid employees to be satisfied, with a slightly better number at East St. Louis, 81 per cent. There are extremely wide variations within the Kansas City plant, from only 25 per cent of the colored men of short service satisfied, to 100 per cent of the colored old-timers, and 100 per cent of the white women of short service. The most critical groups in either plant are once again the colored men of short service and middle service. Repeatedly we have seen the dissatisfaction of these men carrying over from one attitude to the other. It is not surprising that they have the least company allegiance.

The women are slightly more favorable than the men. The reasons for this are: Women rarely have work dealing with the killing of animals, with heavy transportation, or in very cold or very hot rooms. Their work is mostly packing or light knife work in rooms that are quite temperate. Only in rare instances do women packinghouse workers work under very difficult working conditions.

There is some difference by race in the Kansas City plant but not at East St. Louis. Only 53 per cent of the Kansas City Negroes are favorable, in spite of the very satisfied old-timers. This attitude toward working conditions simply reinforces the trend of generally less satisfaction which we have seen among the Kansas City Negro workers.

As for length of service, there is not any consistent trend among the plants. At Kansas City the old-timers are much more favorable than their fellow workers. At East St. Louis there is no service difference.

A loyal old-timer, Clem Haines, a Negro who has worked for forty-three years in the same department, comments on the great improvements Swift made in working conditions over those forty-three years:

Oh say, when I first came here, we didn't hardly even have a place to take a bath. The dressing rooms we had, you had to furnish your own lock. And you couldn't wear no good clothes out here. Somebody'd break your lock open, you'd go down there — 'cause I know — I bought a brand new pair of shoes, like on Saturday, and wore them out on that Monday. I came down that Monday night to change my clothes, the shoes was gone, the lock broken. You couldn't wear nothin' down here. They didn't have no janitor stayin' in the dressing room, cleanin' up. Nothin' like that. . . . Everything is convenient now, to what it was then — no roaches, no mice to get in your pockets.

*Interviewer:* Why do you think those changes came in? Who brought those changes?

*Haines:* Well, it looks like every time they change superintendents or somethin', he improves somethin'. Every superintendent they got in here, look like he make a different improvement. This superintendent they got in here now, he make a lot of improvements. 'Cause he wants a clean plant. He put more men cleanin' up around in the yard. Pickin' up papers.... Yes, they's lots of changes aroun' here. You know — a lot of difference. When you want a drink of water in those days — they have a barrel. Ice and water. A dipper hangin' on each side of it. Thas' the way you got a drink of water in those days. Dip it down in that barrel. Now we got fountains. Showers to take a bath with. Didn' have them in those days. You know that wasn' sanitary neither. That ice was made here. Made a lot of fellows sick.

*Interviewer:* Did it?

*Haines:* Yes, there's whole lots of differences — doctor's office. You can run in and get cough syrup, cold tablets. They have nurses. They used to have what they call an intern doctor to tie up your finger. Now they got everythin', everythin' you want.... I don't think they could make it any better than they got it now.

Among the foremen, East St. Louis supervisors are more favorable (roughly 100 per cent) than the Kansas City supervisors (84 per cent). In both cases, of course, the foremen are more satisfied with working conditions than their own employees are. We would expect this.

The only reversal in the interplant pattern is made by the Local 78 union leaders, with 33 per cent being satisfied about plant working conditions, while Local 12 Kansas City leaders are 63 per cent satisfied. The reasons for this exception are not clear, but are probably the following: These leaders see the whole plant in their travels and therefore are more aware of departments with difficult working conditions. Also, being leaders, they naturally get complaints from workers. Finally, Local 78 leaders are more aggressive than the Local 12 leaders in some ways, and may feel they must constantly press for improved working conditions. In this respect they may be a bit biased in their view of "working conditions," just as the foremen may be somewhat biased in the opposite direction.

Listening to one representative Local 78 steward, for example, Andy Dietz, we can see why the Local 78 leaders are more critical. Dietz is a generally satisfied man, but he is aggressive about working conditions and thinks many improvements should be made:

Very poor for the size of the industry and for the amount of money that enters into it.

*Interviewer:* The locker rooms you mean?

*Dietz:* Everything . . . improvements all over the plant could be made. . . . The negligence, I mean. . . . [He then complains about the administration of the safety system, though this plant has a good record for safety.]

To sum up this three-plant comparison of attitudes toward working conditions, we found that most of the Swift employees are rather satisfied with conditions, some of the old-timers remarking on the great improvements made in the last thirty years. All this in spite of the fact that a meat-packing plant, by the very nature of its operations, cannot be made as pleasant a place to work in as, for example, a radio factory. Once again we find the East St. Louis plant with a slight lead, continuing the pattern. The one exception to this is the Local 78 leaders, and this exception is probably due to their greater aggressiveness regarding Swift.

## THE SUGGESTION SYSTEM

Of all the attitudes reported in this book, the packinghouse workers' views about the Swift suggestion box system are the least important from the point of view of the workers' morale. The suggestion system is obviously not as important to them as their job, pay, advancement, the gang, or company allegiance itself. Nevertheless their attitude toward it is very revealing of the thoughts and fears of the workers. And further, it can give us one more link in the chain of attitudes which will assist us to contrast the three plants with their differing company allegiances.

Swift's suggestion plan enables employees to submit written suggestions for improving equipment, working conditions, or methods. Suggestion blanks, on which the worker writes his ideas, are found throughout the plant. If the company adopts a worker's suggestion, he receives a cash award or, if he prefers, merchandise in place of the cash. In addition, shares of Swift stock are occasionally awarded for the best suggestions received during a given period of time. The value of the awards varies with the savings realized from the suggestion, from a few dollars to thousands of dollars.

Besides providing the worker with a financial incentive, the suggestion system also gives him an opportunity to participate in company affairs. It also provides him with a chance to think. The suggestion system is one of the few remaining institutions in a mass-production plant which might encourage employees at the bottom of the ladder to do original and creative thinking. So we hear one foreman say, "I was right tickled to get the award for something I thought up, something new, see?" There is an element of creativity in making a suggestion. The interviewer occasionally heard a rather reticent worker suddenly speak enthusiastically and in great detail about some suggestion which he had submitted.

What does the suggestion plan mean to the company? Cost savings. In 1953, the Swift organization in the U. S. and Canada saved $428,257 (of which $60,676 was paid out in awards) through employee suggestions.

What does the suggestion plan mean to the worker? Cash, merchandise, or stock. These are one type of reward, material gain. But the worker whose suggestion has been adopted receives additional, intangible rewards. He may receive words of congratulation and recognition from his boss or coworkers. The *Swift News* publicizes some of the suggestions. And when the employee sees one of his own ideas incorporated into the daily life of the plant, his self-confidence is bolstered. His pet idea has been accepted by the company. As a result, he may identify himself more fully with the company. This is advantageous to Swift.

Having a suggestion adopted is regarded by some of the workers as an indication of intelligence beyond the ordinary, as a feat of which one can be justly proud. Long-service worker Jim Udell says:

You got to be pretty smart, you know, to come up with a suggestion that's better than those they got. They have mens that don't do nothin' but studyin' in there: that's their job! You got to be pretty smart to get somethin' better than they already got, see?

Bertha Guzik was pleased when her idea was accepted:

I put it in and got $5 for it. *I didn't know I was that smart.*

Roland Harrison points out that:

I turned in a few suggestions and got a few little rewards . . . *that makes me feel like I know a little something.*

Let us see now how the three workforces differ in their views about the Swift suggestion system.

For the Chicago plant we must be content with "impressions" again. The topic of suggestions came up occasionally in the Chicago interviews. The Chicago workers seemed to have no great interest or confidence in the system, nor did they use it to any great extent. Some were definitely distrustful of it, fearing to make any "efficiency suggestion" lest they suggest themselves out of a job.

As for the other two workforces, we have a more systematic survey with measured attitudes, as shown in Appendix Table VII. Our main finding here is that neither workforce is very favorable toward the suggestion system. Rather both tend toward indifference. Again, the East St. Louis hourly-paid employees are more favorable (2.4) than their fellows at Kansas City (2.9). Nearly three quarters of the former are favorable against about half of the latter. No clear patterns by race, sex, or service are evident: for instance, women are more favorable at one plant and less at the other.

However, when we look at the leadership groups in Appendix Table VII we see a complete reversal of the trend. The Kansas City union leaders (with the perennial exception of the UPWA-CIO group) are more favorable to the suggestion system than the AFL leaders in East St. Louis. Even more important, the Kansas City foremen are nearly twice as favorable to the system as the National Stockyards foremen. The foreman has much to do with the successful administration of the suggestion system. In spite of the less favorable attitudes toward suggestions at Kansas City (due largely to the minority of malcontents in the plant), the Kansas City packinghouse workers actually participate in the system almost three times as much as the National Stockyards people. In Kansas City, for example, there were 21.5 suggestions made for every one hundred employees in 1953. But in East St. Louis there were only 7.8. The attitude of the Kansas City foremen undoubtedly is responsible for the greater number of suggestions made in their plant. Also we must remember that a number of suggestions are put in by the foremen themselves.

In East St. Louis, Local 78 union leaders have helped to keep down somewhat the number of suggestions in their plant. Being rather aggressive unionists, they feel that suggestions, especially work-saving suggestions, might mean less jobs, or might pull the employee's allegiance more toward the company and away from the union. One Local 78 steward, Andrew Dietz, expresses this coolness of the union leaders toward the suggestion system with a curious distinction between science and management. He thinks that workers should talk over their suggestions with a union man first:

*Interviewer:* How does that suggestion system go, I wonder — that box on the wall?
*Dietz:* I'm a union man, remember that!
*Interviewer:* [laughs]
*Dietz:* It's all right — uh — there are little flaws in it. I try to tell all of my people that if ever they have any suggestions, I'd like to see them before they're turned in. They want to know why. I tell 'em, I'd like to see whether you're decreasing employment.
*Interviewer:* Working somebody out of a job?
*Dietz:* Yeh. It's good to make suggestions, but it isn't good to suggest so that somebody isn't able to feed their children at home. . . . I want to increase

employment, not decrease it. And there's a lot of suggestions around here that could be made to probably decrease it. I mean machinery is taking over a lot, over everything. When you suggest something, actually what you're doing is suggesting machinery or a device that would take some of the labor out of the job. And maybe you're suggesting a little device where the company will get an idea from your little device to make a bigger device, and eliminate you altogether by a little push-button.

That could be operated by — well, six or seven push-buttons operated by one man, see? Whereas there were six or seven people operating the job itself. But all in all, the suggestions are all right, provided they're looked over by somebody that has a little authority on whether the job itself is going to be eliminated by it. *I think the union should have somebody there, or suggest to the people to bring it to their stewards or somebody that knows the job before they're ever turned in.*

*Interviewer:* Otherwise somebody might lose a job, eh?

*Dietz:* Uh — I would never — if I could suggest something in science — I would never say 'no' to that, because they're out for something to help everybody, but management is out for something to help themselves.

*Interviewer:* So there's a big difference between science and management?

*Dietz:* There's a big difference. If I could tell one of those big professors how to make a heart tick constantly, I'd tell him. But I wouldn't tell management how to make their machines operate more thoroughly.

That ever-present fear of some new device making one's job unnecessary is common enough among American workers generally. These three East St. Louis workers express such fear: Old-timer, Thomas Leyden says, "I won't turn 'em in where they'll knock three or four men out of work. I never could see that."

Another old-timer, Charles Harwood feels the same way:

Here you may say I'm wrong — I'm not a religious man. But if I'm workin' right along side of you, and I'm a mechanic and you're somethin' else, and if I cut ten men off for $25 or $30 I can't see it . . . if I can improve somethin' to help the men along, I do it. . . . But whenever you cut a man off, you feel bad . . . it may not only hurt him, but it may hurt ten or twelve people.

This fear is deep-seated; it is based on personal experience, on what the workers have seen in their own department. Listen to the views of Florence Crane:

*Florence Crane:* Well, I think suggestions are all right. I mean if they are going to be helpful. But if it's going to hurt some people, I don't think they are.

*Interviewer:* Work them out of a job?

*Florence Crane:* Well, like they're doin' now. Everytime they put a suggestion in and it is followed up, why there's just that many girls out of a job. . . . There's going to be three girls off the line that they're putting in now.

Other reasons for being unfavorable to the system are the view that the awards are not high enough, or that there is too much delay or favoritism in answering the suggestion slips. On the other hand, some employees in all three plants like the system because they think that it does pay good awards, because it gives them recognition, and because it makes for better working conditions for all the employees.

To summarize: While the Swift suggestion system is not of central importance to the packinghouse workers, their attitudes toward it are revealing. One example is their fear of "suggesting" a fellow worker out of a job or out of his previous wage-rate. We saw that in spite of this fear, some workers were rather favorable to the plan, though the average opinion is close to indifference. On a comparative basis, we find East St. Louis workers slightly more favorable in attitude, though they participate much less in the plan, due in part to the unfavorable views of the Local 78 leaders, and also to the fact that their foremen are rather indifferent to the suggestion plan. The greater number of suggestions in Kansas City is to be ascribed mostly to the very high opinion of the system among the foremen there.

We ought now to have a better understanding of what the job and some of its aspects mean to the packinghouse worker. Since these job attitudes also related to company allegiance, this latter concept should also be coming into sharper focus.

What have we found in this chapter? We found that the workers in all three plants are fairly well satisfied with their jobs, taking "job" in the limited sense used in this book. We also found that the East St. Louis plant had a slight lead. Then comparing four more attitudes, primarily between Kansas City and East St. Louis, we saw that the worker's fellow employees are an important aspect of his total job situation, and that significantly enough there is no difference between Kansas City and East St. Louis here. Without dramatic differences, we then found East St. Louis workers slightly more satisfied with their pay, working conditions, and the suggestion system. Clearly, the pattern of East St. Louis' better industrial relations is emerging.

In all these five aspects of the job, we see definite satisfaction. In the next three chapters, however, we shall see three company-related attitudes in which the workers are mostly dissatisfied.

CHAPTER VII

## *The Chance to Get Ahead*

In spite of the company allegiance we have found in varying patterns in the three plants, the packinghouse workers are not satisfied with their chances to "get ahead." In this chapter we shall consider the men's views about their opportunities for advancement, and then the Negroes' comments about equality of treatment.[1]

LIMITATIONS ON ADVANCEMENT

America has built some remarkable traditions about the opportunity of her citizens to move up the economic and social ladder. It is a sociological commonplace that various immigrant groups coming to this country have begun at the "bottom" and seen their grandchildren arrive at the "top." We do not have so rigid a class structure as have the British Isles and the European continent. There is no conclusive evidence that this "upward social mobility," as it is called, is becoming less free in America at least with respect to economic opportunities.[2] Our tradition still maintains that qualified and ambitious people may advance.

As for the packinghouse workers of our three plants, we ask whether or not they see this "American dream" as a possibility in their own lives or in the lives of their children. We want to know whether they care much about advancement, whether this attitude is a factor in their company and union allegiance, and whether it varies among the three plants.

Gustavus Swift had a policy of promotion from within, expressed by the saying: "I can raise better men than I can hire." Do the workers think this policy affects them?

"Attitudes toward the opportunity for advancement" means: Does the packinghouse worker think that there are opportunities for a qualified man to work up to a more desirable or better paying job, and especially into supervision? For foremen, it means their attitude about moving up higher into the ranks of management. We do not necessarily mean the actual wish for personal advancement. A man may realize that he is not qualified for a higher position or he may not want its responsibilities, but he can still express his opinion about the opportunities for advancement for those who are qualified and ambitious. The worker's attitude to his opportunities is what we are talking about and measuring.

The topic of advancement was covered less systematically with the women employees, because women packinghouse workers generally do not care much about opportunities for advancement, at least for themselves.

The principal findings, in Appendix Table VIII, are that the employees have mostly unfavorable thoughts about their opportunities for advancement. In Chicago, 43 per cent are favorable; in Kansas City, 44 per cent, and in East St. Louis, 56 per cent. Thus we see no difference between Chicago and Kansas City, with a small margin of greater satisfaction at East St. Louis. The trend favoring East St. Louis continues.

ATTITUDE OF WHITES AND OLD-TIMERS

Let us look at some of the variations. If we compare the colored men in the three plants, we see Chicago and East St. Louis to be about the same, around 43 per cent favorable. But the Kansas City colored are far lower, only 23 per cent favorable. This time the reason cannot be simply ascribed to the UPWA sympathizers in Kansas City, such as the minorities among the Negro men of short and middle service. The Negro old-timers, though company-minded men indeed, with a company allegiance score of 1.5, are only 28 per cent optimistic about their advancement opportunities. The Negroes' views on advancement are so closely related to their attitudes toward "equal opportunities" that we shall discuss them rather in the second part of this chapter. At East St. Louis, Negroes are significantly more critical than whites.

As for length of service, we see some difference here, at least among the white men and women employees. The long-service people are significantly more favorable and optimistic at East St. Louis. Eighty-six per cent of the white men, fifteen years of service and over, think that advancement opportunities at Swift are good, a very high proportion. They are significantly more favorable than the Kansas City old-timers.

We have seen that the long-service workers are frequently more favorable about many company-related matters. Advancement is no exception. Incidentally, they mentioned adequate education as a requirement for advancement more often than the younger men did. Herman Dudley speaks for these older employees. Mr. Dudley has been with Swift over thirty years. He started out as a laborer and worked up to be an assistant foreman. Now he is doing semiskilled work in the gang itself. He has a number of relatives in the plant, one in supervision. His comments bear out Swift's policy of promotion from within:

*Interviewer:* Well, how about, as far as Swift is concerned, are the chances for advancement, moving up and that?
*Dudley:* Well, I'd say they are excellent. *Ever since I've been here, Swift always goes down through the ranks to bring some one up.* I don't know of 'em *here* ever going outside the organization to, uh, bring somebody in. They take 'em out of their employees. They had a course here, I think they still have it, you can take, an educational course. I took that when it just started.

Oh, they give you foremanship and everything. . . . I don't know what they call it now, "Young Men's Training." They have mathematics and foremanship, plant operation and things like that. It's good. It's educational. You learn a lot. I only went through the eighth grade of school and most of my figuring, my education has been learned here.

A good number of other white men of shorter length of service are as favorable to their advancement opportunities as Mr. Dudley. For example, Frank Fechner. Fechner is young, skilled, and a hard worker. His foreman thinks that he is an exceptionally good all-around man. Fechner never had much education, but we shall see how he makes up for it:

You can really move up if you really want to. You know you can take a chance at steppin' down and doin' it, you could do it. That's with anything else, if you take a chance to it and try . . . only try, you can really do it. . . . I started in here and I really moved up and I stayed in the _____ room and I stuck it out, and I figured I'm gonna try it.
*Interviewer:* You've got a good future here?
*Fechner:* I really have.
*Interviewer:* How about, do you think maybe you'll get in the supervision some day? Think you'll try that?
*Fechner:* Well, I don't know, but at least I'm gonna try to work myself up if I can.

When we listen to the colored workers, however, we hear a very different story:

— There's not too much chance for colored.
— No chance, no future because all I know is work, no education.
— I don't have much chance to advance at all because I'm colored.
— It might be all right for the white boys, but not for the colored; can't be foreman.
— There's several jobs we can't get into even though we have seniority; I can't see no chance for advancement at all.

— A Negro doesn't have much chance of advancing; my job is as far as I can go; there's one guy up there with thirty years and he couldn't get a stuffer's job.
— The farthest we can go is checkers.
— They don't give Negro women a chance.
— Negroes can't get a chance to go to foremen's school.
— There's no place to move up to in the janitor's gang; no place to go; no colored gang leader or colored foremen.
— The colored boys tried to get in the foremen's school, and they wouldn't let them.
— They don't put Negroes on mechanical jobs.
— They tell a man that it's a white man's job.

What the union leaders think about advancement is interesting, for some people think that men go into union political office because they do not find advancement opportunity in their company.[3] We have no specific data about this for Chicago's Local 28 leaders. Half of the leaders of Local 12 definitely favor their advancement opportunities. This is better than the average Kansas City employee. And 57 per cent of the leaders of Local 78 are favorable, about the same as their fellow employees. Of course the UPWA men in Kansas City Local 12 follow their pattern by being very critical, 90 per cent unfavorable. Some of them are union-leadership-minded, partly because they think they cannot advance in Swift. There were also a few Chicago unionists like this. As for the stewards in both plants, they are less favorable than the local leaders primarily because there is a higher proportion of Negroes among them.

To take an example, Local 78 leader, Ted Berghoff thinks that Swift offers a good chance for advancement. He tells how he himself became active in the union, because he was dissatisfied with a grievance:

*Interviewer:* Then there's the question of advancement here for a younger guy, moving up the line. How do you feel about that? Do you feel you have a chance?

*Berghoff:* Oh, yeah, there's — every chance in the world . . . not only — not only as far as the union is concerned — I think that — if he makes himself qualified as a union member and working along those lines of advancement that he has all the opportunity in the world — even to become a management man.

*Interviewer:* It is pretty open?

*Berghoff:* It is, wide open. At least it is that way for the last six years, I'd say. They have taken quite a few members out of our ranks. Our checkoff shows that any number of them that they brought out. . . .

*Interviewer:* They won't be snappin' you up, will they?

*Berghoff:* No, I don't think so. They may not want me. [laughs] There's a lot of 'em. There's salesmen, there's — I guess the sales force has got about six or seven of our [union] people, and —

*Interviewer:* Did they ever try — try to get you in there?

*Berghoff:* No, they never asked me. . . . When the union first started, you know, why — they were given' me a pretty rough go — generally. This was when the job in the _____ Department was in progress, you know. I tried to get some consideration, and I went from one guy to the other to get somethin' done that was the right thing. And, lo and behold they turned their back on me and when they did, why — the — anybody'll swim to a log you know when he's goin' to go down, you know — And these guys were all talkin' about the union, And I said, by gum, I'm gonna see what this is all about.

So our first meeting — we went down there and they had election of officers and they elected me _____ that night and the next morning we come out here and Joe [a certain management man] told somebody, I think it was the superintendent at the time, he says, there's the man that you could have had on your side of the fence. Instead of that, he says, he's goin' to give you a rough way to go. [laughs] He really told 'em the truth about it. He hit the nail on the head so to speak.

For the union leader, advancement means not so much a better hourly-paid job, but promotion into management. For white men of union leadership capability, the ranks of supervision in Swift were quite open.

## Attitude of Foremen

Two facts are important about the foremen's views: the foremen are definitely more favorable to advancement opportunities than the hourly-paid workers; secondly, the foremen of the three plants, unlike their employees, differ greatly, with the East St. Louis foremen being highly favorable (88 per cent), to their opportunities.

Since the majority of the Swift foremen have once worked in the gang, or at least as standards checkers, and have been advanced from this work into supervision, it is not surprising that they are mostly favorable to their advancement opportunities.

Here are some of their comments:

— I feel like Swift's advances people, but it's strictly on the individual and his qualifications.
— My boss has a college education and that will advance him fast.
— I've been pretty fortunate myself; I've come up quick.
— I haven't done too bad; chances are pretty good.
— I've always been treated well; I've moved up fairly well.
— They are good, very good; anyone that gets in and shows any initiative, he's not going to be held back.
— They're wonderful now; they're in desperate need of men coming up; in the last years, promotion and advancements are really coming on.

— I honestly think so; education helps a lot, but if you got common sense, you've got a chance to get ahead.
— Oh, there's a good chance, if you're qualified.

The second main fact is that East St. Louis foremen are clearly in the lead, continuing the pattern of greater satisfaction there. We see a big difference especially between East St. Louis and Chicago, where the foremen were not very favorable at all.

Old-time foreman Joe Hamen from the East St. Louis plant gives his own views on advancement there. He thinks that advancement opportunities are good, if a young man wants to get education and make some effort. He gives quite a talk on education as a requirement for advancing. He also appears to be somewhat insecure in his views, anxious that other people, in this case, the interviewer, should agree with him:

*Hamen:* They want educated people; they want 'em. They want people who can do things. An' I think — honestly, if a man don't advance with Swift & Company, I don't think he would advance with anybody.
*Interviewer:* That's their policy, to promote from within, huh?
*Hamen:* Yes, stay with Swift. They can always train better than they can hire somebody like that. . . . Raise better men than they can hire. . . . And they promote the men from their own ranks. And that old tradition, I think, is followed right down today. I think it is. . . . I think if you don't advance, I think it's because — I always tell these boys, I say, your colleges, and your public schools, the doors are wide open at night, your high school doors are propped open at night, the lights all on. You go to St. Louis and go past the St. Louis University, it's all lit up. You drive past the Washington U., it's all lit up. I say, all you people comin' in here, we try to teach you somethin'; if you'll just come in so we can teach you.

Another view about the importance of education for advancement, especially college education, is expressed by Kansas City foreman Jim Reese. Mr. Reese's comments show why the Kansas City foremen, while favorable to advancement opportunities, are not quite so favorable as East St. Louis foremen.

Jim Reese started with Swift during the first World War as an ordinary laborer. He worked himself up to be a foreman. He thinks that advancement opportunities are good for a man in the gang; he is not so sure about the chances of advancing into supervision. He thinks that the recent trend is to favor college men. But he feels that a man who is qualified and who works up from the gang "makes an awful good mechanical foreman":

Well, for the skilled man or the unskilled man, or the semiskilled, I think it's a wonderful place to build up if you use a little initiative with it. *But for the hourly man now to build up to be a foreman, I don't know. There's a tendency* to fill these departments with college men on the supervisory jobs. . . . A man comes up through the gang, maybe he's a wonderful man, but maybe he isn't a college man. The college man gets — he's the one that's going places around here now. Maybe well, you're a college man, but still I think you understand what it's about. . . .

Of course, he's got the advantage because he's got his college education. *But when it comes to that, I think a man coming up through the ranks, I think he makes an awful good mechanical foreman.*

*Interviewer:* For one thing, he knows men. He knows what it's like to work in a gang.

*Reese:* He knows that, and he knows the plant. This plant's pretty big. Takes a man a long time to learn everything. I mean, the details all over the plant. And I'm not — I wish I'd been a college man. I could be a lot further than I'm now, if I was. Don't get me wrong, I'm not talking about a college education.

*Interviewer:* Well, the old Swift motto was, "I can raise better men than I can hire."

*Reese:* That's the thing I should have said in the first place, and then I wouldn't have had to done all this talking. I forgot about that. I'd go for that 100 per cent.

*Interviewer:* I wonder if they're doing it?

*Reese:* No.

*Interviewer:* So there might be some improvement possible right in there, in advancement?

*Reese:* I think so. Now when it comes to the master mechanic, naturally I'm — anyone would expect him to be a college man. He'd have to be. *But I sure like a good foreman who's come up through the ranks.*

So far as advancement into supervision is concerned, we should note that not all the packinghouse workers, by any means, want to be foremen. At Kansas City, for instance, a rather significant 29 per cent of the white men in our sample spontaneously volunteered the information that they did not want to become foremen. No Negroes made such comments. Some white men would mention the responsibilities of supervision, or that the additional pay would not be enough to make their promotion worthwhile. This question was not systematically explored. If it had been, we might have found a percentage higher than the 29 per cent.

One foreman presents the problem from his observation in the plant. He is Norman Flack, nearing thirty years with Swift, with over ten years as a foreman in Kansas City. He thinks that it is becoming increasingly difficult to get men in the gang to want to seek supervisory positions:

*Interviewer:* How about the chances for moving up, advancement here, for a young fellow like yourself. Do you feel it's pretty good?

*Flack:* Well, I don't classify myself as a young fellow any more. *As far as going up is concerned, I'd say it was pretty good.* For a young fellow, for instance, that'd come in ta start, maybe as a salesman, or a standard checker, or something like that, chances are pretty good. . . . You've got a condition here now, too, that it's been discussed considerably lately, with the union. *It's becoming more and more difficult to git a man to leave the union and go on a supervisory or some sort of a straight time job.* For one thing, the part of it's money. *There isn't too much incentive in the money.* 'Course sometimes a fella looks to the future and forgets about that. Then another thing is the *acceptance of responsibility.*

While it is true that some workers do not care much about personally advancing into more responsible jobs or into supervision, they are in the minority. Advancement opportunities are important to most of the packinghouse workers. For the first time, we find most workers unfavorable. Apparently they do not think that the old Swift maxim "I can raise better men than I can hire" is being borne out in their cases. Attitudes similar to these have been found among auto workers, steelworkers and metalworkers.[4] Incidentally, the packinghouse workers' views about advancement will help to make more meaningful their thoughts about having their children come to work in the plant.

Negroes as Second-Class Citizens

We shall now pinpoint attitudes toward advancement, by hearing the Negro workers' views on equality of plant opportunities as they see it.

What do we mean by this "attitude toward equal opportunity"? It includes both attitudes toward advancement and full acceptance in the life of the plant. The topic of racial relations tends to be a sensitive area for many Negro workers, especially when they are talking to a white interviewer. Frequently the topic was introduced by some phrase like this: "Do you feel that there is equal opportunity here in the plant, regardless of race, creed, or color?" A few Negroes might be favorable to their opportunities and, at the same time, advert to such a situation as the cafeteria segregation at East St. Louis, about which they might sincerely express very little concern. To them, cafeteria segregation is not a "meat-and-potatoes" matter; job promotion is. Such workers might be graded as "favorable" on our scale.

In other words, "equal opportunity" is perceived by different Negro workers with different highlights and emphases, though it is sufficiently constant to be measured for Kansas City and East St. Louis. As for Chicago, we have qualitative rather than quantitative data. The great dissatisfaction of the Chicago Negro packinghouse workers with their opportunities (as of 1950, but greatly improved since then) appears in interview after interview.

Before coming to our findings, we ask: What are the actual degrees of integration or segregation between the races in the three plants and the three local unions? In Chicago, the major discrimination was that very few Negroes were being promoted into the skilled mechanical jobs and none into supervision, the standards gang, or the office. Since 1950, these lines have been crossed. In Local 28, the discrimination, if any, was against the whites, since so many meetings were held in Negro Bronzeville.

As for conditions in the Kansas City Swift plant, Negro men had been hired for many years, beginning well before World War I. Years ago, Negro women were hired. Then for many years none were hired. Beginning again during the second World War, limited numbers of Negro women were hired. The Negro men work in almost all the operating departments, and vary in their proportions from 100 per cent in the Tank House, 92 per cent in the Beef Dressing Department, 89 per cent in the Pork Dressing Department to 18 per cent in the Mechanical and engineers (mostly in mechanical "labor" gang), 1 per cent in the Auto Department and 0 per cent among the ham-boners and the calf-skinners.

The Negro women are rather evenly divided among six departments: the Pork Warm Variety Meats, Pork Packing, Beef Warm Variety Meats, Table-Ready Meats, Cafeteria, and Wrap and Tie. These women were first hired in the cafeteria as cooks, kitchen helpers, and counter attendants.

The over-all plant proportions are white men, 38 per cent; Negro men, 38 per cent; white women, 14 per cent; Negro women, 1 per cent; Mexican men, 10 per cent. Taking the men and women together (1953), the plant is about 40 per cent Negro.

Some other facts are these: There is one Negro in supervision. He is an assistant foreman. There are no Negroes in the Standards Department, nor as office workers in the plant office building. Some years ago there was racial segregation in the cafeteria facilities. There is none at the present time. The Negro women, however, have segregated dressing room facilities.

Local 12 is an integrated local for all business purposes. It avoids union social activities, such as parties, dances, and picnics, where problems of racial relations might arise.

As for Swift East St. Louis, integration conditions are less favorable to Negroes than at the Kansas City plant. East St. Louis has been hiring Negro men for many years, even prior to the first World War. Years ago, Negro women were apparently hired as well. But for many years, since before the depression at least, Negro women have not been hired. (By 1957, womens' seniority lists were depleted and there was talk of hiring some Negro women, but reduced operations have since prevented any new women from being hired.) Negro men now work in almost all the operating departments, but hardly at all in the mechanical departments. There are no Negroes in the Standards Department, or sales, or the plant offices, or in the ranks of plant supervision. Certain departments are almost all Negro, such as the Beef Dressing, Pork Dressing, Beef Fancy Meat departments, and the Hide Cellars.

As butchers, some Negroes in all three plants have risen to top skills with good pay and status. Most are in semiskilled work. The few unskilled jobs are largely Negro-manned. Of course, the proportion of Negroes in the East St. Louis plant is rather high, 44 per cent, considerably higher than the Negro proportion in the surrounding area of East St. Louis. But this follows the pattern of most packinghouses in the north. Since there are many jobs which white people will not take or retain, the Negro people take these jobs. This accounts for the high proportion of Negro packinghouse workers.

Some additional race relations facts are these: The large employees' cafeteria is Jim Crow in practice, but not by any company rule or sign. The serving tables and steam tables are in the middle of the room. The white workers are served and seated on one side with the Negro men on the other. Attitudes toward this situation are expressed in a number of interviews. Occasionally Negro men will break the color line by eating on the white side. No external trouble has occurred, but such efforts have never lasted. These Negro workers are not racially aggressive, as they are in Chicago.

Swift has two rather autonomous, but company-supported employees' social organizations; the Boosters' Club and the Arrow-S Club. The former is all-Negro and the latter is all-white. The various affairs of these clubs, such as the annual Christmas parties, are Jim Crow, though Swift management supports and visits both affairs equally. The segregation of these two clubs is not necessarily a company policy, nor is their desegregation a company policy either.

Regarding the union, Local 78 has integrated union meetings with Negro officers and stewards. It did not have social affairs, such as parties and dances, doubtless because the problem of race relations would then become acute. However, mixed gatherings for stewards and their wives have recently occurred. Local 78 has not taken an aggressive stand regarding racial integration or such matters as the hiring of Negro women and cafeteria integration. If anything, it has been less aggressive than Local 12. Chicago's UPWA Local 28 is, of course, by far the most aggressive, taking after its own International.

### East St. Louis Negroes

While Negroes have the best conditions in Chicago, with Kansas City being superior to East St. Louis, East St. Louis Negroes are, paradoxically, more satisfied than those in Kansas City. Of course the difference between the two plants is very slight. But our main finding is that most Negroes are definitely dissatisfied with their racial status and opportunities in the Swift plants. Appendix Table IX brings this out.

Because of conditions less satisfactory to Negroes at East St. Louis we would expect these people to be less satisfied. Negro women cannot get a job in their plant. The cafeteria is segregated. No Negro has managed to get a supervisor's job. All of these discriminations had been corrected some years previously at the Kansas City plant. Why then do we find the Kansas City Negroes more critical? Partly because the UPWA has made them more conscious of their rights. We recall that many of them are UPWA sympathizers, and that the UPWA has been trying to raid the plant.

In East St. Louis while the next door Armour local was UPWA, no effort to raid Local 78 was made. Indeed, we find a considerable amount of criticism among Local 78 people about the UPWA. Another important reason for the paradox is the fact that a significantly greater number of the East St. Louis Negro packinghouse workers are southern-born. They are more conservative, more content with the *status quo*.

While the number of colored women is small at Kansas City, it is interesting to note that they are only half as favorable (10 per cent) as the men. Paradoxically, they have more company allegiance than the men, but they are more conscious of racial feelings against them. Probably the fact that they were required to use a segregated dressing room caused this attitude, and also the fact that colored women in the past had to have a letter of recommendation to get hired, while white women did not.

Another interesting point is found in Appendix Table IX: The old-timers so favorable to most aspects of their jobs, and usually leading in company allegiance, are even more critical than the younger men about racial equality in the plants. At East St. Louis, the incoming Negro workers with Swift less than two years, are 50 per cent favorable toward their opportunities, while the Negro old-timers are only 29 per cent favorable.

Since we seek understanding of the Negro workers' views, we present three interviews at some length. First is Art Love, twenty years old, and a very recent newcomer to Swift. Love is not typical. Rather of all the people interviewed, he was the most emotionally disturbed about discrimination. Love was born in Tennessee, finished high school, and had some college.

He was recently married and lived in one of the poorest colored neighborhoods of East St. Louis. As the interview began, he sat on the edge of his chair and began talking very emotionally about the whole question of discrimination. Later in the interview he relaxed, but he is evidently a very race-conscious man. Also he had been ill, and once had been dropped from employment because he was unable to work following an operation. His foreman says: "He is one of them smart guys. About the lowest rating. Late and off quite a bit. Always has an excuse." When we study the entire interview we see that Love tends to be very sorry for himself and to make excuses. But we also see some of Love's reasons for this: No hope for the future, as he sees life.

*Love:* The chances for the white to advance are much greater than the chances for the Negro.
*Interviewer:* I see.
*Love:* You understand that?
*Interviewer:* Yeah. How does that work out, Art? That's what I'd like to get at.
*Love:* Well, it's sort of like this. A Negro — he might work here ten years. All right — if he's a good worker and he behaves on the job, he might advance as far as a steward. . . . But usually that's as far as it goes. I mean, the white — here's a fellow — he might work here five years. If he's a white man, he might go as far as able to be a straw boss or foreman. . . .
*Interviewer:* Now, could you move up? You're in — let's say you're in the _____ Department. Could you move up to a higher job?
*Love:* Well, that all depends. Most of it depends on me, see. Like, for instance, if — like I'm doing labor now. And if I never say anything about a higher job, they'll just keep me or leave me. See? I'll just do labor from now on. But if — on the other hand, if I say that — if I get a knife and try to learn how to butcher, maybe I begin to do it pretty good, and I ask the foreman could I get a higher job — if he has an opening. I tell you, see it all depends on the individual.
*Interviewer:* So you can move up within your department, huh?
*Love:* Within the department. . . .
*Interviewer:* But there's discrimination there — is there?
*Love:* There are really discrimination.
*Interviewer:* How does that work out? That's what I'd like to know.
*Love:* Well, you see — well I would say the Negro, coming up through the years, he feels sort of like — well in other words he feels like the white man is *over* him. But the white man *is* over him. There's no doubt about it, see? And whereas one white man can do more with a group of thirty-five, or fifty, or a hundred Negroes than four or five other Negroes can do with them by himself, see? Do you understand that?
*Interviewer:* Yes. . . .
*Love:* Well, I mean we feel that we're just as much as you are. You understand? I feel just as great as you, although my skin is dark. You understand?
*Interviewer:* Sure.

*Love:* It's not that I would want to be with you but it's like this. If we work together in the plant, why couldn't we eat together? You see it's no more than right — see? Not that I feel that it's my duty or something to be over there *with* you, but it's just, that it don't even make sense, to discriminate like that.

Love goes on to talk in greater detail about an episode in the cafeteria where he was requested to move from the white side. He also mentions his desire to go to college. Instead, however, he married recently and his wife is expecting a baby. He continues:

So I said — well — it worries me — I said, I might be stuck here. I might have to do twenty years. Who knows? But I don't want to. And I'm trying as hard as I possibly can to get away from it. But it's one of those things. You got to work. See, I wasn't born rich. . . .

So maybe I wouldn't mind too much doin' twenty years here if I could advance. If maybe I could get to be a foreman. You understand?

*The "Jester" — Two Viewpoints of the Negro.* Leaving the emotional and sometimes inaccurate statements of Art Love, we come to a major reason why people misunderstand each other: stereotyping. Ray Kiley, a Kansas City Swift foreman, brings this out. Mr. Kiley's views are no more typical than Mr. Love's views, but his generalizing about the "Negro jester" is common enough.

Mr. Kiley is a successful foreman in many ways; he is rather well liked by his overwhelmingly Negro gang. Looking at the Negro worker through Mr. Kiley's eyes, we must remember that Kiley has some factual support for his extreme opinion. Undoubtedly in his gang, some Negroes are frequently absent on Monday mornings; some seem irresponsible and act like clowns. What Mr. Kiley fails to see is: (1) not all Negroes, as a race, are like this; (2) the cause for the "jester" role is in part precisely the white stereotypes which keep the Negro from positions of responsibility and dignity. The problem runs in a vicious circle. Mr. Kiley's opinion is as follows:

*Bein's I have to work with colored people, I studies 'em. Because every one is like a child. There is no grown-up colored people.* . . . I've got a couple of pretty good boys there, are just a *little bit* higher class than the white folks. And these two boys are constantly sittin' on the fence, ready to pick up anything that the white folks miss on. . . . Now these two boys I can handle just as easy as pie, but let me be gone, these two guys are in trouble; but to me, don't give me a bit of trouble. . . . You'll find a few that will have responsibility — their over-all period [of work] they don't have them. . . . I would divide 'em up at about 20 per cent very high skilled, and those 20 per cent will learn skills fast. . . . An' then I would class the next 40 per cent as the average skilled. Below that, they're just here. Bales of straw with mighty minor brains.

The second viewpoint of the Negro as a jester is well expressed by Negro Larry Wiggins who does not work, by the way, in Mr. Kiley's department. Mr. Wiggins is a broad-shouldered worker, thirteen years with Swift. He is a Korean War veteran and has had many chances to observe the social relations between white and colored people. He makes these penetrating observations about his fellow Negroes and their occasional role of jester:

I'll tell you something else, too. Take a Negro. He's a funny fellow, being one myself I can say that. If he's given no consideration, given no representation, well in a lot of cases he'll act the jester. He has no sense of responsibility, he's just as carefree as he wants to be — I've seen too many times. I saw it in the Service — I'm not trying to use the Service as compared to Swift & Company, but I can use it to put a few pertinent points over. A man'll come to the army just as trifling as he can be. He don't care whether he goes to the guardhouse or whether just anything. And just as soon as you give him a little responsibility you'll see him change just like day and night. . . .

It's the same way here at Swift Company. . . . Shoot the bull all day long. They don't care. If you tell them what to do then he'll do it. Why accept the responsibility and get gray hairs like you're doing if I'm not going to get the money? I'll use my strength and you use your head. You know that's as far as I'm going. You know they develop that attitude quickly.

But in the same sense of the word, with a little orientation, or a little more or less psychoanalysis of the individual, you could put them in a position of responsibility. And you could get a maximum, I would say.

Mr. Wiggins is certainly not a satisfied man and he has no company allegiance. He would leave Swift, but he says he is too old and has a family to support. He goes on to say:

When a Negro comes to Swift & Company, the ceiling is very low. That is, he has to give manual labor from the time he gets there to the time he dies, or to the time he quits, or leaves the service. There's a very low ceiling. . . . At the same time when Swift hires an employee I think that their mental capacity or their physical capacity should be given a test and regardless of race, color, or creed, they should be in line for a promotion into the category into which they fit. More so, I think instead of, if you have a strong back and a weak mind, there's always a place for a Negro at Swift's.

*But if you're looking for promotion, you know, where you can feel as though you are part of the big movement of Swift & Company and that you feel that the responsibility of certain portions of the company, you know, that you'd like for it to be yours, that you'll accept it and what you might say efficiently execute it; well these positions are never here. . . .*

But, I don't know, not being Caucasian. I couldn't tell what formalities are followed, that is, in all types of employment. I don't know, I may have laid it down in a way that you may think I'm partial, or have a little bias.

*Interviewer:* Not at all. I'm very much interested in what you think.

Turning from rank-and-file Negro employees to Negro union leaders, we find unanimity for the first time, even between the conservative Amalgamated and NBPW leaders, along with the UPWA raiding group at Kansas City. Regardless of union affiliation, 100 per cent of these men are critical, at least of some of the race practices at the two plants. Not one of them thinks that the Negro worker is given conditions and opportunities at the plants equal to those given to the white workers, according to abilities, and qualities, and regardless of race. There is no other attitude in this entire study on which there is such agreement among the Negro workers. This attitude does not mean, however, that the Negro leaders do not recognize advances that have been made. Also, they differ among themselves in their aggressiveness and emotional involvement. On one thing they agree, further advances need to be made before equality of opportunity for the Negro will have been achieved.

One of the most interesting interviews on race relations is this one with Marvin Oliver, union steward in Local 78. Oliver is tall, well built, intelligent, with quite a winning personality. Unlike Art Love, he is not emotionally wrought up about the race question. He is more mature. He does not carry a chip on his shoulder. He gives the impression of being a reasonable person. Except for the matter of discrimination, he is a well satisfied man.

Unlike both Art Love and Larry Wiggins, Oliver has definite company allegiance. For instance, he says:

I like to work for Swift, because I'm making good money. If I lost my job here today I wouldn't know where I would want to go. Because I don't know no other plant where I make as much money, nor where the work is so good.

Steward Oliver definitely has leadership ability, judging by his union activity. During the war, he was a lieutenant in an all-Negro unit of the army. He makes the important point that Negroes sometimes play around because they have no responsible future to look forward to: "That's why I play now. I wouldn't play, if I was tryin' to where I could become a boss. Because I play a lot. Lots of time, like right out here now, they say, you play. Sure, I play. I was in the army. I become an officer in the army. I didn't play in the army. But I played before I thought about becomin' an officer. I did everything. I even went to the stockade because I went AWOL. But after I settled down and knew what I wanted, I went to school, OCS. And I strained. . . ."

*Interviewer:* Sure. How about the chances for advancement around here, Marvin — move up to a better job — over the years here — how do you feel about that?

*Oliver:* Well — the advancement here — I don't know — it's just — you haven't got too much of it — actually. To be frank about it — a colored man, he can't go too far. . . . Well — no — it isn't — it isn't equal here. I imagine in time it will be. But — actually now, I mean, I have a good job — I can't get much better off than I am now.

*Interviewer:* In your department?

*Oliver:* In my department. . . . And well, with other fellows that came in there last week — they can move up, the white boys, they can move up there in an office job. I mean, sometimes that kind of hurts me — I had college education.

*Interviewer:* Did you go to college?

*Oliver:* Yeah. I went to _____ College.

*Interviewer:* Did you? How far did you go there?

*Oliver:* Two years . . . Then I worked. I had to. I got married. [laughs] See, it's just so far, and. . . . Well, we don't have any colored foreman. And that's — that's what hurts. That kind of hurts, but still I always say — I don't pay no attention to it because maybe my son would like to be a foreman, or my grandson. . . .

Oliver continues:

Because — if I — I had the opportunity or chance to become a foreman — it's honest truth that I'd be an altogether different man — than I am now. As far as out here.

*Interviewer:* Is that so?

*Oliver:* Because little things that I might say and do — or might not make — might shirk to keep from doing some work. I would do it, because I'd have somethin' to fight for. But I know I ain't got nothin'.

*Interviewer:* You'd take an interest in the department?

*Oliver:* That's right. Because one of the fellows down there, he don't belong to the union. Fellow I mentioned a while ago, he don't belong to the union — a colored fellow. Now he knows that _____ Department bottom to the top — he knows all of it, but he'll never be the boss — because he's a colored man.

Oliver then talks about the Swift training program for potential foremen. After that I asked him if he would like to have a foreman's job:

*Oliver:* Actually, I'd love it. . . . I would; I'd have somethin' to look forward to. Because then I could say, well, I could come on out here and — in a suit of clothes, I wouldn't have to wear these coveralls.

*Interviewer:* Yeah, that's something.

*Oliver:* And — that's just like — I don't like to be dirty. [laughs] When I'm out in the street I don't go dirty, and I don't like to be dirty on the place here. [laughs]

*Interviewer:* And you feel that you could run the gang?

*Oliver:* I believe, in time, with goin' to classes I could run the gang, and know as much as any of the bosses here . . . 'cause I know how — I'm a man, too, and I know how — I want to be treated. I'm not the type of fellow that likes to holler at nobody. But I don't like nobody to holler at me. And so that's the reason why I know I can run a gang. Because I could talk to a man and get his cooperation. . . . That's right. Because I have as many white friends in the _____ Department as I do colored. I don't believe I have one white fellow down there that would say one word against me, because — I mean, we all laugh and talk.

*The Mexicans.* So far we have talked about Negroes' opportunities. But since 10 per cent of the men employees in the Kansas City Swift plant are Mexicans, it will be interesting to see how these people look at their opportunities. The Mexicans work in most of the departments in the plant. Thirty-one per cent of the men, however, work in the Sweet Pickle Cure Department. Lesser concentrations are in the Mechanical Departments and in the Beef Cutting Department.

Only 31 per cent of the Mexicans in our sample felt that they did not have equal opportunity in the plant. This figure is in sharp contrast to the 78 per cent of the Negroes. Three UPWA-minded Mexicans were sharply critical. Two Mexican Independent Unionists were divided, with one critical and the other favorable.

For example, Juan Gomez, Independent unionist with allegiance to both company and union, thinks that the Mexicans do not get the breaks due them:

*Interviewer:* Do you figure on getting your son in here to work some day —
*Gomez:* Oh, I don't know. If he gets in a good department, it would be all right. But if he gets where I am — I'm in the pickle cellar — I don't think that's a very good place for anybody. That's what I was goin' to say. See, now, the Mexican people, they never give 'em a chance to try for somewhere else, you see.
*Interviewer:* Well, that's a thing I was going to ask you about, Juan, when I mentioned that question of equal opportunity.
*Gomez:* Well, it's like I say, the company is very good, one of the best plants I ever worked in — or places. But as far as opportunity, the Mexicans just don't get it. Of course, I'm here to say what I know. Facts, and no lie about it.
*Interviewer:* You know more than some other people, because you get around on your union job.
*Gomez:* I've been there, and I see — I've been in that same department fifteen years, and there has been fellows that were there when I started, say a month before I got into it, American boys, are all out of there, in better jobs. . . .
*Interviewer:* In other words, there isn't equal opportunity?
*Gomez:* Oh, no! No, no, no! Very far from it. There's Mexicans on the dock here. By now they should have a chance to be a checker. But instead, they take a man there, workin' there for a month. American fellow, with the same schooling, same intelligence, and all that — There are a lot of Mexican boys there in town that have education, and still they don't. . . . That's the reason

they have that against our union here. And I've told \_\_\_\_\_ about it. And he says, "Well, things'll get better as they go along." But I said, "They should get an equal chance."

On the other hand, another Independent Local 12 leader, Fernando Lopez, definitely does not think that the Mexicans have cause for complaint:

Well, it's up to you. That's all. If you want to get the job and ask for your job rights, you'd probably get it. Now that's my opinion of it.

In general, the Kansas City Mexicans are much more satisfied than the Negroes about equal treatment, though, of course, they do not feel that their status is comparable to the non-Mexican whites.

Except for the foreman and the East St. Louis white men, the male workers are pessimistic about their chances to advance with Swift. And the Negro men and women are convinced that they get unequal treatment. Yet most of these same people are fairly satisfied with many other aspects of their jobs and with their company and union. Most of them have company and union allegiance. Such ambivalence need not surprise us. We shall see more of it in the next chapter.

CHAPTER VIII

## *Problems of Wage Incentives*

The Swift wage-incentive plan, called the Standards System, plays a central role in the work-lives of the packinghouse workers and is of moderate importance to them. Now we come to their second most critical attitude,[1] though it is more favorable than the workers' attitudes toward advancement opportunities and toward having their children work in the plant. These views about wage incentives, although considered separately, will help to clarify the workers' other attitudes, especially toward pay, the gang, and the job.

On what common basis do we compare our nearly five hundred packinghouse men and women as to their attitudes toward standards? Our abstraction is a scale of "understanding-trust" ranging over into "misunderstanding-distrust." By understanding, we do not mean an understanding comparable to that of the time-study engineer or of the officials or checkers of the Standards Department. We cannot expect the ordinary employee to have such a technical understanding.

By understanding we simply mean some knowledge of the basic arithmetic involved in the system. Presumably the employee should understand what the standard is; namely, sixty work units per hour. He should understand roughly how much work is required to produce the standard output, and how much work to produce outputs above the standard. He should have some knowledge of the fact that there is a definite relationship between the work he does, the output he makes, and the premium earnings he takes home. By understanding, the employee presumably should be able to read and comprehend the "B-sheet" or Standards Posting Sheet, giving his output record and published weekly on a bulletin board in his department.

What do we mean by "trust"? We mean the employee's confidence and belief in the basic fairness, justice, and honesty of the Standards System and its operation. Trust means that the employee thinks that the standards are set equitably in the first place, and that there is a fair relationship between the amount of work he does and the amount of output and premium earnings he makes.

How do we relate understanding and trust? By understanding-trust we mean an attitude containing a definite relationship between understanding and trust with more or less emphasis on either understanding or trust depending on each employee. Could we not find an employee who has understanding-distrust, and if so how would he be rated on the scale? Such an employee is quite rare and might be a foreman who knows quite a bit about the system and thinks that certain people (perhaps himself) are falsifying records. If such a person has a great deal of distrust, he would be rated on the unfavorable side of our scale, even though he had understanding. If he had very little mistrust and possessed understanding, he would be rated on the favorable part of the scale.

Likewise can we find an employee who has trust but clear misunderstanding of the system? This is more common. How would such an employee be rated? Again, it is a question of degree, after carefully analyzing the total interview. If such an employee has a greatly distorted understanding of the system and just a little trust, he would be rated as unfavorable; this would be rare. If he has rather poor understanding and a great deal of trust, he would be rated as favorable.

Therefore, whether an employee will be rated as favorable or unfavorable depends upon the relative amounts of two closely related attitudes: understanding and trust. This will become clearer as we listen to the people speaking their minds. Only a small minority of the packinghouse workers, incidentally, had so much misunderstanding-distrust that they were against wage incentives as such, preferring straight time pay.

Let us start by looking at the quantitative three-plant comparison as given in Appendix Table X. The percentage figures for all hourly-paid workers, for foremen, and the union leaders are the key figures.

Considering first the hourly-paid employees, we find only 25 per cent of the Chicago packinghouse workers with clear understanding-trust of standards. East St. Louis Swift appears to have the most satisfied employees.

Kansas City (47 per cent) seems to be less favorable than East St. Louis (66 per cent) because of three groups of employees, the white men of short service (18 per cent) and the colored men of short service (29 per cent) and middle service (38 per cent) distort the average score. We saw before that they are the most UPWA-minded men in the plant. If we discount their extremist views, then the Kansas City employees are about as lukewarm to standards as the East St. Louis people. (If we use the joint median of the weighted attitude scores for the employees of the two plants, about the same number of employees in both plants lie above and below the median.) However, the colored men in East St. Louis are significantly more favorable than the Kansas City colored men.

Why might we find differences of "understanding-trust" about wage incentives among the three workforces? Four reasons come to mind:

(1) The varying amount of UPWA-CIO influence in the plant.
(2) The general degree of worker satisfaction, especially with foreman, pay, and so forth.
(3) The time and manner of installing the Standards System.
(4) The efficiency and accuracy of administering standards.

It is impossible, of course, exactly to "weight" the above factors. But in our opinion the UPWA-CIO influence is the strongest one. In Chicago, Local 28 has eloquently criticized the operation of standards for many years in the *Flash*. Also the International UPWA has been critical. In Kansas City, Local 12 has never publicly criticized standards with a union leaflet. However, the raiding UPWA splinter-group in the plant has attacked standards from time to time, especially at election times. Local 78 in East St. Louis has never campaigned against standards and there is no UPWA raiding group there to do so.

Clever leaflets and talk about "speedup," along with incentives-grievances surely influence the packinghouse workers' attitudes, especially when such a campaign is carried on over years. We are talking here about the official union statements. Presently we shall see that the unionists' personal understanding-trust of standards follows a different pattern. But if we look at official union positions, we need not be surprised to find the Chicago packinghouse workers the most critical, along with the UPWA sympathizers in the Kansas City plant.

The second reason for the three-plant difference is the general degree of worker satisfaction. The thoughts of a worker about his foreman, job, advancement, or having his children come to work at the plant influence his thoughts about wage incentives. The reverse is also true. As we study these company-related attitudes, we find that the Chicago workers are, indeed, less satisfied in many ways, thus giving a partial explanation of their greater criticism of wage incentives.

The third factor is the time and manner of installing the Standards System. Standards was installed first in Swift's Cleveland plant and six months later, in 1923, in Chicago. Naturally the Chicago employees and foremen did not get off to as mature a start in their experience with standards as did the people of Kansas City and East St. Louis where standards was installed about a year later, in 1924. The other plants profited from such mistakes as were made in Chicago. Differing traditions of standards administration were established in these plants having some influence over the years. But this factor is probably not nearly as important as the preceding ones.

The last factor, the efficiency and accuracy of administering standards, is probably not very important either. We were not able to observe much difference among the three plants in the abilities of their respective Standards Departments or of their foremen in handling standards operations.

Except for Chicago, the workers are mostly rather evenly divided in their views about standards. When we listen to the workers at greater length we find definite patterns of views emerging. For the unfavorable workers, lack of understanding of standards is paramount. For instance, short-service worker, Marie Dalton, stresses the contentions (among women employees) about standards, and also the fact that she does not understand the system:

*Interviewer:* But the gang on the whole — they get along?
*Marie Dalton:* Well, some of them begrudge the others — if one table makes more B's than the others, well, they will holler about it, you know. But for my part, they don't mean that much to me. I don't want nobody mad at me. I would rather have friendship than all the money.
*Interviewer:* The little petty jealousies are not worth it?
*Marie Dalton:* They're not worth it to me. Now some of them think it's terrible because one girl will go in and say, *Well, I've worked just as hard as that table and we don't make the B's.* Why? Well, it's just something that's happened there. That's all I can say. It isn't the time-study fellow's fault, because when he inspected that job he set that watch there. He isn't going to study one job just because one bunch of girls is given to better standards than is another. . . . Why should he? Because he's working for a living the same as we are.

Mrs. Dalton then went on to talk about the factors that influence standards, such as the kind of meat coming to her department, the weight of the meat and the size of the gang. Then she paradoxically says that standards is "wonderful," but she would be glad to do without it! Incidentally such comments show us very graphically how important it is to study the whole interview with a given employee before attempting to say what the employee thinks and before giving a final attitude score. For in spite of Mrs. Dalton's saying that standards is "wonderful," she does not have understanding-trust of the system:

*Interviewer:* Does the B system work pretty well?
*Marie Dalton:* The B system as a whole is wonderful, I think, but for my part, I think too many girls make B's. You know what I mean? Big B's. *But really I think if it was at an hourly rate, you know, it would be better and I be-*

*lieve* the average worker, not the fast worker or the slow worker, but the average worker would turn out more work than they do even just like it is.

*Interviewer:* You mean just a flat rate without any B's?

*Marie Dalton:* Without any B's — if it was just a flat rate.

*Interviewer:* They would have to have some minimum standard?

*Marie Dalton:* Yeah, have a minimum standard and not have the B's. That's the way I feel about it. I don't think there would be near so much hard feelings, Father. . . .

She goes on to say:

But I have worked piece work all my life. I think the bonus system is better than piece work. Of course, I don't understand the bonus system. In fact, I really don't understand the B's. I don't understand them. I've worked here for seven years and I've never been able to understand them, well, it was six years in June.

*Interviewer:* Did they ever really try to explain it, I wonder?

*Marie Dalton:* Yes. They have tried to explain it to me, and I have had different ones. But what worries me about your bonus, your B system, is one time maybe you'll turn out a certain amount and you make 1.26 or 1.36 — that's times your hourly rate of pay. And maybe the next day you'll come in and you'll turn out just a box or so less, and you won't even make a point! I just can't understand it. I guess it's just something I've never been . . . well, in the first place I just don't take that much interest in the bonus. I want to do a day's work and I'm *going* to do a day's work.

*Interviewer:* Bonus or no bonus?

*Marie Dalton:* Bonus or no bonus.

The following two men workers, similar in their views, make comments that are typical of the employees unfavorable to standards. First, Porter Jackson. He does not have allegiance to Swift. He does not understand how the Standards System works. He states that the company does not tell employees anything about the bonus, and he would like to know how it works:

I know they put a chart and some weeks you work and get the same amount [of product] and still you won't get as many B hours, as we got the week before. Well, I never could understand how it worked. . . . I dunno how they actually figger it, those bonus hours. Because I know some men get a higher bonus 'n another 'n for doin' the same job, see. And I dunno how they figger that. . . . When you're on those high-paying jobs, if you cut more higher, you know, I think they take off a little. That's about the only thing I know about the bonus. But I know they don't get as much as they should, because I know some different people in the plant, you know, on different jobs, some of 'em get more bonus than they get pay. But up there in _____ Department, I don't think they — I don't know how they figger it, but I don't think they get the bonus that they should get.

He states that he thinks it would be better to pay more by the hour and not have a bonus:

Because a person, say they would get more an hour, they'd work probably harder or do better work than they would if they say: "We gonna give you a bonus but you don' know how much the bonus gonna be, so I'm gonna promise you something that you may never get." See? That's the way that bonus is . . . a higher bonus, 'r a lower bonus . . . you don't know what you're gonna git.

Old-timer, Carlton Burke, a distinguished-looking colored man, also thinks that there are considerable inequities in the amount of standards payments among the different departments. He believes that he is working just as hard as men in other departments who make far more premium earnings than he does. Burke is a highly skilled butcher who has fair company allegiance, but feels strongly that Negroes are denied fair opportunities in the plant. About standards, he says:

Well, there are things about the bonus that I don't understand. It's quite a problem to try to figure out, the bonus.
*Interviewer:* How does it work?
*Burke:* Well, just to tell you honestly the truth, I don't know *how* to explain to you how they *do* work it, because now we work *hard* up there on those jobs. And they've got men out in different departments and other places that's making eighty, ninety dollars a week bonus. More than our weekly pay, a forty-hour week! And that's the part I don't understand.
*Interviewer:* Some other departments, they make that much?
*Burke:* Yes, I was just looking at a sheet today where a fella in a different department, he made 3675, 3675 B's, that's the way they count it, and that's multiplied by his rate, and so that will run his bonus, close to eighty-five or ninety dollars, for a week. And that's the *bonus*. . . . The question is, I can't figure how they can make it just one person can make that *much* more than the others, and him working hard too. We have to be able to account for every minute we are down there. Yeah.

The small minority of workers who say they would prefer to do away with standards do not necessarily offer any substitute plan for the system. We do not know whether or not they might become equally dissatisfied with straight-time payments and wish to return to some sort of wage-incentive system. One employee in this minority, Norma Wells, is against the Standards System because she thinks it makes for inequities and jealousy. Though her laughter during the interview indicated that she was not seriously concerned about the matter:

Here in the _____ Department they have what they call the gang, everybody makes the same thing. It's pretty hard to make anything on it there, and none of 'em really likes that. *You know, where some people work pretty hard and then others don't, naturally that pulls the — you know —; I don't understand all about this B System.*

*Interviewer:* Supposing Christmas time comes around and you want to buy a lot of extra presents for all of your relatives. You say, "I'm going to work hard this week and make a lot of B's —"

*Norma Wells:* Well, you can't do that in this [department], but over in the Pork Trim you can do that. . . . I mean, that's individual an' I think that's the way it should be all over — if you're goin' to have the B System. *Of course, it would be all right with me if they did away with it.* [laughs] Because it causes a lot of confusion. . . . Well, you know how some people are. Some of 'em are envious an' jealous, so it does something, 'cause they know what their other friend is making.

Now that we have heard the complaints, we shall hear one of the many employees who are favorable to wage incentives. Most of them mention the extra money they can make because of the system. For example, skilled old-timer, Joseph Hetzel has definite company allegiance though he likes neither his foreman nor his job. Nevertheless, he does like the way the Standards System is operating:

Well — it works fairly well, if you can take a group of men — like I say I got two — I got four workin' for me now and we work for a week; we don't have to work hard. We work at a normal speed, we take off once in a while and we don't injure ourselves working, and we'll do fairly well. But when you run into — we run into quite a considerable amount of trouble, see. Like you take the job we're on now — well, there was a time when we could make more money, but when we're up [doing a certain operation that requires waiting for other workers], we have got to get away and get off the job when that's over with. And then you have considerable amount of lost time workin'. In other words, your production is cut down. And production is what your B system is based on. Some weeks go — oh, above normal. But I couldn't complain about the standards. *It's workin' pretty swell.*

*Interviewer:* You can make maybe ten, fifteen dollars a week on that, can you?

*Hetzel:* Well, we'll average about — oh, I imagine about fourteen a week. And that's — I'd say you're workin' about 55 per cent of your time in actual work. See, the rest is plannin' and study and processin' the different details that come under the standards.

*Interviewer:* Yeah. But you actually like that system pretty well, huh?

*Hetzel:* I think very highly of it. . . . There are certain factors in it: if a fellow's dissatisfied with it he can go to his foreman. And I'd say the foreman generally can go over to the office and find out probably if there's a mistake in the office or the man who's responsible. It's well worth it. . . .

Our original Chicago research disclosed many Chicago craft and mechanical employees to be strongly averse to standards. The Kansas City mechanics were critical, but less so. The East St. Louis mechanical departments were slightly favorable.

Influences of Sex, Race, and Service

We have seen these factors as an important influence on certain attitudes, but they do not much affect the packinghouse workers' views on wage incentives.

Sex makes the biggest difference. Appendix Table X shows the women workers in both Chicago and Kansas City as more favorable than the men workers. But the differences are slight. The difference in Kansas City appears to be great (women 83 per cent favorable, and men 41 per cent) but the men's score is distorted. If we consider the median scores instead of the mean scores, then the women are only slightly more favorable. As for East St. Louis, the men have more understanding-trust of standards, primarily because an important group of women there, the white women of middle service, are quite critical of standards.

The reasons why women are somewhat more favorable in Chicago and Kansas City are these:

(1) Many women work in such departments as Sliced Bacon and Pork Trim where high premium earnings are often made. (One such operator in Kansas City made higher earnings than her general-foreman, thanks to standards!)
(2) No women have mechanical jobs, and we have seen mechanics to be critical.
(3) Women are more likely to be on individual application rather than large group application. Individual application often makes standards more attractive and understandable to the employee, since he can more readily relate his earnings to his personal output.

Here are the opinions of some women workers. First, Jane Klir. Mrs. Klir is a meat worker, about eight years with Swift. She works on an individual standards application and is quite favorable to the system:

*Interviewer:* Do you like that system of having a bonus?
*Jane Klir:* Yes, I think it's nice. Because *you don't have to worry about — this person's playin' around while you're workin' tryin' to get the work out — when you're workin' you're workin' for yourself.* And if the other person wanta make just the standard and no extra money — well that's them. *But if you wanta — now like myself — I like to keep mine about the same — I work about the same all the time because I want my check to be about the same. So that's the way I figure.*
*Interviewer:* I'm glad to get your opinion on that bonus. Do you understand it?
*Jane Klir:* Yes. We have a chart out — every can of meat we turn in, it's

wrote down and we see it at noon and then we see what we finish up with in the evening. And then they give us a standard on it — how much premium B's, or make so much money. . . .

*Interviewer:* You're buying your home?

*Jane Klir:* Yes. And so as far as to remarry right now, I'm not interested until I get the home paid for — in about two years I'll have that paid for so she'll [her mother] have some place to stay. If I go *any*where I'll know that she's taken care of. That's my point of makin' those B's and workin' every day. Because I've been here — it'll be eight years in February — and I haven't lost a month's time since I've been here.

Race is not a factor in the workers' views about standards. True, some Negro men tend to be on large-group applications of standards, at least in the pork and beef-dressing departments, and may not make as much premium earnings as men with more skilled jobs having individual applications. Yet other Negroes have such high-premium jobs as beef-boning. Then too, the white men have most of the mechanical jobs, and the men on these jobs tend to be critical of standards. We do see some racial differences in Kansas City, where the Negro men of short and middle service have only 29 and 38 per cent understanding-trust. But these men are critical of many things besides standards. Their UPWA-mindedness is an influence. Most of the workers who say "I don't understand the B System" come from these two groups of men.

As for the influence of length of service, we have complete data only regarding East St. Louis and Kansas City. For Chicago, we estimate that the middle-service group (mostly mechanics) is the least favorable. Appendix Table X shows practically no service difference for East St. Louis. But for Kansas City, we see some unusual variations, with the old-timers very much more favorable (70 per cent) than the younger workers (from 38 to 42 per cent). The white old-timers are a big reason for this score, with 79 per cent of them having understanding-trust. In sharp contrast to them, the Kansas City white workers of two through seven years' service are the most unfavorable of all the groups of men in the plants (18 per cent)! General dissatisfaction and UPWA-CIO-mindedness are the reasons for this. Their company allegiance, as we saw, is the lowest in all three plants.

Attitudes and Output Behavior

Trying to relate a worker's attitudes to what that worker actually does can give us a better picture of both attitudes and behavior. An acid test of the validity of an attitude is the behavior related to it. In two plants of this study we can relate the workers' output, as independently measured by the standards department, to the attitudes tapped by our interviews.

Tables 27 and 28 show two departmental comparisons. The design of this research did not focus on a comparative study of departments. Our sampling was taken from the entire population of each plant and not from the lists of a given department. Nevertheless, our sampling in these given departments was fairly representative of the proper proportion of men, women, colored, white, short, and long service, and so forth. The number of workers interviewed in some departments is small and therefore, these comparisons are not conclusive. But they are suggestive.

Table 27. *Departmental comparison relating output with other variables in five major departments in Kansas City Swift plant, 1953.*

| Dept. | Average standards output | Employees interviewed | Attitudes toward: Standards | Pay | Foreman | Job | Per cent on individual application |
|---|---|---|---|---|---|---|---|
| A | 76 | 9 | 1.3 | 1.3 | 1.7 | 1.5 | 78 |
| B | 70 | 9 | 2.2 | 1.9 | 1.2 | 1.7 | 0 |
| C | 69 | 5 | 2.5 | 2.1 | 1.3 | 1.3 | 0 |
| D | 66 | 5 | 3.6 | 2.0 | 1.8 | 3.3 | 0 |
| E | 62 | 5 | 3.3 | 2.5 | 2.6 | 2.6 | 0 |

Rank-order correlation between:

| | |
|---|---|
| Output and attitudes toward standards | .9 |
| Output and attitudes toward pay | .9 |
| Proportion on individual application | .75 |
| Output and attitudes toward foreman | .7 |
| Output and attitudes toward job | .6 |

Table 27 shows a rather high relationship in Kansas City between output (60 being the standard) and the workers' attitudes toward the Standards System itself and toward pay. There is also a relationship between output and the type of standards application the employee has — individual bonus or group bonus.

As for East St. Louis, shown in Table 28, the highest correlation is between standards output and the attitude of each department foreman toward the Standards System. (Unfortunately, we do not have comparable data for Kansas City.)

It is certainly plausible, both from observation and from listening to the packinghouse workers, that the foreman could greatly influence the understanding and trust of his employees regarding the Standards System. It is the foreman's job to explain the system to a new employee and to adjust workers' complaints about premium earnings. If the foreman himself is skilled at standards, perhaps because of his previous experience in the

Table 28. *Departmental comparison relating output with other variables in eleven major departments in Swift East St. Louis plant, 1953–1954.*

| Dept. | Average standards output | Employees interviewed | Attitudes toward: Standards | Pay | Foreman | Job | Per cent on individual application | Attitude of foreman to standards |
|---|---|---|---|---|---|---|---|---|
| A | 77 | 6 | 2.5 | 1.5 | 1.5 | 2.0 | 100 | 1.0 |
| B | 73 | 7 | 2.6 | 2.1 | 2.1 | 1.9 | 29 | 1.0 |
| C | 73 | 12 | 2.8 | 1.6 | 1.2 | 1.5 | 17 | 1.0 |
| D | 71 | 10 | 2.8 | 1.8 | 3.2 | 1.9 | 0 | 1.0 |
| E | 71 | 7 | 2.3 | 1.9 | 2.5 | 1.9 | 14 | 1.0 |
| F | 70 | 5 | 2.6 | 1.7 | 1.3 | 1.8 | 0 | 2.0 |
| G | 69 | 5 | 2.2 | 1.7 | 1.9 | 1.8 | 40 | 1.0 |
| H | 68 | 7 | 3.0 | 2.0 | 1.7 | 2.0 | 14 | 2.0 |
| I | 68 | 4 | 2.5 | 1.5 | 1.3 | 1.0 | 25 | 4.0 |
| J | 67 | 7 | 2.2 | 1.7 | 1.6 | 2.4 | 0 | 2.0 |

Rank-order correlation between output and:

| | |
|---|---|
| Attitudes toward standards | .06 |
| Attitudes toward pay | .30 |
| Attitudes toward foreman | .16 |
| Attitudes toward job | .33 |
| Per cent on individual application | .58 |
| Attitude of foreman toward standards | .79 |

Standards Department, then he can explain and adjust better. Our East St. Louis findings bear out such reasoning. On the other hand, we cannot rule out the possibility that both foreman and workers are more favorable in those departments to which standards are more adaptable.

Another important factor in satisfaction with standards is the type of application. When the employee works just for himself, on an individual standard, he can readily see how more work leads to more premium earnings. But if he works on a large gang incentive, with some employees working hard and some loafing, and with the size of the gang greatly affecting the total amount of earnings, then it is much harder for the individual employee to relate his own work to his own earnings. In East St. Louis, we do find a moderate association between output and type of application, with a correlation coefficient of .58. For Kansas City, the figure is higher: .75.

The other Kansas City correlations are rather high, though they are low in East St. Louis. One would think, for instance, that the employees' understanding-trust of standards would greatly affect their own output record. We find such an association in Kansas City; we do not find it in East St. Louis. No doubt part of this variation is due to the inadequacy of our departmental sampling. But we must remember that other variables also enter in: especially the foreman's attitude toward standards, and the type of standards application. These two variables will have the greatest influence on output. The employee's attitude will also be a factor.

We have one other statistical approach for exploring the relationship between attitudes toward standards and individual versus group application. Suppose we arrange the packinghouse workers in our regular pattern by sex, race, and service. Further, let us see how such factors affect the type of standards application the worker may have — individual, small-group, or large-group. (See Appendix Table XI.)

Now let us secure the attitude scores toward standards for the employees on individual application as opposed to those on group application, applying a statistical "t-test" to see if the differences might be due to the type of application, or to chance.

The results are illuminating.[2] We find that the white men in both Kansas City and East St. Louis are significantly more favorable to standards if they are on an individual application as opposed to being on a group standard. As for the white women, we also find a significant difference in favor of the individual application at least for the Kansas City workers. We find no real difference among the East St. Louis women.

With due caution, we can say that two different comparisons, the rank-correlations and the t-tests show an employee on individual standards application as more likely to understand and trust the system than an employee on group application. The earnings of the individual-type employee will be affected by the amount, weight, and quality of the product coming to him. He may not understand how these factors affect his earnings, but at least the variables of changing gang size, underworking, or overworking fellow employees will not be present. Seeing a direct relationship between the work he does and the premium earnings he makes, such an employee on individual wage incentives is more satisfied with the wage incentive system.

Could Swift, or other packers, take advantage of this finding and put all employees on an individual standard? The standards people say that this would be very difficult, really impractical. However, it may well be that some jobs at least could be changed from group to individual application.

Incidentally, setting up standards is much more difficult and complex for some departments and jobs (welding as opposed to bacon wrapping), than for others. The objective fairness of the standard varies somewhat from department to department. This factor of standards applicability must also be considered.

## Union Leaders and the Standards System

In most of the attitudes we have explored, the union leaders are not too different from the rank and filers in their views, but regarding standards, we see wide variations. Of the Chicago Local 28 leaders, only 14 per cent had understanding-trust. Some reasons for this were the presence of leftwingers among the local leaders and the generally critical position of the UPWA. We see the UPWA leaders in the Kansas City plant following the same pattern. But here they are 100 per cent unfavorable.

On the other hand, Local 12 leaders in Kansas City think about the same (44 per cent favorable) as the rank-and-file workers (47 per cent). The National Brotherhood has never taken a stand against standards, nor have the Local 12 leaders criticized the system in their newssheets. However, when Swift offered to train one of their members to become a union time-study man, they refused saying: "Why should we jeopardize our position with our members by having a standards man? . . . Let Swift run its Standards System."

The views of the Local 78 leaders are rather paradoxical. Out of seven men, only one (14 per cent), manifests "understanding-trust" of standards. Local 78 has never attacked standards in leaflets; nor has it fostered grievances on standards. In fact Local 78 had the University of Illinois conduct time-study classes in the Local hall for its own leaders and stewards. Furthermore the International Amalgamated Meat Cutters' Union is definitely sympathetic to the idea of wage incentives, recently setting up its own Engineering Department, with John Powderly, former President of Local 78, as industrial engineer. Yet the fact that Local 78 has never taken an officially critical position of the Swift Standards System does not keep the Local 78 leaders from being personally critical.

One Local 78 leader, Paul Kirkland, gives us an idea of this criticism. Though a strong union man, Kirkland is quite favorable to Swift. But he feels that the standards earnings are not equitable:

I make B's — but I don't know whether I get 'em or not — because I can't figure them B's. My job is so varied. I'm not on like a machine operator that punches out a certain thing all the time. I'm unloadin' a million different kind of products.

*Interviewer:* A variable job, it's hard to figure the B's, huh?

*Kirkland:* It's hard. And they get it set up where it's packages — the average weight per package — and they throw them together in a group. Fellows that are [doing one operation] and the fellows [doing another operation], separating the orders, then we're all throwed together, and my job is throwed in with 'em. And then you're — it seems like one day you're not workin' hard at all. You know, an average day. You'll come up with a big B. You'll make a lot of B's. And the next day you're breakin' your neck killin' yourself — it seems like you got twice as much work as you did the day before, and there you come up with a low B hour. . . . And then you question it. And they tell you: Well, you got so many hours, had extra help. The foreman turns in the B dope and he might show that some guy that — well — workin' out somewhere else — he'll show him on our B's. Unless you start a grievance and go through all that procedure, root it out. All that fightin' over that! I say to hell with it, let it go as it is!

*Interviewer:* It causes some confusion?

*Kirkland:* It does. And it causes hard feelings, too. 'Cause I know — take in the _____ Department — the fellow that bones or rounds — seems like — we work forty hours, and I know damn well that I work just as hard, if not harder, the work I do out on the dock, unloading _____. He'll come up with $35 a week B's or $50 a week B's. And I come up with measly $5.00, $6.00, $7.00!

Probably Local 78 leaders like Kirkland feel that because of their official union role they should be critical of standards, at least of the way it operates. Though satisfied in general, these men are aggressive trade unionists. But they have not taken an official union position about standards, and apparently their personal criticism has not much affected the views of the rank and file. Indeed their own stewards are much more favorable than the leaders.

We might sum up the position of the union leaders like this:

Local 28 — personally critical and openly hostile.
Local 78 — personally critical but cooperative.
Local 12 — personally indifferent and cooperative.

Local 28 leaders have most affected the views of the rank and file. They and the Local 78 leaders vary in their views about standards from their own rank and file.

FOREMEN AND THE STANDARDS SYSTEM

Since the foreman's knowledge of standards and his attitude toward it can greatly influence the thinking and productivity of his gang, it is important to know the foremen's views. Appendix Table X shows that the foremen are really quite favorable to standards.

Unfortunately we do not have exact figures for the Chicago foremen. But at least a majority would be favorable to the way standards is being run. The National Stockyards foremen are slightly more favorable than the Kansas City foremen, 74 per cent as opposed to 67 per cent. This difference is very small. But when we see this small difference being repeated in so many attitudes it would seem scarcely due to chance alone. The main thing, though, is that the foremen are so favorable.

Of course in each plant we find some of the hourly-paid employees more favorable than the foremen. This need not surprise us. These people may be making very good premium earnings, even more than their foreman. In their department, the system may be working smoothly with few complaints. On the other hand, some one foreman may be having trouble with standards or with the Standards Department. Such a foreman may think that the standards are not correctly set in his department, so that his output record is unfairly lower than the record of comparable departments. Or perhaps he has trouble with some of his employees or stewards over standards. For these and other reasons, a minority of foremen do not have understanding-trust of standards.

Foreman Andy Helinski can speak for the foremen generally and give us an idea why most of them like the Swift wage-incentive system. He also feels that individual or small-group application would help:

Some of the employees are knockin' it. They don't understand it, you know. But I do understand it myself, see. And it is there for — not only for the company's benefit, for the benefit of the company, because after all they do have to make money — but at the same time the employee can help himself to more earnings there. Why, I understand there's — there's way better conditions over here at Swift than it is at Armour's. The only thing is over here, too, I think that they would benefit — the Company would benefit more — if they would have individual B's in certain places. There's certain jobs —

*Interviewer:* Could they do that in your department?

*Helinski:* Well — at one time they had it like that. And why they discontinued, I don't know. I guess they know more about it than I.

Helinski then goes on to discuss the practical problem of trying to educate the employees toward better understanding of standards:

*Helinski:* They don't understand it. [The employees].

*Interviewer:* You think they could have some kind of system of teaching them more?

*Helinski:* No, you can't teach 'em. You can't teach 'em.

*Interviewer:* They can't?

Helinski then says that changes in the size of the gang make a difference.

*Interviewer:* A big gang will make less B's than if you got a small gang?

*Helinski:* Well, if you — well, it's all depends, *if you're short of help, well naturally your B's are goin' to go up because everybody's cuttin' in. If you're short of help — the size of the gang,* sure.

*Interviewer:* All those things are hard to explain, I suppose?

*Helinski:* Well, they are — you can't — like we have men, or they're sick. And they should have them come in on us, and we have extra men that we just hire the day before, why it's pretty hard there — get rid of 'em. Sometimes other departments are all filled up, we can't transfer 'em out, so we have to absorb 'em some way, and that will naturally pull down the B's. *But I, myself, think that that Standard System is wonderful.*

In spite of the difficulties of explaining standards, Swift in recent years has developed a program for trying to get the main points of wage-incentive theory across at least to the foremen themselves. The hope is that then the foremen will successfully explain standards to their own employees.

Standards are important to the men and women we have observed in this book, but we must not exaggerate their importance. The other company-related attitudes have their place. Wage incentives are the second problem area uncovered in this research. If incentives are truly to be psychological inducements to work, then the workers of all three plants still need much more understanding and trust in the system. It may be, as foreman Andy Helinski stated, that worker education in wage incentives is a hopeless task, yet surely improvement is still possible, even though the Swift Standards System is complicated to explain.

What light has this chapter thrown on our three-plant comparison? The main insight is the influence of the UPWA on attitudes toward standards. We find the Chicago workers and the Kansas City UPWA-minded minority by far the most critical of standards. The influence of the United Packing-house Workers is surely the main reason for this.

The pattern of lesser satisfaction among the Chicago workers continues. We do not find much difference between Kansas City and East St. Louis, though the foremen of the latter plant are slightly more favorable, continuing the superior position of that plant.

CHAPTER IX

*Aspirations for His Children*

This last of our company-related attitudes is unique. By it, the packinghouse workers tell us what they think of their work-life in the company, not for themselves, but for their children; they also reveal something about their attitude toward the plant for themselves. A double standard is quite possible, and prevalent.

The packinghouse workers perceive the idea of "children here" in personal and unique ways, and yet they provide an attitude common enough to talk about and to measure. A worker whose teen-age son is about to be graduated from high school will have a clearer attitude than a young worker with no children, or an older worker whose children have grown up. Still, the speculations of these latter also have significance.

When we speak of "children here," we mean working in the plant itself, not in the office. A few workers might say they wanted their children to work in the office, but not in the plant. Very few made such a comment. They would be graded unfavorable on our scale, for they do not want their children to be packinghouse workers.

The findings set forth in this chapter should be understood in the light of an important fact: All three Swift plants are intertwined with family relationships. Worker after worker would have a father, son, brother-in-law, sister, mother, uncle, brother, even grandfather either now working, or who had previously worked in the plant. These family relationships, often extending from hourly-paid worker into management or office personnel, are not an insignificant factor in the company allegiance we found. There are quite a few children of Swift workers actually working in the plant. But this fact is not incompatible with the unfavorable attitudes we find.

EAST ST. LOUIS AND CHICAGO

Putting together our attitude findings, as seen in Appendix Table XII, the great majority of the packinghouse workers want their children to work elsewhere than in Swift packinghouses. The Chicago workers, only 18 per cent favorable, and the East St. Louis workers, 47 per cent favorable, are at the poles in their thinking about their children for packinghouse work. For the hourly-paid workers, at least, the patterns of our earlier company-related attitudes are strongly reinforced in this chapter, giving East St. Louis the most satisfied people, with Kansas City next, and Chicago last.

What groups of workers are responsible for the considerable differences we see between the plants? Unfortunately, we have no solidly accurate breakdown data in Chicago by sex, race, and service.

But if we look at Kansas City, we see that the women improve the average. Certain groups greatly lower the Kansas City score: the colored men of short and middle service and the white men of short service, with only 7, 17, and 23 per cent favorable to bringing their children into the plant. But we cannot blame the rather low total of Kansas City on these groups alone. Even the white men of middle service, many of whom work in the mechanical gangs, are only 15 per cent favorable. Finally, the colored old-timers, who have loyalty to Swift, are not much more favorable, 27 per cent. Seventy-three per cent of the white old-timers stand out in sharp contrast; they are the only really favorable group in the plant.

How do some of these variables affect the East St. Louis percentage? The sex difference works in just the opposite way there. The women are less favorable than the men, with the outstanding exception of the women of long service, who are 70 per cent favorable. There is not a very marked race difference, but again it reverses the Kansas City findings, for the East St. Louis Negroes are more favorable to having their children come to the plant than the whites in the same plant. This finding reinforces our earlier findings that the East St. Louis Negroes are generally more satisfied workers than the Kansas City Negroes.

As for length of service, we find consistent trends among the two plants: The new workers are less favorable; the longer-service workers are definitely more favorable. Why is this difference? The younger workers, just because they are young, are probably ambitious for their children. Also they have not had the chance to see the advantages of factory work, and to develop as much allegiance to Swift. So they are less likely to want their children in the plant.

First let us consider the minority of workers who do want their children to come to Swift and be packinghouse workers. The factors influencing these people are Swift's generally good treatment and pay. Some of them also mention advancement possibilities.

Frank Fechner, for instance, is a skilled worker in the East St. Louis plant. He has a happy disposition and a high degree of satisfaction with almost everything connected with his job. We are not surprised to hear him say that he would like his son to come to Swift. He has one boy, aged three. During this part of the interview he took a picture of the boy out of his wallet and proudly showed it to the interviewer. Such showing of pictures was quite common. When asked about whether or not he planned to bring his son to work in the plant, Mr. Fechner said:

I hope to. I really do. I would think if he would follow along like I did it'd be swell. I'd really like it. 'Cause I started down here, and I got interested in the stuff, where I went along, and I really like it. If he can build hisself up, there's a lot of different ways he could build hisself up in the industry. Like Swifts here, like bein' a welder or anything like that. And I would think it'd be a good deal. 'Cause I liked it right off at the start and I still like it.

*Interviewer:* Maybe you'll make a _____ [the job Mr. Fechner now holds] out of him, huh?

*Fechner:* I hope to, if he'd follow along as a _____, it'd be swell. 'Cause I don't see nothing — you know it's hard work, you know it's all work as far as that goes, but it ain't too hard, it's hard but it ain't hard as a lot of things. You know, like we went around into the field [on the farm] and that. We done a lot of hard work out there.

We saw that the East St. Louis Negroes, paradoxically enough, are more favorable than the Kansas City Negroes. Curtis Neace brings out some reasons for the considerable satisfaction of the East St. Louis workers. Mr. Neace is forty-five years old, though he has not been long with Swift. He has loyalty to both company and union. Also, he is one of the few Negroes who felt that opportunities were about as good for colored as for whites. He definitely wanted his son to come to Swift:

I got my boy workin' right here with me, —

*Interviewer:* You got your boy here, have you?

*Neace:* He's workin' right here. I'd been with them for a while, and I went down and talked to them and they told me to bring him out here. . . . And I was glad to bring him, because I make my livin' here and I think he can make his livin' here, too. He started down in the janitor gang. Liked the plant so well, he said: Dad, I believe I want to be a man just like you, be a man and get out in the plant and learn somethin' 'bout the job outside — outside in the plant — more than a janitor. Anybody can be this. He got the right idea. So he went down and talked to the boss and told him. And they transferred him on out to the cutting room at nights. He worked here every night and he really liked the job. . . . He works long hours and he stays right on. He really likes the job. He draws nice big checks down and tells me about it all the way home [laughs]. . . . .

*Interviewer:* So that as far as opportunity, you feel that a colored man has got about the same opportunities as a white man here?
*Neace:* I — think so.
*Interviewer:* On the whole, you think so?
*Neace:* I think so, I think so, yes.

The long-service East St. Louis women are 70 per cent favorable. The Swift "family spirit" is one influence here. For instance old-timer Myrtle Miller says:

My son-in-law works here. And my son, he worked here before he went in service. . . .

Then the possibility arose of some of her six grandchildren coming to Swift:

Oh, well, I wouldn't be surprised, because I think it kinda grows on people. . . . I've had several of my brothers who have worked out here and years ago, my older sister worked out here. So. . . .

Appendix Table XII shows that many of the old-timers are more likely to want their children to work at Swift than the younger workers. Two long-service men from Kansas City bear this out. First, Mexican Juan Manzanilla, who is sixty-four but looks younger. Mr. Manzanilla is a very happy employee and this doubtless affects his thinking:

Oh, sure. Yeah. If I had sons, they'd come over here, work here. It's a good place to work. If you got sons, it's all right. I recommend the company to every friend I got.

Colored Swift veteran James Waller says he is raising two of his grandsons himself:

One is fifteen and the other's twelve.
*Interviewer:* You're raising them yourself?
*Waller:* Yessuh. I've had 'em all since they was born. . . .
*Interviewer:* Do you figure on getting them in here to work some day?
*Waller:* Well, I hope so. One of 'em now, he wants to come to work but he's a little too light yet. The oldest one. And I don't care 'bout him startin'. Little too early yet. He ain't quite fifteen. He'll be fifteen in, ah, first of September.
*Interviewer:* Later on you expect to bring him in here?
*Waller:* I hope to.

Reasons why the majority of Swift workers in all three plants want their children to go elsewhere for jobs can be gathered into three groups: lack of advancement opportunities at Swift; difficult working conditions; the desire to have one's children get a better education which they think would be prevented in packinghouse work. Of course, behind these surface reasons are the more complex reasons of prestige and power for their children in the community. The community's frequently lower evaluation of factory work, especially in packinghouses, is probably the major influence over the aspirations of these people for their children.

Negro worker John Edwards brings up both advancement and education. Mr. Edwards came to Swift at only nineteen, right after the first World War. He is a definitely satisfied employee, even loyal. But he would not bring his children to the plant to work. He feels they would not be given equal opportunity to advance because of their Negro race:

*Interviewer:* Did you figure on getting any of your boys in here to work at all?
*Edwards:* Well, uh, I thought, I decided that I would rather not.
*Interviewer:* Yes?
*Edwards:* You see, you know, I think that parents should look forward to their children to their betterment and not bring them right . . . in . . . the . . . you know. . . . That's the way I, that I see it. . . . That's the way I see it, because there isn't any advancement here. . . .

Mr. Edwards, in talking about Swift, says that it is: "a wonderful place to work." The conversation continued:

*Interviewer:* So, if you were doing it all over again would you still come out here?
*Edwards:* Yes, I would, yes I would, I would. But I wouldn't like for my children to follow in my footsteps.
*Interviewer:* No?

Mr. Edwards concludes:

Now, it isn't a thing that I fight, it's just a thing that I study, I don't never talk these things. I don' never talk 'em. 'Course at home, sometimes, I know some years ago, well, the boy would say, "Dad, why not take me over some time [to the company]?" I said: "No, I don't want you to go." Because I want them to be two or three steps ahead of me.

Skilled white worker Tom Leyden, with Swift for many years, is also generally satisfied for himself, but he would not want his children here. He stresses the need for education which he did not have himself. With an education, he says, a boy need not come to do factory work.

*Interviewer:* If you had a son, Tom, would you bring him in here to work?
*Leyden:* Nope. I don't think I would. It would be in the Standards Department or in the office, yeah.
*Interviewer:* Not in the plant?
*Leyden:* Not a plant job, no. I've got too much of the plant. . . . And a kid, nowadays, if he doesn't get an education, he's foolish.

Short-service man Robert Thompson has only recently come to Swift, although he is forty-six years old. Being white, he has no racial reasons for not wanting his children to come to Swift, but he mentions difficult working conditions, along with advancement:

*Interviewer:* Think he'll [your son] come into the packinghouse?
*Thompson:* I don't know, I don't know. But it is kind of a bad job in the packin'house for him. I'd rather have him, I'd rather for him to have a different kind of advancement than in the packin'house. It's too wet and damp and cold here.

The most unfavorable groups in the entire study are some of the colored workers in Kansas City. It will be worth our while to hear these extreme views. First George McCarthy:

Naw. Uh, uh. I have no intention of — if they come this way, it'll be no choosin' of mine. 'Cause I'm on my way out of it fast as I can get out. [He plans to quit and get into tailoring work.] This isn't the kind of set-up for an up an' coming youngster. If a person can do better, I surely want to see 'em.

And Porter Jackson:

No. Nowhere near. I don't think no one else would want their children workin' up there. It's just not a good place, tha's all. Only time a person come in to work is jus' like if you wanted to get a little foundation, a little money in your hands. Far as a man comin' here fixin' to get it in his mind that he gonna settle down here — No.

Basil Hanniford mentions health conditions:

After I've worked here so hard in packin', that if I could find anything else for 'em to do, I'd try to find somethin' else for 'em to do, other than to bring 'em here. I want to make it possible better providing my kids for the future than what I came up under. The packin' house is a little bad to a person that's not real well an' take care of theirselves good.

Some of the Kansas City Mexicans feel about the same way as the Negroes. For instance, short-service employee Julio Contreras says about bringing in his children:

No. I hope not, Father. . . . Packinghouse work is for the people that don't have enough sense to work anywhere else, mostly. . . . They don't have no chance. . . . I couldn't go — even if I worked twenty years I couldn't be an electrician. I couldn't be a painter. I couldn't be a. . . . We [Mexicans] have no other choice, Father. [He laughs slightly.]

Some of the people we have quoted, of course, are dissatisfied with their work at Swift for themselves too. But the majority are not. They simply have a double standard, one for themselves, and one for their children, as John Edwards said: "I would [come out here if I had it to do over again], but I wouldn't like for my children to follow in my footsteps."

INDEPENDENT UNIONISTS

We find some unusual variations among the local union leaders. Only 17 per cent of the Independent union leaders from Kansas City want their children to come to Swift. However, these are only estimated figures and might be incorrect. Even allowing for some errors, however, the Local 12 leaders appear to be definitely less favorable than the average of all Kansas City workers. One reason for this may be that some of these leaders are Negroes, and we have seen that the Kansas City Negroes are less favorable.

Here is one Local 12 steward, a white woman, Anna Larson. Paradoxically, Mrs. Larson had definite company allegiance for herself, but not for her children. As for bringing them to work in the plant, she says:

Dear God no! No, I believe I'd break both legs. No sir, I wouldn't even want them to smell Swift's as they went by. I wouldn't want my children working here; regardless of whether it was in the office. 'Cause if they get here they'd never leave, and they're in a rut.

The Kansas City UPWA-CIO leaders are the most critical of anyone in the three plants. One such leader, Juanita Mendozo, who has strong opinions on many things about the company, also strongly opposes her children coming to Swift:

No. There's no future for them there. [She has two young children.]. . . Because they will *not* hire Mexican boys in the office and will not hire Mexican girls in the office. . . . Have you walked through their office? You will see nothing but redheads and blonds! You will never see a dark-skinned person. An olive-skinned person, or a Negro woman. That's something you'll never see. . . .

Well, \_\_\_\_\_, he used to be [a certain executive] of the plant. . . . He started here as a worker in this plant. Now I could never look for *that* kind of a future for *my* boy. No. Unless times have changed by the time he was able to work, that they should say: "Well, there's equality regardless of who you are, if you're capable and you've got the, let's say, the brains to do that job," — then he will.

As for East St. Louis, we find the Local 78 leaders about as favorable as the rest of their workforce. They are slightly more favorable than their own foremen. Also, they differ sharply from their own stewards, who are only 20 per cent favorable. One reason is that these men are nearly all longer-service people, and we have seen that the workers of more than eight years' service are more favorable. Another reason is that these leaders are more satisfied than the union leaders of the other two plants, at least with respect to many attitudes. Already we have seen them to be more satisfied about advancement opportunities. As for the Chicago Local 28 leaders, we have no precise figures, though the majority would be unfavorable.

ATTITUDES OF FOREMEN

The views of the Swift foremen should contribute to our interplant comparisons. But looking at Appendix Table XII, we may be surprised to find no sizeable differences among the supervisors from the three plants. We have seen such definite differences among the hourly-paid employees, with the East St. Louis workers being the most generally satisfied, that we might also expect to find the same differences among the supervisors. As a matter of fact, we did not see such large differences among the foremen of the three plants for the other company-related attitudes either. There were differences, of course, and the East St. Louis foremen seemed to have a slight edge of greater satisfaction. But it was very slight. Now we find about the same evenness, regarding these men, in their not wanting their children to come to Swift — ranging from only 32 to 36 per cent favorable.

Even more important than the lack of interplant differences among the foremen is the fact that the foremen are so generally unfavorable. In East St. Louis, they are even less favorable than the hourly-paid employees and the Local 78 leaders. This fact does not mean that the foremen do not have company allegiance. It does not mean that the foremen are dissatisfied men. We have seen the company allegiance and the satisfaction, especially of the East St. Louis foremen.

The finding means this: The foremen are definitely ambitious for their sons. Especially, they want their children to get office jobs or professional jobs.

For instance, East St. Louis foreman Frank Letto makes some interesting comments about the importance of education for his own son. Mr. Letto is not exactly a typical foreman. He is a hard worker, but quite high-strung and dissatisfied with his salary, standards, the government inspectors, and with a certain higher supervisor. Undoubtedly these attitudes color his attitudes about having his son come to Swift. But his comments on education are typical enough:

I tell you, Father; I come from a pretty large family of six boys and one girl, and things was pretty rough, you know. And we never had too much — we always had somethin' to eat and a clean place to live in. But as far as that, that was about as far as it went. Now I got two children now; I got a boy three and a half and I got a boy one and a half, and I try to do everything in the world for those kids. I give them anything they want. In fact, it cost me quite a bit of money. They cost me all I make.

*Interviewer:* Do you figure on gettin' them in here some day?

*Letto:* No, I don't, Father. I tell you what I'm doin'. I buy war bonds. I have $2.50 a week taken out of my pay every week; I don't even miss it. It's for the kids' education. I got about — oh I guess I got 25 or 26 of those $25.00 bonds, and that money I won't touch. I'll have to be awful hard up before I'll touch it. That's for the kid's education. . . . I figure on the kids livin' like — like they should, and not have to put up — I don't want 'em workin' in a packin'house.

If Swift packinghouse workers do not want their children to work in the plant — and they do not — then their clear company allegiance must be understood with this fact in mind. This finding does not mean that the company allegiance we found is a fiction. Workers make distinctions, and we must do so also.

Our results, moreover, are borne out by the few other studies investigating this interesting question. The Seidman group's study of six local unions of miners, steelworkers, metalworkers, knitting mill workers, telephone workers, and plumbers found that most of these people liked their companies and jobs. But with the notable exceptions of the "white collar" telephone workers, and the craft-conscious plumbers, the majority of the other workers did not want their children to come into their plants and do the work they were doing. A typical comment was: "I'd like to have my boy get an education so he wouldn't have to beat his brains out on piecework. . . . I would like him to be a draftsman, or a building engineer — some profession like that." [1]

Also Chinoy's study of a sample of autoworkers, in a UAW local, found that "there was an almost universally expressed desire that their sons not go into the factory, that they do 'better than that.'" One strong comment of a line repairman about his son graduating from high school sounds like packinghouse steward, Anna Larson: "If he goes into the factory, I'll beat hell out of him." [2]

The future of a workingman's son or daughter touches upon an important, personal area of his life; his aspirations and ideals. In America, where we have "The American Dream" of anybody's son rising to any height, Americans commonly hope that their children will "do better" than they did. Considering the prestige our culture attaches to white-collar jobs and to the professions, it is not surprising that many working people wish their children to achieve such jobs and professions.

The findings of this chapter are somewhat disturbing. They may indicate a false view of manual labor, and a false idealization of the white collar job and a college education. They may indicate that in spite of company allegiance, and the packinghouse workers' superficial satisfaction with their jobs, pride in the dignity of their work in a packinghouse may well be lacking. At any rate they have no desire to urge their sons to choose the same career.

Yet certainly many children of these packinghouse workers will end up in factory jobs somewhere, if not in a packinghouse. Not all can go to college, and be doctors or lawyers. Since our American communities put such value on white-collar and professional jobs where are we to get the manual workers of the future? For in spite of automation, some manual workers will always be needed. What will happen to the relative wage scales of the semiskilled and unskilled factory workers of the future? Will there be still greater increases? And since really few jobs are open at the top what will happen to the possibly frustrated aspirations of the factory workers of the future? Our data raise these questions, though we cannot answer them here.

Apart from such speculation, these findings certainly add a new dimension to our view of the packinghouse workers' company-related attitudes. In their indirect way, these views show the continuing pattern of the East St. Louis workers' greater satisfaction.

### THE TEN COMPANY-RELATED ATTITUDES

We have compared the packinghouse workers as to their company allegiance and nine other company-related attitudes. It is important now to pull together the comparisons we have seen. Table 29 gives a ranking of the plants for all ten attitudes.

It is clear from Table 29 that the people at East St. Louis are the most satisfied with Swift and with the other aspects of their work.[3] The relative positions of Kansas City and Chicago are not so immediately evident. If we take the company allegiance of the hourly-paid workers, Chicago has slightly more company allegiance than Kansas City. Then, if we rank Kansas City with Chicago on the five attitudes first listed in Table 29, along with company allegiance, we find Kansas City having a slightly more favorable score, 2.33 as opposed to 2.58.

A complete interplant comparison must take account not only of the hourly-paid workers generally, but also the key leaders of both company and union; the local officers and the foremen. Among these groups, Kansas City definitely leads Chicago. Finally, if we combine the relative standings for the two plants, giving hourly-paid workers, union leaders and foremen equal weight in our comparison, we find that Kansas City is definitely

Table 29. *Ten company-related attitudes: a three-plant ranking.*[a]

| Attitude | Hourly-paid workers ||| Union leaders ||| Foremen |||
|---|---|---|---|---|---|---|---|---|---|
| | E.S.L. | K.C. | Chgo. | E.S.L. | K.C. | Chgo. | E.S.L. | K.C. | Chgo. |
| 1. Company allegiance | 1.0 | 3.0 | 2.0 | 1.0 | 2.0 | 3.0 | 1.0 | 2.0 | 3.0 |
| 2. Foreman | 1.5 | 1.5 | 3.0 | 1.0 | 2.0 | 3.0 | | | |
| 3. Standards | 1.0 | 2.0 | 3.0 | 2.5 | 1.0 | 2.5 | (1.0 | 2.0 | —) |
| 4. Job | 1.0 | 3.0 | 2.0 | 1.5 | 1.5 | 3.0 | 1.0 | 3.0 | 2.0 |
| 5. Advancement | 1.0 | 2.5 | 2.5 | (1.0 | 2.0 | —) | 1.0 | 2.0 | 3.0 |
| 6. Children to Swift | 1.0 | 2.0 | 3.0 | (1.0 | 2.0 | —) | 2.0 | 1.5 | 1.5 |
| Average rank: | 1.08 | 2.33 | 2.58 | 1.50 | 1.62 | 2.87 | 1.25 | 2.12 | 2.37 |
| Combined rank: | 1.25 | 2.07 | 2.60 | | | | | | |

*East St. Louis and Kansas City only:*

| | E.S.L. | K.C. | E.S.L. | K.C. | E.S.L. | K.C. |
|---|---|---|---|---|---|---|
| 7. Gang | 1.5 | 1.5 | 1.0 | 2.0 | 1.5 | 1.5 |
| 8. Pay | 1.0 | 2.0 | 1.0 | 2.0 | 1.0 | 2.0 |
| 9. Working conditions | 1.0 | 2.0 | 2.0 | 1.0 | | |
| 10. Suggestion system | 1.0 | 2.0 | 2.0 | 1.0 | 2.0 | 1.0 |
| Average rank: | 1.13 | 1.88 | 1.50 | 1.50 | 1.50 | 1.50 |
| Combined rank: | 1.36 | 1.63 | | | | |

[a] Ranking: First gets a score of 1.0; tie for first, 1.5; second, 2.0, and so forth. The lowest score available means the plant having the most favorable attitudes; here it is East St. Louis. Where parentheses are used, the attitude is not scored because of a lack of data in one plant or another. "Combined rank" includes the ranking of hourly-paid workers, union leaders and foremen, all equally weighted.

ahead of Chicago with a score of 2.07 as opposed to 2.60. East St. Louis, of course, is first, with a still more favorable score of 1.25.

Looking at the second part of Table 29, where we compare certain attitudes between East St. Louis and Kansas City (since for these attitudes we have no quantitative data in Chicago), East St. Louis has a slight lead. This is due to the hourly-paid workers, not to the leadership groups.

We may now ask: Why do we find the greatest satisfaction at East St. Louis, with Kansas City and Chicago following in order? A combination of factors accounts for these differences: The past and present management leaders; the past and present union leaders; the different makeup of the workforces; finally Chicago as a metropolis. Other differences are less important. Practically the same kind of work is done in each plant. Each plant has about the same type of working conditions.

The key people, the men in positions of leadership, have much to do with the differences we find. As far as higher management is concerned, we cannot make any definite statements. Regarding the foremen, we saw that there is really very little difference in their acceptance by the three workforces, though if we take the combined attitudes of the hourly-paid workers and the union leaders there is probably a slight edge in favor of East St. Louis.

We are left then with the union leaders. These men, with their differing philosophies of union-management relations, are an important clue to the differences we have found. So far as the Kansas City NBPW Local 12 leaders are concerned, we must remember that their position is greatly affected by the UPWA raiding group in their midst.

The makeup of the workforces is another factor in the differences. Sex, service, nationality, age — these are not very important. But the differing racial proportions, and also the differing racial attitudes, greatly affect our findings. Chicago not only has a large Negro proportion, but much more aggressive Negroes, at least through their control of the local union. The East St. Louis Negroes are the most satisfied in many ways, due in part to their southern background. This is in spite of the fact that the status, employment and advancement-opportunities of these Negroes are the lowest of the three plants.

Finally, the fact that Chicago is a metropolis, with many of the attendant problems of a very large city, makes for one more influence. This largeness affects the living habits of the people; it affects the prestige of the Stockyards; it affects the status and prestige of the local union. In some ways, our findings for the Chicago plant are least favorable precisely because of the big city itself. There is little difference between the cities of Kansas City and East St. Louis in their influence upon the findings.

So far, we have often talked about the workers' "satisfaction" or lack of it. We are aware that the satisfied workforce is not necessarily the "best" workforce for itself, the company, the union, or the community. Peasants in India might be satisfied. But their poverty would only be remedied by their developing some dissatisfaction. Indeed we found the packinghouse workers to be dissatisfied generally in three out of the ten company-related attitudes. Their satisfaction with the other seven attitudes, at least, appears to be genuine enough and not a rationalization leading them to passive acceptance of a work-life basically disadvantageous for them.

The differences we have seen among the Chicago, East St. Louis and Kansas City packinghouse workers are significant and illuminating. But they must not be allowed to obscure the equally important similarities. The workers' company allegiance, for example, originally found in Chicago, is found in greater strength in Kansas City and in East St. Louis.

PART THREE

His Role as Unionist

CHAPTER X

# The Worker Looks at His Union

With this chapter, we turn to the second main area of the packinghouse worker's work-interests: his union. Since the union is a different kind of institution from the company, we shall naturally be tapping some different kinds of thoughts and sentiments.

## UNION ALLEGIANCE AND SEVEN OTHER RELATED ATTITUDES

By union allegiance we mean "general satisfaction with the union *as an institution*," or "belief in the necessity and existence of a union in the plant." We do not mean that a worker who has union allegiance necessarily approves of the local or international leadership of his union. Nor do we mean that such a worker will like everything about the organization, and practices of his union, or necessarily have a deep loyalty to the trade union movement. We do not mean that active participation in union affairs or even actual membership in the union are requirements for union allegiance.[1]

Naturally, however, the union's leadership, grievance and strike policies, and other practices will influence the worker in his union allegiance, just as attitudes toward various aspects of his job influence his company allegiance. In the case of both the company and the union, the worker can and does distinguish between the institution and its practices.

Union allegiance is a simpler concept than company allegiance because the union is a simpler kind of institution. The union offers the worker protection and status, as opposed to the more complex returns of job satisfaction and a livelihood offered by the company. Before looking at our comparative findings of union allegiance in detail, we shall consider a summary of our eight union-related attitudes taken together, as seen in Table 30.

Four of the attitudes in Table 30 can be compared quantitatively only for Kansas City and East St. Louis, since precise data is missing for Chicago. However we shall bring in qualitative impressions about these attitudes for

Table 30. *Summary of union-related attitudes.*
*Chicago, 1950; Kansas City, 1953; East St. Louis, 1953–4.*

| Attitude | Chicago, UPWA Local 28 ||| Kansas City, NBPW Local 12 ||| East St. Louis, AMC&BW Local 78 |||
|---|---|---|---|---|---|---|---|---|---|
| | *Hourly-paid* | *Union ldrs.* | *Fore-men* | *Hourly-paid* | *Union ldrs.* | *Fore-men* | *Hourly-paid* | *Union ldrs.* | *Fore-men* |
| Union allegiance (For foremen, union endorsement.) | 2.1 79%[a] | 1.0 100% | 2.4 54% | 1.3 95% | 1.0 100% | 1.5 90% | 1.2 100% | 1.0 100% | 1.7 76% |
| 1. Toward employee representation plan | 50% | | | 73% | 0% | 62% | 22% | 0% | 29% |
| 2. Toward the union shop | | | | 30% | 20% | | 78% | 100% | |
| 3. Toward union leaders | 3.5 26% | 1.5 (4.5) (right) (wing) | 4.2 5% | 2.4 63% | 1.5 (4.9) (CIO) | 1.6 95% | 1.6 96% | 1.9 | 1.4 100% |
| 4. Toward the UPWA | | | | 29% | 9% | 0% | 27% | 0% | 14% |
| 5. Toward (a) Grievances | | | | 2.4 65% | 100% (12%) (CIO) | | 1.4 98% | 95% | 100% |
| (b) Stewards | | | | 2.5 62% | 100% | 90% | 1.7 93% | 84% | 83% |
| 6. Toward strikes | | | | 3% | | | 3% | | |
| 7. Participation behavior. | 3.4 | 1.0 2.0 (stewards) | | 4.2 | 1.1 2.7 (stewards) | | 4.4 | 1.0 1.2 (stewards) | |

Scale: 1.0 Very favorable; 2.0 Favorable; 3.0 Neutral; 4.0 Unfavorable; 5.0 Very unfavorable.

[a] Percentages mean per cent favorable. For some attitudes we have both the numerical scale and the per cent favorable. For other attitudes we present only one measure.

Chicago. Participation behavior, the seventh item, is not really an attitude; it is our rating of each employee's degree of participation in union affairs, judging by his comments in the interview.

The main fact evident in Table 30 is that the Local 78 union members from East St. Louis are the most union-minded and the most satisfied with their local union. Next in order comes Local 12 of Kansas City. The Chicago packinghouse workers are the least content with the idea of unionism and with Local 28 although in some ways they are the most active in union participation. The detailed examination of these various union attitudes, and especially their relationship to union allegiance, will be treated in this and the following four chapters.

East St. Louis

Why do many working people want, support and join unions? Our comparative findings of union allegiance, presented in Appendix Table XIII, show that most of the hourly-paid employees do have union allegiance, and secondly, that the East St. Louis workers have the strongest union-mindedness and the Chicago workers the least. The scores of 2.0 for Chicago, 1.3 for Kansas City, and 1.2 for East St. Louis need to be interpreted in the light of our statistical tests of significance. Such tests show, at least for the men, that Chicago is significantly less favorable to having a union than either Kansas City or East St. Louis. Also we find that the East St. Louis men are more favorable than the Kansas City men. In short, East St. Louis leads and Chicago is last.

These comparative differences are changed somewhat if we include the women workers, because in some cases they reverse the relationship. For example, the Kansas City women are slightly more union-minded than the East St. Louis women. But since the women form only 14 to 15 per cent of the workforce in any of the plants, we can afford to omit them in making our comparative ratings.

Why do we find so much less union allegiance in Chicago? Four reasons come to mind:

(1) The serious failure of the UPWA's 1948 strike.
(2) The fight between Local 28 and the International UPWA, creating the impression of two unions in the plant.
(3) The capture of Local 28 leadership by the Communist Party.
(4) The race issue.

These four problems, greatly affecting the workers' union allegiance, have not seriously bothered either Local 12 or Local 78. In Chicago, some of the packinghouse workers were so aroused by these issues that they were actually against the idea of having any union in the plant at all (union disallegiance). We found not a single employee in the other two plants who was positively against the idea of having a union.

In 1955, over five hundred workers withdrew from Local 28 to work toward building the kind of union they wanted. However, these people were definitely union-minded. They had union allegiance. And as for the 1956 and 1959 UPWA-Swift strikes, they did not seem to make the Chicago Swift-UPWA workers more satisfied with the UPWA. While there might be more union allegiance among the Chicago workers in 1960 than there was in 1950 and 1951, it is doubtful that the Chicago union allegiance would be as strong as the allegiance we find in Kansas City and East St. Louis.

Why should East St. Louis have a slight edge over Kansas City? Probably because Local 12 has been under siege by the UPWA, making it less secure than Local 78. Then, too, the Amalgamated Meat Cutters tend to be more militant than the National Brotherhood. The following chapters should make Local 78's position clearer, for we shall see that the East St. Louis workers are more satisfied with other aspects of their union as well as with its existence as an institution in the plant.

It is worth our while to listen to these people in greater detail to understand why they want a union, especially the workers from East St. Louis, since 100 per cent of them have union allegiance. First, we come to Charlie Bloomer, of East St. Louis. Bloomer is young, thirty-two, and has worked in fourteen departments in only six years. Still, he says he never had a grievance. He is not satisfied with everything about the union. But his union allegiance is strong:

*Interviewer:* Well, coming to the union, Charlie — do you figure it's a good thing, then, to have some kind of a union in the plant?

*Bloomer:* Oh, definitely. I would hate to think about being without a union [laughs].

*Interviewer:* How does it help here, do you think?

*Bloomer:* Well, mostly I would say on wages and — and relationships. They can't just walk up and fire a man. Then I think the union has its drawbacks, too, 'cause — I have seen cases where men — refused to do what the boss told them and if you fire 'em, they come back to work.

And I mean, I think there should be a limit on that. But still a man comes in and gets seniority and can hold his job. I mean I think that's wonderful, because otherwise the boss will hire a friend of his in — and when the work gets slack he'll lay off a man that's been here for twenty years; and they tell me it happened a lot. That was before my time; I mean, I wasn't workin' before the union. And I've also heard that they used to come — they told them to come in to work, and they'd work 'em a couple hours if they wanted to, and then send 'em home. They got credit for two hours.

*Interviewer:* So it's really brought a lot of changes?

*Bloomer:* I'm definitely in favor of the union.

Middle-aged packer Pearl Halliday gives two reasons for her union allegiance: seniority and wage protection.

Here's the thing I think about the union. There's some things has come up where maybe uh jist say fer instance now, like there's a lay-off comin' Friday. This last Friday. Well, now, if it wasn't fer the union, a lotta the girls, they could stay on, where a lotta the other girls would have to come out. See what I mean?

*Interviewer:* Seniority makes a difference?

*Pearl Halliday:* Seniority makes a difference. And then fer instance say that they overlooked it some way or another. And, say there's a girl come out *over* me and I stayed on. If she'll look into it, they'll have to lay me off and take her back. Well, there's where the union goes in and fights fer the rights of the girl. So, and another thing, too, say fer instance, like in our department, the girls is on a different job and there's another job open. Well, they'll tell us if this job is open. Our steward generally does that.

It's s'posed ta be posted but there's never been any job, one job, posted in there since I've been in there that I know of. But she generally always tells the girls. And then, say if they say they won't do it but if I want the job then I could go in. And they couldn't take it away from me. Unless, we keep it fifteen days, and then in fifteen days why the job is ours. But in the meantime, if we find out we don't want it, then if one of the younger girls wants it, it's still all right. But uh . . . as far as the union, I think it really has done wonders for us.

*Interviewer:* It's a good thing to have a union?

*Pearl Halliday:* Yes, I think so. I really do. 'Cause I'll tell ya why. My sister lives in the south. And uh, their quotas go *so* high, fer 'em ta get out and all, where I told 'em if they had a union they could go in there and they'd break that down into a scale, and they wouldn't have to work so hard. And they only make 75¢ an hour, and I almost double her.

*Interviewer:* Where does she work?

*Pearl Halliday:* At uh . . . some garment factory in South Carolina. See, they don't have no unions down there at all. Well, just whenever they get ready ta lay off, they ain't got nothin' ta say, all they have ta do is take their layoff. And if there's a young girl on the job why she gets ta stay and the other girl has ta leave.

*Why Do They Want a Union?* The union allegiance of the packinghouse workers is in some ways unique to each man or woman. But we can distinguish at least four principal patterns of reasons why these people believe in the need for some union: (1) the union helps seniority; (2) the union is a restraint on the foreman; (3) the union gives the worker a voice in his affairs — grievance machinery; (4) the union is a wage instrument.

(1) *The union helps seniority.* It is interesting to notice how common this facet of union allegiance is among the women workers. As we saw in discussing the social life of the department or gang, women tend to have jealousies and rivalries. Seniority somewhat regularizes these tensions.

Semiskilled, young meat worker, Ruth Ewing, speaks of seniority:

*Interviewer:* Do you think it's better to have some union, than no union at all?
*Ruth Ewing:* Oh, yes! I think you should.
*Interviewer:* Why — what do you think is the reason for that?
*Ruth Ewing: Well, I think, well, if you wouldn't have any seniority or anything like that, if you didn't have the union, I don't imagine. . . .*

(2) *The union is a restraint on the foreman.* While this comment is close to the next one about the grievance procedure, we can separate the two. Here, the worker wants a union because it protects him from a possibly domineering foreman. The union acts as a restraint upon the foreman. Many workers give this reason for their union allegiance.

Independent union leader, Juan Gomez explains why he thinks a union is necessary:

*Interviewer:* Is it good to have some kind of a union?
*Gomez:* Oh, yes. Very much.
*Interviewer:* Why is that?
*Gomez:* Well, you have more rights. *You know, if we wouldn't have a union, they'd probably get every right you have in the world.* They wouldn't even give you merits. If a foreman just *took a notion to fire you, or abuse you, or overwork you, well, he could do it for meanness.* Because you know, they're cursed that way. They just — I notice here, right here, every once in awhile, a foreman gets something on some man, he just makes it harder and harder.

Old-timer Willie Wolley, an expert mechanic, is a short, fat, agreeable man. He has clear dual allegiance. He continues Gomez' theme about the union being a restraint on the foreman:

*Wolley:* Well, it [the union] kinda keeps ah, in fact it *keeps the boss on the line,* and you know they show a little partial — And I've seen places where I've worked where there was favorites. But they claim it's a pretty good place to work now. I was playin' ball and I was in the clique [the Masons]. If you wasn't in there why there wasn't much hope for ya.

(3) *The union gives the worker a voice in his affairs — grievance machinery.* This is also an important factor in union allegiance for many workers. They mean different things by "voice in affairs." Some would be

thinking of the national union's collective bargaining with the Swift Chicago office. Others would be thinking of local bargaining arrangements. But most would be thinking of the grievance procedure by which they may voice a complaint or make a request and have someone standing behind them, "going to bat for you."

Short-serviced colored worker, Nora Wilcox, newly elected union steward, makes much of the grievance procedure in her thoughts about the union:

*Interviewer:* Well, I'd like to get your ideas on the union, Nora.
*Nora Wilcox:* Well, I think it's good to have some kind of a union.
*Interviewer:* Why — because?
*Nora Wilcox:* Well, *seems like their grievances is easier handled, where you can go to somebody and get it settled.* Where if you, I imagine if you don't have a union, you just argue with yourself and don't get any place at all. . . .

Charles Landez, a butcher, tells an interesting anecdote about two men caught stealing ham and how the union helped one by "talking for him." Although he is uninformed about the actual labor law involved, the incident impresses him, and partly explains his union allegiance:

*Landez:* It's good to have some union.
*Interviewer:* Why?
*Landez:* Because you have a little — you have somebody to speak for you, even if the union is no good. Al'right, let's say somebody say that the union is no good and all that. Al'right, it might not be good but there may be a time when you get in some kind of a jam and you *need* the union — *you need somebody to speak for you.*

Like for instance there was two fellas over here in the freezer. They happened to have a ham. Al'right, this fella was stealing a ham, and they [the company] caught him. One of the fellas belonged to the Union, and one didn't. Al'right, so they [the company] fired both of them.

Well, one fella didn't belong to the union an' the other one did — they were both Mexicans. An' the steward always told the one fella — he says: "come on, join the union, join the union, why not?" [The nonunion employee said] "Oh, what do I want the union for?" He says, "Just because you wear that [steward] button you don' pay no union [dues] — you're gettin' paid — that's why you want me to join so's you can git more money outa' the union." The steward says: "Oh, but it's good to be together."

Well, so he [the nonunion member] didn't do it [join]. And when they caught the men stealing the ham, they fired 'em both. Well, they're both fired an' then they [the union] came over an' talked to the superintendent, well, to bring [the union member] back. But the other one didn't come back. . . . Didn't come back, ya see, *that's why I say it pays to have somebody talk for you.*

(4) The union is a wage instrument. Obviously one reason working people want a union is because they believe that it will look after their wage

interests. We found in the Chicago study that this was not the major factor, except perhaps for the younger men. But it is a definite component of union allegiance, nevertheless.

Clarence Dodge, an older worker near retirement, brings out the wage influence as one component of his union allegiance:

Yes, it's a good thing to have a union. *If you didn't have a union whatsoever, why the company would probably run over the men, see. And they prob'ly wouldn't give 'em as much money, an' prob'ly wouldn't give 'em a fair deal, somethin' like that, see.* It's good to have some kind of union. If we don't have this union we have, it's good to have the CIO or AF of L or somebody in order to take care of the men.

Tractor man Gerald Culpepper, with Swift about ten years, also brings up pay, in his feeling about the need for a union:

*Culpepper:* Well, a union *is* good one way, and in another way it *ain't* good. [What he means here is that he is pro-CIO rather than pro-Independent.] *It's good on the rate of pay, which we wouldn't be gettin' the rate if it wasn't for the union,* because companies pay ya just the way they want ta, and work ya as long as they want ya to work, ya see. But they is got it at a certain amount of time you've got ta work [referring to the contract provisions on hours of work] and they gotta pay ya. They can help thataways. . . .

For East St. Louis, we are able to define more sharply the workers' thinking about the need for a union, as shown in Table 31.

Table 31. *What the union means to the East St. Louis Swift-Local 78 workers, 1953–1954 (in per cent).*

| | |
|---|---|
| A "voice in the affairs" that affect the worker | 40 |
| A wage instrument | 16 |
| Seniority and job protection | 15 |
| Protection from unfair treatment by foremen | 11 |
| Better working conditions | 9 |
| Insurance and hospitalization | 2 |
| No qualification | 2 |
| Miscellaneous safety, discrimination, etc. | 5 |

Those categories are not perfectly water-tight. Several of them overlap into that most important area — a "voice in the affairs that affect the worker."

*Influences of Sex, Race, and Service.* While these variables have affected many attitudes, they do not influence much the amount of union allegiance a worker will have. Let us consider sex first: In Chicago, we found some of the women, the long-service colored and white women, with very weak union allegiance. These people might confirm the common opinion that women in many industries are less union-minded than men. But the middle-service and short-service women in Chicago were some of the most active unionists in the plant. In a word, we cannot make the generalization that the women, as such, have less union allegiance in Chicago. In both Kansas City and East St. Louis the women packinghouse workers strongly support the idea of having a union. Indeed the small group of Negro women of middle service in Kansas City have the strongest union allegiance (1.0) of any group outside of the local union leaders themselves.

Incidentally, we saw that regarding company allegiance, the women are generally more favorable, except at East St. Louis.

Race is important only in Chicago's Local 28. After a minority of racially aggressive Negroes, along with some leftwingers, gained control of Local 28, and of District One of the UPWA-CIO, many white workers (with colored workers too) were alienated from the union.

Dissatisfaction with the way things were being run in the local carried over, affecting the very union allegiance itself of the union members. In neither of the other two locals do we find any such distinction between white and colored in their union-mindedness.

In Chicago, the old-timers definitely were less union-minded, except among the colored men. For Kansas City also, we see, in Appendix Table XIII, some trend toward less favorable union views among the long-service workers. But here the difference is slight. We see no service difference in Local 78. All the packinghouse workers there have strong union allegiance.

As for company allegiance, we found that service does make a difference in all three Swift plants. The old-timers are clearly more company-minded. Evidently being more company-minded for these people does not necessarily mean being less union-minded. Here is a further manifestation of dual allegiance.

Attitude of the Union Leaders

Obviously a worker would hardly sacrifice his time and convenience to become a local union leader if he did not believe in the union movement, and if he did not think that a union was a good and necessary institution in the industrial plant. We are not surprised to find that the leaders and stewards of all three local unions are 100 per cent union-minded. They all have union allegiance, including the anti-UPWA Chicago leaders, who withdrew from Local 28 and who were actively working toward a new union there. The factors making up the union allegiance of the union leaders are about the same as those influencing the rest of the work force:

protection, wages, fringe benefits. But the protection-status factor is by far the most important.

Just taking two local union leaders at random, we see the same reasons for wanting a union that the rank and file expressed. For instance, Negro unionist, Marvin Oliver, says:

> If it wasn't for the union, I don't know. Actually, I believe if it wasn't for the union I don't believe I'd be here. Or a whole lots of 'em. Because I wouldn't be makin' $1.67 an hour. [He laughs]. . . . And you got to have a union, because I believe that — just like now I was puttin' praises on the company a while ago. But if we didn't have a union, the packin' house wouldn't be half as clean as it is. . . . 'Cause I know they'd say, well *maybe a foreman might say: Well, I have a cousin out there, and I'm gonna bring him in here and fire you.*
> *Interviewer:* Favoritism?
> *Oliver:* Yeah. When you got a bunch of the people together, everybody's not tryin' to look out for the public. They're tryin' to look out for their own selves.

Unionist Jack Lang stresses the pay benefits he thinks the union has brought:

> *Interviewer:* Do you figure it's a good thing to have some kind of a union?
> *Lang:* I think so, in a way. Because it always helps out. Of course, now I guess it's — take it one way or the other — *if it wouldn't be for the union maybe we wouldn't get as much money.* And another thing, with a lot of guys, of course, this way, you know, a lot of guys wouldn't be workin' here, I guess. If it wouldn't be for the union, they'd get laid off or fired or somethin'. But this way, you know, they always got a chance. But I think a fellow should feel this way: union or no union, if you got a job and you like it and you should take care of it. There's a lot of people come in here half stewed but this way, well, they might be laid off for a week or so; and they have to take 'em back.

### ATTITUDE OF THE FOREMEN

It may seem strange that foremen, representatives of management, think that having a union among their employees is a good idea. But this is exactly what we found for most of the foremen. This attitude of the foremen we call their "union endorsement." (To avoid confusion we do not call it their union allegiance, for this latter is a self-directed attitude of the hourly-paid employees in the sense that it concerns an institution which they can join.) The union endorsement of the foremen means their favoring the presence in the plant of a union for their employees. Foremen with union endorsement support the union by explicit statements of approval to the interviewer and often to the employees.

Union endorsement, however, is not to be confused with support of the current local union leaders and their policies. Rather it refers to the institution of unionism in the plant. The Chicago foremen, for example, were strongly opposed to the leftwing Local 28 leaders, but a slight majority of these same foremen thought that having a union was a good thing. This is an important finding.

Many foremen were themselves once in the union and still have sympathy for it. That is one reason for the endorsement we find. Furthermore, the foremen see that the union can help them in the disciplinary matters of the plant. Finally, the Swift foremen, at the time of the field work for these studies, got raises when the union won raises. This policy has since been changed, but it was one more factor in the foremen's union endorsement.

Now let us see in Table 32 how the views of the foremen in the three plants compare.

Table 32. *The foremen's union endorsement (per cent with endorsement).*
Sample of 32 Chicago foremen, 1950; 19 Kansas City foremen, 1953; 25 East St. Louis foremen, 1953–1954.

|  | Chicago | Kansas City | East St. Louis |
|---|---|---|---|
| Favorable | 57 | 90 | 76 |
| Neutral | 16 | 0 | 12 |
| Unfavorable | 27 | 10 | 12 |

The main thing in Table 32 is that we actually do find a majority of the foremen in each plant expressing views of union endorsement, with the later studies strongly reinforcing the Chicago study. The second main point is that all three plants differ from each other. The Chicago foremen are by far the least sympathetic to having a union in the plant. The reasons for this are about the same as those explaining why the Chicago hourly-paid employees have less union allegiance. We saw earlier that the Chicago foremen have the least company allegiance of the three plants.

There is not really a great amount of difference between East St. Louis and Kansas City, but the Kansas City foremen are more favorable toward having a union nevertheless. What is the reason for this? The Kansas City Swift foremen are aware of the fact that they are dealing with a definitely procompany union, in Local 12. Local 12 has never had a strike or slowdown, while nearby UPWA locals, in the former Cudahy plant and at Armour and Wilson, have often had both. By this sharply contrasted behavior the foremen see that they have a cooperative union reasonably willing to recognize the problems of management.

Local 78 also was viewed by the foremen more favorably than the UPWA Armour local next door. But Local 78 has been more militant toward Swift than Local 12. The Kansas City foremen have all the reasons that we have already enumerated for favoring the idea of having a union. In addition, they are definitely satisfied with the conduct of Local 12 and with the National Brotherhood of Packinghouse Workers generally. While this is an attitude toward union leaders and policies, it naturally influences the foremen's union endorsement.

Also the Kansas City foremen are more favorable than the East St. Louis foremen to the previous Employee Representation Plan. In the foremen's eyes, the Representation Plan worked better in Kansas City than in East St. Louis. Doubtless, the Kansas City foremen have more union endorsement partly because Local 12 evolved out of this plan which they favored.

Listening to several foremen, we shall easily see why they support the idea of having a union in the plant. Harold DeCamp, for example, an East St. Louis foreman bases his union endorsement on the fact that a union guarantees a "fair deal" for the worker:

I think the union has been a very helpful thing for the company and for the men.
*Interviewer:* Do you?
*DeCamp:* Very much.
*Interviewer:* How has it helped?
*DeCamp:* How has it helped? It's helped this way: it's helped people get a better deal in anything that comes up and I think — I think in general that people in this plant are sure to get — to get a fair deal if in practically — if there's any question at all, they're pretty sure that they'll get the large end of it, every time. Which is a good thing. On the other hand, why — there's a few abuses — because of the union power — but on the whole it probably balances up pretty good.

We might expect youthful foreman Andy Halusek to have union allegiance, for he was once very active in the present union, Local 78, before he entered supervision. Some observers might expect the opposite, however; namely, that Mr. Halusek might turn against unionism. Here is what Halusek actually thinks:

*Interviewer:* Well, coming to the union, now, how do you feel about that? You've had a lot of experience on both sides of the fence.
*Halusek:* Yes. We have to have a union — or else it would be back to where it was . . . [the boss] told you that evenin' that you didn't do enough work today — you better do more tomorrow or you wouldn't have no job. That's the truth. You actually — next day you went out and you worked hard. You had so much to do, of course, I did. You had so much to deliver every hour, regardless — if the elevator was crowded you had to make it up. You did it on — the noon hour, if the elevator run, or you start early, you start five to 7:00, you start before

12:30, and you work past 3:30. Say, five minutes here, five minutes there, you make your quota. If you didn't, you turn your list in, and the next day he'd say: Hey, not enough production here! Let's go tomorrow! If you don't, you don't have no job. And they did. They lay you off — they hire you today and lay you off at noon.

*Interviewer:* So it is better to have some kind of a union?

*Halusek:* Yeah. I figure it makes it better for the foremen and everything.

Not all the foremen have union endorsement. We shall let William Kinsey speak for the foremen who do not. Although Kinsey is from Kansas City, his views are typical enough of the foremen in all three plants. He is a gray-haired, rather distinguished-looking man who is well spoken and moderate in his views. He thinks that the presence of a union keeps men from taking an interest in their work and from trying to advance on the basis of their own merits.

Well, I was here before they had unions, and since. And I think the company — of course, I know we can't go backward — but the company as a whole was far better off before we had the unions. I don't care whether it's independent, or what union it is.

*Interviewer:* They had the assembly plan. . . .

*Kinsey:* Yes we had that.

*Interviewer:* How did that work?

*Kinsey:* It worked fairly good. But it was something a little bit like the union — about the same thing. Well, I think, they'd be better off without any union, as far as the company's concerned. I don't know whether it would be better for the workers, but I think this company'd be better off. *For this reason: here's what I want to bring out. Every foreman knows men that's tryin' to do the right thing, that wants to get ahead and take an interest in their work, and so forth. The way the setup is now, the foreman don't have no choice but just work. Give the next man a job, regardless of whether a man's capable, or otherwise you've still got to give him a chance. And then he may not be interested in it.*

Before, a man took an interest in it. And I know myself, on most of the jobs — I've been on all the jobs there is down there — and when I'd have a little time, I'd get in on them jobs and try to train myself.

You know what I mean, without any company givin' me anything. I was interested in it at that time, and tryin' to get ahead . . . but now they know that they automatically go. . . .

## The Former "Company Union"

After the first World War, Swift established throughout its plants a plan for giving the employees some voice in plant matters that concerned them. This plan was called the Employee Representation Plan. By our present day standards, nearly forty years later, we would probably call this a company union, though it was not started to defeat any existing effort to unionize Swift.

The Swift ERP is important for many reasons. One is the fact that the National Brotherhood of Packinghouse Workers, an independent union legitimately certified under the Taft-Hartley Act, grew up out of the leaders and practices of the ERP. The National Brotherhood represents seven Swift local unions, and more than six thousand packinghouse workers. Evidently the ERP was satisfactory to many Swift employees since they supported the subsequent independent union.

Of course only the old-timers could have an opinion about the ERP today, since the ERP was dissolved soon after the Wagner Act in 1935 and 1937. Now what is the relationship between an old-timer's opinion about the ERP and his union allegiance? We must not exaggerate the relationship but it probably does exist. A worker might approve of the ERP and still have union allegiance. Such a man would think that the ERP did a good job in its time, but that now it is good to have a union. Yet approval of the ERP might also mean less union allegiance for today, or even a lack of union allegiance. Such a worker would think that the ERP did such a good job that it is really unnecessary now to have an outside union.

This latter worker is quite rare in our three studies. Approval of the ERP gives evidence of somewhat less union-mindedness in most workers. With caution, we can say that more support for the ERP means less union allegiance, with the single exception of Kansas City. Before we attempt to clarify these points, let us see how the people of the three plants compare in Appendix Table XIV.

The main thing to note in this table is the rather good support (50 per cent) for the ERP in Chicago and the poor support (22 per cent) in East St. Louis. Many of the Chicago old-timers had less union allegiance than the other workers, and their approval of the ERP might partly account for this. Even though half of the Chicago old-timers thought the ERP was quite satisfactory, there was never a serious contest in the Chicago plant between the incipient UPWA and the independent union in the post-Wagner Act days.

The reason for the lesser approval of the ERP at East St. Louis is not entirely clear. At least it manifests one thing: The East St. Louis old-timers (and their foremen) apparently feel that the Employee Representation Plan in their plant was not too successful. The generally good relations between East St. Louis Swift and Local 78, and the workers' strong union allegiance, probably lead many of these people to think less favorably of the ERP, as they reminisce about it. Yet when Local 78 began, it was very nearly defeated by the independent union growing out of the ERP. The ERP evidently had many supporters in 1935, especially among the women. Let us quote one East St. Louis worker, Charles Renault, as typical of the majority of old-timers. Renault is critical of the ERP:

I just caught the tail end of that [the ERP]. I couldn't tell you much about it. I mean, they were just gettin' established. And I was just a young fella at that time, eighteen years old; but I did hear that it wasn't the best thing, because naturally people are human. Well, a company union — they're gonna look out for theirself first and then the individual next, you know. That's the way I would say it, you know.

As for Kansas City, nearly three-fourths of the old-timers are favorable to the ERP. For most of these people, such approval does not mean less allegiance to having a certified union now. The very fact that Local 12 grew out of the ERP might well account for their high approval of the ERP. The following comments of one of the Local 12's leaders (who certainly has union allegiance) about the old Employee Representation Plan will clarify the point we are making.

*Interviewer:* You were in the old Assembly, weren't you?
*Walter Cobb:* The old Assembly. . . .
*Interviewer:* How did that thing go?
*Walter Cobb: Fine.* It was ab-so-lute-ly fine. . . . We got justice there that uh . . . wasn't due us. I can say that. I can *truthfully* say that. We have had — I have won cases in the old Assembly that I didn't think I could win. I really have did that. And I take it absolutely, would win on sympathy. And the human care that the management has for the pa'tic'lar group involved. *Not* the man that I was representing, but for the one that *was putting the case befo' them.* Ah often think that a lotta times Mr. \_\_\_\_\_ and Mr. \_\_\_\_\_, that group, I feel it, that a lotta things they went along with, was entirely because it was us, not because they figgered that what we was puttin' over to them was the best. They knew better. They knew better. And ah 'preciate that.

In spite of the Kansas City exception, we shall assume that more approval of the ERP means somewhat less union-mindedness. Using this assumption alone and starting with the most union-minded members, we might rank the locals in the following order: Local 78; Local 28; Local 12. This assumption gives us another clue to the differences among the workers in their attitudes toward their unions.

VIEWS ON THE UNION SHOP

Our meaning of union allegiance and our comparative findings for two of the plants becomes clearer by considering the packinghouse workers' views on union security. In view of the current agitation about "right-to-work" laws, the thinking of these people becomes important.

Almost all the packinghouse workers understood what was meant by "union shop." Where they did not, the interviewer would clarify: "Do you think they should have to join the union after thirty days?" Since this topic was not covered quite so systematically in the Kansas City study as it was in East St. Louis, the Kansas City figures must be taken with caution. Substantially they are correct, but we must not stress the precise percentages given. Appendix Table XV shows a remarkable difference between the two plants.

Only 30 per cent of the Kansas City unionists want to have a union shop in their plant as opposed to 78 per cent at East St. Louis. Even making an allowance for an error of 10 or 20 per cent at Kansas City, we still have a big difference in the thinking of these two groups of packinghouse workers. At East St. Louis we have the data broken down by race, sex, and service (excluding workers under two years' service). But the differences are not significant.

The East St. Louis workers tell us why they feel so strongly about having a union shop: It is not fair to receive the benefits the union wins without paying the same dues everyone else has to pay. Curtis Neace, for instance, brings this out:

*Interviewer:* Do you think they ought to have union shop, Curtis, where everybody would have to join a union after thirty days?

*Neace:* I do, I do, I do. I don't think anybody should have to wait thirty days, I think anybody should come right in and have to sign up a union card. He tells me yeah, and I go up and see him now. I walked over all the plant tryin' to find him. I find these guys 'cause I know 'em. I say, "How long have you been here?" I told them about the union and meetin's and I take them a card and get them to sign it. I think that's good, myself.

*Interviewer:* You're helping the stewards?

*Neace:* Yeah, I helped 'em.

*Interviewer:* Even though you're not a steward, yourself?

*Neace:* No. See, I just helps them. I think it's important. If a guy comes in and works with you, even if you gets a raise, he gets one. *And if he's not in the union, I don't think it's fair.*

On the other hand, the majority of the Kansas City workers think like John Bradley. Mr. Bradley says that he does not favor the union shop:

No. 'Cause a person's got a right to join or not, accordin' to whatever he wish — even in church. But to enforce a person to do something is kinda silly. A new boy come to work there an' he says: "I was goin' out to lunch, a guy come up to me an' asked me if I belonged to the union. And I said: 'No.' An' he stuck a red button on me an' he said: 'Now you belong to the union.'" Well, that's kinda high-handed, high pressurin'.

Why is it that the Kansas City unionists do not favor the union shop, while the Local 78 unionists do? The answer probably lies in two or three areas. For one thing, there is a distinct difference in local support for local union leaders between the two locals. We saw that while 96 per cent of the rank and file favor their local leaders in Local 78, 73 per cent are favorable in Local 12. Very likely the workers in Kansas City who oppose their union leaders are also cool to the idea of having Local 12 as a union shop. Such people are the UPWA-minded workers in the plant. If the UPWA were in control of the local, then these people would probably support the idea of a union shop.

We have seen that the people of the two locals also differ significantly in their approval of the old company union, the Employee Representation Plan, with the Local 12 people being much more favorable. If we accept the assumption that more support for the former company union means less strong union allegiance, then the greater support for the ERP by Local 12 people might give some idea as to why they are less aggressive about having the union shop. On the other hand, if we look at the union allegiance scores alone, we find scarcely any difference between the two locals, both having high union allegiance among their members.

Probably the most important clue to the differences we find is to be noted in the very different attitudes of the union leaders themselves, with Local 12 leaders only 20 per cent favorable, and the Local 78 leaders 100 per cent favorable to the union shop. Surely these leaders have influenced the thinking of their members.

We must still answer the question of why the Independent union leaders are not favorable to the union shop. The answer lies in the fact that these men are independent-minded. They do not support the big organized labor movement. They believe in competition among unions, as in competition among managements. Perhaps they are more inclined to accept management thinking which usually opposes the union shop. They are more management-minded than the Amalgamated (and certainly more than the UPWA) leaders. For these reasons, the Local 12 leaders are less inclined to such objectives of the general labor movement as the union shop.

Neither Local 12 nor Local 78 has any urgent need for the union shop to give themselves security. Eighty-five to 95 per cent of the Kansas City Swift workers have belonged voluntarily to Local 12. Over 95 per cent in East St. Louis belong to Local 78. In the past, neither union had pressed for the union shop in negotiations, though in 1956 and 1959, Local 78, as part of the UPWA-Amalgamated joint bargaining group, sought and failed to win the union shop in the national contract negotiations.

There are two important findings in this chapter: the packinghouse workers, and even a majority of their supervisors, really do believe in having a union in their plants; and secondly, they differ significantly in how much they support this idea of unionism.

The union allegiance originally found in Chicago, is found even more strongly in both Kansas City and East St. Louis. Not all the rank and file, but clear majorities in all three plants, want to have a union representing them. Also the union endorsement of the Swift first-line foremen found originally in Chicago, is underlined in East St. Louis, with 76 per cent, and even more dramatically in Kansas City, with 90 per cent favoring unionism in the plant.

The variables introduced into this research such as three different unions, three different cities, and so forth, definitely affect the degrees of union allegiance we find. Chicago, with Local 28 in a state of the greatest insecurity and turmoil, finds fewest workers supporting the idea of having a union. Kansas City, with Local 12 more secure, but threatened by the raiding UPWA, definitely has more union allegiance, though less than we find in East St. Louis where a strong and secure Local 78 holds sway.

The degree of union freedom from turmoil and threat is only one major cause of the different union allegiance findings. We have seen the influences of company attitudes, too. In the following chapters we shall see the effects of the workers' other union-related attitudes, especially about their leaders.

CHAPTER XI

## *Union Member and Union Leader*

Of all the union-related attitudes, besides union allegiance, the attitude of the packinghouse workers toward their union leadership is the most important. Just as we saw the foreman influencing the worker's feelings about his company and his job, so the union leader influences the rank and filer's views about the union.

We saw that a worker distinguishes between the company and its management, especially its foremen. Likewise the worker distinguishes between the union as an institution, and its leaders. Members with union allegiance may like, or not like, the way their union is run. Some workers do not come into much contact with the union officers. A minority, especially those with less than two years' service, do not know enough about their local leaders to have any attitude about them at all. Such workers are not scored in our results for "all hourly-paid workers." But most of the other union members do have a positive attitude.

By attitudes toward union leaders, we mean the worker's opinion about his local officers, and about the way they conduct the affairs of the local. (We do not mean the worker's views about the international union and its leadership.) In most cases, a packinghouse worker's attitude toward his local leadership can be rather easily assayed. Some workers might approve one union officer and disapprove of another. However, careful analysis of these views nearly always gives us a definite attitude toward the over-all leadership of the local. Both the personalities of the local leaders, and their policies in managing union affairs, will influence the worker's attitude toward local union leadership. Also the worker's attitude toward his own department steward, or his personal experience with the grievance procedure, union meetings, strikes, and so forth, will influence his views toward the local leadership.

The packinghouse workers in our three different unions have decidedly different views about their local leadership, as shown in Appendix Table XVI.

The hourly-paid workers, that is, the rank and filers, are moderately unfavorable to their leaders in Chicago, with a score of 3.5. Only 26 per cent of the Chicago workers are clearly favorable. In Kansas City, on the contrary, the workers are rather favorable, with a score of 2.4. Seventy-three per cent favor Local 12 leadership. Finally, at East St. Louis we find the very high score of 1.6. Ninety-six per cent of the union members are favorable.

These differences look like steps of stairs and they dramatically reflect the varying degrees of security of the three locals. The Chicago Local in 1950 (and also to a lesser degree in 1960) finds itself beset with an aggressive, radical core, and also with racial tensions. The Chicago leaders were able to hold their power only because of the apathy or dissatisfaction of the rank and file, and also because of the support from District One and from the International UPWA.

The leaders of Local 12 in Kansas City, on the other hand, are moderately popular with their union members. Considering the fact that a minority of UPWA-CIO-minded people have come to the plant in recent years since the 1951 closing of the neighboring Cudahy plant, it is not surprising that the support of the Local 12 Independent leaders is only moderate. Yet 73 per cent support is strong enough. The costly efforts of the UPWA to raid the local have met with poor success.

When we come to East St. Louis, a local, secure for many years and with little factionalism, we are not surprised to find such strong support for its leadership as 96 per cent of the membership in favor. The 1956 strike may have alienated some of the members from their leaders. It is probable that some union members saw no necessity for that strike. It is also possible that they did not like the local's conduct of the strike. The 96 per cent would perhaps be somewhat reduced if the major field work for our study had been done in 1956 or later instead of in 1953 and 1954 because recently there have been some complaints about union finances and grievance handling. Nevertheless, there can be no doubt that Local 78's leaders are definitely the most popular of the three locals.

Listening first to the Local 78 union members, since they are so favorable, we find that most of them like the union leadership because it is conservative but still gets results. First, Dick Roe, a skilled craftsman. Mr. Roe has definite union allegiance and also moderately approves of the leadership of Local 78. He prefers the AFL to the CIO, because he says that the CIO is too radical:

*Roe:* We got a good union. We got a good union.

*Interviewer:* They're running it pretty well?

*Roe:* That's right. They're not radical. That's one thing I like about 'em. And ah, I cain't say anything wrong about it. They, of course, there's a lot a people, it's just like everyplace, they got a lot a jealous men, you know what I mean? One guy like to cut the other one's throat. As far as our union, I think Local 78's all right, myself, the AFL, I like it. It's not radical or anything of the kind.

Former Mississippi farmer, Curtis Neace, is loyal to both union and company. Part of the reason for his considerable satisfaction with Local 78 leadership is because he is a close friend of two leaders:

*Neace:* I don't know — the philosophy — it's good to be in this [the AFL], because it all works the same way, I imagine. Yeah, it's good to be in, because they will see yo' problems better than you see it. On the problem you want to solve, why they will tell you just what you should do, an' if you cooperate with them, they'll cooperate with you.

*Interviewer:* Sure.

*Neace:* And they'll help you on the job. Yes, time and time again, I saw the union officials go down to Chicago, come back — nobody go outside [on strike].

*Interviewer:* Uh-huh.

*Neace:* I think that's remarkable. And I have to put flowers on the AF of L, because that's my union. And I have a feeling that they do fair. I don't say you get what you should have. Nobody gets what you should have at all times. You have to make the best out of it you can, 'till you can do better. And they's improvement to it all the time. If they tell you if you go back to so and so, and so and so, we go back to that for a while. And then you get a little raise in wages. That's the way you get it. . . .

Mr. Neace goes on to talk about what the Local 78 officers have done for the membership. Then he continues about his personal friend, one of the leaders:

That guy — I really like him. He and I gets coffee sometimes, and sit down, talkin' things over. Why he can show you a point that makes you understan' what he's tryin' to tell you! You can stop by and have a conversation with him anytime. He has got his mind deep in the union, and he wants to do a good job. And I think he's a good guy to work with.

A few Local 78 members do not favor their leaders. One of them, Charles Bloomer, mentions a complaint mentioned only by a small minority. We quote Mr. Bloomer simply because his complaint manifests one perennial problem of the union leader: The fear that if he is friendly with management, his union constituents will "talk." Bloomer is one of those who do "talk." He had just been talking to the interviewer about the few strikes at East St. Louis:

I been here — I think this is my eighth year now, and we haven't been out [on strike] since I been here. And that seems pretty efficient — a fairly good union, or else we're knucklin' down too easy, I don't know.
*Interviewer:* Well, how would you say the company and the union get along here, Charlie?
*Bloomer:* Well, it seems like to me that — I tell you what — this reminds me: I would much rather see an outsider president of our union, rather than a workin' man. Because I don't know if you're aware of it or not, but our president is elected from the plant. He holds his seniority while he is president. When his term expires, or he's defeated, he goes straight back to his job with his full seniority. But that's wonderful protection for that man. But I would rather have a member outside the plant that knows the conditions of the packin' house as the president. Because that man knows he can't come back here to work, and I think he'd buckle down.

I mean, he bends under to 'em just a little bit too much. Because I've got a report from the last dance we had — of this Arrow — this dance, I think it was — that there were certain high officials in our union that went around to the tables of the bosses and had a jolly good time and ignored the people. And you know very well they're all workin' people. I don't like that. I say, mix with anyone. I mean, if you know a person, if they call you the boss, it doesn't mean you shouldn't talk to him, or anything. But to go over to his table and sit down and drink with him and have a good time and not even see the workers — I don't think it's right. *I think they're pretty well tied in with the company, to tell you the truth.* I believe — one of the big reasons we haven't had any strikes.

Actually, the Local 12 leaders have to be more careful than the Local 78 leaders about alleged overfriendliness with management, because the UPWA-CIO sympathizers in their plant are quick to charge them with "company unionism." While the Local 12 leaders are fairly popular with their constituents, they are definitely behind Local 78 in this. A considerable and growing minority in Kansas City is opposed to the Local 12 officers. Short-service Negro men are the core of this minority.

Negro worker Jack Reeves, a former steward in Local 12, expresses this criticism, although he is not personally a UPWA sympathizer:

Well, my idea about the union is that the Independent Union is all right if they would push the cases . . . [about the CIO] Well, I don't know. I just believe, from the looks of it, the people would lose. . . . In most places, the way I understand it from people who work under the CIO, that changes the whole setup. And they're always pullin' strikes when just the same it could be settled while the gang was workin'. Why, they'd pull a strike two or three days to get a thing settled.
*Interviewer:* Where did that happen here?

*Reeves:* Oh, in both plants here [Cudahy and Armour].... As I said before, there's nothing wrong with the Independent Union. They're just not enforcing it.... I think if they could get a new set of officers that would kind of stir things up a little bit. *The representative is too close to the foreman.*

Coming to Chicago, we find only 26 per cent of the workers in 1950 satisfied with their local leaders. Four factors account for this dissatisfaction: (1) the unsuccessful 1948 strike, blamed, perhaps unfairly, on the local leaders; (2) the anticompany attitude of many of the leftwing leaders; (3) the leftwing and radical policies of the leaders; (4) the strong pro-Negro bias of the Local's officers. The number of people remaining out of Local 28, the apathy at election times, back-to-work movement during the 1959 strike, and several other indications, give probable evidence of dissatisfaction with Local 28 leadership in 1960 as in 1950.

Another aspect of the leaders' popularity in our three locals is the attitude of the union leadership core itself toward its own leaders. Most people in power in each local are generally satisfied with their fellow union leaders and their policies, though there will always be some rivalries, dissidents, and factions. Such factions are especially found in Local 78.

Also it is obvious in the locals, split by rival factions with radically different ideologies, that the faction out of power will be most critical of the leadership in power. We see this in Chicago where the rightwing group has no use for Local 28 leadership, having an attitude score of 4.5. Also we find the UPWA-CIO leaders in Kansas City even more dissatisfied about the Local 12 Independent leadership, with a score of 4.9. There are no such radically differing factions in Local 78.

The steward bodies in the three locals are mostly satisfied with their local leadership, but they tend to be more critical than the local leaders themselves. This is because the steward bodies are large and include some people not necessarily in sympathy with the men in union office. The stewards are usually elected by their own fellow employees in their own department. Such elections, based on the personal popularity of the steward, may not always follow the party lines of the union officers elected for the whole plant.

If we probe a bit into the data of Appendix Table XVI we shall get a better picture of the workers who support, and those who oppose, their union leaders. The factors of sex, race, and service do not affect these attitudes in a systematic way. For instance, the race factor reverses itself. In Chicago, the Negroes are more favorable to the (mostly Negro) union leaders than the whites are.

In Kansas City, the Negroes are less favorable to the Local 12 leaders than the whites are. The colored men of short and middle service, and the white men of short service, are among the least favorable. These same groups were the lowest in company allegiance. They are partly the UPWA-minded minority in the plant. There is hardly any difference between colored and white at East St. Louis.

As for differences according to one's sex, the Kansas City women, especially the white women, are more strongly favorable to Local 12 leadership. The men are more critical, especially those men already mentioned. But at East St. Louis the opposite pattern prevails, with the men more satisfied than the women.

Service, like race and sex, reverses its influence. In Chicago, we find the old-timers opposing local leaders. In Kansas City and East St. Louis, it is the old-timers who are among the most favorable. The latter is probably the normal condition in most locals which are not going through crises such as Local 28 has suffered. The old-timers have had more time to get to know the union leaders personally. In Chicago, however, the old-timers were mostly white and conservative; they resented the radicalism of the Local 28 leaders. Incidentally, we did not find such service differences in union allegiance as we find in these attitudes toward union leaders.

### The Foremen View Local Leaders

As the first-line representatives of management, the foremen's views about local union affairs are important. Most of the foremen favor the idea of having a union, even a slim majority of the Chicago foremen being favorable. But this does not mean that the foremen are favorable to the local union leadership. In Chicago, while 57 per cent of the foremen had union endorsement, only 5 per cent approved the 1950 leadership of Local 28. In the case of the other two locals, the foremen are very favorable indeed, with practically no difference between them: 95 per cent and 100 per cent.

These foremen are quite a bit more favorable to the local union leaders than they are to the idea of having a union. Such a fact is understandable, since the union leaders are persons whom the foremen know and like, and not an idea representing an institution. It is interesting to note that in Kansas City, the foremen are more favorable (1.6) to the Local 12 leadership than the rank and file are (2.4). The UPWA minority among the Kansas City rank and file is the main reason for this difference.

With practically all the East St. Louis foremen favorable to Local 78 leadership, we should be curious to know why. Several reasons emerge: The supervisors see the Local 78 leaders as willing to cooperate. They find the union stewards rather experienced and well trained. The union grievance committee is cooperative with the company. Though there have been three strikes, stoppages are almost unheard of. The Swift foremen clearly preferred the generally smooth union-management relations they had with Local 78, to the many problems they heard besetting the Armour foremen with the UPWA local next door.

Letting a few foremen express these ideas in their own words, we come to Ross Ludwig. Mr. Ludwig is a big, good-natured foreman who has had a lot of experience in dealing with employees and with the union. He thinks Local 78 leaders are good, on the whole. Especially he says that they have been cooperative in safety work:

―――――, to me, I think, was the best man they ever had. Then there was a lotta times something would come up with ―――――. He wouldn't even bother about presentin' it. Because he'd tell the man: Why, look a-here, you haven't got a leg to stand on! Why — why do somethin' about it — when there isn't any chance of your gettin' anything for it? That's the only difference between him and ―――――. ――――― brings up everything! . . . Oh, he goes along fairly well on — on different things. We had him in on this safety inspection.

*Interviewer:* Safety inspection?

*Ludwig:* You see, that's composed of different teams. You have a management — one management man, and then from — one from the union. And he went along a lot. In fact, he sat in with the meetings we had before we started it out. And he said it was a very good idea.

Also Kile Ritchie, a young foreman with definite dual allegiance to both company and union, thinks that the Local 78 leaders are fair, peaceable, and reasonable:

*Interviewer:* And then there's the question of the officers — of the union, Kile, how about them? The leadership of Local 78; how do you feel about their leadership?

*Ritchie:* The few dealings that I've had with them, I — think they've been very peaceable — fair, a tendency to look at both sides of the question — and reach a fair decision.

*Interviewer:* If you were to describe them to somebody outside, how Local 78 and Swift get along, how would you say it?

*Ritchie:* I would point with pride to the fact that we do have peaceable relations. . . . And the national industry as a whole. Well, I don't say that we're the only one that has peaceable relations — Swift, themselves can't say that — but I think locally, here, we can. . . . I go back to ―――――, a fellow who I have the utmost respect for — and admiration. Many a case I have been in on, with him. He was always — he didn't come out and actually say it in so many words — but it wasn't *who* was right, but *what* was right — always —regardless of who it affected — what was right. And he handled cases time and time again — with, I think, a remarkable success — in view of the apparently muddled condition. He really was gifted — in straightening things out.

The Kansas City foremen are practically just as favorable to the leadership of Local 12. The same general reasons are given, and here we should recall that Local 12 has never had even one strike. Incidentally these reasons, and these interviews, give support to the findings that the foremen favor having a union in the plant.

Kansas City Swift foreman Jim Reese talks about the old days when he was in the gang. He goes on to show his satisfaction with Local 12:

*Reese:* I would like to tell you this. Before we had the union, it was pretty rough. It was pretty rough.
*Interviewer:* You were in the gang in those days?
*Reese:* I was in the gang then. That was from — oh about 1916. . . . Well, let's see. I was here during the war. I left here and went to the army. And we had some kind of a union then, I don't know what they called it. Everybody called it a company union. Which it done a little good, but it didn't — they had no contract nor nothin'. It didn't do too much good. And, after the war a while, they organized a union again, and I can't think what year that was. I believe it was up in the '30's somewhere. And we got along from there on. We got along pretty good.
*Interviewer:* So it's going well now?
*Reese:* I think the union is trying to do a good job for the employees, and I think the company is cooperating the best they can. Of course, they don't all agree on everything — they couldn't. Wouldn't do the company no good if they done that. But I think they cooperate well, excellent.

Finally, foreman Steve Giles sees the leadership of Local 12 in contrast to the militant policies of the neighboring packing unions. This comparative way of evaluating is quite common, as we see. Mr. Giles likes Local 12's leaders because they avoid strikes:

You couldn't work without a union . . . Well, now if you didn't have no union, the boys'd all feel like they was pushed around and nobody'd uphold 'em, and stuff like that. . . .
Just like I say, if they think they're mistreated or somethin' like that, or somethin's put on them that's more than they're supposed to do, why, they take it up with the union. And they'll talk it over, and — *I think it's swell that we've got this kind of union.* . . . They don't have to make no trouble.
*Interviewer:* That's good. . . .
*Giles:* Best union ever I've seen. Now, you take, like these boys come from Cudahy's and Wilson's over here. The CIO of course. If I was workin' somewhere and had to belong to the CIO to make a livin', I'd just have to do it, you see, like anybody else did. But they put their men out on strike. They said, "Giles," they said, "they're supposed to call a vote on it. And they didn't ask none of us to vote. They called a strike; now we're out on the street."
I was talkin' to one guy, and he said, "I had around a thousand dollars saved up, and a little place out here in the country. Come in here and get a room and go home on weekends. And they kept me out on strike over here till I

spent my thousand dollars and then I had to go and mortgage my place to live on." And the boys that come from there over here, some of 'em working for me, said just like ———— over here — a while ago — They like it swell over here. Said, "If I'd known it was this kind of place to work here, where everybody gets along, I'd of been over here a long time ago!"

To sum up, we find both East St. Louis and Kansas City foremen quite satisfied with the leadership of the local unions they deal with — mainly because the local leaders are cooperative. We find the Chicago foremen dissatisfied because they feel that Local 28 has been too radical and uncooperative.

The situation in East St. Louis may have changed somewhat because of the 1956 strike. Local 78's conduct of that strike caused ill feelings, and may have cooled the East St. Louis foremen's enthusiasm for the local officers. Just as the Kansas City foremen have more union allegiance than the East St. Louis or Chicago foremen, today they would probably have more satisfaction with the local union officers. Of course these two attitudes strongly affect each other.

## Attitudes Toward the UPWA

One of the purposes of this book is to contrast the three unions in the meat packing industry. Therefore we shall be interested to know what the Amalgamated and Independent packinghouse workers have to say about the United Packinghouse Workers of America. Since the UPWA is attempting to raid NBPW Local 12 in Kansas City, it is especially important to know what the workers there think of the UPWA.

There is still another reason for the relevance of these attitudes: the proposed merger between the Amalgamated Meat Cutters and the UPWA. In the past these two unions had been keen rivals seeking to win exclusive jurisdiction of the basic meat packing industry and competing against each other for the loyalty and allegiance of the packinghouse workers by raids and leaflets. In recent years the enmity ceased, no-raiding agreements were set up and the way smoothed for the merger. Yet the merger has been repeatedly delayed.

Finally, the reasons given by the workers for their views about the UPWA are indirectly very revealing of their opinions on the kind of unionism and union policies they want.

What do we find? According to Appendix Table XVII, there is hardly any difference at all between the people of Independent Local 12 and Amalgamated Local 78, when it comes to the UPWA-CIO. They are both very critical. Two-thirds of the workers dislike the UPWA.

Surprisingly, there is practically no difference among the leaders of the two locals. Since the UPWA has never raided Local 78, one might expect that the Local 78 leaders would be at least indifferent to the UPWA, even though the Local 12 officers would understandably be opposed. This is not the case. Both sets of officers are strongly opposed.

As for the foremen, we cannot well compare them since so many of the Kansas City foremen are in the "neutral" category. It may be that the interviewer did not present this matter to the foremen of the two plants in precisely the same way. If we further pursued this question with the Kansas City foremen, it is possible that we would find them quite as critical of the UPWA as the East St. Louis foremen.

The UPWA is in plants, neighboring Swift, in both Kansas City and East St. Louis, and the workers form their opinions from the behavior of those locals. Since the UPWA has been trying to raid Local 12, the Kansas City people frequently see UPWA leaflets attacking the Independent union. The workers object to the frequent walk-outs of one or another department that occurred in the UPWA locals at the Armour plant in East St. Louis, and the Cudahy, Armour, and Wilson plants in Kansas City. In East St. Louis the workers are unfavorable to the UPWA especially "because it is too radical" and "because it means strikes."

Listening to the Local 78 rank-and-file members at greater length, we hear complaints of radicalism, strikes, communism. Since the issue of strikes is so important we shall return to it later. Unionist Roland Harrison, for instance, is in favor of a merger between the AFL and the CIO, but he does not like the UPWA-CIO:

*Interviewer:* Well there's the CIO, Roland, do you have any opinions on them at all? . . .

*Harrison:* I personally know a lot a' people that work at Armour's that would much rather be at work than to be on strike when they go out just for some little wildcat strike.

*Interviewer:* They have a lot of those, haven't they?

*Harrison:* CIO, they walk out . . . just drop your hat an' they're gone. Well, I admire AFL for that, because they don't, they don't do it. They don't. They will talk about it. An' when the right people get to talkin' about something, why you get it straightened out with all, without all that. I think if . . . AFL was CIO, or CIO was AFL, all one organization, then they wouldn't have no right to go out down there, without this plant goin' out with 'em. This plant would stay in and they'd stay in, too, until they settled whatever was necessary to be talked about.

Walter Fox, a new man with Swift, says:

I like the AF of L.

*Interviewer:* Do you? .... They've got the CIO over at Armour's; I think that's the only place they are here [in packing in St. Louis area].

*Fox:* It seems like over there at Armour's — I don't know — *every time somebody blows their nose or somethin', they're on a strike.*

Another new employee, John Cainski, says:

I would guess that this is better than the CIO. *There's too much communism in the CIO.* I never did like it. An' every time — when I used to work at Armour's, we got a 50¢ raise — not a 50¢ raise, say about 8¢ raise, or maybe about 4¢ or 5¢, well, they'd raise our dues about 50¢. They thought they was doin' somethin' big for you. Well, the company gives it to you, and they take is away. They weren't doin' nothin'.

Old-timer Leyden in Local 78 continues this same theme:

*Leyden:* If I had my choice, it'd be AF of L. .... I've noticed they're not so radical. I mean they're more broad-minded or somethin' to me. *It seems they study things over and try to cooperate* ... it takes cooperation. If there's no cooperation, if one side is goin' to be stubborn with the other, you're not goin' to get nowhere.

*Interviewer:* They give and take?

*Leyden:* That's right. Just like anywhere else; you got to give and you got to take.

Here is an exception among the women, Mary Martin. She is favorable to the CIO:

CIO, I like them well. Some people knock the CIO, but they don't know what they're talking about. Just like people talk and they don't know what they're talkin' about. But if you have the right kind of leadership in any organization, it will be o.k. Your leadership is what makes your organization.

Finally, Mary Ranson continues the unfavorable comments of so many women:

*Interviewer:* How about the CIO, Mary? Do you have any preference about them at all, or do you know anything about them?

*Ranson:* Well, I don't know too much about 'em, but I like this union better.

*Interviewer:* They have that over Armour's — the CIO.

*Ranson:* Uh-huh. But seems like they go on strike more. Something — seem like we can always settle ours an' get along, you know, an' work. .... An' I don't like to strike.

Coming to Kansas City, we find very much the same theme among the workers about the United Packinghouse Workers. Here are two employees whose views are typical enough of the others. First, Mrs. Martha Richardson. Mrs. Richardson had just said that the women from the former CIO Cudahy plant are against the CIO:

*Interviewer:* Well, why do those girls feel that way about it [CIO]? Perhaps they were thinking about that 1948 strike?

*Martha Richardson:* Well, that had a whole lot to do with it. The way I understand it: The CIO, when they had a grievance — say I had something wrong with my department — and I went to my foreman with my story about it. Instead of just my foreman and I talking about that, and iron it out, I understand over there [at the Cudahy plant] that the whole department went [out on strike]. And between me and you, I think that's one reason why they never opened back up [after the flood]. I think it was the CIO that kept them from opening back up.... I really believe it. I believed that happened many times.... Because I'll tell you, Father, I don't care who it is, there ain't no cooperation in letting somebody else tell you how to run your business. And I believe in organized labor, but I don't believe in organized labor to the extent that they're, just like I say, one grievance for the foreman and six people have to go, and everybody stops working.... There's no reason for that. That's just too much. A company can't stand it.

Negroes and the UPWA

Looking back to Appendix Table XVII we see the sharp contrast between the white and Negro packinghouse workers in their views about the UPWA. The colored workers are just as favorable toward the UPWA as they are unfavorable. It is about half and half. They are, significantly, much more favorable at both Kansas City and East St. Louis than the white workers there. At Kansas City 46 per cent of the Negroes and only 17 per cent of the whites are favorable; at East St. Louis it is about the same, 42 per cent of the Negroes, and 16 per cent of the whites being favorable to the UPWA.

The relatively high amount of approval for the UPWA among the colored workers does not surprise us by this time. The UPWA has been more aggressive than either the Amalgamated or the National Brotherhood in promoting equal opportunity for Negroes. Moreover, the UPWA has given more publicity to the whole civil rights question, by antidiscrimination conferences, leaflets, and so forth. Many Negro packinghouse workers believe that the UPWA will do more for them than the other meat-packing unions. On the other hand, some of these same Negroes have mixed feelings, for they do not like the radicalism and aggressiveness of the UPWA, especially regarding slow-downs and strikes. Here is one typical comment showing why many colored workers like the UPWA:

Well there ain't but one thing about the CIO. The CIO behind anybody, white, colored, women and men!

One Local 78 worker, Leroy Foreman has some interesting comments that highlight the thinking of many Negro workers about the UPWA. Foreman has been with Swift in East St. Louis only about one year. He is now doing unskilled labor. He worked at both the Armour plant (CIO) and the Swift plant (NBPW) in St. Joseph, Missouri. Hence he has had experience with all three unions of the meat-packing industry. Of the three, he prefers the UPWA-CIO because he feels that it is more interested in advancing the cause of Negro rights. Foreman feels very strongly about this latter question, and spent quite a bit of time during our interview discussing it. He says:

Well see.... *I* like the CIO better than I do this one here, because they're gonna do a little bit more fightin' for ya. But the company's union has always been on the steward's word.... You're right in with the company. Just like if you go right over there to the Independent [in St. Louis], well that's the company's union. If the foreman figgers you're gonna be fired, and you go on to the steward — maybe you and the steward talk face to face right then — well right after then it goes, you know, closed doors. And you're in the foreman's favor then. Well, *without* that, you're in the man's favor, see? And then they tell you one thing and when it comes from push to shove, you're out of a job. You're too smart, and they can't use you. But they don't *tell* it to you like that. They tell it to you in a roundabout way. But you still have no job.

*Interviewer:* The company union doesn't really fight for you?
*Foreman:* No *sir*. It fights, but not nothin' like the CIO does.
*Interviewer:* Of course here you've got the AFL.
*Foreman:* Yes.
*Interviewer:* Would you say that's kind of a company union?
*Foreman:* Yes, it's just like a company's union. [Of course, most of the Negroes would not agree.] To a certain extent, there. Now see at Swift's at St. Joe, you just had one fella to represent the whole plant. And if the foreman said you were fired, and went to the steward, that was almost like not seein' anyone. Because the steward'd get together and said he's fired. And he would tell you, the steward would tell you, "well I'm doin' all I can for you." But that would be very little. See, he'd tell you to your face....
*Interviewer:* Well, how would you rate the AFL here? Is it about the same as that one, or....
*Foreman:* No, this one's a little bit better than that one.
*Interviewer:* A little better than the Independent?
*Foreman:* Yes.
*Interviewer:* But still the CIO you'd rate a little higher?
*Foreman:* Yes. It's even better.... It's more equal rights on that thing.
*Interviewer:* Equal rights?
*Foreman:* Yes *sir*. See now if the CIO was here, they would almost demand that colored women be hired. If she can qualify for that job, they want her to have it. Company's union don't. If you qualify or not, just ... complexion.... You just can't get it.

*Interviewer:* So the CIO would be more aggressive?
*Foreman:* Yes sir. Yes *sir.*

Finally, coming to Kansas City, butcher John Johnson continues the same theme: The UPWA-CIO will be more aggressive, especially for the colored:

They haven't done anything. I dunno. There's not much they c'n do. The Independent union can't do anything. Nobody'll say nothin'. If you *say* anything, you jus' as well not, because ain't nobody gonna pick it up. . . . They won't push for you. . . . The representative, he won't push. . . . I spoke to several (about the CIO). And these young fellas who come in here, and haven't been in here mo' than three or fo' or six months, well they're the strongest for the CIO. They're stronger than the older men. Older men been here twenty-five, thirty years, well they, you know, they didn't want it. But these younger boys, workin' now, they wanted it . . . they wanted the CIO.

Johnson is no doubt correct that the younger men, especially the younger colored men, favor the CIO and oppose the leadership of Local 12.

To sum up, we found a high percentage of the packinghouse workers in both plants unfavorable toward the UPWA, with the union leaders and foremen even more unfavorable. We might have expected some differences between Local 12 and Local 78 but we found none. In view of the fact that even in 1953 the ground was being prepared for the proposed merger of the Amalgamated and the UPWA, we might have expected the Amalgamated Local 78 people to be more favorable to the UPWA than the Local 12 people. Of course, publicity about the merger had not been much spread by 1953 and 1954. It is possible that we might find somewhat more favorable attitudes in East St. Louis today. Nevertheless, our findings point up the problems at the local level, of bringing about a merger between the AMC&BW and the UPWA.

One conclusion from this chapter is the fact that the packinghouse workers want reasonable, middle-of-the-road union leadership. They do not like strikes, radicalism, or work-stoppages. They want their union leaders to try to "work things out." This does not mean that the workers will not strike; but they mostly prefer peace, cooperation, and give-and-take between company and union. So many interviews clearly pointed to this fact.

The thinking of many Negro workers does not follow the pattern of white workers. The majority of the Negroes do not favor the UPWA. But many more of them than the whites think that the UPWA-CIO, and not the Independent, or the Amalgamated, will be the champion of their rights.

However, in Local 78's moderate leadership, most workers find the greatest satisfaction. In one more important attitude we find this local maintaining its leadership position among the three. Chicago's Local 28, because of its radical leaders, has the least satisfied membership. Kansas City comes between the two. In a way, these three degrees of leadership popularity reflect and cause the three degrees of local union security.

CHAPTER XII

## *Grievances*

Having a union-management grievance procedure means much to the American worker. One major component of union allegiance is the worker's desire for a built-in structure to handle his problems if they should arise. Not only does he want a grievance procedure, but also one that will process grievances promptly and fairly. We shall see how these wants are specifically shown in Kansas City and East St. Louis. Comparing these plants on attitudes to the grievance procedure gives us another link in our over-all comparison. We do not have quantitative data for the Chicago packinghouse workers' views, but we have observed that they were quite critical of the way grievances were handled and quite critical of their stewards.

ATTITUDE OF LOCAL 78

As shown in Appendix Table XVIII, Local 78 workers are much more favorable (90 per cent), toward the way their grievances are being handled than the Local 12 workers, 65 per cent of whom are satisfied.

These percentages are almost the same for attitudes toward the steward. They also closely resemble the workers' attitudes toward their local union leaders. We saw Kansas City people to be 63 per cent favorable to their union leaders, and East St. Louis people, 96 per cent favorable. It is only natural that the workers' views about local leaders and about the efficiency of their grievance procedure and stewards should tend to coincide. The main job of the local union is to handle grievances, and one criterion the worker has for appraising the leadership of his local is the grievance-service it provides for him. If we projected the union leadership figures for Chicago we could say, with perhaps not too much error, that the Chicago packinghouse workers are only about 26 per cent favorable toward their grievance handling and stewards.

What is the reason for the greater satisfaction at East St. Louis? It is principally due to the absence of any UPWA-CIO raiding group. In Kansas City, the UPWA sympathizers do not favor Local 12's leadership, nor do they favor its stewards and their grievance handling. Outside of this minority, the rest of the packinghouse workers in Kansas City do not differ much from those at East St. Louis. Appendix Table XVIII shows only 12 per cent of the UPWA leaders in Kansas City favorable to the way Local 12 handles grievances. These leaders have undoubtedly influenced the UPWA-minded rank and filers appearing in our random sample.

We would expect the local union leaders to be favorable to the way their local handles grievances. Both Local 12 and Local 78 are 100 per cent favorable. It is more unusual, however, to find the foremen so favorable: 95 per cent for the East St. Louis foremen. Apparently Local 78 and Swift East St. Louis have harmonized well on their mutual handling of grievances.

There are differences between the locals and plants, but we should not overlook the fact that most of the workers in both places are definitely satisfied with this important part of their working lives.

Listening to Local 78 members we can readily see why they are so satisfied with the grievance handling in their plant. For example, short-service employee, Kurt Wolf has definite dual allegiance, and is quite satisfied with his steward and the grievance procedure. The steward has helped him several times with problems, rather than with formal grievances:

Well, yes, they have several times. When my pay's been messed up or somethin'. Maybe I'd say somethin' to the steward and he'd go right then and if there was no one else asked about it, he'd just take my slip, and next week he'd straighten up on my pay. It seemed to me like they loaned me out or somethin', and I wasn't totally satisfied with it, and he straightened it out.

John Cainski shows his confidence in the system:

*Interviewer:* Well, coming to the union, John, how do you feel about that? Do you think it's good to have some kind of a union here?
*Cainski:* Oh, yeah, a union's a very good thing to have — it gives you protection if you're right. And if you're wrong, well, it's your fault, and the union can't help you much on that kind of thing if you're wrong.
*Interviewer:* But it gives you protection?
*Cainski:* It does. *It helps you out — you know, just like a case or somethin'.* And they see whether you're right, and if you're wrong, then there's nothin' they can do.
*Interviewer:* Then there's the — did they ever help you on any cases or grievances?
*Cainski:* No never.
*Interviewer:* Never been in trouble, huh?

*Cainski:* I never tried to get in trouble or anything like that. I always try to figure things out myself, see. Maybe this is right and this is wrong. And if I'm wrong and I think I'm wrong, I'm gonna ask the next fellow and the next one and the next one. And if it's three against one — I know I'm wrong. [laughs] I won't say nothin' about it. *But if I need help or somethin' like that very bad, you know — I can turn to 'em.* I don't get in no trouble.

As for Kansas City workers being rather less satisfied than Local 78 people, the reason frequently given was the delay in grievance-procedure processing. Actually a higher percentage of Kansas City grievances are settled at the first step than is the case in East St. Louis; nevertheless Kansas City has many more first-step grievances presented. With dissatisfied people, delays are an easy complaint.

Kansas City old-timer Warren Moore stresses this point of delays. He is not typical, but does speak for the dissatisfied minority. Mr. Moore has clear dual allegiance. He is not satisfied with the raiding CIO. Nor does he like the leadership of Local 12, and this probably is his real reason for complaint about grievance handling. He remembers with satisfaction the operation of the old ERP. The main thing that bothers him is one of his own grievances that has not been settled in the last six months:

*Interviewer:* Do you figure that it's necessary to have a union?
*Moore:* Yeh, well — it'd be necessary, yes. But not the CIO! . . . Some kind of union — it would be best to have a company union like they had befo'! . . . That old assembly would be the best thing that ever happened. . . . Because, when you had *that,* we could reach everybody. Could reach Chicago an' everybody in this plant . . . within a few minutes. We didn' have to wait no two — three weeks or somethin' to hear from 'em. If a case come up, you could find out the next two — three hours.
*Interviewer:* And now it's kind of slow?
*Moore: Slow!* This case I been tellin' you about been six months an' I haven't — over six months, eight months — an' haven't paid nothin'!
*Interviewer:* How far did that grievance go?
*Moore:* Well, it's supposed to go to the third step here an' then go on to Chicago. But they don' let it get no further than here. Ain't nothin' goin' up. . . .

Of course Mr. Moore is not typical of the majority of Kansas City workers, for they are quite favorable to the operation of the grievance procedure.

What the worker thinks about his shop steward is an important attitude, and closely related to attitudes about the grievance procedure. Just as the foreman is the worker's main contact with the company, so the steward is the worker's main contact with the union. The steward can do much to make a satisfactory, or unsatisfactory, grievance procedure. It is a difficult role, because the steward must try to please both worker and foreman. He is a "man-in-between." Whether or not an employee has a good grievance, he expects his steward to win the grievance. Naturally, what an employee thinks about his steward will modify what he thinks both about the way the union is being run (its local leadership), and about the efficiency of the grievance procedure.

Appendix Table XIX shows East St. Louis leading Kansas City again, having 93 per cent of its membership satisfied with the stewards, as opposed to 62 per cent satisfied in Kansas City. These figures closely follow the previous attitude scores for the workers' attitudes toward the grievance procedure itself.

There is one difference. We find the Local 78 union leaders slightly less satisfied with their stewards than the Local 12 leaders in Kansas City. The difference is not great and may be due to the somewhat greater factionalism among the Local 78 leaders. A union leader might well be critical of one of his stewards because he belongs to an opposing faction. Differences among the foremen are negligible.

The two main findings of Appendix Table XIX are that most of the union members are satisfied with their stewards, and secondly, that these attitudes closely parallel the workers' other attitudes both toward the grievance procedure and their local leaders, the Local 78 people continuing to be the most satisfied.

Many reasons will account for the Local 78's success and for the differences we find among the three local unions in the effectiveness of their stewards, and grievance handling. One of these reasons is very likely the differences in steward organization.

The Local 78 steward organization is quite different from both Kansas City NBPW's Local 12 and Chicago's UPWA Local 28. Chicago had many stewards, sometimes several in each department. Local 12 has about one steward per department. But Local 78 allots several departments for each steward. Thus at East St. Louis the steward has more importance, but less personal contact with the workers not in the actual department where he is working himself. Then too, the Local 78 stewards are paid for attending stewards' training meetings; the stewards in the other locals are not paid. There is much less turnover in the steward body in both Local 78 and Local 12 than in Local 28. As a result, a fair number of the Local 78 stewards have had many years' experience in handling grievances and interpreting the contract. These facts account in part, at least, for Local 78's success.

The East St. Louis workers explain how the Local 78 stewards try to take a real interest in the worker with a grievance. For instance, old-timer, George Kasten thinks his steward is a pretty good persuader:

*Interviewer:* How about your steward? How do you feel about him, have you got a good steward?
*Kasten:* Sure, I think we've got a wonderful fellow. . . . Doing a swell job.
*Interviewer:* Grievances are going pretty well?
*Kasten:* Yeah, all of 'em. He usually gets together with the boss and the man. Whether the man is wrong, he'll straighten it out or whether the boss is wrong, he'll get *that* part straight. Two to one the man goes back to work. I've seen some grievances where the man was at fault and he goes back to work. I've seen some grievances that the boss was at fault and he goes back to work, so that seems that both of 'em to be cooperatin' together.

And Charles Martin, a Negro, continues this same theme:

*Martin:* And our steward's name is _____. Now, he is one of the swellest guys. Right and right only. If you go to _____ no lies in your mouth, you go to _____ with the right in fact. _____ fight for you until he goes down. A very fine fellow. . . . He really helps the colored, and there have been cases that he know the fellow was wrong. And he have went to the boss and practically on his knees, to spare this man just because he got a family and the poor devil and he done wrong and give him another chance. . . . But when he got a case that look like a losing case, he go on the mercy of the court. He don't go in a case swinging at nobody. Oh, he is a swell guy, that _____! There ain't no question about it.

FOREMEN AND STEWARDS

If the foremen's union endorsement seems surprising, these views of the East St. Louis foremen about their stewards ought to show why such support is really not surprising. And the Kansas City foremen's remarks come to the same thing.

For one thing, a steward can be a real asset to a foreman in solving the human relations problems involved in running a gang. Foreman Harry Bouk makes this point:

He [the steward] cooperates all right. . . . In the first place, he helps me a lot.
*Interviewer:* Does he help you? How is that?
*Bouk:* Well, he helps the gang to get it going. . . . Yeah if you get on the good side of them guys, you're all right.

(Foreman Bouk has not had a third-step grievance in years — a remarkable record.)

While expecting the steward to be sensible toward the foreman, the foremen, in turn, show appreciation for the problems the stewards face. They understand that the steward is a "man-in-between" like themselves. For example, foreman Kile Ritchie says about his steward, a woman:

She has a double role. She goes on that side of the fence as a steward and back on this side as an operator. And I say it's hard for both of us to make that adjustment. All in all, I think our dealings have been peaceful enough. I think our dealings have been above average, as far as being peaceful. . . . I know this to be a fact, that I think she does squelch a grievance when she thinks it unjustified. I do not know that she had did that.

One final point should be made, showing why Local 78 and Swift East St. Louis have generally had such good mutual relations. Both the foremen and the stewards here have tried to see each other's point of view in dealing with grievances. We shall quote a steward and a foreman who mention this. First, Local 78 steward Joseph Rudolph. Mr. Rudolph was asked how the grievances were going:

*Rudolph:* They've been going good, I guess. I've been getting good cooperation.
*Interviewer:* Are the foremen cooperating?
*Rudolph:* Oh yes. We have a wonderful foreman. Anytime I want to talk over anything with him, why he's never too busy to sit down and talk, or stand and talk to you. And he seems to do everything he can to correct the situation. He even goes out of his way to correct something. He's not the type that will jump on you and say well I've got no time now, put it off 'til later. Until you get somebody else mad at you, because you're not doing anything about it. He's not that type. I think he's a wonderful foreman.

And Foreman Frank Letto, on his part, thinks that the Local 78 stewards cooperate with the foremen:

I mean they [the stewards] try to work with the company, not against the company. Whenever you've got to figure that this company is in business to make money and you're here workin' to make a livin', you've got to lean on that company and that company has got to lean on you. I don't see any point in the union tryin' to buck the company, instead of tryin' to work with it.

Apropos of such mutual cooperation, it is interesting to notice this paragraph in the *Local 78 News,* for November 1957:

The Local Union will not be responsible or handle any grievances concerning pilfering because it is very expensive to the company and is an uncommendable act.

So far, we have found, in comparing Local 12 and Local 78, that the Amalgamated unionists are the most satisfied with both their stewards and the handling of grievances, though the majority of workers in both plants is favorable. Chicago lags far behind the other plants, at least according to our general impression.

## Comparative Number of Grievances

Actual grievance statistics bear out many of the attitudes of the packinghouse workers that we have seen. Let us consider the third-step grievances. These are grievances that have reached the highest level possible for adjustment in the local plant; namely, the local union grievance committee and the plant superintendent's labor relations specialist. Since many rather inconsequential or obviously one-sided grievances get weeded out in the first or second steps, the third-step grievances make a better basis of comparison. Table 33 gives us the comparative picture.

First of all, Table 33 shows a sharp difference among Chicago and the other two plants, with Chicago's Local 28 having nearly twice as many third-step grievances. There is a small difference between the other two

Table 33. *Third-step grievances, 1954 (in per cent).*

|  |  | Chicago | Kansas City | East St. Louis |
|---|---|---|---|---|
| Number of grievances per 100 employees |  | 1.35 | .77 | .67 |
| The sex of the grievants:[a] | Male: | 85 | 100 | 91 |
|  | Female: | 15 | 0 | 9 |
| The race of the grievants: | Negro: | 82 | 66 | 36 |
|  | White: | 18 | 34 | 64 |
| The service of the grievants: | Short (under 5) | 24 | 61 | 55 |
|  | Middle (5–15) | 44 | 28 | 18 |
|  | Long (over 15) | 32 | 11 | 27 |
| The age of the grievants: | Under 20 | 0 | 0 | 0 |
|  | 20–29 | 20 | 28 | 36 |
|  | 30–39 | 30 | 28 | 18 |
|  | 40–49 | 30 | 28 | 36 |
|  | 50–59 | 17 | 16 | 10 |
|  | Over 60 | 3 | 0 | 0 |
| Classification of grievances: |  |  |  |  |
| Discipline and discharge |  | 43 | 31 | 14 |
| Union and management status |  | 4 | 0 | 0 |
| Union security |  | 4 | 0 | 14 |
| Employments rights |  | 20 | 6 | 22 |
| Work schedules and premium pay |  | 15 | 0 | 36 |
| Wage structure |  | 14 | 63 | 14 |

[a] Figures in these sections regarding the grievants exclude "gang" grievances for which accurate data are not available.

plants, East St. Louis leading with the smallest number: .67 per 100 employees.

Regarding sex of grievants, we should remember that women make up about 14 to 15 per cent of the workforces. In both Kansas City and East St. Louis the women are underrepresented among the grievants, remarkably so in Kansas City where we do not find a single third-step grievance involving a woman employee in 1954. This behavioral fact bears out the high company allegiance we found among these women. In Chicago, however, the women are fully represented. Most of these are colored women who were quite aggressive in the Chicago plant. The Table Ready Meats Kitchen with its several departments accounted for a large share of these grievances of the colored women. Other high frequency departments, involving men, were the Soap House, Smoke House, and 115-House Loading Dock, the latter two now being shut down.

Regarding the race of the grievants, we must be careful to relate these figures to the quite different racial proportions of the three plants: 55 per cent colored in Chicago; 38 per cent in Kansas City; 44 per cent in East St. Louis. Making a proportion of the percentage of Negro grievants in Chicago and the percentage of Negroes in the plant as related to the percentage of Negroes in the Kansas City plant, we would expect that about 57 per cent of the Kansas City grievants would be Negroes. Actually we find that 71 per cent are Negroes. These figures suggest that the Kansas City Negroes are even more racially dissatisfied and aggressive than the Chicago Negroes, in so far as such aggression is measured by third-step grievances. We have already found their attitudes to be more critical.

Obviously, the Negro proportion of grievants in East St. Louis is far less than either of the other two plants. This fact supports our attitude findings where we learned that the East St. Louis Negroes are more satisfied, even though they have less opportunities.

Regarding the service of the grievants, we see that more of the older workers are involved in grievances in the Chicago plant. This fact is partly because the Chicago workers are actually older in service and age. But another reason is the greater union aggressiveness of the older Chicago workers. As for Kansas City, we find the largest number of short-service workers among the grievants. Very likely these short-service, predominantly Negro grievants, are among the UPWA-CIO sympathizers in the plant. We already saw the greater dissatisfaction of these men with company, job, and foremen.

One final fact in Table 33 is noteworthy: the pattern of discipline and discharge grievance cases. Here the pattern follows the same pattern of employee satisfaction. Most satisfied, East St. Louis with 14 per cent of such cases; Kansas City next with 31 per cent of such cases; Chicago last with 43 per cent of such cases.

## Settlement of Grievances

Speed and prompt handling of grievances is important to the workers who have complaints. The employee wants to get an answer soon, even if it is unfavorable. Table 34 compares the three plants, especially as to the percentage of cases they settle at that important first step, between the worker and the foreman.

Table 34. *Comparative steps of grievance adjustment.*

|  | 1950 | 1951 | | 1952 | | | 1953 | | 1954 | |
| --- | --- | --- | --- | --- | --- | --- | --- | --- | --- | --- |
|  | Chgo. | Chgo. | K.C. | Chgo. | K.C. | E.S.L. | K.C. | E.S.L. | K.C. | E.S.L. |
| Step 1 No. cases presented | 367 | 364 | 75 | 380 | 127 | 57 | 104[a] | 62 | 352[a] | 85 |
| No. cases settled | 191 | 195 | 44 | 217 | 106 | 38 | 47 | 21 | 292 | 27 |
| % settled here | 52 | 53.3 | 58.7 | 57 | 83.5 | 66.7 | 45 | 33.9 | 83 | 32 |
| Step 2 No. cases presented | 174 | 168 | 31 | 163 | 21 | 19 | 51 | 41 | 60 | 58 |
| No. cases settled | 74 | 76 | 23 | 72 | 13 | 14 | 33 | 9 | 39 | 45 |
| % settled here | 20.2 | 20.8 | 30.7 | 19 | 10.2 | 24.6 | 32 | 14.5 | 11 | 53 |
| Step 3 No. cases presented | 98 | 91 | 8 | 91 | 8 | 5 | 18 | 32 | 21 | 13 |
| No. cases settled | 41 | 49 | 7 | 56 | 6 | 5 | 18 | 32 | 14 | 13 |
| % settled here | 11.2 | 13.4 | 9.3 | 15 | 4.7 | 8.7 | 17 | 51.6 | 4 | 15 |
| Step 4 No. cases presented | 16 | 39 | 1 | 35 | 2 | 0 | 0 | 0 | 1 | 0 |
| No. cases settled |  |  | 1 |  | 2 | 0 | 0 | 0 | 1 | 0 |
| % settled here |  |  | 1.3 |  | 1.6 | 0 | 0 | 0 | 3 | 0 |
| Step 5 No. cases presented | 5 | 5 | 0 | 0 | 0 | 0 | 0 | 0 | 0 | 0 |

[a] Six of these cases had **not** been settled at that period of time.

The figures in Table 34 most pertinent for our present discussion are the 1952 figures, comparing all three plants and locals. Here we see that Kansas City is outstanding, with 83.5 per cent of its cases settled in the first step. East St. Louis and then Chicago follow. In the following years, Kansas City continues to lead East St. Louis. These figures would seem to indicate a more efficient grievance procedure in Kansas City. But we must note that Kansas City has from two to four times as many grievances as East St. Louis has. This fact points to lesser satisfaction at Kansas City than at East St. Louis. Probably, just because there are few grievances at East St. Louis, Local 78 leaders and stewards feel that they must make more of them, and push them up to the third step, rather than settling them in the first step.

## GRIEVANCES

In this chapter, we found that the East St. Louis packinghouse workers are the most satisfied with grievance handling and that they have far fewer grievances. Next comes Kansas City. Far behind in last place comes Chicago. Less grievances may not mean greater employee satisfaction, if we can find evidence that some grievances are being bottled up or suppressed. But we could find no such evidence in East St. Louis. The lower number of grievances, and the distinctly greater satisfaction of the Local 78 union members with their grievance handling and stewards, support the favorable attitude we have already seen these employees to have toward both company and union.

CHAPTER **XIII**

## *Patterns of Rank-and-File Union Participation*

In this chapter we are concerned with the comparative behavior of the packinghouse workers rather than with their comparative attitudes. Knowledge of their behavior comes to us as described in the interviews, and secondly, as we have observed it in the three plants. It is hardly necessary to stress the importance of worker participation in local union life and affairs. Seeing the different patterns of behavior of the packinghouse workers in their union affairs will give us the last piece of evidence about their union-related attitudes, and especially about their union allegiance.

Each interviewed worker was rated on his degree of "union participation," using the following criteria,[1] not given in any order of importance: (1) attendance at union meetings; (2) reading union literature; (3) talking about the union; (4) doing union work; (5) voting in union elections; (6) in grievances, using the services of the steward; (7) wearing a union button; (8) membership in the union.

The parts of the interview in which most of these activities were covered, together with the entire impression of the interview, formed the basis for the rating. Admittedly, what a worker actually does, and what he says he does, may not always coincide. Yet in most of the interviews there was no evidence of an intent, conscious or unconscious, to deceive the interviewer. A bigger problem is really how to "weight" the participation criteria given above. Other researchers might give different weights from those we gave. But our weighting is fairly consistent among the three locals, and therefore it should give us a reliable comparison.

VARIETY OF UNION ACTIVITY

Our main comparative findings are shown in Appendix Table XX, those concerning "All hourly-paid" workers. Here the Chicago workers are more active than those of the other two locals: 3.75 as opposed to 4.2 at Kansas City and 4.4 at East St. Louis. However, we must use these comparative figures with caution, because it is hard to give the same "weights" consistently to the eight participation criteria, and also because the interviewer slightly changed his weight-value on the sixth criterion, "voting in union elections." This criterion was given less weight or importance in the Chicago ratings, and therefore the Chicago workers, who vote less actively, received a somewhat inflated participation activity score, compared with workers of the other two locals.

Actually there is not much difference in the amount of rank-and-file participation in union affairs among Local 28, Local 12 and Local 78. There is a difference in the kind of participation. "Attendance at union meetings" is about the same, quite inactive. "Reading union literature" is much more active in Chicago, where rival factional newssheets are constantly warring with each other. Kansas City, especially in 1956, had a similar degree of activity. Local 78 was the least active in this type of participation. "Talking about the union" is probably more active in Chicago. "Doing union work" is about the same in all three locals. "Voting in union elections" is most active in Local 78 and least in Local 28. "Using services of the steward," in the sense of going to the union for help, is certainly most active in Chicago, together with "Wearing a union button."

"Membership in the union" is, by far, least active in Chicago, as another table will show. But this criterion is only an indirect criterion, and that is why we dropped it from the scales used in the Kansas City and East St. Louis studies. At these latter locals, practically all the workers belong to the union. But in Chicago's Local 28, one-third of the people in the bargaining unit dropped out of the unions after the 1948 strike and at the time (1949-1951) of the major field work for the Chicago study. Local 28 was able to win back much of its membership. But then again, in 1955, over one-fifth of the people in the bargaining unit led by the "Real Unity Committee," withdrew from the UPWA-CIO to campaign for union reform. Strictly speaking, these people are participating actively in union affairs, though they are not even members of Local 28. In 1950, however, if a worker did not belong to Local 28, this fact was at least a partial indication of his lack of participation in union affairs. In short, if we compare the three locals solely on the basis of "membership in the union," then Chicago was least active in 1950, though about the same as the other two locals in 1956 and 1957, since the Chicago nonmembers were at this time active unionists.

How do race, sex, and length of service affect participation in local union affairs? We see in Appendix Table XX that Negro workers are far more active in Chicago's Local 28 than the white workers. This racial split in participation is a serious problem for the future of the local. In Kansas City's Local 12, the colored workers are slightly more active than the whites. The difference in Local 78 is hardly noteworthy. Women are traditionally less active unionists than men in industrial locals such as these. Our figures bear this out, with the women consistently less active in all three locals. Length of service does not seem to make much difference, except in Chicago where the old-timers, who are mostly white, are definitely less active than the other workers.

To return to the matter of participation in local union meetings, the interviewer attended Local 78's regular monthly meetings during part of 1953 and 1954. Taking these meetings as a roughly adequate sample, we find that from 1½ to 2 per cent of the membership attend, that is, from about thirty to forty-five people. The women members are well represented, by about 15 per cent. This is approximately the same as the women's percentage in the local. Negroes are not so adequately represented. About 20 per cent of those attending meetings are colored, while the colored make up about 44 per cent of Local 78's membership. The reason for this may be that Local 78 hall is at some distance from the Negro Southend. In a word, we find that the rank and file generally are quite inactive about attending regular meetings. This is in accordance with the findings of others, such as Sayles and Strauss,[2] and the Seidman group.[3]

In addition to the regular membership meetings, Local 78 has special meetings, such as the meeting held in September 1953 at the local hall. International President Jimerson, Secretary-Treasurer Gorman, and Vice-President Hook among others, were present at this meeting to explain the problems and terms of the current contract negotiations between the AMC&BW and Swift & Company. A strike vote was taken at this meeting. Over fourteen hundred Local 78 members attended (over half the membership), so that people were no longer able to jam into the Union Hall. This remarkably high attendance shows that on special occasion Local 78 members will attend meetings in large numbers.

As for the stewards' meetings, time study class meetings, executive board meetings, and so forth, these are generally rather well attended by the small number of key unionists involved. The stewards are paid for attending meetings, and this fact helps to produce better attendance. The local now has several compulsory meetings annually. Failure to attend means incurring a small fine.

As for the differences among the locals in the participation of the local union stewards, we find Local 78 most active (1.2); Local 28 next (2.0, converted score); and Local 12 last (2.7). The reasons for these differences are not entirely clear. The small number of stewards in Local 78, the fact that only this local has a full-time paid business agent who can organize steward activities, along with the fact that the stewards are paid a small amount for attending meetings — these probably account for the greater activity of the Local 78 stewards. The Chicago Local 28 stewards were far more numerous than in any of the other locals and their activity was partly motivated by the various factional conflicts within the local.

The local union leaders and officers are the very active core-group in every local. In Chicago, of course, there were several factions, principally the rightwingers who have withdrawn from Local 28, namely the Real Unity Committee. However, other rightwingers, not in complete sympathy with this committee, remained in the local and tried to oust the leftwingers from within. Hence in Chicago there were about three separate cores of active union leaders. In Kansas City, there are two: the Local 12 leaders and the UPWA-CIO leaders. In East St. Louis, while there are certainly political differences among the local leaders in and out of office, yet we could not call these "factions" in the same sense as in the other two locals.

Some additional, independently based data will help to complete our comparative picture of union participation. For instance, Table 35 shows the Chicago bargaining unit to be somewhat less unionized than Kansas City, with Local 78 far in the lead.

Table 35. *Percentage of workers unionized, 1950–1958 (in per cent).*

| Chicago UPWA Local 28 | | Kansas City NBPW Local 12 | | East St. Louis AMC&BW Local 78 | |
|---|---|---|---|---|---|
| 1950 | 69 | 1950 |    | 1950 | 71 |
| 1953 | 86 | 1953 | 84 | 1953 | 94 |
| 1954 | 86 | 1954 | 84 | 1954 | 97 |
| 1955 | 77 | 1955 | 84 | 1955 | 97 |
| 1956 | 81 | 1956 | 85 | 1956 | 97 |
| 1957 | 80 | 1957 | 95 | 1957 | 96 |
| 1958 | 70 | 1958 | 97 | 1958 | 96 |

We have already seen the reasons for Local 28's position. For some years after the 1948 strike, the workers were dissatisfied and many withdrew. Some returned. But in 1955 a rightwing faction again withdrew. These people were quite active in promoting unionism, but not in promoting UPWA policies. There is a bigger difference between Local 12 and Local

78. It is obvious that a union shop agreement would mean little in East St. Louis, where only 3 per cent do not belong to Local 78. These unionization figures contribute one more piece of evidence to the superior strength and security of Local 78 among the three locals of this study.

A very important criterion of membership participation is voting in the local union's annual or biennial elections for local officers. We cannot expect many members to come regularly to union meetings or to read the union literature carefully and regularly. But since the health of a union depends on the interest of the rank and file in securing good leadership and in keeping a check on that leadership through the periodical use of its electoral power, we should expect the rank and file to vote. Table 36 shows some spectacular differences in our three locals.

Table 36. *Percentage of membership voting in annual or biennial elections of officers, 1947-1958 (in per cent).*

| Chicago Local 28 | | Kansas City Local 12 | | East St. Louis Local 78 | |
|---|---|---|---|---|---|
| 1947 | 32 | | | | |
| 1948 | 20 | | | | |
| 1949 | 60 | | | | |
| 1950 | 54 | | | | |
| 1951 | 38 | | | | |
| 1952 | 36 | | | 1952 | 86 |
| 1953 | 48 | | | | |
| 1954 | 42 | | | 1954 | 83 |
| 1955 | 35 | | | | |
| 1956 | 41 | 1956 | 73 | 1956 | 87 |
| 1957 | 31 | 1957 | 65 | | |
| 1958 | 44 | 1958 | 65 | 1958 | 91 |

The membership of Local 28 is by far the least active in union affairs, and the Local 78 members are the most active, slightly more so than those of Kansas City Local 12. Local 78's record is considerably better than the voting record of our American national political elections. By putting its voting van almost at the East St. Louis Swift plant gate (though not on company property), Local 78 is able to get nearly all its members to stop and vote either during their lunch hour or on the way to or from work. The high voting record of the Local 78 unionists confirms our findings of strong union-mindedness among the rank and file, and their support for local union leaders and practices. The low voting record at Chicago partly reflects the dissatisfaction and factionalism of so many members with the politics and conduct of the Local.

To sum up, we found that the kind, rather than the amount of worker participation varies. Most of the rank-and-file workers in all three locals are best described as "rather inactive." Voting behavior in the local elections is the main exception. We found the Local 78 people quite active, and leading the other locals, with Local 12 not far behind.

Reasons for the worker's general inactivity are about the same in all three locals, though in Chicago we have additional problems of the political conflict and racial differences within Local 28. Apathy, the distractions of television, sports, family obligations, and distance from the union hall — all these factors keep down the workers' union activity, especially regarding union meetings. This lack of participation, while undesirable, is not incompatible with the high union allegiance we have generally found.

The Amalgamated Meat Cutters, among other unions, is very concerned about member apathy. In a *Butcher Workman* editorial for August 1957, entitled "Half Empty Halls," the Amalgamated stated:

Regrettably . . . attendance of the members at meetings does not receive serious attention. . . . An old-fashioned revival in the labor movement is necessary. It is about time that in addition to organizing the unorganized, we should start a vigorous campaign to organize the organized, because they are only half organized now. . . . Only then can we feel that this great nation of ours is safe.

The Amalgamated's Local 78 has meetings about as poorly attended as those of the other two locals. But at least in the remarkable voting activity of Local 78 members, instead of apathy, we find a healthy leadership.

THE NINE UNION ATTITUDES

In the last four chapters we sought a better understanding of what packinghouse workers expect and want from their unions. To get a clearer picture of what the union means to these men and women, we put side by side their views about three very different unions, representing the three major union groups of the meat packing industry, the CIO, the AFL, and the Independent. Briefly, what have we learned and found?

First of all, allegiance to the union is a persistent finding. Although union allegiance is weaker in Chicago's Local 28 because of the many troubles there, the union allegiance in the other two locals is truly remarkable. We saw that even the foremen have union endorsement, especially in Local 12 and Local 78. The reasons why the workers want to have a union should now be clearer. These reasons vary somewhat from local to local. We have seen how the other union-related attitudes affect union allegiance.

If we rate the three locals according to the packinghouse workers' union allegiance, attitudes toward their union leaders, the former Employee Representation Plan, and their participation in union affairs, we find that East St. Louis' Local 78 has the lowest, or most favorable, score: 1.63. Table 37 presents the ratings.

Table 37. Nine union-related attitudes: a three-local ranking.[a]

| Attitude | Hourly-paid workers | | | Union leaders | | | Foremen | | |
|---|---|---|---|---|---|---|---|---|---|
| | E.S.L. | K.C. | Chgo. | K.C. | Chgo. | E.S.L. | K.C. | E.S.L. | Chgo. |
| 1. Union allegiance | 1.0 | 2.0 | 3.0 | 2.0 | 2.0 | 2.0 | 1.0 | 2.0 | 3.0 |
| | | | | | | | (union endorsement) | | |
| 2. Employee Representation Plan | 1.0 | 3.0 | 2.0 | | | | (1.0 | 2.0 | —) |
| 3. Union leaders | 1.0 | 2.0 | 3.0 | 1.5 | 1.5 | 3.0 | 2.0 | 1.0 | 3.0 |
| 4. Participation | 2.0 | 2.0 | 2.0 | | | | | | |
| Average rank: | 1.25 | 2.25 | 2.50 | 1.75 | 1.75 | 2.50 | 1.50 | 1.50 | 3.00 |
| Combined rank: | 1.63 | 1.94 | 2.64 | | | | | | |
| E.S.L. Local 78 and K.C. Local 12 only: | | | | | | | | | |
| 5. Grievances | 1.0 | 2.0 | | 1.0 | | 2.0 | 1.0 | 2.0 | |
| 6. Stewards | 1.0 | 2.0 | | 1.0 | | 2.0 | | | |
| 7. Strikes | 1.5 | 1.5 | | | | | | | |
| 8. UPWA | 1.5 | 1.5 | | 2.0 | | 1.0 | 1.0 | 2.0 | |
| 9. Union shop | 1.0 | 2.0 | | 2.0 | | 1.0 | | | |
| Average rank: | 1.20 | 1.80 | | 1.50 | | 1.50 | 1.0 | 2.0 | |
| Combined rank: | 1.45 | 1.55 | | | | | | | |

[a] Ranking: First gets a score of 1.0; tie for first, 1.5; second, 2.0, and so forth. The lowest score means the local union having the most favorable attitudes. Where parentheses are used, the attitude is not scored because of a lack of data in one local or another. Combined rank includes the ranking of hourly-paid workers, union leaders and foremen, all equally weighted.

The three locals are comparable on four categories in the upper half of the table. If we arbitrarily equate the opinions of the hourly-paid workers with those of the union leaders and the foremen, then Local 78 is first, Local 12 is second, and Local 28 is third.

Table 37 also compares Kansas City and East St. Louis according to five attitudes, for which numerical data is unavailable at Chicago. Again, Local 78 is first,[4] taking the opinions of the hourly-paid workers alone, and also combining their ratings with those of the union leaders and the foremen.

Two categories, attitudes toward the Employee Representation Plan and attitudes toward the UPWA-CIO, are reversed in the valuation in the table. This means that if the workers are more favorable toward the ERP, or the UPWA, we assume that they are less favorable toward their own union. Hence we give them a lower score. While this assumption is only partially true, it is sufficiently valid to be included in the table. If we were to eliminate the two items in question, Local 78 would still come out ahead.

It is interesting to note that the attitudes of the union leaders regarding their unions do not differ very much. In the case of each local, its union leaders are about equally union-minded. We would expect this. The foremen differ, but only regarding Chicago, toward whose local they are definitely less favorable. The hourly-paid workers, that is, the rank-and-file unionists, differ among all three locals. They are most satisfied with Local 78. Next comes Local 12. Local 28 comes last. This order of preference was the same for company allegiance and the company-related attitudes. We will now turn our attention to the influence of a strike crisis on these attitudes.

PART FOUR

His Actions and Reactions

CHAPTER XIV

*Strikes and Allegiance*

We have seen the packinghouse workers' views about their unions, and the growing pattern of allegiance to both their unions and to Swift, namely, dual allegiance. A crucial factor in our theory of dual allegiance, however, is a strike-conflict situation between company and union. What happens to dual allegiance then? One observer, Robert Kahn, puts it this way:

> But what of a time of dispute or strike? It seems to me that dual allegiance is feasible at some times, but not at others. It may be a kind of equilibrium or steady state which is subject to periodic disruption over issues which make the demands of the two institutions no longer compatible. When a strike-bound management urges its workers to return to their jobs and a striking union exhorts them not to cross a picket line, what becomes of dual allegiance? A possible answer to this question is that even in such extreme situations, dual allegiance persists, in the sense that the majority of workers still favor the continued existence of both company and union.... Data collected during a time of stress, or better still data for the same population collected at different times and in different circumstances with respect to union-management relations would illuminate further this area.[1]

Kahn's point is well made and fortunately we are able to present the attitudes and behavior of some of the packinghouse workers both during a strike situation and also over a period of time. The 1956 and 1959 strikes occurred during the field work done for this book, and we were able to gather some interesting data. This material is limited in extent, but it should throw light on the whole question of what happens to dual allegiance in a stress situation.

Before coming specifically to the 1956 strike, let us see what the workers have to say about strikes in general. Some of their critical views have already been expressed as a major factor in their suspicion of the UPWA-CIO.

STRIKES AND PICKET LINES

A few workers might like a strike because they want some time off from work, or at least a bit of excitement. But we know in advance that most workers do not "like" strikes any more than they like being drafted to fight in a war, or having to go to the hospital for an operation. Yet the more precise nature of the packinghouse workers' attitudes toward strikes can be very informative. We have rather specific data here for Kansas City and East St. Louis, along with more general attitudes for Chicago, especially about the 1948 strike.

We found that 97 per cent of the packinghouse workers in both Kansas City and East St. Louis were unfavorable to strikes. Because these packinghouse workers are unfavorable toward strikes does not mean that they will not strike if they think it urgently necessary to do so in order to get what they need. The following qualifications of the East St. Louis people undoubtedly approximate the thinking of the Kansas City workers too: "I don't like strikes" (No further elaboration) (18.4%); "I don't like strikes, but I would strike if necessary" (71.3%); "I would never favor a strike" (7.0%); "I think you've got to strike to get labor's fair share" (3.3%).

Only the last group who say "I think you've got to strike to get labor's fair share," is the group we call "favorable" to strikes. These workers, mostly the younger ones, would be quick to strike and to see in the strike a force to be readily used. The great majority of the workers are unfavorable to strikes but would probably strike (at least for a short period) if the union's strike vote and the union's leaders ordered the strike.

The important fact is that we find no difference between the two plants. Because the Local 78 people belong to a more aggressive union, we might expect them to be more strike-minded. Local 78 has had three strikes (1946, 1956 and 1959) in its brief history, while Local 12 has never had one strike. Nevertheless, the packinghouse workers in both plants have remarkable agreement in their attitudes.

As for their behavior, the difference is due to the very different strike philosophies of the Amalgamated Meat Cutters and the Independent Union. While more reluctant to strike than the UPWA, the Amalgamated is much more likely to call a strike than the Independent. Once the international and local leaders plan a strike, the outcome of the local strike vote for supporting the strike is often a foregone conclusion. Hence while the workers are no more strike-minded at East St. Louis than they are in Kansas City, when the Amalgamated International planned three strikes, the Local 78 workers supported them.

As for Chicago's Local 28, we have qualitative data at least. The Chicago packinghouse workers were clearly opposed to the ill-fated 1948 strike. Dissatisfaction with this strike (which the Local 28 rightwing leaders tried to avert) was one of the main reasons for the Chicago-Swift packinghouse workers' dissatisfaction with their union leadership. We shall discuss the 1956 strike below.

Listening to the workers, we hear East St. Louis craftsman, Charles Renault, say that he would strike if necessary, but he would prefer to avoid it:

Well, if the time comes where you just have to strike, I would say go on. But normally a strike hurts the individual. I mean, you have to get quite a raise to make up for the difference that you actually lose, you know, and if you can't get together, you should try everything until the last resort, to get together on a deal, I think. If they feel like they can give it to you, and you feel like you're not asking too much. It should really be studied out. I do believe they wait a little too long. You know, last time they waited and waited and waited till the last minute before they confronted 'em with a contract, and a —

*Interviewer:* Settle it a little faster, huh?

*Renault:* Yeah, and I mean, they should start from the time the contract's over, they should start figurin' for the next contract, and put it before 'em an' let 'em figure it over, how they, what they can do for us, you know. If they're makin' money and it helps the individual to get a little more raise, why, and they feel like they can handle it, I say, that's what they should do, you know. It's no more than right.

And Homer Warren, a short-service employee, says:

Well, I don't think I care too much for strikes — for this reason: I know Armour's went on strike, 'bout four or five months, and they went back to work for the same thing. If I get out on a strike, I want to wait before it gets settled before I come back. I don't want to come out for four or five months then have to go back for the same thing.

Another employee, Sally Moore, only recently come to Swift, believes in strikes at least as a last resort:

*Interviewer:* How do you feel about striking, Sally?

*Moore:* Well — I, a — I figure that it hurts you in the long run, but this is a free country and if you intend to stand up for your own rights and you think you're right — I think that that's the only way you can get anything.

*Interviewer:* If you have to do it. . . .

*Moore:* If you *have* to do it — I figure well then that's one way of getting half what you want anyway.

Generally, we find the short-service workers more favorable to the idea of striking than the old-timers. The long-service people may be more satisfied. Certainly they are more conservative. Then too, the newer workers may have never gone through a strike, and therefore would tend to be less opposed to one.

Virgil Lighty, a very new worker with Swift, expresses a sentiment fairly common among the younger workers:

Well, if they don't get it, I feel they should go on strike until they get it. That's the way I see it. . . . The way I figure it, if they don't get it, sit down and make them give it to us.

Most of the long-service workers would strike if necessary, but their comments do indicate a very different attitude. They are more cautious and would prefer strikes only as a last resort. Old-timer Frank Fale, for instance, shows this:

*Interviewer:* They had a big strike vote meeting. [Fall, 1953] Did you get over to that?
*Fale:* Yeah.
*Interviewer:* They had a big crowd there.
*Fale:* I didn't vote with the majority. [He laughs.]
*Interviewer:* Well, I guess they figured they could work it out?
*Fale:* Maybe they figured just to kind of push to company a little bit. More or less, I don't know much about that stuff. But you know, as far as a strike is concerned, the way I feel about it, you lose more than you gain when — when you strike. Because — well, whatever you lose is gone. And even if you do get what raise you fight for, that's money that's still gone, and nine chances out of ten, before there's any negotiatin' goin' on, why you have to come back to work 'fore they start negotiatin'.

Roland Harrison has conservative views about the union. But in saying: "I wouldn't favor a strike no matter what happened," he is being unusually conservative:

*Interviewer:* And then they haven't had many strikes, they've had only one, I think.
*Harrison:* At this plant they haven't, because those guys, as I say, they control that, and when they go to talk about strike, why they get together. An' they call a meeting to decide whether or not it's worth while. An' they usually, when the people go out on a strike, they lose more than they gain to go. There's a lot of people that don't wanta go on strike. *Me myself, I wouldn't favor a strike no matter what happened.* I think when it comes time for a thing like that, why people should talk to management and get together with 'em.
*Interviewer:* Work it out?
*Harrison:* Because if the company can afford to do whatever the union or the people are askin' for, they will. If they can't, they're not goin' to. That's the way this setup here is, to my thinkin'.
*Interviewer:* They'll go as far as they can and try to help you, huh?
*Harrison:* That's right, they'll go as far as they can. We got people here that disagree with me considerably. Oh, I'm very much against strike, I don't know. I don't believe in my strikes. I honestly believe that a company that is doin' as big as Swift or Armour or Wilson plant, I think that they're, they're pretty good

gentlemen, or they wouldn't be as big as they are. A man don't just grow up with a lot of money just over night, he might beat people out of it but he doesn't rob a bank or somethin' to get it. All the world's pretty fair, that's my opinion on the thing, I mean I think it takes honesty in corporations, personality, it takes everything.

As for the Kansas City workers, we saw earlier that they oppose the UPWA because they think it means strikes and slow-downs such as at the former Cudahy plant across the street. A young colored meat worker, Mrs. Dolly Harris, brings out this idea with a remark that is quite typical:

I think the CIO is a good union. I really do. But I am Independent. I think the CIO is a nice union, but the reason I'm not in it — I don't see why, I just don't like the striking that they do. If you work, if you have to work, if you need a job, well, all the striking and things are not helping any. I mean, a lot of things that they go on strike for I don't think is necessary. But I think the CIO is okay. Last year, when they were trying to get in, I voted for the Independent Union.

*Interviewer:* Have you changed your opinion since then?

*Dolly Harris:* Well, I feel the same as I felt about it [before]. Because, I don't know, you think about the strikes the CIO has — I guess that's the main thing that stayed on my mind. . . .

Finally, we come to Lawrence Wiggins who is dissatisfied with Swift and his job mainly because of his feeling that he cannot advance because of his race. He has clear union allegiance and favors the Independent although he feels that it needs a sweeping-out. He does not prefer the CIO in spite of the race question:

Well, just like I said, this union [the Independent], doesn't have much voice in settling disputes or anything like that. The CIO, I think, has a little too much [voice]. Look at the lot of money and time the poor fellows lose working in industries that are too eager to strike. . . . I'm not saying that a union should be powerless to strike, but they should be less eager. I, frankly speaking, think that the CIO is a little too eager. . . .

The packinghouse workers mostly agree in being scarcely enthusiastic about striking. The fact is, however, that they will strike if necessary. How this fact relates to their dual allegiance we shall see presently.

## THE 1956 STRIKE

In two ways the 1956 strike against Swift & Company was unusual in the three-quarter-century history of the meatpacking industry: for the first time Swift alone among the Big Four or the Independents was struck; two unions, the Amalgamated, and the United Packinghouse Workers bargained as one team and struck Swift together. This was the seventh major strike in the

American history of the industry, preceded by strikes in 1948, 1946, 1921, 1904, 1893 and 1886.

The year 1956 was a fairly good year for the meat packing companies. In 1954, Armour had reversed the past and became the first meat packer to settle with the UPWA, setting the "pattern" for the industry. Some meat packing managements felt that Armour was too soft with the union and Armour was not particularly anxious to be the pattern-setter again in 1956. Pattern-setter it would be, however, because Swift had decided to be a tougher bargainer that year. Armour & Company was reducing its debt and wanted no strike in 1956.

The UPWA and the Amalgamated, with the merger convention set for October 1956, prevailed on the packers to accept one joint union bargaining committee. At first Swift and Armour opposed this, but when they saw that the contracts would probably have to be merged anyway shortly after negotiations, they agreed to accept one bargaining group for the first time.

One of the bargaining issues brought up by the unions was the demand for the union shop. Armour was not strongly opposed to the idea of the union shop, which idea had already become the pattern in the auto and steel industries among others. But Swift decided to be a crusader against the union shop and sent a letter to all its employees during the negotiations with these comments:

Now on the question of Union Shop — The Unions are attempting to force the company to deny employees the right and freedom to choose for themselves whether to join or not to join a Union. This right is the declared policy of the Labor-Management Relations Act which also provides that if a state law prohibits a Union Shop, the state law will prevail. Seventeen states in which we have sixteen meat packing plants prohibit the Union Shop.

But the company feels that even in those states where it is permissible to have a Union Shop, it is unfair to individuals to force them to join the Union to retain their job. The basic principle of all our freedom is the freedom of choice. Would you be free to choose if you were forced to join the Union to keep a job? The Company's position boils down to this — We feel very strongly that every employee should continue to have the right to decide for himself whether he wishes to join the Union or not. This position is in your own best interests.

Swift felt that it was defending an important principle of liberty. To Swift, the union shop bargaining issue was a major point. It may well have been only a minor point with the two unions, especially with the Amalgamated who would hardly gain much by having union shops among its meat packing locals.

One union man, a key member of the bargaining team, stated that

Swift never would have been struck on the union shop issue alone. He thinks that the other issues were more important to the unions. He cites the fact that Wilson was not struck, even though Wilson refused to agree to the union shop. The unions did answer Swift's letter with a release of their own to all locals:

Although Armour & Company and Cudahy Packing Company have offered a modified union shop, Swift & Company has stood unalterably opposed to any kind of union security. This has been true in spite of the fact that all the major industries, including steel, auto, rubber, aluminum, and others now have some form of union shop provision. Over 92 per cent of Amalgamated packinghouse contracts provide for a union shop. Swift & Company told us that it is "immoral and un-American" to agree to a union shop. By this attitude they imply that General Motors, Ford, U. S. Steel, and many others are un-American and morally defective.

Three other matters completed the four major issues of the stalemated bargaining between Swift and the Amalgamated-UPWA: Swift's proposal to convert the clothes-changing-time allowance into the regular hourly rate. Swift's other proposal to lengthen the time off from work before sickness and accident payments would start to be paid. This latter was to avoid abuses of sick pay. The final major point was a difference of opinion on the reduction of the north-south pay differentials.

Only Swift, of all the packers, made the clothes-changing time and sickness-and-accident proposals. To the union leaders, these meant an apparent loss of previous gains, taking away something that they had won. Several union spokesmen felt that these two issues were much more important to the unions than the union shop question. They also felt that Swift had become very aggressive in its industrial relations policy and needed to be taught a lesson. There were other issues, of course, as well as the matter of an across-the-board wage increase.

We shall not try to evaluate the relative importance of the four main issues. The fact was that Swift and the unions could not agree on them and a national strike was declared to start at 12:01 A.M. on the morning of Thursday, September 20, 1956. Thirty-nine Swift plants throughout the country went out on strike.

Swift made no effort to work its plants during the strike or to persuade its employees to return to work. Swift did inform its people of the progress of the strike, and of negotiations, in order to convince them that the strike was not necessary. But the only work done in the plants was necessary maintenance, clean-up work, and the moving out of products already partly processed.

The UPWA and the Amalgamated set out their picket lines. There were few reports of violence. The Teamsters cooperated with a number of the local unions in refusing to drive their trucks across the picket lines.

The National Brotherhood of Packinghouse Workers, meanwhile, continued its negotiations with Swift. While the NBPW locals had given "votes of confidence" to their own leaders' bargaining, the NBPW did not think that a strike was necessary and refused to go out. Therefore Kansas City Local 12 continued its strikeless record.

By the time the strike was a week old, Armour reached an agreement with the UPWA-Amalgamated, granting among other things a modified union shop. The next day, on September 28, Swift and the NBPW reached an agreement that did not include the union shop. (The NBPW had not demanded it.) Swift's policies of clothes-changing time and sickness-and-accident payments, both of which seemed reasonable to the NBPW, were retained.

Armour's settlement, along with that of Cudahy, followed by Swift's settlement with the NBPW, indicated that the struggle between Swift and the UPWA-Amalgamated was about over. An agreement was reached just a day later, and the 1956 strike ended on Saturday afternoon, September 29, just ten days (eight working days) after it began. The agreement, like Armour's, gave a 10¢ wage increase across the board, along with automatic wage increases of 7½¢ per year in 1957 and 1958.

It is always hard to say who wins a strike, since all parties, including the general public, sustain losses. But just looking at the four main issues in collective bargaining, Swift won on the union shop issue, but lost on the clothes-changing time, and sickness-and-accident issues. The geographic differentials issue was compromised. The unions claimed a "tremendous victory," though Swift officials doubtlessly thought that their stand on the union shop issue was vindicated. Swift undoubtedly resented the strike and as a result may have further tightened interpretations of its industrial relations policy in such matters as the administration of sickness-and-accident benefits against abuses, and so forth.

Whether the strike helped or hurt the proposed merger between the UPWA and the Amalgamated is not easy to decide. In some ways the strike solidified relations between the two unions since they struck against a common opponent. It showed the possibilities in unity.

Finally, the strike brought out clearly how relationships had changed in the meat packing industry from the 1940's. Swift had usually been the pattern-setter in collective bargaining and the union leaders had usually put Swift above Armour in their estimates of smoother industrial relations.

But by this time Armour had become the pattern-setter, and the union leaders, at least, claimed smoother relations with Armour than with Swift.

## Behavior of Local 28

The 1956 strike affected two of the three locals whose story is told in this book. Let us consider first the UPWA Local 28 in Chicago. Fortunately we have information from interviews and observed behavior gathered during the stressful time of the strike itself, and also gathered from some of the same people who were interviewed six years before, at a time of relative peace.

At the time of the short 1956 strike, it was not possible to do an extensive interviewing program of a sample of all the hourly-paid members of Local 28. For various reasons, use of a questionnaire was rejected. There was time only to interview a small but influential group. To test the dual allegiance concept most rigorously, under a conflict situation, we wanted a group that would definitely have company allegiance, and might be presumed to be unsympathetic to the strike.

The best possibility was the rightwing leader group. (While both rightwingers and leftwingers themselves had several factions, we are justified in using the general terms, right and left.) These rightwingers definitely had company allegiance in 1950, even though they were aggressive unionists. Quite inaccurately, but significantly, the leftwingers used to call them "company stooges." These people had opposed the last strike in 1948. They were mostly against the current leftwing Local 28 leaders, the District One leaders and also against the International union which, along with the Amalgamated, was supporting the 1956 strike. Some, the Gantt faction, had actually dropped out of Local 28. It was a reasonable supposition that if any group might be unsympathetic to the strike, it would be these people. The anatomy of dual allegiance under conflict could best be seen by interviewing and observing the behavior of these leaders.

What did we find? A clear majority, 64 per cent, were against the strike, though a solid minority supported it. But in spite of these mostly unfavorable attitudes, and much to the surprise of the leftwingers, and of many in Swift management, the rightwing local leaders observed the Local 28 picket line to a man! Why did they do so, and how does this relate to their company and union allegiances and to their other company and union-related attitudes? To get the answer, let us listen in detail to these men and women.

Starting with the minority of rightwing leaders who were in favor of the strike, we come to Ordway White, first interviewed in his southside home six years previously. Mr. White has worked many years with Swift. He is not an aggressive man, but has been active in union affairs for many years. About the 1956 strike he says:

It's the most effective strike we've ever had. Very effective! Very few people worked in the plant and were not on strike. The AFL and the CIO were in on it together. People didn't cross the picket line. It showed us the strength of the union.

The strike was more effective than we thought it would be because the people out of the union [the Gantt faction], they went out and stayed out too. That's what surprised us so.

Mr. White was then asked how the workers generally felt about the strike. He answered:

Oh they didn't seem to feel too proud about it. [He laughs. By this he means they don't approve it much.] But yet an' still, they said they didn't have no other alternative. The Company was taking away a lotta gains they had made in the past. . . . I think the strike in the end, you know, will serve will do a lotta good. Because on the Chicago plant, the Company doesn't recognize the union much at all. . . . I feel the union will be stronger after the strike. A lot of people didn't have confidence. They didn't think the strike would be as effective as it was.

Mr. White goes on to say this about the matter of confidence:

We did not have too much confidence in our leaders, local and international. We did have confidence in the AFL. There was somebody else at the head that we can appeal to.
*Interviewer:* Why didn't the people come back to work?
*White:* Even the nonunion people know what it means to have a union. They just know. They don't feel we can get along in this plant without a union.
*Interviewer:* Suppose the strike goes on more than a week?
*White:* It's hard to determine. The packinghouse workers don't have any money. . . .

Big Tom Rose, an active man on Local 28's grievance committee for many years, agrees with White about the necessity for a strike:

The people are not in favor of the strike. But strike is the only thing left to do. . . . The people are aroused at the position the Company is taking in negotiations. . . .

Swift makes no effort to get the people back to work. But we couldn't hold our people out [beyond a week].

Finally we come to Fred Strauss who was not active in Local 28's leadership in 1950, but who has recently become very active indeed. Strauss says that:

# STRIKES AND ALLEGIANCE 231

The strike is necessary. . . . Even Armour is helped by it. . . . The biggest issues are the wage issue and the union shop. . . . We figure a short strike to be effective. In a long strike people are greedy for money and they scab. They have no principles about them. There is a rumor that many employees anticipate going back to work on Monday, even if the strike is on. I could excuse a down-and-outer, but. . . .

We have 60 to 65 per cent in the union. The others are out. I expected Ralph Gantt's group to back up the union's demands. His going out [on strike] helped materially. Management was surprised at that.

In sum, we see these rightwing leaders favoring the strike, though two of them think that the workforce generally was against it. Three of the four think that a back-to-work movement would have been inevitable, had the strike gone beyond a week. Since these men are surprised at the support of the Gantt faction, let us listen to Mr. Ralph Gantt.

Ralph Gantt (with permission, his real name is used here) has been active in Local 28 since its original charter in the Wagner Act days. As we saw, he led a faction out of the union in 1955, endeavoring to get affiliation with the Amalgamated Meat Cutters. Gantt is definitely a procompany man in the sense that he has company allegiance and is satisfied with his job and service with Swift. Indeed the leftwingers repeatedly called him a company stooge. But he has always been a militant unionist, and has never hesitated to criticize Swift & Company when he felt such a criticism justified. Let us listen to Mr. Gantt's views about the 1956 strike. Especially, we shall be interested to know why he observed the picket lines of local officers whom he opposed, in a strike he was definitely against.

The workers are sore about the strike. . . . I talk to a lot of men around this plant, man to man. And the average guy is mad about being out. . . . That strike vote meant nothing. Few were there. You can fix it as you want.

*Interviewer:* How is it that most of them have company allegiance and yet they strike?

*Gantt:* They'll go out for one or two weeks. They don't want to be called a scab. Your pride costs you money. . . .

Gantt went on to say that the general satisfaction of the workers with conditions at Swift would influence how long the workers would be willing to stay out on a strike of which they disapproved. He made much of the fact that the UPWA would not have been able to hold the Chicago Swift workers out beyond a short strike of a week. He mentioned a probable back-to-work movement for the Monday of October 1, if the strike had not been settled by that time.

Gantt repeated that "the workers disapproved of the whole thing. It's a useless strike." Gantt himself, like the majority of the Local 28 rightwing leaders, disapproved of the strike personally. He puts his reasons for observing the strike quite succinctly:

> The leftwing crowd didn't think I'd strike with them. [Neither did some of the rightwingers.] But I won't go to work in any plant that's legally on strike. Even if I don't like the issues.

Ralph Gantt had a major reason for observing the picket lines. As a militant union leader for much of his life, scabbing was naturally repugnant to him. But his main reason was this: He wanted to retain his influence in the union movement among union leaders, especially among the leaders of the Amalgamated Meat Cutters with whom he hoped for an affiliation for Local 28. If he were a scab he would ruin his chances with these people. Any future good he hoped to do for Local 28 would depend on his supporting a strike called by the two international unions, the UPWA and the Amalgamated.

As a union leader, Gantt wanted to keep his status with the union movement. This desire was stronger than his combined disapproval of the union's strike position and of his own company allegiance. Of course, the rank-and-file workers have no such desire to keep status with the union movement, to the same extent, as a union leader like Ralph Gantt. Later, we shall enumerate their motives for observing the picket lines of a short strike. Coming now to rightwing leader Jack O'Brien, we hear that:

> Nobody knows the real reason why we're striking. [Though the UPWA did distribute leaflets.] Therefore it's like the 1948 strike in a way. . . . I'm amused how everybody went out. No arguments. No roughness. All seem to support the strike. It's gay along Ashland Avenue. Whiskey and so forth. The Real Unity Committee [the rightwing leaders' group] voted not to pass the picket lines, though they are not in favor of the strike.
>
> *Interviewer:* Why do people obey the union order to strike?
> *O'Brien:* Well, they'd rather have a sound head than a split head. There is naturally some fear of a picket line. Then too they can do work at home. They respect the top people. "Let them work it out." Then they hope it won't be a long strike.

O'Brien also noted that Swift made no effort to try to operate the Chicago plant:

> Some foremen said to their gangs: "We're not going to operate unless there's a complete gang." They take care of sanitation, and so forth. Their implication is: "Don't come back to work right away."

Back in 1950, local leader Della Harris was very outspoken in her criticism of the leftwing union leadership in Local 28 and in UPWA District

One. She had said that these leaders were too hot headed and radical: "You supposed to *think* — I tell 'em. Listen and then think. Don't just rush into it. The Lawd done give you five senses an' one of them is *think*. An you s'posed to think about these things!"[2] Miss Harris is just as critical in 1956. She says:

The way they got that strike off! The peoples in there now [in Local 28 leadership] are awful. The foremens say they wish they could get the plant back the way we [the rightwingers] had it. . . .

I said before the strike: "We're not going to get no union shop." The place is divided, and the company know it! Peoples don't agree on the union shop. Some want the freedom to do what they want to do. 'Most everybody *would* join the union if it was a good one. But they're ign'rant. The meetings are no good. No intelligence. They get the District there. They can't run in themselves.

Della Harris is very cynical about the strike vote:

They say they had a big vote an' it was "yes." But the real vote was "no." They always say the people voted yes, but they didn't. . . . If the strike went on three weeks or a month, the peoples would have broke the strike. I know that definite. . . . If we on strike they [the higher union leaders] still get their salaries. They pull us out on strike for nothin'! We get a raise and food prices go up!

The peoples are against the strike. But when you belong to the union, whether you like it or not, you go along with the union. You go along with the big guy. You know you don't want to say you didn't go along with the union. Nobody likes to be a scab. . . . Some of the foremen said: "Don't come in here and work. You're hurtin' yourself and us."

When Della Harris says "You go along with the union," she means that few workers like to cross a picket line. She does not mean that the worker who is reasonably well satisfied with his company and working conditions and who has company allegiance will not oppose leaders who are too quick to strike. Her own union example over many years is proof of this.

Rightwinger Mike Osborne dropped out of Local 28 with the Gantt faction, but he is still an active unionist. He says:

The majority didn't want to strike, no. The strike vote don't mean much. The union shop is the big issue. The only way to make us join was to get the union shop. . . . The majority of the people aren't interested in the union shop. They're interested in the union. . . . You hate to cross a picket line. But as far as I can hear the people are planning to come back in on Monday [October 1].

We come now to Ted Kurowsky, one of the early organizers of Local 28 who said in 1950: "In '37 and '38 I was laid off twenty-one times! . . . But they never fired me for union activities." Ted has company allegiance along with his strong union allegiance, though he was very critical in 1950 of the Swift Standards System. He has high blood pressure and is approaching retirement. For these reasons he is not active in union affairs now.

*Interviewer:* How do the people feel about the strike?

*Kurowsky:* Well, I'll tell ya. Not too good. They didn't care too much for it. They didn't like what Swift offered them, and they didn't like the strike. There doesn't seem to be the enthusiasm, you know. They [the union] haven't got the worker after that ten week strike we lost [in 1948]. They taken the heart out of us. They [the people] don't seem to care.

*Interviewer:* But they voted to go out?

*Kurowsky:* I'll tell you: your guess is as good as mine. Because last time [in 1948] we didn't vote to go out. I think the vote was fifty-six to four against it in Local 28. But the vote don't mean nothin'. As far as you and I are concerned, if you had my honest opinion, if the vote was ten to one against the strike, but it was sent to the national office, the national office is going to use that vote just the way they see fit.

Kurowsky further develops the idea of financial need affecting the packinghouse workers during a strike:

They got large families, the packinghouse workers. You know the colored boys. Not that I'm trying to run 'em down you know. . . . Somebody, some guy told me he had a family of five children. And he had one of these big union buttons that said: 'Don't ride; Join the union! Don't be a free rider!' By gosh he didn't strike. His wife told him he'd have to have something to feed the kids. He went to the union four or five days after the strike started. The union said we can't do nothing for you in four or five days! He came back [to work].

*Interviewer:* What if the strike goes on?

*Kurowsky:* My guess is as good as anybody's. I think we'd have a *big* back-to-work movement.

Mr. Kurowsky was asked about the matter of dual allegiance and the strike. However, the interviewer used the word loyalty. Kurowsky answered:

This is a pretty ticklish question: loyalty to the company, loyalty to the union. You've got to work to live. And if you've got to work to live, whether you got loyalty [to the union] or not, you gotta come back. You know they don't work for the company because they're loyal to the company. They work fer the company because it's a matter of life and death. You either live or you don't.

Kurowsky, of course, does not speak for most of the workers when he says that. He speaks only for himself and indeed he seems to admit to some company allegiance though not to loyalty:

They're just as satisfied with Swift as any company. You know what I mean. This place and the working conditions are not bad. Swift isn't a bad company to work for.

Finally we hear Jay Corbett, very active in UPWA affairs for many years. While Corbett is a rightwinger and opposed to the leftwingers in Local 28 and in District One, yet he thinks that the Gantt faction made a mistake in withdrawing from the local. He thinks that the only way to oppose the leftwing is from within the local itself.

*Interviewer:* How do the people feel about the strike, Jay?
*Corbett:* How do the fellas feel about it? Well, it was surprising all the free riders that stayed out [on strike]. In my department, it was about fifty-fifty. I expected to see people walking back in more when I got down to 43rd and Ashland. They held out pretty good. I was surprised.

The interviewer then asked Mr. Corbett about the strike vote. He said:

Yeah. But who counts 'em? [He laughs.] I went over and voted. Yeah, who counts 'em? See, even if they voted *not* to strike, which I think they did, they'd call a strike regardless.
*Interviewer:* You think Local 28 voted *not* to go out then?
*Corbett:* I'd say they did. Very few voted. Very few. If you don't vote, you're voting *for* it. I went over and cast my vote against the strike. I thought one strike in packing was enough for twenty years! [He refers to the 1948 strike.] . . .
*Interviewer:* If the strike goes on long?
*Corbett:* I think they'd come back.
*Interviewer:* Even across a picket line?
*Corbett:* Oh, yes. See, the busses were crossin' the picket lines. The CTA busses. This year all the foremen stayed in the plant. The last time, in '48, the foremen called the people back in to work. I think Swift knew that it was time killin' in this [1956] strike and probably wouldn't go on for long. . . .
*Interviewer:* Do you think the union is stronger or weaker because of the strike?
*Corbett:* In our plant the union was weak before and it's still weak. . . . But I think the faction out of the union done a very wrong thing. . . .

What have we learned about dual allegiance in crisis from the rightwing leaders? These people had allegiance to both Swift and to the union. Most of them opposed the strike, but they observed the picket lines because they are strong-minded professional unionists and wished to stay that way. They knew that crossing the picket lines would spoil their chances to retain their leadership position, at least with the International officers of both the UPWA and the Amalgamated. We recall that some Local 28 rightwing leaders had been hoping to quit the UPWA and get an Amalgamated charter. In spite of these motives, some of the rightwingers would very probably have led a back-to-work movement if the strike had gone on much longer than a week. Plans for this had already been laid.

The rightwing local leaders also say that the Chicago workforce generally was unsympathetic to the strike. That is only their opinion. The leftwing leaders would have probably said the opposite. We were not able to sample the opinion of the workforce as a whole. We do know that most of these people had company allegiance and were fairly well satisfied with their jobs in 1950. We also know that they observed the 1956 picket lines. Some additional facts will help to clarify their probable attitudes and their behavior.

The last week in September is fairly busy in the Swift meat packing houses, but it is not the peak time of the year. Swift made little effort to urge its employees to return to work. For instance, one Chicago plant official stated:

We had a much better start on retaining personnel at the beginning of this strike than in 1948. Then, in '48, nobody was in the plant from the workforce on the first few days of the strike. This year about 150 from the UPWA and about 200 from the AFL, electricians [not involved in the strike], truck drivers, and so forth, reported from the start. That is, they never struck. This improved slightly during the seven days of the strike.

The company made no effort to get the strikers to return. Some people applied for jobs during this time [maybe they were sent by the union?] and we said: "We're not hiring now. Wait until after the strike." We did no production work in Chicago during the strike, no killing, or processing. Not even much repair work. Just maintenance to preserve the products in the coolers.

Also it was easier [for the strikers] to get other work in '56 than in '48, though it should also be said that the picket lines were easier in '56 than in '48. I think the union did not really want an all-out strike this time.

On the other hand, one of the letters Swift sent out to its employees during the strike may have made a few workers think that their E.B.A. benefits, group insurance and hospital benefits might be forfeited unless they returned to work. Swift had no intention, however, of interfering with these benefits, but was reminding its employees that they must keep up their membership payments even though on strike.

Why did the Chicago workforce strike? Perhaps many felt that the major collective bargaining issues were worth a strike, though they were well aware that packinghouse workers at Armour next door did not have to go out on strike. Also, quite humanly, they did not like to cross the picket lines, partly out of fear of physical harm, but more because of possible ostracism by fellow workers later. Then too, some workers were glad to have this unexpected "leave of absence" in order to clean up around the house, or even to take a short vacation. The weather was warm and comfortable during that last week of September 1956. Finally, they did not mind too much sacrificing one week's pay for the general raise in pay Swift had already offered and which would come to them, once the strike was settled.

However, there would have been a strong urge to go back to work on Monday, October first, if the strike had not been settled by that time with the prospect of a second weekly paycheck to be missed. As one unionist put it: "We could not have held them out much longer." Asked why, he answered: "Because they are satisfied with the collective bargaining issues and with the company."

Evidently many factors besides company and union-related attitudes and allegiances were influencing the Chicago packinghouse workers during the 1956 strike. These factors need to be considered along with dual allegiance if we want to understand the workers' strike behavior.

*Behavior of Local 78.* Leaving Chicago and coming now to East St. Louis, we shall see how the second local union of our study conducted itself during the 1956 strike. We will draw our evidence mostly from observed behavior, and a few interviews with some key people on both sides.

In spite of the excellent relations at East St. Louis among employee, Swift, and Local 78, we find much more aggressive strike behavior than we found in Chicago especially in mass picketing and in prevention of refrigerator car shipments.

As one plant official said to the author shortly after the strike:

All is smoother now than before. But it looks as if some of the kinks will take a lot more hammering, then polishing. I thought, for a while, that we had wrecked your book.

The aggressiveness of the Local 78 leaders during the 1956 strike seems very surprising, but there is no basic contradiction. First, we consider the rank-and-file workers. It is not surprising that the average worker observed the Local 78 picket lines and stayed out on strike.

(1) We recall that Swift made no effort to recall the employees to do regular plant operations during the strike.

(2) The strike was short, and most workers could find things to do at home or find part-time work.

(3) Mass picketing, along with the fact that East St. Louis police had no jurisdiction in the town of National City, Illinois, made few people inclined to go through the lines. Moreover, since East St. Louis is an extremely prolabor town, and since some Local 78 leaders are in local politics, it is unlikely that the East St. Louis police would have helped, even if they had jurisdiction. The National City police are a token force only.

(4) We should note, though, that no actual violence was reported. While the rank-and-file workers had a slight but definite lead in company allegiance

and general job satisfaction as among the three plants, they had a much bigger lead in their union allegiance and satisfaction with union affairs. Because of their support for the union shop that we saw earlier, they may have sympathized with the strike more than the Chicago packinghouse workers. However, the average worker probably knew little about the issues.

(5) As for Local 78's massed-picketing tactics (stopped after an injunction), most of the workers were not involved in this. The maximum number of pickets was one hundred, around 5 per cent of the membership. These pickets were undoubtedly the steward body, executive board, and the small core of very active union people.

Secondly, we come to the Local 78 leaders and active core. These men, too, have company allegiance and are generally satisfied men. But they also have strong union allegiance. Once the plans for the strike had come from Chicago, it is not at all surprising that their roles as local union leaders would lead them to support the strike.

But the aggression of these men in blocking railroad shipments and preventing office people and supervisors from entering or leaving the plant may be more puzzling. The following reasons give the best explanation:

(1) There was no police interference in such a labor town as East St. Louis.
(2) The alleged union agreement with Swift about not shipping out meat was very important to these leaders. They doubtless believed that the Swift office workers and supervisors were loading the meat to be sent out to NBPW plants (not on strike) to be processed there. Hence, they felt that such shipments would weaken the force of the strike.
(3) One or several of these leaders, having the power to cripple the Swift plant, wanted to use that power to gain personal prestige in the eyes of fellow unionists. It is important here to note that Thomas Hubert, former president of Local 78 was narrowly defeated in January, 1956, because (according to some people) he was too pro-Swift. The winning officers probably wished to give strong evidence against possible charges of collusion with the company, by their extra militancy during the strike.
(4) Within five days after the mass-picketing began, the Local 78 leaders at least freely reversed this policy after Swift filed a petition for a second injunction. The union and Swift reached an agreement making the injunction unnecessary.

Probably the most important of those reasons is the ambition for prestige on the part of a very few Local 78 leaders. Strike behavior and policy based on this narrow focal point does not upset our other findings; that industrial relations between employees, union, and company at East St. Louis were very good.

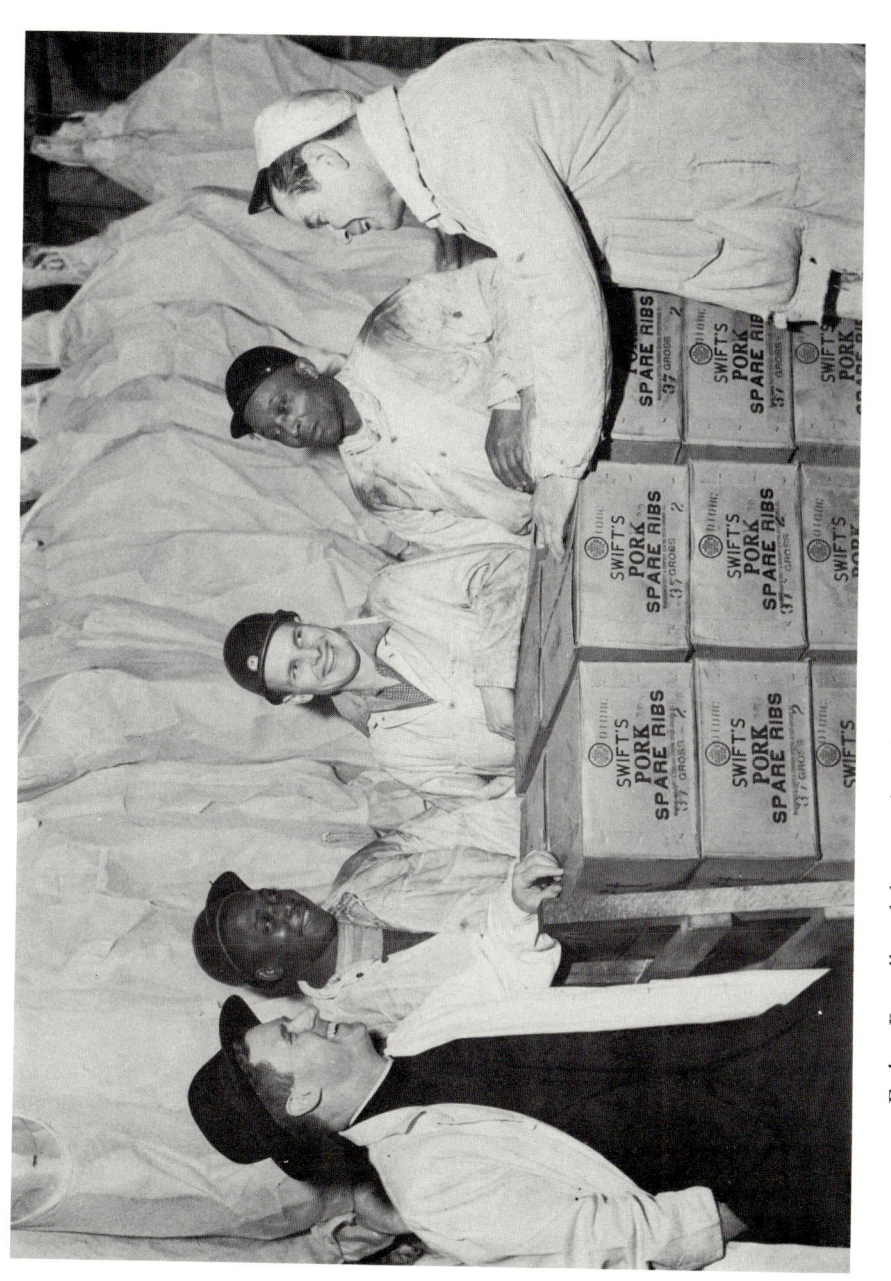

Father Purcell and four workers interviewed at East St. Louis Swift and Local 78.

Packingtown has become a ghost town and Chicago is "hog butcher to the world" no longer. Here the great Armour Chicago plant falls to the wreckers' ball.

The meat packing industry has decentralized into small, efficient, one-storied units such as this new Wilson, N. C., Swift plant — a bone of contention in the 1959 strike.

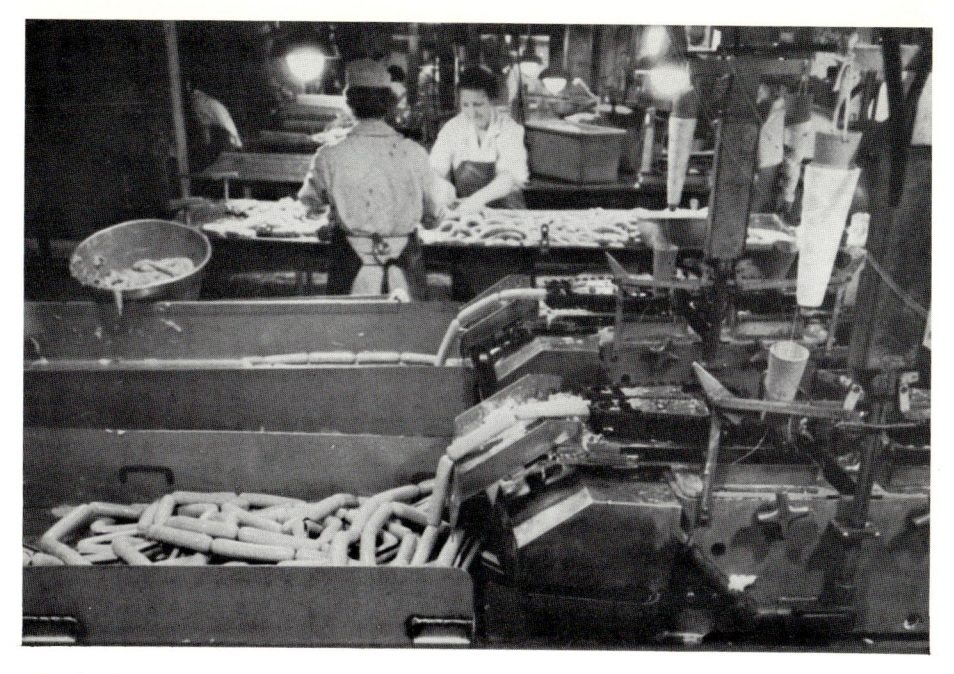

In the last ten years the meat packing industry has become more automated than in the previous twenty-five. In the foreground this efficient, new continuous-flow-sausage-stuffer displaces five manual operations of the women in the background. Photograph courtesy *Business Week*.

The back-breaking work of the splitter on the hog dressing line is now done easily by this man with his electric cutter and counterbalanced moving assembly. Photograph courtesy *Business Week*.

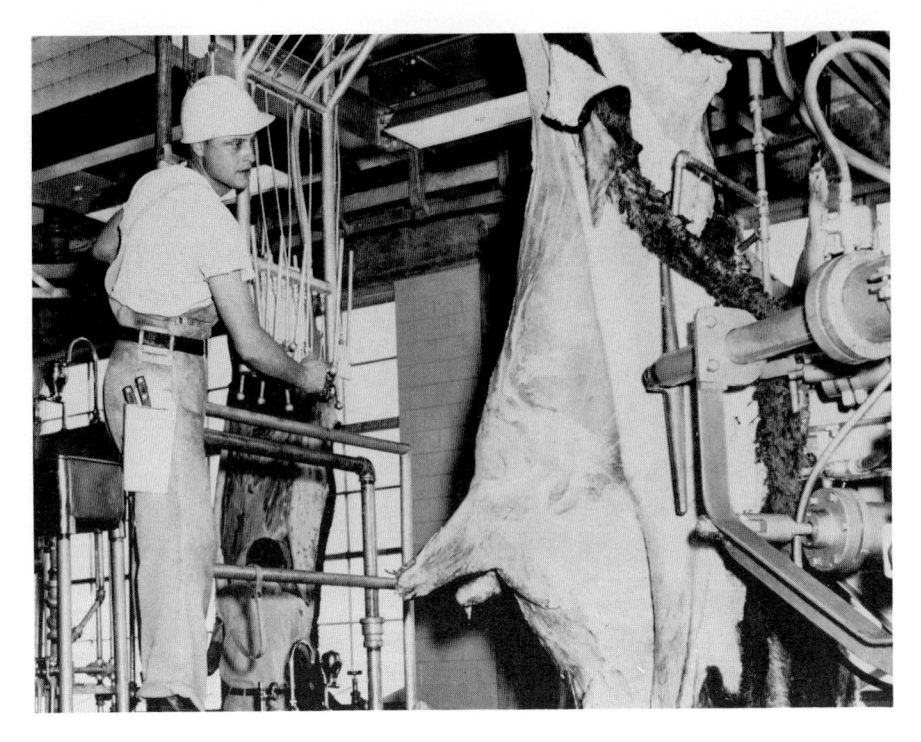

This operator runs "Gorgeous George," the new automatic hide removing machine that displaces the ancient knife skill of the floorsman.

Beef branders mark the clean sides of beef.

A UPWA Chicago picket comes to grips with a policeman in the 1956 packinghouse workers' strike.

President Tony Kleine and pickets in the 1959 strike.

Strikers picket Swift in the 1959 strike.

Two separate lines of argument in the 1959 negotiations divide Swift and the UPWA-Amalgamated teams.

The dual allegiance of these rank-and-file packinghouse workers needs to grow into "deeper and more meaningful dual loyalties."

THE 1959 STRIKE

Some issues of the 1956 strike had not been settled. They came back to haunt the Chicago Morrison Hotel bargaining tables at contract renewal time in 1959. The meatpacking industry was continuing its rapid change. Armour had shut down six large plants across the country. The Chicago Swift plant had reduced operations. Small, modern, one-story, small-town plants were sprouting among the independent packers. Mechanization was constantly advancing.

Such a climate led the meatpacking unions in 1959 to strive for job security and a shorter work week to spread jobs. Armour again became the pattern-setter. Armour did not want to accept a shorter work week, was seriously concerned with the unions' other demands regarding separation pay and employment guarantee, but did recognize the problems of lost jobs due to mechanization and plant movements. So, in the last week of negotiations, Armour countered the unions' proposals with its novel "automation fund" idea, partly influenced by a plan of the Pacific Maritime Association, but mainly planned and written out by the Armour bargaining team.

*The Armour Plan.* The automation fund idea was to be a company-financed fund plus a special labor-management committee so that "every effort will be made to cushion whatever unemployment may arise through the introduction of automation. Specifically, the agreement looks toward the financing of studies of this problem, programs to retrain and/or relocate workers thus affected and other solutions."[3] The fund was to be financed by the company up to $500,000 over the next two years. The labor-management committee was to be composed of union and management members with an impartial chairman. The findings of the committee were not to be binding on the parties and were to be presented at least six months before the end of the contract.

After little hesitation, both unions accepted the Armour automation fund idea. The idea then became a pattern for the industry and a key issue in the Swift strike to follow. The automation fund idea attracted unusually favorable comment across the nation. Most of the major packers accepted the automation fund and committee plan. Swift, however, thought it was bad business to tie up half a million dollars in some vague plan to do what Swift felt it was already doing. Since 1938, Swift had a plant-wide seniority system and displaced workers had been trained for new jobs at least within the same plant at company expense.

Certainly the automation idea was new and untried. How much benefit it would have for displaced workers remained to be seen, for many packinghouse jobs are semiskilled and quickly learned. The unions hoped that future bargaining would strengthen the plan, especially for transferring a worker from one plant to another after a shutdown or reduction. Whether valuable or not, the plan publicly announced Armour's concern with job displacement. The unions liked the plan and they rejected Swift's alternate savings plan.

*The major 1959 strike issues.* The Armour package amounting to about 23¢ per hour, was soon accepted by Cudahy, Morrell, Oscar Mayer, Rath, and Hygrade. Hormel and others accepted modifications of the package. Swift and Wilson held out. Wilson offered as a bonus each year two cents more than the pattern, but refused the automation fund, union shop, and other items. Because of this offer, the company's apparent willingness to bargain, and the expense of two strikes, Wilson workers continued to work without a contract, while Swift alone was struck on September 4 by the UPWA and the Amalgamated acting jointly. After the Swift settlement, the UPWA struck Wilson. The 109-day Wilson-UPWA strike lasted twice as long as the Swift strike. Unlike Swift, Wilson seriously tried to enlist strikebreakers, promising permanent work to over 3000 people, mostly young farmers. The strikers, even oldtimers with Wilson, feared they would lose their jobs. But the arbitration board set up by the final agreement decided on a single seniority system so that strikers would be rehired and scabs "bumped." The exceptions were cases of picket line violence. The AFL-CIO and the Amalgamated Meat Cutters supported the UPWA, but the NBPW began a raid, attempting unsuccessfully to organize the Wilson locals. The strike was bitter and costly for both sides. It would take a long time for the wounds to heal.

Wages were not an issue in the Swift strike. Swift agreed to a 15¢ raise over two years, the same as the Armour settlement. The issues involved several differences of principle among Swift and the two unions: (1) the southern plants' wage differential; (2) the automation fund and committee; (3) the Swift savings plan; (4) the union shop; (5) company right to discipline on wage incentive cases involving slowdowns; (6) putting the Swift pension plan into the contract; (7) including new plants such as Wilson, N.C. in the master agreement; (8) voluntary overtime; (9) separation pay after two years' layoff.

The southern plant problem was perhaps the greatest single issue, especially between Swift and the Amalgamated. Of all the big packers, Swift had by far the largest number of plants in the South, at least eleven, some of considerable importance. The wage differential problem was minor for Armour, Cudahy, and the others.

Over the years the unions had managed practically to eliminate wage differentials between North and South. The result, according to Swift, was that its southern competitors, some having contracts with these same unions, others unorganized, sometimes paid wages from 69¢ to 95¢ lower than Swift wages, and often paid no fringe benefits.

Swift felt that this put its southern plants in an unfair competitive position. In six Swift plants in the South, employment had dropped 39 per cent from 1956 to 1959, though part of the reason for this was the shortage of cattle and the growth of small independent plants. At the start of negotiations Swift proposed that the northern wage-increases not be given in the South and indeed that southern wages be reduced. To this the unions replied in a strike bulletin of September 9:

The Swift plants can . . . compete effectively with nonunion firms because Swift workers have considerably higher productivity. Wage costs might be higher in these plants, but total production costs are not. And it is total production costs which count.

Swift replied in an employees' letter on September 15:

We want to keep our plants open and keep Swift people at work. But, we also know that something must be done about these problems. . . . We proposed that employees at the southern plants forego any general wage increase for the present. . . .

As in 1956, the union shop was again an issue, more important to Swift by far, than to unions, though some members of both UPWA and Amalgamated were anxious to win it.

The Swift savings plan had been partly borrowed from the General Electric plan (not accepted by the electrical workers). This carefully worked-out plan gave the employee the right to contribute a small sum each week, one-half of which the company would match. These combined savings, as a trust fund, would be invested in U. S. Bonds or in Swift stock. The employee must not withdraw his savings for three years (if he were to get the company's share), though special provisions would apply for layoffs or unusual circumstances. (The time was reduced to two years in the Swift-NBPW settlement.) This plan was not an "automation fund," but was to further savings and provide for the future of all Swift employees, displaced or not. Swift believed that this plan was well tailored for its own employees.

The unions' reaction was critical. In a strike bulletin of September 8 they said:

The plan has a lot of strings attached. Swift would kindly let an employee take his own money out of the fund, but he could only have part of the company contributions at three year intervals.

The plan offers immediate tax benefits for Swift, but only potential benefits for workers. What's more, it does not make up for the parts of the Swift proposals which fall far below the Armour pattern.

As for the wage-incentives issue, the unions claimed that Swift was trying to claim the right to discipline workers for failing to make more than the standard (60) B-hour. Swift replied that it was only trying to get contract language to cover slowdowns, such as the serious one occurring at the Denver plant just before the strike. The company stated in its October 13 employees' letter:

It should interest you that slowdown tactics are only experienced at plants represented by the UPWA, and that we have never had this difficulty with either the AMC&BW or the NBPW. Such tactics gain nothing and can only bring hardship and loss of earnings for the employees involved.

The issues were sharply opposed. Swift proposed its package and the unions proposed theirs: the Armour pattern. A long and rather bitter strike began at midnight, September 4, involving around eighteen thousand Swift workers in thirty-seven meat packing plants, in thirty-five cities, twenty-six branch houses and seven poultry plants. Around six thousand strikers belonged to the Amalgamated and around twelve thousand to the UPWA. The National Brotherhood with its seven thousand workers did not strike, but made an interim agreement with Swift, accepting some of the company's proposals, but continuing to negotiate.

While it seemed in May 1959 that the UPWA and the Amalgamated would never bargain together, the summer negotiations soon brought the two unions together and they bargained for the second time in their history with joint teams led by Lloyd of the Amalgamated and Helstein of the UPWA, with Helstein handling most of the discussions.

*The conduct of the strike.* The Federal Mediators called sessions, but the strike wore on with agreement seemingly far off. Before the beginning of the strike Swift began a policy of informing its employees of strike developments by letters mailed to their homes. These letters were skillfully written, couched in moderate language and appeared nearly every day — twenty-seven letters from September 3 to October 15. The unions, calling Swift's letters "Dear John" letters, countered with their own letters and leaflets in less restrained language indicating the bitter feelings that arose. For example, this letter from the Amalgamated on September 11:

Some people who are normally decent, turn dirty and vicious the minute they get into a fight. Whatever Swift may be normally, it is certain that its management people have become dirty and vicious in this strike situation. Today, for example,

Swift management officials in a number of spots spread the rumor that Swift workers in other spots had become scabs and returned to work. Some Swift foremen have even called workers' wives with reports that workers in one or another area have gone back to work for Swift. All of this is complete falsehood.

One purpose of the Swift letters was of course to encourage a back-to-work movement. But for most of its plants, especially in the North, Swift did not try to break the strike by firing strikers and hiring new workers. "Work" was offered strikers who would return. But there was no effort at a general resumption of meat slaughtering and processing operations. Some Swift officials were probably surprised at the failure of the general back-to-work movement. One stated that perhaps the workers' union allegiance was greater than their company allegiance. But the relative strength of the two allegiances is not to be measured primarily by striking versus scabbing behavior. As we saw in the 1956 strike, other important short-run factors will more greatly affect the workers' strike behavior.

The Amalgamated locals were all tightly shut down. At the East St. Louis plant, the foremen (not harassed as they were in 1956), aided by office people, and salesmen, shipped at least fifty carloads of product. Some office girls did minor sausage operations. The Chicago Swift-UPWA plant, however, was 85 to 90 per cent in operation, with most of the Chicago workers crossing the picket lines and coming back to work. Several facts may explain this.

The Chicago cut-back had reduced the plant workforce to only about nine hundred workers, especially in the soap, sausage, margarine, mechanical, and dog food departments. These were mostly older workers, concerned lest the entire plant be shut down. "Swift would use the strike now to close the plant." Many workers had dropped out of Local 28. Many, as we have seen in our past studies, were not favorable to the UPWA or to Local 28 leadership. Some comments were: "To hell with John Lewis' strike." (Lewis was President of Local 28.) "The Company and the Union are both bull-headed." Finally, the picketing was poorly organized. Indeed, with stockyards workers, and workers from other packers, going in the many gates of the huge stockyards area, picketing would have been difficult at best. Swift's "Dear John" letters kept the Chicago workers well informed, in sharp contrast to poor communications from the UPWA.

Toward the end of the strike on October 20, the Swift Chicago G. H. Hammond plant was about 20 per cent in operation, as were Moultrie, Georgia, and Jersey City. The Atlanta plant, with its UPWA local, was about 50 per cent in operation, with the whites returning to work and the colored observing the picket lines. The small Swift-Amalgamated Ocala plant in Florida was about 100 per cent in operation. The controversial new Wilson, N.C. Swift plant was 100 per cent in operation. This plant had just recently been organized by the UPWA by a majority of 139 to 98. It was not called out on strike at the start. Later some workers struck. New workers were hired. The UPWA very much wanted this plant included under the master agreement. Swift refused.

The sizable NBPW plants never struck. Thanks to the over-time work of these plants, plus the slight return to work in some UPWA plants, plus supervisor labor, Swift was able to maintain about 40 per cent of its normal output nationwide. This was an important factor in its ability to sustain alone a strike of such duration. The strategic importance to Swift of the sympathetic NBPW is evident. The NBPW signed an interim agreement at the beginning of the strike, and though continuing to negotiate, waited out the seven-week power struggle among Swift, the UPWA, and Amalgamated, finally accepting the southern wage increase. The NBPW would very probably never have received the raise for its southern locals had it not been for the other two unions. This NBPW bargaining pattern points to the less militant bargaining policy of the independent union.

In view of the merger failure between the UPWA and the Amalgamated, and yet the joint bargaining in 1959, it is not surprising that Swift hoped it might get a separate settlement with the Amalgamated. On September 22, 23, and 24, Swift met separately with the Amalgamated. Progress seemed to be made. Then, according to Swift, the UPWA returned and all parties were all back where they started. These events were reported in a Swift employees' letter of October 3:

We told the AMC&BW in our discussions of Wednesday that the developments were most unusual. Never before in the history of our relations with AMC&BW had we reached the point of being told that we had a tentative agreement and it would be recommended, etc., and then had it fail to go through. We have our own ideas on the reason for these actions on the part of the AMC&BW representatives. However, rather than make assumptions, we would only suggest that you think seriously about what has happened and draw your own conclusions.

In unusually strong language, the Amalgamated replied in a public letter of October 6:

Among these putrid weapons in the traditional strike-breaking arsenal of Swift & Company are the honeyed letters to the employees, visits by foremen to the homes of employees, circulation of rumors, public calls for "back-to-work" movements and threats of discharge and replacement.

Swift & Company is evidently using the despicable divide and conquer tactics

... the attempt to create a wide rift between our organization and the UPWA, which have been closely cooperating during all of the negotiations and which cooperation has continued through the duration of the strike.... Make no mistake that the unions involved in this controversy will continue to be in full cooperation until a contract is consummated which we can honorably accept.

Clearly any thought that the Amalgamated and the UPWA might be split was inaccurate. They were in the strike together, though different issues affected each union. The southern differential most affected the Amalgamated. The automation fund, wage-incentives issue, and the Wilson, N.C. plant most affected the UPWA. Yet the 1959 strike by no means advanced the merger of the UPWA and the Amalgamated. The Amalgamated itself had very divided views about the strike and negotiations. As one Amalgamated leader said regarding the UPWA: "The honeymoon's over."

*Final agreement.* The strike ground into its seventh week before settlement was reached. None of the parties showed the inflexibility of the marathon steel strike of 1959. Both Swift and the unions yielded, and the strike ended on Sunday, October 25 after fifty-one days. Swift won its issues of the union shop, voluntary overtime, separation pay, wage-incentives grievances, and exclusion of the Wilson, N.C. plant from the master agreement.

The unions won a compromise on the controversial southern differential and took improvements in vacation and separation pay. As for the South, Swift had begun negotiations by denying any raise or escalator. The settlement gave the southern plants 8½¢ in two years plus the escalator (as opposed to 15¢ and the escalator in the North).

President Lloyd of the Amalgamated and President Helstein of the UPWA stated:

Our unions have negotiated substantial wage increases and substantial improvements in benefits. We did not win all of the objectives we sought, but we have successfully reversed the company's program for heavy wage cuts and drastic reductions in workers' benefits.[4]

Richard Tagg, the Swift negotiator, stated:

The agreements preserve management rights which we believe are essential for efficient operation and best possible service to customers and consumers. These refer to assignment of work to employees, the amount of work performed and scheduling of hours.... There is no provision for a union shop or agency shop. This continues our policy under which employees are free to choose whether they wish to become union members.[5]

Thus both sides could claim gains and losses in the long, bitter, and costly strike, costing the workers around $13,000,000 in lost wages and probably as much for Swift in lost customers and lost profits.

The company's and unions' emotions and perceptions of the issues were clearly different. Swift stated in its employees' letter of September 23: "Swift insists that its management people, not the union leaders, retain the right to run the business.... It appears quite obvious that the union leaders are seeking a part in business management for themselves, more than financial benefits for their members." And again on September 25: "... the union insists that we 'rubber stamp' and accept conditions that are not in the best interest of employees and the company." The unions saw this as arrogant paternalism and stated in their release of October 2: that "They scorned the 'Father knows best' attitude of Swift & Company in its attempt to dictate the terms under which its employees will work."

In our analysis of strikes and allegiance, we found that the attitudes of the packinghouse workers (and very likely any workers) toward strikes are generally not favorable. But these people will strike for issues they, or their leaders, believe in. There is little difference between our three plants in such attitudes.

Also, we found some differences between UPWA Local 28 and Amalgamated Local 78 in their 1956 and especially their 1959 strike behavior. In 1956 both observed the strike. Local 78 was more militant; while Local 28 members might have later crossed the picket lines, this would never have happened in a prolabor town like East St. Louis. In 1959, Local 28 was 85 to 90 per cent back to work, while Local 78 members were 100 per cent on strike.

The reasons for these differences were largely in the type of local leaders, the presence or absence of factional splits, geography, different picket-line strategies, and so forth, though the lesser union allegiance in Chicago played its part. Of course the nonstriking behavior of Kansas City Local 12 was due to the very different labor philosophy and policies of the NBPW people.

In a word, the packinghouse workers' strike behavior, is greatly influenced by the policies and enforcements of key international and local union leaders. The rank and file tend to follow. This does not mean that company allegiance and other company-related attitudes, union allegiance and other union-related attitudes of the rank and file are not important in predicting behavior. They are. But their influence will rather affect the long-run policies of the union. For example, the continuing critical attitudes and behavior of the Gantt group in Chicago toward the International UPWA and District One began in 1948 because of dissatisfaction with interference by the Communist Party in the internal affairs of Local 28. Such attitudes have greatly affected Local 28 for over ten years. The average worker's allegiances are important during a strike, but they must be viewed in the light of other powerful, short-run influences.

CHAPTER XV

# Three Patterns of Dual Allegiance

As we come to the end of this book, we need to bring together what may seem to be a great mass of attitudes and factual data.

Company allegiance appears to be a more complex attitude than union allegiance. By company allegiance we mean partly a summation of the worker's company-related attitudes, and partly the worker's perception of "the company as such." By union allegiance we mean the worker's approval of the idea of having a union to represent him in the plant community. In either case, it was clear that a worker might be dissatisfied in one or several company-related or union-related attitudes and still have company or union allegiance, but he would not have these allegiances and still be dissatisfied in many subordinate attitudes. Company and union allegiance are the unifying concepts of this book. Before giving our own results, let us glance at what others have found.

We will cite twelve studies of dual allegiance with rather similar findings, and four studies that do not find such duality. These studies have used somewhat different research methods, and only a few of them use the same theoretical language, such as "allegiance," which is used in this book. Nevertheless, there is real comparability among them, if we go behind the words to the underlying ideas. All the studies are concerned with the attitudes and behavior of workers regarding both union and company. All are concerned primarily with industrial relations at the local union, local plant level.

First we come to Ross Stagner, co-author of *Illini City*, a University of Illinois study of eight firms and unions in Illinois. Stagner and his colleagues, using the language "attitudinal climate," find that this climate embraces both company and union. Stagner says:

The workers do not accept the inevitability of conflict, nor do they accept the necessity of binding themselves to one group or the other. Apparently they look at the whole relationship, including company and union, as a single unit. They accept the status of dual allegiance and, at least under normal conditions, seem to experience no internal stress as a result.[1]

The *Illini City* studies comes to conclusions very similar to ours.

Lois Dean conducted a study at Cornell of three New York state factories under conditions of conflict. She concludes that:

positive attitudes toward management may be related to positive attitudes toward the union, regardless of the degree of conflict in the union–management relationship.[2]

In Japan, Kunio Odaka, of the University of Tokyo, directed a research study of a Japanese steel mill and a coal mine, "designed to examine worker identification with union and management." His results show that "positive identification with both union and management was the most numerous class of response." [3]

The Seidman group's University of Chicago study of six local unions also comes up with findings similar to our own. Most of the workers were satisfied with both their unions and their companies. For example, Seidman says about the steelworkers in his study:

The steel workers as a group, it is evident, think highly of their company as an employer, and highly of their union as an agency to insure fair treatment.

Also regarding the coal miners:

With only rare exceptions the miners thought highly of their company, most of them pointing to fair treatment as the factor that they liked. "They treat you like human beings" was a common remark.

Yet the miners were also union-minded:

For most of the miners unionism was a normal and natural part of the environment in which they grew up, an institution to be accepted and identified with almost in the way that one's church is accepted.[4]

Seidman states that "most of our good union men, loyal but critical members, and crisis unionists would show dual loyalty" in the sense used in this book, though he does not use our dual allegiance terminology. Interestingly enough, like ourselves, Seidman finds some workers who "have little use for either company or union. . . . Perhaps 'dual disloyalty' is the term that best describes workers such as these."

After surveying local union research in recent years, John R. Coleman describes one characteristic of the union, as a decision-making body, as follows:

The local industrial union is dependent upon the loyalty of members who not only have all of the normal multiplicity of loyalties to be found in our society, but who have a particular loyalty to that very institution, the company, of which the union arose to fight and lived on to restrain.[5]

Coleman goes on to suggest that craft unions "will differ from the industrial unions. . . . Where there is no continuing relationship between one employer and his employees, dual loyalties are presumably unimportant." However, Seidman found a definite loyalty between the plumber and the employing master plumber.[6] At any rate, Coleman supports our findings for the industrial-type unions.

Miller and Young's study of six local unions in Columbus, Ohio, found that:

While some degree of dual allegiance to both employer and union was noted among all groups, skilled workers showed more consciousness of employer problems.[7]

In another study by Miller and Rosen, one large industrial local union, called "Local X," the researchers found "that union 'solidarity' [or prounion attitudes] does not necessarily mean antagonism to employers."[8] This finding is rather similar to our own findings of dual allegiance.

In his study of St. Louis Teamsters' Local 688, Arnold Rose asks whether there is class-struggle thinking among the union members, making them anticompany. But this finding is equivalent to a kind of dual allegiance:

The evidence which arises from this study seems to suggest that there is no inflexible antagonism toward employers on the part of the large majority of workers. If anything, the evidence supports the opposite contention that the union movement is a buttress for the free enterprise system.[9]

The Michigan Survey Research Center's Daniel Katz studied several hundred workers in an automobile plant. His findings continue the same theme of dual allegiance:

The great majority of workers see no fundamental conflict between the aims of the company and the aims of the union. . . . A majority believe that the company is interested in the welfare of the union, and that the union is interested in the welfare of the company. . . . They see no essential reason why both management and the union cannot achieve their goals, but they recognize that each side may have to give up something in the process.[10]

Another Michigan study by Kahn and Tannenbaum of four industrial-type local unions located in the state of Michigan, comes to similar conclusions:

Differences were expected in attitudes toward the companies, but with few exceptions this expectation was not borne out. Active union members as a group do not express more hostility toward the company than do the inactive members.

They both generally feel that the company is cooperating with the union and is being fair to its employees. This perhaps is an expression of dual loyalty on the part of many but not all actives. It is further support to the generally held view that union action is not premised on a basic antipathy toward management.[11]

In 1954, the National Labor Relations Board gave a ruling affecting the Studebaker South Bend plant and its United Auto Workers Local Union manifesting the practical dual allegiance of many workers there. It seems that in 1953, nineteen Studebaker workers drove automobiles other than Studebakers, in violation of an old tradition among UAW Studebaker employees that they drive Studebaker cars only. The company suspended the nineteen employees not because they refused to drive Studebaker cars, but because the other employees refused to work with them. Unfair labor practice charges were filed by one of the dismissed workers but the NLRB cleared the corporation of any such charges. The trial examiner stated:

It appears to stem not only from a sense of loyalty to the company and pride in its product, but from a belief that it is in the economic self-interest of the employees to support the company product.[12]

While this is not a research report, it is an interesting sidelight on dual loyalty.

Finally, John W. Riegel's study of eight manufacturing firms and six local unions found that these companies were fairly well able to interest their employees and union leaders in the financial prospects and success of the companies. From which finding he concludes:

A contest between the managers of a successful or prospectively successful company and the officers of a union for the exclusive loyalty of the company's employees would be a mistake. . . . Although the employees have a partisan interest in increasing their share of the earnings of the company, they have an equal interest in increasing the total of those earnings and in the reinvestment of a portion of the earnings to strengthen further the company's competitive position.[13]

Four studies find a majority of the workers giving their allegiance either to the company or to the union, rather than to both. For example, John LaPoint[14] studied a small Illinois firm whose management was strongly opposed to the union, rendering the union very insecure. Feelings ran high. LaPoint's findings were that workers who favored the company were strongly antiunion. These findings are not surprising in such a situation of conflict.

In a rather similar situation of deepseated opposition and a very insecure union, Francis X. Paone found the *unionized* Western Electric engineers in the famous Hawthorne plant of Chicago to have very strong unilateral allegiance, this time to the union, the independent Council of Western Electric Technical and Professional Employees:

The specific hypothesis explored may be stated as follows: "The industrial condition referred to as dual allegiance will be found to exist among a majority of the unionized Western Electric engineers." This hypothesis was not borne out by the findings which indicated that 43 per cent of the engineers in the sample had union allegiance but no company allegiance while less than 10 per cent had company allegiance but no union allegiance. Only 38 per cent were classifiable under the dual allegiance category. The balance of the engineers had allegiance to neither institution.[15]

Kornhauser, Sheppard, and Mayer's study of Detroit United Auto Workers in 1956 found that most of the workers tended to vote Democratic rather than Republican and that they trusted the union's political recommendations more than management's. They conclude that the unionism of the UAW members is far "from the currently popular philosophy of emerging unity, basic harmony, and dual allegiance."[16] In other words, these workers do not have dual political allegiance.

However, this study needs to be more cautious in some of its generalizations. The UAW is an unusually active union in its political education. Moreover, Detroit auto workers are hardly typical, even of factory workers. In St. Louis, the Rosens[17] found that 45 per cent of the members of the Machinists' Union were adverse to their union telling them for whom to vote. Furthermore, the fact that laboring people tend to vote Democratic, and management people tend to vote Republican, is not new and does not lessen in any way the importance of the inplant dual allegiance we have found so far.

Finally, Eugene Jacobsen's study of some Michigan auto workers[18] resulted in findings not exactly of unilateral allegiance, but that company or union allegiance was very dependent on the worker's degree of participation in the decision-making of the foreman or of the shop steward. Such findings are in line with our own, where we learn that both foremen and stewards tend to be pulled more toward their respective institutions (though having dual allegiance) than the rank-and-file workers.

It is obvious, of course, that findings of dual allegiance will be mostly absent where there is no union in the plant, such as in the Burroughs Adding Machine plants in Detroit or in the Motorola plants in Chicago.

We have found a fair amount of research with highly related findings about dual loyalty or dual allegiance. While it is true that most of this research does not treat the concept in a strike crisis situation, the findings

Table 38. *Dual allegiance (I).*
Random samples of hourly-paid workers in three plants: Chicago — 192; Kansas City — 121; and East St. Louis — 152 (in per cent).

|  | Chicago | Kansas City | East St. Louis |
|---|---|---|---|
| Unfavorable to both company and union | 0 | 0 | 0 |
| Neutral to both | ½ | 0 | 0 |
| Favorable to company and neutral to union | 0 | 4 | 0 |
| Favorable to company and unfavorable to union | 13 | 0 | 0 |
| Favorable to union and neutral to company | 0 | 7 | 0 |
| Favorable to union and unfavorable to company | 13 | 11 | 1 |
| Positively favorable to both — dual allegiance | 73 | 78 | 99 |

|  | Men | | | Women | | |
|---|---|---|---|---|---|---|
|  | Chgo. | K.C. | E.S.L. | Chgo. | K.C. | E.S.L. |
| Unfavorable to both | 0 | 0 | 0 | 0 | 0 | 0 |
| Neutral to both | ½ | 0 | 0 | 0 | 0 | 0 |
| Neutral to company, favorable to union | 4 | 8 | 0 | 0 | 0 | 0 |
| Neutral to union, favorable to company | 8 | 6 | 0 | 4 | 2 | 0 |
| Neutral to union, unfavorable to company | ½ | 0 | 0 | 0 | 0 | 0 |
| Favorable to company, unfavorable to union | 12 | 0 | 0 | 24 | 0 | 1 |
| Favorable to union, unfavorable to company | ½ | 12 | 1 | 0 | 0 | 0 |
| Dual allegiance | 74 | 74 | 99 | 71 | 98 | 99 |

|  | Colored | | | White | | |
|---|---|---|---|---|---|---|
|  | Chgo. | K.C. | E.S.L. | Chgo. | K.C. | E.S.L. |
| Unfavorable to both | 0 | 0 | 0 | 0 | 0 | 0 |
| Neutral to both | 0 | 0 | 0 | 1 | 0 | 0 |
| Neutral to company, favorable to union | 4 | 9 | 0 | 2 | 6 | 0 |
| Neutral to union, favorable to company | 3 | 5 | 0 | 10 | 4 | 0 |
| Neutral to union, unfavorable to company | 1 | 0 | 0 | 0 | 0 | 0 |
| Favorable to company, unfavorable to union | 10 | 0 | 0 | 20 | 0 | 0 |
| Favorable to union, unfavorable to company | 1 | 18 | 2 | 0 | 6 | 0 |
| Dual allegiance | 80 | 68 | 98 | 67 | 84 | 100 |

Table 38. *Continued*

|  | Short service | | | Middle service | | | Long service | | |
|---|---|---|---|---|---|---|---|---|---|
|  | *Chgo.* | *K.C.* | *E.S.L.* | *Chgo.* | *K.C.* | *E.S.L.* | *Chgo.* | *K.C.* | *E.S.L.* |
| Unfavorable to both | 0 | 0 | 0 | 0 | 0 | 0 | 0 | 0 | 0 |
| Neutral to both | 0 | 0 | 0 | 2 | 0 | 0 | 0 | 0 | 0 |
| Neutral to company, favorable to union | 5 | 11 | 0 | 4 | 0 | 0 | 2 | 6 | 0 |
| Neutral to union, favorable to company | 5 | 6 | 0 | 5 | 0 | 0 | 11 | 8 | 0 |
| Neutral to union, unfavorable to company | 2 | 0 | 0 | 0 | 0 | 0 | 0 | 0 | 0 |
| Favorable to company, unfavorable to union | 7 | 0 | 0 | 10 | 0 | 0 | 27 | 0 | 1 |
| Favorable to union, unfavorable to company | 2 | 17 | 3 | 0 | 9 | 0 | 0 | 0 | 0 |
| Dual allegiance | 79 | 66 | 97 | 79 | 91 | 100 | 60 | 86 | 99 |

are quite significant, though further research for crisis situations is still called for. Our own analysis of allegiance in relation to the 1956 and 1959 meat packing strikes should be a step in this direction. Now let us look to our own findings and see how they compare with others.

We bring together our two basic concepts into one final and unifying concept, dual allegiance. The heart of our entire three-plant, three-union study can be found in the following two tables. Table 38 is concerned with the average, hourly-paid packinghouse worker.

The most important figures in Table 38 are those showing dual allegiance. Here we find that the dual allegiance of 73 per cent of the Chicago packinghouse workers is not only repeated, but intensified in both of the subsequent studies done three years later. Seventy-eight per cent of the Kansas City packinghouse workers have dual allegiance, and in East St. Louis, the very high number of 99 per cent have it. In spite of differing conditions, plants, and especially local unions, we find that dual allegiance persists as our main finding.

There are evident differences in the amount of dual allegiance between the three plants. The reason for the lowest score in Chicago lies in the fact that about 13 per cent of the workforce have allegiance to the company, but fail to have union allegiance, while another 13 per cent have opposite views. Kansas City is somewhat higher, with 78 per cent of the hourly-paid people having dual allegiance. But there, the picture is different. Eighteen per cent of the people are anticompany, but prounion. Four per cent are antiunion and procompany. In other words, while the people not having dual allegiance in Chicago are evenly divided in their company and union view, the Kansas City workers without dual allegiance are mostly lacking in company allegiance. Their union allegiance is quite strong, significantly more than their company allegiance, while union allegiance in Chicago is rather weak.

When we come to East St. Louis the picture is almost completely different: 99 per cent of the workforce have allegiance to both company and union (though again, significantly more to the union). Here we find no dissatisfied minorities to bring down our high scores of both company and union allegiance.

Which groups tend to bring down the dual allegiance findings and for what reasons? First, regarding the sex of the workers: We note in Table 38 that there is very little difference by sex in the dual allegiance of the Chicago workers, but a very large difference among the Kansas City employees. In Kansas City, the women are definitely more satisfied with both their company and their union. In Chicago most of the women (especially the whites) are deficient in union allegiance.

Secondly, race influences dual allegiance but in exactly opposite directions in Chicago and Kansas City. In Chicago, it is the colored who have the most dual allegiance; the whites have less because they are less union-minded. In Kansas City, it is the whites who have the most dual allegiance; the colored have less mostly because they are less company-minded. In either case, we see that race makes an important difference. The opposite directions of its influence bring out dramatically the very different situations of the two plants and the two local unions regarding their white and colored social relations.

Thirdly, length of service as a factor also works in opposite directions in Kansas City and Chicago. In Chicago it is the old-timers who are lowest in dual allegiance because of their dissatisfaction with unionism. In Kansas City, it is primarily the young workers who are lowest because of their dissatisfaction with the company.

In a word, we find that sex, race, and service are important variables affecting the attitudes of the workers, and in opposite directions. The reasons for these opposite influences should be clear. For instance, Local 28 in Chicago is a colored-dominated union in a colored-majority plant, and the whites are dissatisfied — therefore their dual allegiance is lower. In Kansas City, Local 12 is a white-dominated union in a white-majority plant — consequently some colored are dissatisfied and have less dual allegiance.

We should not oversimplify this. There are other factors, such as the presence of a UPWA-CIO minority in the Kansas City plant, anxious to cooperate with the UPWA International's efforts to raid NBPW Local 12. It is not just because many people in this UPWA minority are colored that they have less company allegiance, but also because they are being influenced by the anticompany propaganda of the UPWA. In East St. Louis, we have a white-dominated local and a fairly large white majority in the plant, yet the Negro workers do have dual allegiance.

To give life to these statistics about dual allegiance, let us listen to one of the packinghouse workers expressing dual allegiance in his own words. Millwright Charles Renault is a rather well satisfied employee of the Swift East St. Louis plant and a member of Local 78. Renault is in his early thirties and has had a high school education. He definitely has dual allegiance, though his union allegiance is somewhat stronger than his company allegiance.

*Interviewer:* And then the company as a whole, Charles, how about Swift's as a place to work? You know, putting it all together.

*Renault:* Well, years ago, back before I went in the service, I used to think it was pretty lousy. I mean I don't pull no bones about nothing. I mean I'll just tell you how I feel about it. But you begin to grow up and you begin to get interested in your company, begin to realize things that, how the plant operates, they have to make money, and you see some of their problems, too. You know. And as a whole, I believe we have some pretty good conditions here. Now the union has brought a lot of these conditions in here. Packin' house used to be rough. They used to be, people had little education an' they only knew nothin' but work, you know. Now whether the union has brought all of it in, now I've, I was here since they had the company union.

*Interviewer:* How did that work?

*Renault:* I just caught the tail end of that. But ah, I couldn't tell you much about it, I mean, they were just gettin' established. And I was just a young fella at that time, eighteen years old, but I did not hear that it wasn't the best thing, because naturally people are human! Well a company union, they're gonna look out for theirself first and then the individual next, you know. That's the way I would say it, you know.

*Interviewer:* Sure. But the union has helped, huh?

*Renault:* Oh, I think they have, and it's proven out in a, well, we've had a union. I'd say around twelve years, I guess, somewhere in that vicinity, I would, somewhere in there. And a, things have been better.

Another important way of inquiring into dual allegiance at our three plants is to seek out the attitudes of the key people in company and unions.

We see in Table 39 that a remarkably high percentage of the union leaders in Kansas City and East St. Louis have dual allegiance: 100 per cent! Although these people are official representatives of unionism (therefore certainly having union allegiance), they all have company allegiance

Table 39. *Dual allegiance (II)* (*in per cent*).

| Union leaders | Chicago UPWA | Kansas City NBPW | Kansas City UPWA | East St. Louis AMC & BW |
|---|---|---|---|---|
| Favorable to union and neutral to company | 34 | 0 | 9 | 0 |
| Favorable to union and unfavorable to company | 0 | 0 | 55 | 0 |
| Positively favorable to both — dual allegiance | 66 | 100 | 36 | 100 |

| Union stewards | Chicago | Kansas City | East St. Louis |
|---|---|---|---|
| Favorable to union and unfavorable to company | 12 | 0 | 7 |
| Positively favorable to both — dual allegiance | 88 | 100 | 93 |

| Foremen | Chicago | Kansas City | East St. Louis |
|---|---|---|---|
| Neutral to company and favorable to union | 3 | 0 | 4 |
| Neutral to union and favorable to company | 12 | 0 | 12 |
| Neutral to union and unfavorable to company | 3 | 0 | 0 |
| Favorable to company and unfavorable to union | 25 | 10 | 12 |
| Positively favorable to both — dual allegiance | 57 | 90 | 72 |

too. Not to our surprise, we find the Chicago union leaders much lower in dual allegiance: 66 per cent. The reason, of course, lies in their critical views of Swift.

The union stewards differ somewhat from their leaders. There is some political unity among the local union leaders actually in office. But opposing factions are often represented among the steward body. Some of the stewards in Chicago, for instance, were rightwingers with no doctrinaire opposition to the company. Hence the Chicago stewards had more dual allegiance than their own leaders.

The dual allegiance of the opposite leadership group, the foremen, is also significant. We might expect the foremen to be antiunion. We saw before that most of the foremen profess union endorsement. Here in Table 39 we see that 90 per cent of the Kansas City foremen, 72 per cent of the East St. Louis foremen, and 57 per cent of the Chicago foremen have dual allegiance. Why does Kansas City stand so far out in the lead? Because only 10 per cent of the Kansas City foremen fail to support the need for unionism in their plant (and most of them, of course, have company allegiance). This figure compares with 24 per cent of the East St. Louis foremen. The reason for the much lower dual allegiance of the Chicago foremen is because a scant majority of these men feel that having a union in the plant is a good thing. They were so dissatisfied with the conduct of Local 28 that many failed to have any union allegiance at all.

Most of the foremen in all three plants have allegiance to the company. It is regarding the union where they differ. The differences of dual allegiance among the foremen are much greater than the differences among the local union leaders.

An important question now arises: If we are to rank the three plants and locals as to their dual allegiance, what weight shall we give to the hourly-paid, rank-and-file employees, and what weight to the union leaders and to the foremen? There is no single answer or method. Our two sets of findings differ. East St. Louis is far in the lead in dual allegiance among the workforce as a whole, with 99 per cent. But if we consider the union leaders, we see no significant difference between East St. Louis and Kansas City, both having 100 per cent. Finally, if we take the foremen, Kansas City is in the lead, with 90 per cent. In every case, of course, Chicago is in third place.

Probably the most important percentage is that representing the hourly-paid workforce as a whole. This represents the largest group of people. In many ways it is the most important group. Yet we cannot ignore the fact that dual allegiance follows a different pattern among the leader groups who have influenced and will influence the thinking and behavior of the workforce as a whole. We have said that East St. Louis Local 78 people were the most satisfied and had the best industrial relations. Our findings on dual allegiance confirm this, with the exception of the foremen's dual allegiance (best in Kansas City), and the union leaders' dual allegiance (the same in both locals).

The differing patterns of dual allegiance among the foremen and union leaders bring out more than anything else the different status and security of the three local unions. Local 28 is the least secure. Local 12 is very cooperative with Swift (and the Kansas City foremen know this). The local is secure, but is threatened by a UPWA minority group. This threat makes for a certain instability in rank-and-file union relations. Consider, for instance, the very low dual allegiance of the CIO leaders in Kansas City: 36 per cent.

Taking all these factors and putting them together: the dual allegiance of the rank and file, plus the other company-related and union-related attitudes of the workforce and of the union leaders and foremen, plus the security of the unions, our conclusion is that the people at East St. Louis–Local 78 are the most satisfied with both company and union. It is true that Local 12 has never had a strike, while Local 78 has had three. It is true that the Kansas City foremen are more satisfied with Local 12 than the East St. Louis foremen are with Local 78. It is true that Local 12 has done more for its Negro members than Local 78 has done. Yet because of the many other facts, and attitudes scores favoring East St. Louis, we conclude that the packinghouse workers themselves are most satisfied with Swift East St. Louis and with Amalgamated Local 78. Chicago Swift–Local 28 has the least satisfied people.

While these three allegiances are the unifying theme of this book, they are only part of the story. Company allegiance does not perfectly sum up all the company-related attitudes, nor union allegiance the union-related attitudes, nor does dual allegiance perfectly describe the interrelations between the two. This does not mean that the dual-allegiance theory fails to make an important contribution to understanding the American worker as employee and unionist. It does. But we cannot expect a single theory to explain completely the complex relationships of the modern industrial plant. That is precisely why we have brought so much other data into our three comparative case studies.

For instance, we studied carefully those few company- and union-related attitudes which involved problems and which were not always in line with the company and union allegiance we generally found.

Fortunately, we were able to study dual allegiance over time and especially during the crisis situation of the 1956 and 1959 strikes. We saw other powerful influences over the short-run behavior of the workers during those strikes: The fact of triple unionism in the meat packing industry; the stalled merger between the UPWA and the Amalgamated; the very different policies and philosophies of the United Packinghouse Workers, the Amalgamated, and the Independent Brotherhood affecting the calling or not calling of the strikes; differences in the local union leaders, especially regarding factions; differences in the cities, and so forth — all these factors, in addition to company and union allegiances, affected the packinghouse workers.

The relative amounts of the three dual allegiances would not have perfectly predicted the 1956 strike for example. Kansas City had less dual allegiance than East St. Louis, mostly because the Kansas City workers had slightly less company allegiance. Yet Kansas City did not strike and East St. Louis Local 78 did. The main reason for this short-run difference lies in the different policies of the two international unions.

But the allegiance attitudes do affect the long-run activities of the unions. We recall the formation of the Gantt faction in Local 28 and the continued resistance in Local 12 to the UPWA raiding.

Strike behavior is only part of industrial relations. Turnover, productivity, grievances, race relations, and other matters are equally important in both the short run and the long run. In these areas we have seen definite relationships between the packinghouse workers' attitudes, allegiances, and the behavior involved.

The three allegiances, along with the other company- and union-related attitudes, are only a part of the story. But they are an important part.

SIX PROBLEM AREAS

We found most of the packinghouse workers clearly satisfied with company and union, but we noticed a few attitudes on both sides that were unfavorable, three regarding the company, and three regarding the unions. More research and improvement in these six areas would be fruitful.

As for the company, the workers mostly had misunderstanding or mistrust of the Swift wage-incentive system. The white men were scarcely optimistic about their chances for advancement and the Negroes were definitely dissatisfied with equality of opportunity. Finally, a majority of the employees did not want their children to come to work in the Swift packinghouse.

This latter attitude points to an absence among many workers of pride in the dignity and importance of their work. Difficult as it may be, improvement in this area should prove especially rewarding.

As for the union, dissatisfaction with the UPWA leadership was common among many workers. This was pronounced in Local 28. But in the locals of the other two unions, we also noted distrust of the UPWA, giving one clue, incidentally, to the failure of the merger. A major reason for this distrust was the reluctance of the packinghouse workers to have slowdowns and strikes. The overwhelming desire of the workers to have their problems settled peaceably over the bargaining table rather than militantly over the picket line is the second problem area concerning the unions.

The third area concerns the workers' behavior more than their attitudes; namely, their lack of participation in union affairs. We have seen good reasons for this inactivity and the concern, especially of the Amalgamated, about improving the participation of its members. The problem remains less acute for the three locals of this study than for many other local unions, but it is still a problem if democracy and health are to prosper in the three locals.

Finally, an additional problem-area was shown by this research: the need for wise and mature leadership of the international unions, especially of the UPWA. If the merger between the UPWA and the Amalgamated is off for good, and if the National Brotherhood maintains itself, then the meat packing industry will have three international unions dividing the jurisdiction. This situation need not make for instability, or for the companies playing one union against the other. As a matter of fact, the major companies of the industry have never bargained as one, any more than the three unions have done.

If the UPWA can rid itself of some hotheads and radicals, if the Amalgamated can preserve its democracy and leadership, if the NBPW can become more of a typical trade union even though independent, then greater industrial peace can come to the meat packing industry.

On the other hand, Swift may need to take a more understanding attitude toward the trade unions it deals with. One case in point is the company's crusading and rigid stand on the right-to-work issue. In addition, we cannot ignore the growing competition in the meat packing industry, especially among the small independents. Profit margins could surely be improved and this would improve many management attitudes. While this research has not centered on a study of the politics and problems of the three international unions involved, nor on the problems and policies of the Swift general office in Chicago, changes in some of these matters, along with the six problem areas mentioned earlier, should encourage even better industrial relations than the good local relations we have actually found.

Have we done what we set out to do in this book? We sought a better understanding of the thoughts, fears, aspirations, and behavior of some American workers in their dual role of employees and unionists. Our approach was an industrial "gestalt," studying the whole range of the packinghouse workers' attitudes in their work life, rather than one part. There are omissions, inevitable in a single research project. We have not studied the decision-making process of top management and union leaders, especially in collective bargaining. We have not investigated the politics or the leisure time activities of the workers. But we have tried to take an overview of the inplant life of the workers.

The unifying theme for company-related attitudes was company allegiance, and for union-related attitudes, union allegiance. We have sought better understanding of how these apparently opposing allegiances might interact.

We have especially wanted to see what would happen to allegiance in a time of crisis. The opportunity was given to us, quite without advance planning, by the 1956 and 1959 strikes. The allegiance concept alone could not give a complete explanation of the packinghouse workers' behavior during those strikes. The important influences from the Swift general office and from the international unions were also needed. Admitting its limitations, there was fruitfulness in the dual-allegiance concept even for a time of crisis. Dual allegiance was not simply an absence of class-warfare thinking among the workers. It was a positive concept giving us a more unified understanding of working people, and clues especially to their long-range behavior.

Using a comparison of three case studies we sought to clarify dual allegiance by examining the differences we might find. Differences there were, but they do not obscure the repeated finding of dual allegiance in all three plants.

As we reflect over our dealings with these packinghouse workers — some of whom the author has known for ten years, and whose children he has seen grow up into manhood and womanhood — we are led to ask: What portrait of the American worker have these men and women painted by their words in this book?

Like any aspect of life, it is a picture with light and shadow. The light is found in the roots of industrial peace growing sturdily in Chicago, Kansas City, and East St. Louis — roots shown by our repeated findings of dual allegiance among the workers there. It will be up to the top leaders of both company and unions to be more aware of those roots and to encourage their healthy growth.

The shadow is in the problem-areas. More than anything, there is need to convert the dual allegiance we found, into deeper and more meaningful dual loyalties. Regarding Swift, this will mean helping to develop among the workers a true pride in the dignity of their work with the company. Regarding the three unions, it will mean the workers' active participation in the work and life of the union.

Some say that our mass-production factory system on the one hand, and the large impersonal union on the other, make deep, dual loyalties very difficult. Perhaps. But here is the precise challenge to the top leaders of both company and unions: to show that factory work and dignity are not incompatible, that large organizations, and individual freedom and participation, can still be reconciled.

# APPENDIXES
# NOTES

APPENDIX I

# Statistical Tables

Appendix Table I. *Attitudes toward the company.*
Random sample of workers in three plants, Chicago — 192; Kansas City — 121; East St. Louis — 152, stratified by service, sex, and race, including union leaders and foremen.

|  | Chicago | Kansas City | East St. Louis |
|---|---|---|---|
| Men | 1.6 | 2.0 | 1.5 |
| Women | 1.3 | 1.3 | 1.4 |
| Colored | 1.7 | 2.2 | 1.6 |
| White | 1.5 | 1.6 | 1.4 |
| Under 2 years' service |  |  | 1.7 |
| Short service | 1.7 | 2.1 | 1.7 |
| Middle service | 1.6 | 1.8 | 1.4 |
| Long service | 1.4 | 1.5 | 1.2 |
| *All workers* | 1.6 | 1.9 | 1.5 |
| Foremen | 1.6 | 1.4 | 1.3 |
| Local 28 leaders, right wing | 1.6 |  |  |
| Local 28 leaders, left wing | 2.3 |  |  |
| Local 28 stewards | 2.0 |  |  |
| Local 12 leaders |  | 1.4 |  |
| Local 12 stewards |  | 1.5 |  |
| (CIO leaders) |  | 3.1 |  |
| Local 78 leaders |  |  | 1.3 |
| Local 78 stewards |  |  | 1.8 |
| *Attitude scale* |  |  |  |
| Very favorable | 1.0 |  |  |
| Favorable | 2.0 |  |  |
| Neutral | 3.0 |  |  |
| Unfavorable | 4.0 |  |  |
| Very unfavorable | 5.0 |  |  |

## APPENDIX I

Appendix Table II. *Attitudes toward the foremen.*
Random, stratified sample of 192 workers in Chicago, 121 in Kansas City and 152 in East St. Louis, plus union leaders and stewards.

| Group[a] | Chicago | Kansas City | East St. Louis |
|---|---|---|---|
| White men under 2 years' service |  |  | 1.4 |
| White men short service | 1.8 | 2.2 | 2.0 |
| White men middle service | 1.8 | 1.9 | 1.7 |
| Colored men under 2 years' service |  |  | 2.2 |
| Colored men short service | 2.0 | 2.6 | 1.4 |
| Colored men middle service | 1.7 | 2.1 | 1.9 |
| Colored men long service | 1.6 | 1.2 | 1.7 |
| White women under 2 years' service |  |  | 2.0 |
| White women short service | 1.4 | 1.3 | 1.8 |
| White women middle service | 1.9 | 1.7 | 2.6 |
| White women long service | 1.6 | 2.2 | 1.5 |
| Colored women short service | 1.3 | 1.3 |  |
| Colored women middle service | 1.3 | 1.9 |  |
| Colored women long service | 1.5 |  |  |
| Men | 1.9 | 2.1 | 1.7 |
| Women | 1.5 | 1.5 | 2.0 |
| Colored |  | 2.1 | 1.7 |
| White |  | 1.9 | 1.9 |
| Short service |  | 2.2 | 1.7 |
| Middle service |  | 1.9 | 1.9 |
| Long service |  | 1.7 | 1.7 |
| *All workers* | 1.8 | 2.0 | 1.8 |
| Local 28 leaders, left wing | 2.3 |  |  |
| Local 28 leaders, right wing | 1.6 |  |  |
| Local 28 stewards | 2.3 |  |  |
| Local 12 leaders |  | 2.0 |  |
| Local 12 stewards |  | 1.9 |  |
| (CIO leaders) |  | 3.5 |  |
| Local 78 leaders |  |  | 1.6 |
| Local 78 stewards |  |  | 1.8 |

(Scale: 1.0 very favorable to 5.0 very unfavorable)

[a] This detailed breakdown of our data by sex, race, and service is given here simply to illustrate the sources for our analysis in the text. Such data has been omitted from other tables.

STATISTICAL TABLES

Appendix Table III. *Attitudes toward the job.*
Random sample of workers in three plants: Chicago — 192; Kansas City — 121; East St. Louis — 152, stratified by service, sex, and race; also union leaders and foremen.

| Group | Chicago | Kansas City | East St. Louis |
|---|---|---|---|
| *All hourly-paid workers* | 1.8 | 1.9 | 1.6 |
| Men | 1.8 | 2.0 | 1.6 |
| Women | 1.5 | 1.4 | 1.6 |
| Colored | 1.8 | 2.4 | 1.7 |
| White | 1.8 | 1.6 | 1.6 |
| Short service |  | 2.0 | 1.7 |
| Middle service |  | 1.8 | 1.5 |
| Long service |  | 1.5 | 1.7 |
| Foremen | 1.9 | 2.0 | 1.8 |
| Local 28 leaders, left wing | 2.3 |  |  |
| Local 28 leaders, right wing | 1.8 |  |  |
| Local 12 leaders |  | 1.6 |  |
| Local 12 stewards |  | 1.4 |  |
| (CIO leaders) |  | 2.9 |  |
| Local 78 leaders |  |  | 1.6 |
| Local 78 stewards |  |  | 1.7 |

(Scale: 1.0 very favorable, 5.0 very unfavorable)

Appendix Table IV. *Attitudes toward the gang.*
Random sample of workers in three plants: Chicago — 192; Kansas City — 121; East St. Louis — 152, stratified by service, sex, and race; also union leaders and foremen.

| Group | Chicago | Kansas City | East St. Louis |
|---|---|---|---|
| *All hourly-paid workers* |  | 1.9 | 1.9 |
| Men |  | 1.8 | 1.9 |
| Women |  | 2.1 | 1.8 |
| Colored |  | 1.7 | 1.8 |
| White |  | 2.0 | 1.9 |
| Under 2 years' service |  |  | 1.9 |
| Short service |  | 1.9 | 1.8 |
| Middle service |  | 2.1 | 1.9 |
| Long service |  | 1.6 | 1.8 |
| Foremen | 2.4 | 1.7 | 1.7 |
| Local 12 leaders |  | 1.6 |  |
| Local 12 stewards |  | 1.7 |  |
| Local 78 leaders |  |  | 1.4 |
| Local 78 stewards |  |  | 1.8 |

### Appendix Table V. *Attitudes toward pay.*

Random sample of workers in two plants: Kansas City — 121; East St. Louis — 152, stratified by service, sex, and race; including union leaders and foremen.

| Group | Kansas City | East St. Louis |
|---|---|---|
| *All hourly-paid workers* | 2.1 | 1.9 |
| Men | 2.2 | 1.9 |
| Women | 1.5 | 1.6 |
| Colored | 2.4 | 2.0 |
| White | 1.9 | 1.8 |
| Under 2 years' service | | 2.1 |
| Short service | 2.4 | 2.0 |
| Middle service | 1.9 | 1.9 |
| Long service | 1.7 | 1.7 |
| Foremen | 2.0 | 2.0 |
| Local 12 leaders | 1.8 | |
| Local 12 stewards | 1.6 | |
| (CIO leaders) | 3.0 | |
| Local 78 leaders | | 1.7 |
| Local 78 stewards | | 2.3 |

### Appendix Table VI. *Attitudes toward working conditions.*

Random sample of workers in two plants: Kansas City — 121; East St. Louis — 152, stratified by service, sex and race; including union leaders and foremen (in per cent).

| Group | Favorable K.C. | Favorable E.S.L. | Neutral K.C. | Neutral E.S.L. | Unfavorable K.C. | Unfavorable E.S.L. |
|---|---|---|---|---|---|---|
| *All hourly-paid workers* | 73 | 81 | 3 | 0 | 24 | 19 |
| Men | 68 | 78 | 4 | 0 | 28 | 22 |
| Women | 92 | 93 | 0 | 0 | 8 | 7 |
| Colored | 53 | 81 | 8 | 0 | 39 | 19 |
| White | 83 | 80 | 0 | 0 | 17 | 20 |
| Short service | 63 | 81 | 6 | 0 | 31 | 19 |
| Middle service | 68 | 83 | 0 | 0 | 32 | 17 |
| Long service | 94 | 70 | 0 | 0 | 6 | 24 |
| Foremen [a] | 84 | 100 | 11 | 0 | 5 | 0 |
| Local 12 leaders | 63 | — | 0 | — | 37 | — |
| (CIO leaders) | 22 | — | 0 | — | 78 | — |
| Local 78 leaders | — | 33 | — | 0 | — | 67 |

[a] Estimated.

## STATISTICAL TABLES

Appendix Table VII. *Attitudes toward the suggestion system.*

Random sample of workers in two plants: Kansas City — 121; East St. Louis — 152, stratified by service, sex, and race; including union leaders and foremen.

| Group | Kansas City | East St. Louis |
|---|---|---|
| *All hourly-paid workers* | 2.9 | 2.4 |
| Men | 2.9 | 2.3 |
| Women | 2.5 | 2.6 |
| Colored | 2.9 | 2.1 |
| White | 2.8 | 2.5 |
| Under 2 years' service |  | 2.5 |
| Short service | 3.0 | 2.3 |
| Middle service | 2.7 | 2.3 |
| Long service | 2.7 | 2.5 |
| Foremen | 1.3 | 2.6 |
| Local 12 leaders | 3.0 |  |
| Local 12 stewards | 2.8 |  |
| (CIO leaders) | 4.5 |  |
| Local 78 leaders |  | 3.4 |
| Local 78 stewards |  | 2.9 |

Appendix Table VIII. *Attitudes toward advancement.*

Random sample of workers in three plants: Chicago — 192; Kansas City — 121; East St. Louis — 152, stratified by service, sex, and race; including union leaders and foremen (in per cent).

| Group | Favorable | | | Neutral | | | Unfavorable | | |
|---|---|---|---|---|---|---|---|---|---|
|  | *Chgo.* | *K.C.* | *E.S.L.* | *Chgo.* | *K.C.* | *E.S.L.* | *Chgo.* | *K.C.* | *E.S.L.* |
| *All men* | 43 | 44 | 56 | 7 | 3 | 3 | 50 | 53 | 41 |
| White men | 42[a] | 60 | 70 | 15[a] | 1 | 6 | 43[a] | 39 | 24 |
| Colored men | 43[a] | 23 | 42 | 5[a] | 8 | 0 | 52[a] | 69 | 58 |
| Men under 2 years' service |  |  | 60 |  |  | 0 |  |  | 40 |
| Men short service |  | 38 | 53 |  | 0 | 0 |  | 62 | 47 |
| Men middle service |  | 44 | 48 |  | 5 | 7 |  | 51 | 45 |
| Men long service |  | 53 | 71 |  | 6 | 0 |  | 41 | 29 |
| Foremen | 52 | 72 | 88 | 18 | 0 | 0 | 30 | 28 | 12 |
| Local 12 leaders |  | 50 |  |  | 0 |  |  | 50 |  |
| Local 12 stewards |  | 25 |  |  | 0 |  |  | 75 |  |
| (CIO leaders) |  | 10 |  |  | 0 |  |  | 90 |  |
| Local 78 leaders |  |  | 57 |  |  | 0 |  |  | 43 |
| Local 78 stewards |  |  | 33 |  |  | 0 |  |  | 67 |

[a] Estimated.

# APPENDIX I

Appendix Table IX. *Attitudes toward equal opportunity.*

Random sample of workers in two plants: Kansas City — 55; East St. Louis — 56, stratified by service, sex and race; including 21 union leaders and stewards (in per cent).

| Group | Favorable K.C. | Favorable E.S.L. | Neutral K.C. | Neutral E.S.L. | Unfavorable K.C. | Unfavorable E.S.L. |
|---|---|---|---|---|---|---|
| Colored men under 2 years' service |  | 50 |  | 0 |  | 50 |
| Colored men short service | 21 | 36 | 0 | 0 | 79 | 64 |
| Colored men middle service | 23 | 21 | 8 | 0 | 69 | 79 |
| Colored men long service | 14 | 29 | 0 | 0 | 86 | 71 |
| Colored women short service | 13 |  | 0 |  | 87 |  |
| Colored women middle service | 0 |  | 0 |  | 100 |  |
| Colored men | 21 | 28 | 2 | 0 | 77 | 72 |
| Colored women | 10 |  | 0 |  | 90 |  |
| NBPW leaders (colored) | 0 |  | 0 |  | 100 |  |
| (CIO leaders) | 0 |  | 0 |  | 100 |  |
| Local 78 leaders & stewards (colored) |  | 0 |  | 0 |  | 100 |

Appendix Table X. *Attitudes toward the Standards System.*

Random sample of workers in three plants: Chicago — 192; Kansas City — 121; East St. Louis — 152, stratified by service, sex and race; including union leaders and foremen.

| Group | Understanding-trust Chgo. | K.C. | E.S.L. | Neutral Chgo. | K.C. | E.S.L. | Misunderstanding-distrust Chgo. | K.C. | E.S.L. |
|---|---|---|---|---|---|---|---|---|---|
| *All hourly-paid workers,* weighted totals | 25 | 47 | 66 | 20 | 6 | 6 | 55 | 47 | 28 |
| Men | 23 | 41 | 66 | 19 | 6 | 7 | 58 | 53 | 27 |
| Women | 36 | 83 | 69 | 28 | 0 | 0 | 36 | 17 | 31 |
| Colored |  | 40 | 72 |  | 13 | 0 |  | 47 | 28 |
| White |  | 51 | 63 |  | 2 | 9 |  | 47 | 28 |
| Under 2 years' service |  |  | 56 |  |  | 3 |  |  | 41 |
| Short service |  | 38 | 62 |  | 8 | 0 |  | 54 | 38 |
| Middle service |  | 42 | 68 |  | 4 | 11 |  | 54 | 21 |
| Long service |  | 70 | 70 |  | 3 | 4 |  | 27 | 26 |
| Foremen |  | 67 | 74 |  | 5 | 0 |  | 28 | 26 |
| Local 28 leaders, left wing | 14 |  |  | 0 |  |  | 86 |  |  |
| Local 28 stewards, left wing | 6 |  |  | 13 |  |  | 81 |  |  |
| Local 12 leaders |  | 44 |  |  | 0 |  |  | 56 |  |
| Local 12 stewards |  | 50 |  |  | 0 |  |  | 50 |  |
| (CIO leaders) |  | 0 |  |  | 0 |  |  | 100 |  |
| Local 78 leaders |  |  | 14 |  |  | 0 |  |  | 86 |
| Local 78 stewards |  |  | 31 |  |  | 0 |  |  | 69 |

Appendix Table XI. *Percentages of workers on various types of standards application.* 152 East St. Louis-Swift workers; 121 Kansas City-Swift workers (1953–1954).

|  | East St. Louis ||||  Kansas City ||||
|---|---|---|---|---|---|---|---|---|
|  | Individ- ual | Small group | Large group | Non- standard | Individ- ual | Small group | Large group | Non- standard |
| *Negro men* | | | | | | | | |
| Under 2 yrs. | 14 | 7 | 79 | 0 | — | — | — | — |
| Short service | 7 | 36 | 57 | 0 | 0 | 14 | 86 | 0 |
| Middle service | 7 | 36 | 50 | 7 | 7 | 21 | 65 | 7 |
| Long service | 0 | 7 | 86 | 7 | 0 | 29 | 71 | 0 |
| *White men* | | | | | | | | |
| Under 2 yrs. | 22 | 7 | 64 | 7 | — | — | — | — |
| Short service | 22 | 14 | 57 | 7 | 21 | 7 | 43 | 29 |
| Middle service | 36 | 21 | 29 | 14 | 43 | 14 | 43 | 0 |
| Long service | 7 | 36 | 36 | 21 | 29 | 43 | 21 | 7 |
| *White women* | | | | | | | | |
| Under 2 yrs. | 20 | 50 | 10 | 20 | — | — | — | — |
| Short service | 10 | 50 | 40 | 0 | 25 | 25 | 38 | 12 |
| Middle service | 30 | 30 | 30 | 10 | 50 | 0 | 50 | 0 |
| Long service | 20 | 60 | 10 | 10 | 38 | 12 | 50 | 0 |

Appendix Table XII. *Attitudes toward having their children work at the packinghouse. Random sample of workers in three plants: Chicago — 192; Kansas City — 121; East St. Louis — 152, stratified by service, sex and race; including union leaders and foremen (in per cent).*

| Group | Favorable ||| Neutral ||| Unfavorable |||
|---|---|---|---|---|---|---|---|---|---|
|  | Chgo. | K.C. | E.S.L. | Chgo. | K.C. | E.S.L. | Chgo. | K.C. | E.S.L. |
| All workers, weighted totals | 18 | 26 | 47 | 9 | 8 | 7 | 73 | 66 | 46 |
| Colored men |  | 14 | 57 |  | 6 | 6 |  | 80 | 37 |
| White men |  | 31 | 45 |  | 6 | 11 |  | 63 | 44 |
| Colored women |  | 27 |  |  | 0 |  |  | 73 |  |
| White women |  | 32 | 30 |  | 16 | 0 |  | 52 | 70 |
| All men |  | 24 | 51 |  | 6 | 8 |  | 70 | 41 |
| All women |  | 31 | 30 |  | 16 | 0 |  | 53 | 70 |
| All under 2 years' service |  |  | 21 |  |  | 18 |  |  | 61 |
| All short service |  | 16 | 34 |  | 9 | 9 |  | 75 | 57 |
| All middle service |  | 17 | 54 |  | 9 | 9 |  | 74 | 37 |
| All long service |  | 52 | 55 |  | 0 | 0 |  | 48 | 45 |
| Foremen | 33 | 36 | 32 | 17 | 19 | 8 | 50 | 45 | 60 |
| Local 12 union leaders[a] |  | 17 |  |  | 17 |  |  | 66 |  |
| Local 12 union stewards |  | 17 |  |  | 0 |  |  | 83 |  |
| (CIO leaders) |  | 0 |  |  | 0 |  |  | 100 |  |
| Local 78 union leaders |  |  | 50 |  |  | 33 |  |  | 17 |
| Local 78 union stewards |  |  | 20 |  |  | 0 |  |  | 80 |

[a] Estimated.

## APPENDIX I

Appendix Table XIII. *Attitudes of union allegiance.*

Random sample of workers in three plants: Chicago — 192; Kansas City — 121; East St. Louis — 152, stratified by service, sex and race; including union leaders and foremen.

| Group | Chicago | Kansas City | East St. Louis |
|---|---|---|---|
| *All hourly-paid workers* | 2.0 | 1.3 | 1.2 |
| Men | 2.0 | 1.3 | 1.2 |
| Women | 2.2 | 1.3 | 1.2 |
| Colored | 1.8 | 1.3 | 1.1 |
| White | 2.5 | 1.3 | 1.3 |
| Short service | 1.8 | 1.3 | 1.1 |
| Middle service | 2.1 | 1.2 | 1.3 |
| Long service | 2.3 | 1.5 | 1.3 |
| Foremen (union endorsement) | 2.4 | 1.5 | 1.7 |
| Local 28 leaders, left wing | 1.0 | | |
| Local 28 leaders, right wing | 1.0 | | |
| Local 28 stewards | 1.0 | | |
| Local 12 leaders | | 1.0 | |
| Local 12 stewards | | 1.0 | |
| (CIO leaders) | | 1.0 | |
| Local 78 leaders | | | 1.0 |
| Local 78 stewards | | | 1.0 |

(Scale: 1.0, very favorable to 5.0, very unfavorable.)

Appendix Table XIV. *Attitudes toward Employee Representation Plan.*

Random sample of long service workers: 64 in the Chicago, 36 in the Kansas City, and 38 in the East St. Louis plants, including 12 union leaders and 30 foremen (in per cent).

| Group | Favorable Chgo. | Favorable K.C. | Favorable E.S.L. | Neutral Chgo. | Neutral K.C. | Neutral E.S.L. | Unfavorable Chgo. | Unfavorable K.C. | Unfavorable E.S.L. |
|---|---|---|---|---|---|---|---|---|---|
| Long service white men | | 23 | | | 15 | | | 62 | |
| Long service colored men | | 17 | | | 0 | | | 83 | |
| Long service white men | | 43 | | | 0 | | | 57 | |
| *All hourly-paid, long service* | 50 | 73 | 22 | 0 | 15 | 8 | 50 | 12 | 70 |
| Foremen | | 62 | 29 | | 38 | 0 | | 0 | 71 |
| Local 78 leaders | | | 0 | | | 0 | | | 100 |
| Local 78 stewards (estimated) | | | 0 | | | 0 | | | 100 |

Appendix Table XV. *Attitudes toward the union shop.*

Random sample of hourly-paid workers in two plants: Kansas City — 121; East St. Louis — 114; and union leaders (in per cent).

| Group | Favorable K.C. | Favorable E.S.L. | Neutral K.C. | Neutral E.S.L. | Unfavorable K.C. | Unfavorable E.S.L. |
|---|---|---|---|---|---|---|
| Men |  | 76 |  | 7 |  | 17 |
| Women |  | 86 |  | 0 |  | 14 |
| Colored |  | 84 |  | 3 |  | 13 |
| White |  | 74 |  | 8 |  | 18 |
| Short service |  | 80 |  | 3 |  | 17 |
| Middle service |  | 80 |  | 8 |  | 12 |
| Long service |  | 72 |  | 5 |  | 23 |
| *All hourly-paid workers* | 30 | 78 | 10 | 5 | 60 | 17 |
| Local 12 union leaders | 20 |  | 0 |  | 80 |  |
| Local 12 union stewards | 22 |  | 11 |  | 67 |  |
| Local 78 union leaders |  | 100 |  | 0 |  | 0 |
| Local 78 union stewards |  | 93 |  | 0 |  | 7 |

Appendix Table XVI. *Attitudes toward union leaders.*

Random sample of workers in three plants: Chicago — 192; Kansas City — 121; East St. Louis — 152, stratified by service, sex, and race; including union leaders and foremen.

| Group | Chicago | Kansas City | East St. Louis |
|---|---|---|---|
| *All hourly-paid workers* | 3.5 | 2.4 | 1.6 |
| Men | 3.5 | 2.6 | 1.6 |
| Women | 3.4 | 1.8 | 1.8 |
| Colored | 3.2 | 2.8 | 1.5 |
| White | 3.9 | 2.2 | 1.7 |
| Short service | 3.0 | 2.7 | 1.8 |
| Middle service | 3.6 | 2.3 | 1.6 |
| Long service | 3.8 | 2.1 | 1.5 |
| Foremen | 4.2 | 1.6 | 1.4 |
| Local 28 leaders, left wing | 1.5 |  |  |
| Local 28 stewards | 2.7 |  |  |
| Local 28 leaders, right wing | 4.5 |  |  |
| Local 12 leaders |  | 1.5 |  |
| Local 12 stewards |  | 1.8 |  |
| (CIO leaders) |  | 4.9 |  |
| Local 78 leaders |  |  | 1.9 |
| Local 78 stewards |  |  | 2.0 |

(Scale: 1.0 very favorable, to 5.0 very unfavorable.)

Appendix Table XVII. *Attitudes toward the UPWA-CIO.*
Random sample of workers in two plants: Kansas City — 121; East St. Louis — 152; stratified by service, sex, and race; including union leaders and foremen (in per cent).

| Group | Favorable | | Neutral | | Unfavorable | |
|---|---|---|---|---|---|---|
| | K.C. | E.S.L. | K.C. | E.S.L. | K.C. | E.S.L. |
| *All hourly-paid workers* | 29 | 27 | 5 | 7 | 66 | 66 |
| Colored | 46 | 42 | 5 | 12 | 77 | 81 |
| White | 17 | 16 | 6 | 3 | 49 | 46 |
| Local 12 union leaders | 9 | | 9 | | 82 | |
| Local 12 union stewards | 19 | | 0 | | 81 | |
| (CIO leaders) | 100 | | 0 | | 0 | |
| Local 78 union leaders | | 0 | | 17 | | 83 |
| Local 78 union stewards | | 7 | | 14 | | 79 |
| Foremen | 0 | 14 | 62 | 0 | 38 | 86 |

Appendix Table XVIII. *Attitudes toward grievance handling.*
A random sample of hourly-paid workers in two plants: Kansas City — 121; East St. Louis — 152; stratified by service, race, and sex; including union leaders and foremen (in per cent).

| Group | Favorable | | Neutral | | Unfavorable | |
|---|---|---|---|---|---|---|
| | K.C. | E.S.L. | K.C. | E.S.L. | K.C. | E.S.L. |
| *All hourly-paid employees* | 65 | 98 | 4 | 0 | 31 | 2 |
| Local 12 union leaders | 100 | | 0 | | 0 | |
| Local 12 union stewards | 100 | | 0 | | 0 | |
| (CIO leaders) | 12 | | 0 | | 88 | |
| Local 78 union leaders | | 100 | | 0 | | 0 |
| Local 78 union stewards | | 80 | | 0 | | 20 |
| Foremen | | 95 | | 0 | | 5 |

Appendix Table XIX. *Attitudes toward the stewards.*
A random sample of workers in two plants: Kansas City — 121; East St. Louis — 152; stratified by service, race and sex; including union leaders and foremen (in per cent).

| Group | Favorable K.C. | Favorable E.S.L. | Neutral K.C. | Neutral E.S.L. | Unfavorable K.C. | Unfavorable E.S.L. |
|---|---|---|---|---|---|---|
| *All hourly-paid workers* | 62 | 93 | 5 | 0 | 33 | 7 |
| Local 12 union leaders | 100 | | 0 | | 0 | |
| (CIO leaders) | 12 | | 0 | | 88 | |
| Local 78 union leaders | | 83 | | | | 17 |
| Foremen | 90 | 84 | 0 | 0 | 10 | 16 |

Appendix Table XX. *Packinghouse workers' union participation.*
Random sample of hourly-paid workers in three plants: Chicago, Kansas City, and East St. Louis, stratified by service, race, and sex; including union leaders and foremen.

| Group | Chicago[a] | Kansas City | East St. Louis |
|---|---|---|---|
| *All hourly-paid workers* | 4.5 (or 3.75) | 4.2 | 4.4 |
| Men | 4.5 | 4.2 | 4.4 |
| Women | 4.8 | 4.4 | 4.8 |
| Colored | 4.1 | 4.0 | 4.3 |
| White | 5.3 | 4.4 | 4.5 |
| Short service | 4.2 | 4.3 | 4.5 |
| Middle service | 4.5 | 4.1 | 4.4 |
| Long service | 5.1 | 4.2 | 4.4 |
| Local 28 leaders, left wing | 1.0 | | |
| Local 28 stewards | 2.4 (or 2.0) | | |
| Local 28 leaders, right wing | 2.6 | | |
| Local 12 union leaders | | 1.1 | |
| Local 12 union stewards | | 2.7 | |
| (CIO leaders) | | 2.0 | |
| Local 78 union leaders | | | 1.0 |
| Local 78 union stewards | | | 1.2 |

[a] For Chicago Local 28 we use here a 6-point scale; for the other locals a 5-point scale is used. If we adjust the "All hourly-paid" score in Chicago of 4.5 from a 6-point to a 5-point scale, the mean participation score for Chicago becomes 3.75.

APPENDIX II

# The Nonparametric Statistics and the Joint-Median Test Used in This Research

Statistical techniques for evaluating differences observed in quantitative data drawn from samples are often based upon an assumption that the samples have been drawn from a normal population. Whenever such an assumption concerning the form of the population distribution is untenable, nonparametric (or distribution-free) methods may be applied to the data.

Nonparametric, or distribution-free statistical tools are especially valuable because they do not rest on any assumptions concerning the form of the population distribution. Neither do they demand that estimates of the population be obtained.

After evaluating the quantitative data of this research, we noted that the distributions were usually quite skewed. Hence we believed that an assumption of underlying normality was unreasonable. Psychological insights gained from the interviews supported this view. Hence we decided to use a nonparametric test in analyzing the data, and the median test appeared to be the most suitable.

The median test for two samples involves the determination of a joint median for the two distributions. The numbers of cases within each sample distribution that fall above and below the joint median are then counted. This provides data for a fourfold contingency table. The contingency table is then evaluated by means of the Chi Square statistic. The fourfold contingency table has one degree of freedom. (Since row and column totals are fixed, we are "free" to determine at will a value for only one of the four cells. Once this value has been determined, the values of the other three cells are fixed.) For Chi Square, the critical ratio at the 5 per cent level of confidence, for one degree of freedom, is 3.841. In all tests used in this analysis, the 5 per cent level critical ratio was the minimum value allowed for determining significance. Results that might happen only five times out of 100 or fewer by chance were called statistically significant, or not to be ascribed to chance alone. We considered any values of Chi Square smaller than 3.841 to be statistically nonsignificant, giving us no solid basis for inferring that the differences observed were real differences rather than due merely to chance.

# APPENDIX II

In a few instances, cell frequency fell below 10. In these cases, Yates' correction for continuity was applied. In applying this correction, each obtained frequency larger than expected is reduced by 0.5, and each frequency smaller than expected is increased by 0.5. The over-all effect is the reduction of each discrepancy between obtained and expected by 0.5. Hence the size of Chi Square is reduced.

Computation by formula provides for continuous variations. Chi Square varies in discrete jumps. Should the frequencies be large, this is a relatively unimportant consideration. However, when the frequencies are small, a change of 0.5 becomes more important, particularly if the value of Chi Square should fall in the neighborhood of the critical ratio set as division point between areas of rejection and nonrejection.

An example of the median test.

| Attitude Scores | Sample A f | Sample B f |
|---|---|---|
| 5.0 | 5 | 14 |
| 4.5 | 4 | 6 |
| 4.0 | 2 | 3 |
| 3.5 | 3 | 1 |
| 3.0 | 2 | 0 |
| 2.5 | 4 | 5 |
| 2.0 | 8 | 3 |
| 1.5 | 6 | 5 |
| 1.0 | 6 | 3 |
|  | N = 40 | N = 40 |

The joint median of the two distributions, combining Samples A and B, is 2.75.

|  | Above median | Below median | Total |
|---|---|---|---|
| Sample A | 16 | 24 | 40 |
| Sample B | 24 | 16 | 40 |
| Total | 40 | 40 | (80) |

$$\chi^2 = \frac{80[|(16)(16) - (24)(24)|]}{(40)(40)(40)(40)} = 3.20$$

This value of Chi Square is not statistically significant. Hence the hypothesis that the median is the same for both populations is not rejected.

APPENDIX **III**

## *Intercomparisons of Company and Union Allegiance and of All Other Attitudes*

Using the joint median test already described, we can examine the interrelationships of all the attitudes measured in this research. Our results are shown in Appendix Table XXI below.

Any given box in the table refers to two attitudes, one printed at the side, and the other printed at the top of the table. If the box contains an asterisk, then the attitude marked with an asterisk is the more favorable of the two and significantly so at the 1, 2, 3 or 5 per cent level, depending on the number in the box. If the box is marked with a plus sign, then the attitude so marked is the more favorable. If the box is empty, then there is no significant difference between the two attitudes.

For example, in Appendix Table XXI-1, we may compare the workers' company allegiance with their attitude toward their local union leaders. This comparison (like all these comparisons) can be found in either of two boxes in the table. One box has a plus sign, the other an asterisk. But in each case company allegiance is indicated as the more favorable attitude, and at the one per cent level of significance.

The two attitudes could both be favorable, of course, or both unfavorable, or one favorable and one unfavorable. The asterisk or plus sign simply indicate which of the two is significantly more favorable than the other.

In Appendix Table XXI-1 (simpler because of less quantified data being available for Chicago), we see two areas standing out. First, the Chicago packing-house workers are significantly less favorable to their union leaders than to the other four aspects of their life with company and union.

Secondly, participation in local union affairs stands out as different. Strictly speaking, this is not an attitude but rather a description of behavior. Also, it is not precisely favorable or unfavorable, but rather active or inactive. Hence this comparison is unique in the table, as it is also unique in Appendix Table XXI-2 and 3. It simply means that the degree of union participation is significantly less active than the parallel degree of approval for the various company and union attitudes.

## APPENDIX III

In Appendix Table XXI-2 for Kansas City, we see that among the company-related attitudes, advancement, equal-opportunity, children-to-Swift and, to some extent Standards, stand apart as less favorable. Among the union-related attitudes we see more differences than among the company-related attitudes. Attitudes toward strikes, the UPWA and the union shop are notably unfavorable. Also participation in union affairs is inactive.

In Appendix Table XXI-3 for East St. Louis, we notice slightly more differences than at Kansas City within the company-related attitudes. Especially East St. Louis has many more differences than Kansas City *between* the company-related and the union-related attitudes.

We note that company allegiance at East St. Louis is significantly more favorable than such other favorable attitudes as gang, pay, working conditions. Naturally it is more favorable than such unfavorable attitudes advancement, equal-opportunity, Standards and children-to-Swift. These latter show up clearly on the table as less favorable than many other attitudes.

As for the union-related attitudes, we see the strong union allegiance of the East St. Louis packinghouse workers. Also their aversion to the Employee Representation Plan, strikes, and the UPWA is evident. The union leaders are more approved than several other aspects of work in the plant.

Appendix Table XXI.

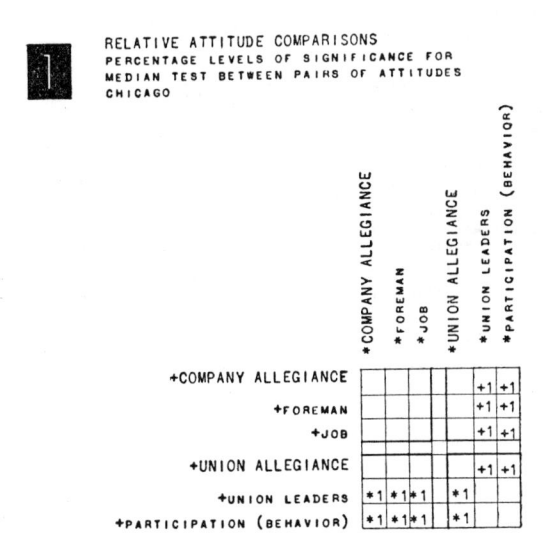

RELATIVE ATTITUDE COMPARISONS
PERCENTAGE LEVELS OF SIGNIFICANCE FOR
MEDIAN TEST BETWEEN PAIRS OF ATTITUDES
CHICAGO

|  | *COMPANY ALLEGIANCE | *FOREMAN | *JOB | *UNION ALLEGIANCE | *UNION LEADERS | *PARTICIPATION (BEHAVIOR) |
|---|---|---|---|---|---|---|
| +COMPANY ALLEGIANCE |  |  |  |  | +1 | +1 |
| +FOREMAN |  |  |  |  | +1 | +1 |
| +JOB |  |  |  |  | +1 | +1 |
| +UNION ALLEGIANCE |  |  |  |  | +1 | +1 |
| +UNION LEADERS | *1 | *1 | *1 | *1 |  |  |
| +PARTICIPATION (BEHAVIOR) | *1 | *1 | *1 | *1 |  |  |

## 2 RELATIVE ATTITUDE COMPARISONS
PERCENTAGE LEVELS OF SIGNIFICANCE FOR
MEDIAN TEST BETWEEN PAIRS OF ATTITUDES
KANSAS CITY

|  | *COMPANY ALLEGIANCE | *FOREMAN | *JOB | *GANG | *PAY | *WORKING CONDITIONS | *SUGGESTION SYSTEM | *ADVANCEMENT | *EQUAL OPPORTUNITY | *STANDARDS | *CHILDREN TO SWIFT | *UNION ALLEGIANCE | *UNION LEADERS | *EMPLOYEE REPRESENTATION PLAN | *GRIEVANCES | *STEWARDS | *STRIKES | *UPWA | *UNION SHOP | *PARTICIPATION (BEHAVIOR) |
|---|---|---|---|---|---|---|---|---|---|---|---|---|---|---|---|---|---|---|---|---|
| +COMPANY ALLEGIANCE |  |  |  |  |  |  | +1 | +1 |  | +1 |  |  |  |  |  |  | +1 | +1 | +1 | +1 |
| +FOREMAN |  |  |  |  |  |  | +1 | +1 |  | +1 |  |  |  |  |  |  | +1 | +1 | +1 | +1 |
| +JOB |  |  |  |  |  |  | +1 | +1 | +1 | +1 |  |  |  |  |  |  | +1 | +1 | +1 | +1 |
| +GANG |  |  |  |  |  |  | +1 | +1 |  | +1 |  |  |  |  |  |  | +1 | +1 | +1 | +1 |
| +PAY |  |  |  |  |  |  | +1 | +1 |  | +1 |  |  |  |  |  |  | +1 | +1 | +1 | +1 |
| +WORKING CONDITIONS |  |  |  |  |  |  | +1 | +1 |  | +1 |  |  |  |  |  |  | +1 | +1 | +1 | +1 |
| +SUGGESTION SYSTEM |  |  |  |  |  |  |  | +1 | +1 | *3 |  |  |  |  |  |  | +1 | +1 | +1 | +1 |
| +ADVANCEMENT | *1 | *1 | *1 | *1 | *1 | *1 | *1 |  | +2 |  |  | *1 | *1 | *1 | *1 | *1 | +3 |  |  | +1 |
| +EQUAL OPPORTUNITY | *1 | *1 | *1 | *1 | *1 | *1 | *1 | *2 |  | *1 | *2 |  | *1 | *1 | *1 |  |  |  |  | +1 |
| +STANDARDS |  | *1 |  |  |  | +3 |  | +1 |  |  |  | *1 |  | *3 |  |  | +1 | +2 | +3 | +1 |
| +CHILDREN TO SWIFT | *1 | *1 | *1 | *1 | *1 | *1 | *1 | +2 |  |  |  |  | *1 | *2 | *1 | +1 |  |  |  | +1 |
| +UNION ALLEGIANCE |  |  |  |  |  |  | +1 |  | +1 |  |  |  | +3 |  | +2 | +2 | +1 | +1 | +1 | +1 |
| +UNION LEADERS |  |  |  |  |  |  | +1 |  |  |  |  | *3 |  |  |  |  | +1 | +1 | +1 | +1 |
| +EMPLOYEE REPRESENTATION PLAN |  |  |  |  |  |  | +1 | +1 | +3 | +1 |  |  |  |  | +1 | +1 | +1 | +1 | +1 | +1 |
| +GRIEVANCES |  |  |  |  |  |  | +1 | +1 |  | +2 |  | *2 |  | *1 |  |  | +1 | +1 | +1 | +1 |
| +STEWARDS |  |  |  |  |  |  | +1 | +1 |  | +1 |  | *2 |  | *1 |  |  | +1 | +1 | +1 | +1 |
| +STRIKES | *1 | *1 | *1 | *1 | *1 | *1 | *1 | *3 |  | *1 | +1 | *1 | *1 | *1 | *1 | *1 |  |  |  |  |
| +UPWA | *1 | *1 | *1 | *1 | *1 | *1 | *1 |  | +2 |  |  | *1 | *1 | *1 | *1 | *1 |  |  |  | +1 |
| +UNION SHOP | *1 | *1 | *1 | *1 | *1 | *1 | *1 |  |  | *3 |  | *1 | *1 | *1 | *1 | *1 |  |  |  | +1 |
| +PARTICIPATION (BEHAVIOR) | *1 | *1 | *1 | *1 | *1 | *1 | *1 | *1 | *1 | *1 | *1 | *1 | *1 | *1 | *1 | *1 |  | *1 | *1 |  |

### RELATIVE ATTITUDE COMPARISONS
PERCENTAGE LEVELS OF SIGNIFICANCE FOR MEDIAN TEST BETWEEN PAIRS OF ATTITUDES
EAST ST. LOUIS

|  | *COMPANY ALLEGIANCE | *FOREMAN | *JOB | *GANG | *PAY | *WORKING CONDITIONS | *SUGGESTION SYSTEM | *ADVANCEMENT | *EQUAL OPPORTUNITY | *STANDARDS | *CHILDREN TO SWIFT | *UNION ALLEGIANCE | *UNION LEADERS | *EMPLOYEE REPRESENTATION PLAN | *GRIEVANCES | *STEWARDS | *STRIKES | *UPWA | *UNION SHOP | *PARTICIPATION (BEHAVIOR) |
|---|---|---|---|---|---|---|---|---|---|---|---|---|---|---|---|---|---|---|---|---|
| +COMPANY ALLEGIANCE |  |  | +1 | +1 | +3 | +1 | +1 | +1 | +1 | +1 | +1 | *2 |  | +1 | +1 | +1 | +1 |  | +1 | +1 | +1 |
| +FOREMAN |  |  |  |  |  | +1 | +1 | +1 | +1 | +1 | +1 | *1 |  | +1 | +3 |  | +1 | +1 | +1 | +1 |
| +JOB |  |  |  |  |  | +1 | +1 | +1 | +1 | +1 | +1 | *1 |  | +1 |  |  | +1 | +1 | +2 | +1 |
| +GANG | *1 |  |  |  |  |  |  | +1 |  | +3 |  | *1 |  | +1 |  |  | +1 | +1 |  | +1 |
| +PAY | *1 |  |  |  |  |  | +5 | +1 |  | +1 |  | *1 | *5 | +1 |  |  | +1 | +1 |  | +1 |
| +WORKING CONDITIONS | *3 |  |  |  |  |  |  | +3 | +1 |  | +1 | *1 |  | +1 |  |  | +1 | +1 |  | +1 |
| +SUGGESTION SYSTEM | *1 | *1 | *1 |  |  |  |  |  | +1 |  |  | *1 | *1 | +1 | *3 | *3 | +1 | +1 |  | +1 |
| +ADVANCEMENT | *1 | *1 | *1 |  | *5 | *3 |  |  | +1 |  |  | *1 | *1 | +1 | *2 | *3 | +1 | +1 | *3 | +1 |
| +EQUAL OPPORTUNITY | *1 | *1 | *1 | *1 | *1 | *1 | *1 | *1 |  | *1 | *1 |  |  | +1 | *1 | +1 | +1 |  | *1 | +1 |
| +STANDARDS | *1 | *1 | *1 |  |  |  |  | +1 |  |  |  | *1 |  | +1 | *2 | *3 | +1 | +1 | *1 | +1 |
| +CHILDREN TO SWIFT | *1 | *1 | *1 | *3 | *1 | *1 |  | +1 |  |  |  | *1 | *1 | +1 | *1 | *1 | +1 | *1 | *1 | +1 |
| +UNION ALLEGIANCE | +2 | +1 | +1 | +1 | +1 | +1 | +1 | +1 |  | +1 |  |  | +1 | +1 | +1 | +1 | +1 |  | +1 | +1 | +1 |
| +UNION LEADERS |  |  |  | +5 |  | +1 | +1 |  | +1 | +1 |  | *1 |  | +1 |  |  | +1 | +1 | *1 | +1 |
| +EMPLOYEE REPRESENTATION PLAN | *1 | *1 | *1 | *1 | *1 | *1 | *1 | *1 | *1 | *1 | *1 | *1 | *1 |  | *1 | *1 |  |  | *1 | +1 |
| +GRIEVANCES | *1 | *3 |  |  |  | +3 | +2 | +1 |  | +2 | +1 | *1 |  | +1 |  |  | +1 | +1 |  | +1 |
| +STEWARDS | *1 |  |  |  |  | +3 | +3 | +1 |  | +3 | +1 | *1 |  | +1 |  |  | +1 | +1 |  | +1 |
| +STRIKES | *1 | *1 | *1 | *1 | *1 | *1 | *1 | *1 |  | *1 | *1 | *1 |  | *1 | *1 |  |  | *1 |  |  |
| +UPWA | *1 | *1 | *1 | *1 | *1 | *1 | *1 | *1 |  | *1 | *1 | *1 | *1 |  | *1 | *1 |  |  | *1 | +1 |
| +UNION SHOP | *1 | *1 | *2 |  |  | +3 | +1 | +1 |  | +1 |  | *1 | *1 | +1 |  |  | +1 | +1 |  | +1 |
| +PARTICIPATION (BEHAVIOR) | *1 | *1 | *1 | *1 | *1 | *1 | *1 | *1 | *1 | *1 | *1 |  | *1 | *1 | *1 | *1 | *1 |  | *1 | *1 |  |

# Notes

CHAPTER I  *Workers' Tale of Three Cities — A Comparison*

1. John T. Dunlop, "Research in Industrial Relations: Past and Future," *Proceedings of the Seventh Annual Meeting* (1954), Industrial Relations Research Association, p. 99. Mr. Dunlop goes on to say: "Study the labor factor comparatively in a limited number of industrializations. Compare the growth and evolution of a number of international unions or local unions in the same international. Compare the industrial relations policies of a number of companies in the same industry or locality. The comparisons are designed to highlight the factors which are strategic to the different experiences. The comparative method yields rich returns but requires greater knowledge since a variety of cases are examined. This greater range of experience requires more maturity." Dunlop suggests another point that we have stressed in this research: ". . . there is need to follow industrial relations events over time, discerning the consequences of a variety of factors: inflation, unemployment, changes in leadership, variations in legislation and political atmosphere."

2. Both the UPWA and the AMC&BW are affiliated with the AFL-CIO. But since these rival unions have not yet merged, we retain their original affiliations as a convenient way of distinguishing them. In May 1960, at its twelfth constitutional convention, the UPWA voted to change its name to United Packinghouse, Food and Allied Workers, but also to retain the initials UPWA. In 1960, the UPWA claimed around 150,000 members in the United States and Canada in approximately 300 locals. Around 80,000 of these were in the meat packing industry, with several thousand others in sugar refining, food canning or agriculture. The UPWA also claimed around 55,000 members in Puerto Rico on a lower dues-paying basis. (The American paid membership of the UPWA dropped from 118,000 in 1955 to 87,000 in 1959.) The Amalgamated claimed around 350,000 members in nearly 500 Locals. Around 100,000 of these were in meat packing. About 150,000 were retail butchers and about 40,000 in the fur-making and leather-processing industries. Most of the latter had been members of the International Fur and Leather Workers' Union, which had been expelled from the CIO. In 1955, the Amalgamated took over the Fur and Leather Union, dropping some of the key leftwingers in the process. The Amalgamated also includes seafood and poultry workers. This diversity gives the Amalgamated a greater membership strength than the UPWA. This is an important difference, especially in view of the recent employment cutbacks in meat packing due to the cattle shortage, the 1958–1959 recession, and to technologically improved productivity. The National Brotherhood has only around 7000 members in seven locals, almost all in the Swift Chain.

3. Some of this research is as follows: Leonard Sayles and George Strauss, *The Local Union* (Harper & Brothers, New York, 1953); W. E. Chalmers *et al., Labor-Management Relations in Illini City* (University of Illinois Institute of Labor and Industrial Relations, Champaign, 1953); Joel Seidman, Jack London, Bernard Karsh, Daisy Tagliacozzo, *The Worker Views His Union* (University of Chicago Press, Chicago, 1958); Arnold Rose, *Union Solidarity* (University of Minnesota Press, Minneapolis, 1952); Fred H. Blum, *Towards a Democratic Work Process* (Harper & Brothers, New York, 1954); Hjalmar and R. A. H. Rosen, *The Union Member Speaks* (Prentice-Hall, New York, 1955); Ely Chinoy, *Automobile Workers and the American Dream* (Doubleday, Garden City, 1955); Charles R. Walker and Robert H. Guest, *The Man on the Assembly Line* (Harvard University Press, Cambridge, 1952); Charles R.

Walker, Robert H. Guest, Arthur N. Turner, *The Foreman on the Assembly Line* (Harvard University Press, Cambridge, 1956); John W. Riegel, *Employee Interest in Company Success* (Bureau of Industrial Relations, University of Michigan, Ann Arbor, 1956); also journal articles by John P. Caldwell, Glenn W. Miller, and others. Arnold S. Tannenbaum, Robert L. Kahn, *Participation in Union Locals* (Row Peterson and Company, Evanston, Illinois, 1958).

4. The interviews quoted in this book bear fictitious names and are disguised.

5. "Two Experiments with an Anti-Semitism Poll," *Journal of Abnormal and Social Psychology,* 41: 136–144 (1946).

6. Social scientist Joseph H. Fichter, studying a Catholic parochial school as a social system, finds no difference in honesty or openness of response of Catholic parents when interviewed by laymen or by Catholic priests. "It is significant that the respondents seemed to have about the same amount of trust in both the lay and clerical interviewers" (p. 279). See Joseph H. Fichter, S.J., "Priests as Interviewers," *Social Order,* 9:275–9, no. 6 (June 1959). See also Joseph H. Fichter, *Parochial School: A Sociological Study* (University of Notre Dame Press, Notre Dame, Indiana, 1958).

CHAPTER II  *Plants and Unions*

1. Walker *et al., The Foreman.* . . .

2. See Theodore Vincent Purcell, *The Worker Speaks His Mind* (Harvard University Press, Cambridge, 1953), pp. 52–3.

3. *Report of National Conventions* (National Brotherhood of Packinghouse Workers, Des Moines, 1954).

4. The First NLRB election was held on September 24, 1941. 1305 ballots were cast, 578 for the Amalgamated, 408 for the Packinghouse Workers Organizing Committee, CIO, 213 for the Swift Employees Association and 106 for no union. The second election was held on November 7, 1941. Out of 1179 ballots, 442 went to the Amalgamated, 385 to the PWOC and 352 to the SEA. In the third and final election 1079 ballots were cast, narrowly divided, 556 to the Amalgamated and 523 to the Swift Employees Association.

5. For two accounts of why the merger failed see *Work* (January 1957) (the publication of the Chicago Catholic Council on Working Life); also, "Unity in Meat Packing: Problems and Prospects," by Joel Seidman in *New Dimensions in Collective Bargaining,* H. W. Davey, H. S. Kaltenborn and S. H. Ruttenberg (Harper, New York, 1959), pp. 29–43.

6. Reported in the *Packinghouse Worker* (July 1958).

7. Editorial in the *Butcher Workman* (June 1959).

8. See John Hope, II, *Equality of Opportunity* (Public Affairs Press, Washington, 1956).

9. Letter from George A. Meany to Patrick E. Gorman, December 20, 1954, quoted in Philip Taft, *The A. F. of L. from the Death of Gompers to the Merger* (Harper & Brothers, New York, 1959) pp. 434–5. For another account of the merger between the Fur Workers and the Amalgamated Meat Cutters, see David J. Saposs, *Communism in American Unions* (McGraw-Hill, New York, 1959), pp. 256–9.

10. See the *Chicago Daily News,* October 24, 1956.

11. For an account of Communist activity in Chicago District One of the UPWA during the years 1949 to 1953, see Purcell, *The Worker Speaks* . . . , pp. 64–72.

12. Saposs, *Communism* . . . , pp. 202–4.

13. Mimeographed letter to President George L. Meany, October 22, 1958.

14. Congressional Record — House, May 14, 1959, pp. 7371-7372.

15. "Report of AFL-CIO Executive Council Subcommittee to President Meany." Typescript, August 1959.

CHAPTER III  *Neighborhoods and Packinghouse Workers*

1. For a fuller description of Back-of-the-Yards and Bronzeville, see Purcell, *The Worker Speaks* . . . , pp. 38–42.
2. "Employment Characteristics in the Greater Kansas City area," Report by the Inventory Committee, Community Unity Conference, Kansas City Human Relations Commission, 1950, page 8. (Typescript.) This estimate was based upon a study made for the National Urban League by Richardson Wood, a former editor of *Fortune* magazine. "This figure is a conservative estimate of the additional amount that could be earned by Negro workers if they were permitted to work at all jobs for which they can qualify."
3. *East St. Louis Journal*, p. 8A, October 15, 1953.
4. Milton Derber, *Union-Management Relations in East St. Louis* (Institute of Labor and Industrial Relations, University of Illinois, Urbana, 1957), p. 32.

CHAPTER IV  *The Worker Looks at His Company*

1. The word allegiance comes from the Old French and from the Latin. Its meaning first crystallized in the feudal period and connoted the relation of a feudal vassal to his superior or liege lord. After feudal times, allegiance applied rather to one's political duties to the king or state. The word has evolved, and now has several nuances of meaning, such as the obligation of fidelity in general to any superior, or to some principle, or to something that is worthy of respect (e.g., allegiance to science).

Allegiance usually connotes some sort of obligation toward an institution. We think of allegiance to our country, for example. We are not watering down this meaning. Company allegiance does involve obligations toward the company, and union allegiance involves obligations toward the union, or at least toward the union movement in general.

The concept of loyalty is somewhat akin to allegiance. For an interesting and thorough treatment of loyalty, especially of its political overtones, see John H. Schaar, *Loyalty in America* (University of California Press, Berkeley, 1957).

2. For a discussion of our statistical methods see Appendix II.
3. Walker and Guest, *The Man on* . . . , p. 120.

CHAPTER V  *Foreman and Worker*

1. B stands for Bedaux, who was a time-study engineer whose system forms the basis of the Swift Standards (wage-incentive) System. Under the system, the Swift worker should produce 60 work units per hour. This is the standard. In addition, the worker is expected to produce extra units above the standard, "premium units," later converted into "premium hours." For example, a worker might make a 65 or 70 "B-hour." On this surplus, the worker is paid premium pay above his regular hourly base rate. The workers often call such premium earnings their "bonus." Employees may be on individual, small-group or large-group applications of Standards. The Swift Standards System is described in greater detail in Purcell, *The Worker Speaks* . . . , pp. 236–7.
2. A Yale research group, studying every work moment of fifty-five auto plant foremen found that these foremen spent more than half their time interacting with other people. See Walker, *et al., The Foreman on* . . . , pp. 86–7. The Swift foremen would be about the same.
3. See Theodore V. Purcell, "Observing People," *Harvard Business Review*, 33: 90–100 (March–April 1955).

## Chapter VI  Five Aspects of the Job

1. Peter Drucker, *The Practice of Management* (Harper, New York, 1954), p. 303.
2. The Bureau of Labor Statistics *Community Wage Studies* for these communities shows a considerable differential between men and women doing office clerical work. There is not such a wide differential in the Swift meat packing plants between men and women doing semiskilled work. The principle of "equal pay for equal work" has narrowed the gap between men and women packinghouse workers. Also, thanks to the Swift wage-incentive system, the women often make considerable premium earnings.

## Chapter VII  The Chance to Get Ahead

1. The essential contractual provisions for promotions in the Swift-UPWA, Swift-Amalgamated and Swift-NBPW collective bargaining agreements are as follows: ". . . Promotion shall be made according to department seniority, provided the employee can do the work or learn it within a reasonable time except that, in cases of necessity where no applicants are available who can perform the job, and there is insufficient time in view of such necessity to teach the applicant the job, a new employee may be hired for such vacancy. The foreman shall advise the department steward of any vacancy and state who is being assigned to the job. . . . The Company shall also post such vacancy in the department wherein it exists and an employee with greater seniority in the department . . . shall have forty-eight hours to bid for the job and shall be assigned in line of seniority as soon as practicable, provided he can perform the job or learn it within a reasonable time. . . ." What the workers of the three plants and the three local unions think about the practical implementation of these contractual agreements about promotions is shown in many of the interviews quoted in this chapter.
2. See for example: S. M. Lipset and R. Bendix, *Social Mobility in Industrial Society* (University of California Press, Berkeley, 1959).
3. One study of St. Louis Teamster Local 688, finds that "the great majority of the members see the union as an instrument for achieving common goals. Only a few think of it as an avenue to leadership or personal promotion. This is shown in answers to a question asking whether the member ever thought to become a union officer or staff member. Those who think . . . of trying to become a union official are also the ones who are more likely to think they have a fair or good chance of rising in the management scale." Rose, *Union Solidarity*, p. 150.
4. Chinoy, *Automobile Workers and.* . . . Seidman *et al., The Worker Views.* . . .

## Chapter VIII  Problems of Wage Incentives

1. Formal wage-incentive grievances are not now very numerous in the Swift plants, probably not amounting to more than 10 per cent of all grievances. Of course, when a new operation is set up, such as the recently developed, highly mechanized cattle-dressing lines, a rash of grievances may occur. But this is generally temporary. As shown in Table 33 of Chapter XII, work-schedule and premium-pay grievances ranged from 0 per cent of the total Kansas City third-step grievances to 36 per cent of the East St. Louis grievances in 1954. We do not have data, however, for an adequate interplant comparison of wage-incentive grievances. Some highlights of the labor-management agreement regarding standards are as follows: "When any changes in standards are made or when standards are applied to a new operation, the foreman shall inform the Union Steward of the new production standards. When an operation is to be time-studied, the foreman will inform the operators of that fact. . . . The arbitrator . . . shall have only the power to decide: (1) Whether insufficient credit is

being given in connection with an existing standard. . . . The arbitrator shall have no power by his award to establish, discontinue, or change any production standard. In the event the arbitrator decides the grievance in favor of the union, the Company will change the standard so that it will be consistent with the award of the arbitrator. . . ."

2. Since our sampling is not ideal, our results must be taken with caution. The colored men, for instance, cannot be compared at all, since so few of them, as we see in Appendix Table XI, are on individual standards application. As for the white men, we have in East St. Louis a t of 2.56, significant at the 2 per cent level. The value of t in Kansas City is 1.91, almost significant at the 5 per cent level. For the white women the value of t is 2.7, significant above the 5 per cent level.

### Chapter IX  *Aspirations for His Children*

1. Seidman *et al.*, *The Worker Views* . . . , p. 112.
2. Chinoy, *Automobile Workers* . . . , p. 127.
3. A joint median test for all the company-related attitudes for the men (85 per cent of the workforces), in East St. Louis and Kansas City, shows East St. Louis significantly more favorable. If we included the small number of women, the very favorable Kansas City women would change these results.

### Chapter X  *The Worker Looks at His Union*

1. While we are using allegiance substantially as Stagner does in *Personnel Psychology*, pp. 41–7 (Spring 1954), we do not mean the word necessarily as accepting membership in the group. For example, the Gantt faction in Local 28 withdrew from the local in order to work toward a better union. They did not accept membership in UPWA Local 28, but they had strong union allegiance, in the sense that they were convinced believers in the trade union movement and were working hard for this cause in their plant.

### Chapter XIII  *Patterns of Rank-and-File Union Participation*

1. For a comprehensive and somewhat different treatment of participation see Tannenbaum and Kahn, *Participation*. . . .
2. Sayles and Strauss, *The Local Union* . . . , p. 173.
3. Seidman *et al.*, *The Worker* . . . , p. 186. The authors also found that the Chicago Plumbers' Local Union had an unusually high participation with from 500 to 1500 of the 4400 local union members attending the semimonthly meetings during 1952 and 1953. They found no necessary relationship, incidentally, between wanting the union ("union allegiance") and participation in union affairs. For example, they note that the steelworkers' "appreciation for the achievements of their union in the past, and their reliance on it for benefits and security in the future, are far greater than the low level of formal participation in local affairs would lead one to expect" p. 90.
4. Our joint-median test shows East St. Louis to lead significantly in all union-related attitudes.

### Chapter XIV  *Strikes and Allegiance*

1. Review of *The Worker Speaks His Mind*, Robert L. Kahn, *Journal of the American Statistical Association*, pp. 419–20 (June 1955). See also Bernard Karsh, *American Journal of Sociology*, 61: 269–71 (November 1955); and Hjalmar Rosen, "Dual Allegiance: A Critique and a Proposed Approach," *Personnel Psychology*, 7, no. 1 (Spring 1954).

2. Purcell, *The Worker Speaks* . . . , page 178.
3. *The National Provisioner,* 141: no. 10, September 5, 1959.
4. *Chicago Sun-Times,* p. 3, October 20, 1959.
5. *Chicago Daily Tribune,* p. 1, October 20, 1959.

CHAPTER XV  *Three Patterns of Dual Allegiance*

1. Ross Stagner, "Dual Allegiance as a Problem in Modern Society," *Personnel Psychology,* 7:42, no. 1 (March 1954).
2. Lois Dean, "Union Activity and Dual Loyalty," *Industrial and Labor Relations Review,* 7:535, no. 1 (July 1954).
3. Kunio Odaka, *Sangyo ni okeru Ningen Kankei no Kagaku (Science of Human Relations in Industry)* (Yuhikaku, Tokyo, 1953), Chapter IX.
4. Seidman *et al., The Worker Views . . . ,* pp. 20, 23, 90, 249, 261.
5. John R. Coleman, "The Local Industrial Union in Contemporary Collective Bargaining," *Proceedings* of Eighth Annual Meeting of the Industrial Relations Research Association, in New York City, 1955, edited by L. Reed Tripp, Madison, Wisconsin, p. 280 (1956).
6. Seidman *et al., The Worker Views . . . ,* pp. 53–4.
7. Glenn W. Miller and James E. Young, "Member Participation in the Trade Union Local," *The American Journal of Economics and Sociology,* 15:40, no. 1 (October 1955).
8. Glenn W. Miller and Ned Rosen, "Members' Attitudes Toward the Shop Steward," *Industrial and Labor Relations Review,* 10:531, no. 4.
9. Rose, *Union Solidarity,* p. 66.
10. Daniel Katz, "The Attitude Survey Approach," in *Psychology of Labor-Management Relations,* edited by Arthur Kornhauser (Industrial Relations Research Association, Champaign, Illinois, 1949), p. 67.
11. Tannenbaum and Kahn, *Participation* . . . , pp. 148–9.
12. Vol. 110 NLRB 1307 at page 1311. Also see 346 U.S. 464 for an interesting case involving anticompany handbills and discharge for cause, in NLRB vs. Local 1229 of the IBEW. The U. S. Supreme Court stated on page 472 that there is "no more elemental cause for discharge of an employee than disloyalty to his employer. It is equally elemental that the Taft Hartley Act seeks to strengthen rather than to weaken that cooperative continuity of service and cordial contractual relationship between employer and employee that is born of loyalty to a common enterprise," Other references to this case are 202 Federal and 94 NLRB 1507.
13. John W. Riegel, *Employee Interest in Company Success* (Bureau of Industrial Relations, University of Michigan, Ann Arbor, 1956), p. 296.
14. John D. LaPoint, "Attitudes of Union and Non-union Workers toward Union and Management Issues," unpublished M.A. thesis, University of Illinois (Urbana, 1954).
15. Francis X. Paone, "The Allegiance Patterns of Unionized Professionals," unpublished Ph.D. dissertation, Loyola University (Chicago, 1960), Chapter XI, p. 175.
16. Arthur Kornhauser, Harold L. Sheppard, Albert J. Mayer, *When Labor Votes* (University Books, Inc., New York, 1956), p. 118.
17. Hjalmar Rosen and R. A. Hudson Rosen, *The Union Member Speaks* (Prentice-Hall, New York, 1955).
18. Eugene H. Jacobsen, "Foreman-steward Participation Practices and Worker Attitudes in a Unionized Factory," unpublished doctoral dissertation, University of Michigan, (Ann Arbor, 1951). Also Eugene H. Jacobsen, in Harold Guetzkow (ed.), "Foreman and Steward, Representatives of Management and the Union," *Groups, Leadership and Men* (Carnegie Press, Pittsburgh, 1951).

# Index

Absenteeism, 51, 53, 55, 79
Advancement, attitude of workers toward, 119, 120, 137; education and, 120, 121; Negro workers' attitude toward, 120, 121, 126–136; attitude of union leaders toward, 122, 123; attitude of Mexican workers toward advancement, 135, 136
AFL-CIO Ethical Practices Committee, 37
AFL-CIO Ethical Practices Codes, 40
AFL Executive Council, 37; approves merger of UPWA and Amalgamated, 33
AFL-CIO Merger Convention (1955), 30
Age variable, 50
Agnew, Sam, Local 78 leader (quoted), 23
Alcoa, 47
Allegiance. See Company allegiance, Dual allegiance, Union allegiance
Amalgamated Meat Cutters (AFL-CIO), representation in industry, 4, 19, 24; merger efforts, 4, 5, 29–35, 193, 198, 215, 226, 228, 259; strikes against Swift, 21, 23, 225–229, 239–246; victorious in East St. Louis, 23; characteristics of, 27, 28; cooperation during strike, 29, 30, 225, 226, 228, 242; differences with UPWA, 32, 34, 40; and Senate Rackets Committee, 39; and Standards System, 149; member apathy, 215; 1948 strike, 24; 1956 strike, 225–229; 1959 strike, 239–246 *passim*
Anderson, Cleveland, Local 78 leader (quoted), 22, 23
Anderson, Noreen (interview), attitude toward foreman, 87
Argentine, Mexicans in, 42
Armour & Company, 4, 14, 22, 24, 44; and 1956 strike, 226–229, and 1959 strike, 239, 240
Armour Plan, 239, 240, 242
Armourdale, 5, 11; Mexicans in, 42
"Arrow S," club, 12, 128
Attitude of foreman, toward workers, 91–97; toward Negroes, 92–94; toward Mexicans, 92, 93; toward job, 102, 103; toward wages, 7, 108; toward working conditions, 113; toward suggestion system, 116, 118; toward advancement, 123–126; toward Standards System, 148, 150, 152; toward children following, 160, 161; comparison of attitudes in three plants, 163, 164; toward union, 176–179, 204,

217; toward union leaders, 190–193; toward UPWA, 194, 198; toward grievance procedure, 201; toward stewards, 204, 205
Attitude of Mexican workers, toward opportunities, 135, 136; toward children following, 158
Attitude of Negroes, toward equal opportunity, 126–136; toward children following, 154–158; toward union leaders, 189; toward UPWA, 196–199
Attitude of stewards toward foremen, 205
Attitude of union leaders, toward foremen, 89, 90; toward working conditions, 113, 114; toward suggestion system, 116, 117; toward advancement, 122, 123; toward Standards System, 149, 150; toward children following, 159, 160; comparison of attitudes in three plants, 163, 164; toward union, 175, 176, 217; toward union leaders, 189; toward union shop, 183; toward UPWA, 194, 198; toward grievance procedure, 201
Attitude of workers, toward foreman, 60, 61, 81–89; toward job, 60, 61, 98–118, 162, 163; toward gang, 61, 98, 103–106; toward wages, 61, 98, 107–110; toward working conditions, 60, 61, 98, 99, 111–114; toward suggestion system, 61, 98, 99, 114–118; toward children following, 60, 61, 99, 126, 153–164, 260; toward advancement, 119–136, 137; toward Standards System, 137–148; comparison of attitudes in three plants, 162–164; toward employee representation plan, 168, 180, 181, 216, 217; toward union shop, 168, 181–183, 216; toward union leaders, 7, 168, 183, 185–190, 199, 216, 222, 260; toward UPWA, 168, 193–199, 216; toward grievance procedure, 168, 200–209, 216; toward stewards, 168, 185, 201–204, 216; toward strikes, 168, 216, 221–225, 246, 260; toward union, 169–217 *passim*
Attitudes, 6–9, 10; variables affecting, 48, 49, 51, 67, 69, 70; company related, 60–164 *passim*, 246, 248, 259, 260; and output behavior, 145–148; comparison of, in three plants, 162–164, 215–217; union related attitudes, 167–217 *passim*, 246, 259, 260
Attitudes. See also Satisfaction

## INDEX

"Attitudinal Climate," 248
Automation Fund. *See* Armour Plan
Automobile workers, study of, 250, 251

B-Sheet. *See* Standards Posting Sheet
Back-of-the-yards, 4, 41
Back-of-the-yards Council and Chicago cutback, 14
Baltimore plant, 24
Baron, Louis (interview), opinion of Otto Nagler, 71, 72
Behavior characteristics, 51–53, 55, 260; attitudes during strikes, 145–148, 229–247, 259, 260; and union, 210–215
Belgians in Kansas City, 42
Berghoff, Ted, union leader (interview), attitude toward advancement, 122, 123
Blanchard, Phil, foreman (interview), attitude toward job, 102, 103
Block, Max, 39
Bloomer, Charles (interview), union allegiance, 170, 171; union leaders, 187, 188
"Booster Club," 12, 128
Bouk, Harry, foreman (quoted), attitude toward workers, 91; (interview), attitude toward stewards, 204
Bowski, Stella (quoted), attitude toward foreman, 96, 97
Bradley, John (quoted), and union shop, 182, 183
Bronzeville, 5, 41, 42, 47, 55, 127
Brothers, Robert, 17
Browning, Leonard (interview), attitude toward foreman, 85
Brunswick, Marian (interview), company allegiance, 68
Burke, Carlton (interview), Standards System, 142
Burke, Frank, foreman (quoted), attitude toward workmen, 92
Burroughs Adding Machine plant, Detroit, 252
*Butcher Workman* (quoted), breakup of Amalgamated and UPWA merger, 34, 35; member apathy, 215

Cainski, John (quoted), attitude toward UPWA, 195; (interview), grievance procedure, 201, 202
*The Call,* 42
Chicago, description of, 47, 48; interracial relations, 47, 48; comparison with East St. Louis and Kansas City, 48; neighborhoods 41, 47, 48
Chicago foremen, 86; company allegiance, 78, 79; attitude toward workers, 90–97; attitude toward advancement, 124; and Standards System, 150; union endorsement, 177, 178; attitude toward union, 177; attitude toward union leaders, 190, 193
Chicago Local 28. *See* Local 28
Chicago Negro worker, 129; and equal opportunity, 126; discrimination against, 127
Chicago plant, 3, 5; cutback in operations 13–15, 243; morale, 14; characteristics of, 15; and 1959 strike, 243
Chicago Swift-UPWA Study, 4, 7
Chicago workers, characteristics, 49–55; geographic origin, 51; turnover, 51–55 *passim;* absenteeism, 53, wage assignments, 53; company allegiance, 62–70 *passim,* 162; company disallegiance, 70; attitude toward job, 99, 163; attitude toward gang, 103, 104; attitude toward wages, 107–110; attitude toward working conditions, 111; attitude toward suggestion system, 115, 116; and Standards System, 138, 139, 143, 152; attitude toward children following, 154; attitude toward union, 168–170; attitude toward union allegiance, 10, 168–170, 215–217; and Employee Representation Plan, 180; attitude toward union shop, 168; attitude toward union leaders, 168, 186, 189, 190; attitude toward grievance procedure, 200, 206, 209; attitude toward stewards, 200, 206; union participation, 210–215; attitude toward strikes, 222; and 1956 strike, 236, 237; dual allegiance, 254–260
Children, workers' attitudes on children following, 153–164; and sex, race, and service variable, 154; and community evaluation of factory work, 157
Children following. *See* Attitudes of workers toward children following
Chinoy's study, 161
Circle Packing Company, 44
Civil rights, practice in Kansas and Missouri, 42
Clark, Tom (quoted), attitude toward job, 100
Coal miners, study of, 249
Cobb, Walter (interview), attitude toward foreman, 7; Employee Representation Plan, 181
Coleman, John R., study, dual allegiance, 249, 250
Collective bargaining, views of UPWA and Amalgamated, 33
Communism, Investigation by House Committee, 32, 36; UPWA and Amalgamated differences in dealing with, 33; and the UPWA, 35–40; and the attitude of workers toward the unions, 194
Communist Party, influence on Local 28 leadership, 18, 247

## INDEX

Company allegiance, 59–80, 81, 145, 162, 169, 175, 217, 246, 248, 259; effect of union on, 65, 66; and union leaders, 74–78; and foremen, 78, 79, 177; and Negro worker, 129, 136; and attitude of workers toward children following, 153, 154, 161, 162; comparison of three plants, 162–164. *See also* Dual allegiance
Company disallegiance, 60, 62, 70–72, 217; discrimination and, 72; workers who quit, 72–74
Contract, Swift-UPWA, 18, 27; Swift-NBPW, 27
Contreras, Julio, 72
Corbett, Jay, union leader (interview), 1956 strike, 235
Council of Western Electric Technical and Professional Employees, 252
Crane, Florence (interview), suggestion system, 117
Croatians, 5; in Kansas City, 42, 43
Croden, Tommie, attitude toward foremen, 85
*The Crusader,* 47
Cudahy Packing Company, 4, 11, 20, 52, 66, 225; and 1956 strike, 228; and 1959 strike, 240
Culpepper, Gerald (interview), attitude toward foremen, 88; (quoted), union allegiance, 174
Czechs, in East St. Louis, 44

Daley, Richard, mayor of Chicago, 14
Dalton, Marie (interview), Standards System, 140, 141
Dean, Lois, study, dual allegiance, 249
Debs, Phyllis, forelady, attitude toward workers, 91
DeCamp, Harold, foreman (interview), union endorsement, 178; (quoted), attitude toward foremen, 92
*Democratic Unionism* (quoted), 38
Derber, Milton, study, East St. Louis, 46
Dietz, Andy (interview), attitude toward working conditions, 113, 114; suggestion system, 116, 117
Disallegiance, company. *See* Company disallegiance
District One (UPWA), and Local 28, 16–18; and Communism, 36, 37; and 1956 strike, 229
Dodge, Clarence (quoted), union allegiance, 174
Donelson, Alan G. (quoted), attitude toward foremen, 88, 89
Drucker, Peter F., 98
Dual allegiance, 7, 59, 175, 261, 262; and strikes, 221–247 *passim;* and 1956 strike, 229–238; patterns, 248–260; studies of, 248–252; and politics, 252; and sex and race variable, 255; and union leaders, 256, 257; and stewards, 257; and foremen, 257, 258; in three plant comparison of, 253–260. *See also* Company allegiance, Union allegiance
Dual behavior, 7
Dudley, Herman (interview), advancement, 120, 121
Duro, Roger, union leader (quoted), 77

East St. Louis foremen, 16, 86, 87; company allegiance, 78, 79; attitude toward workers, 91–97; attitude toward wages, 108; attitude toward working conditions, 113; attitude toward suggestion system, 116, 118; attitude toward advancement, 124; and Standards System, 152; attitude toward children following, 160; union endorsement, 177, 178; attitude toward union, 177, 178; attitude toward union leaders, 190–193 *passim;* attitude toward UPWA, 194; attitude toward stewards, 204, 205
*East St. Louis Journal,* 46
East St. Louis Local 78. *See* Local 78
East St. Louis stock yards, 12
East St. Louis, description of, 43–47; interracial relations, 47, 48; comparison with Chicago and Kansas City, 48; neighborhoods, 43–47
East St. Louis plant, 3, 5; characteristics of, 15; struggle to unionize, 23, 24; and Negroes, 127–131; and racial proportion, 128; segregation at, 128, 129; and 1959 strike, 243
East St. Louis Negro worker, 127–131; and equal opportunity, 126, 128; company allegiance, 129; children following, 154, 155; and attitude toward UPWA, 197, 198
East St. Louis Workers, anxiety about jobs, 47; characteristics, 49–55; geographic origin, 51; turnover, 52, 53; absenteeism, 53; wage assignments, 53; company allegiance, 62–65, 70, 79; workers who quit, 72–74; attitude toward foremen, 81–89; attitude toward jobs, 98, 99, 162, 163; attitude toward gang, 103, 104; attitude toward wages, 107–110; attitude toward working conditions, 112; attitude toward suggestion system, 116–118; attitude toward advancement, 120; and Standards System, 138, 139, 144; relation between output and attitudes, 146–148; attitude toward children following, 154–156; attitude toward union, 168, 169; union allegiance, 169, 170, 174, 183,

215–217; and Employee Representation Plan, 180, 181; attitude toward union shop, 168, 182; attitude toward union leaders, 168, 186, 190, 200–203; attitude toward UPWA, 194, 195; attitude toward grievance procedure, 200–204, 205, 209; attitude toward stewards, 201–204, 205; union participation, 211–215; attitude toward strikes, 222–224; and 1956 strike, 237, 238; dual allegiance, 254–260
Education, factor in advancement, 120, 121; workers' attitude toward children following, 160, 161, 162
Education variable, in Chicago, Kansas City, and East St. Louis, 49, 50
Edwards, John (interview), on children following, 157, 158
Elstad, Frank (interview), attitude toward gang, 105
Employee clubs, 12
Employee merit ratings, 94–97
Employees' Protective Association. *See* Swift Employees' Association
Employee Representation Plan, 19; workers' attitude toward, 168, 180, 181; foremen's attitude toward, 178; history, 179–181; and NBPW, 180
Evans, Merle (quoted), attitude toward foreman, 96
*Evening Journal,* East St. Louis, 46
Ewing, Ruth (interview), union allegiance, 172

FEPC legislation, in Missouri and Kansas, 43
Factory workers, study of, 249
Fale, Frank (interview), strikes, 224
Fair Labor Standards Act, 19, 20
Fechner, Frank (interview), advancement, 121; children following, 155
Fellow workers. *See* Gang
Flack, Norman, foreman (interview), attitude toward advancement, 125, 126
*Flash,* Local 28's weekly newsheet, 14; (quoted), 17, 18; Standards System criticized, 139
Foreman, Leroy, Negro (interview), attitude toward UPWA, 197, 198
Foremen, company allegiance, 78, 79; attitude of workers toward, 81–89; background, 86; attitude of union leaders toward, 89, 90; attitude toward employees, 90–97; attitude toward negroes, 92–94; attitude toward Mexicans, 92–93; attitude toward jobs, 102, 103; attitude toward wages, 108; attitude toward working conditions, 113; rating of workers, 94–97; attitude toward suggestion system, 116, 118; attitude toward advancement, 122–126; Negro, 127, 134; attitude toward standards systems, 148, 150–152; and Standards System, 146, 147; attitude toward children following, 160, 161; comparison of attitudes in three plants, 163, 164; attitude toward union, 176–179, union endorsement, 176–179, 184, 204; attitude toward union leaders, 190–193; attitude toward UPWA, 194, 198; attitude toward grievance procedure, 201; attitude toward stewards, 204, 205; and dual allegiance, 257, 258. *See also* Attitude of foremen
Foster, Alta (interview), company allegiance, 68
Frigo, Jack, foreman (quoted), attitude toward workman, 91
Fur and Leather, division of AMC, 33, 34

Gang, workers' attitude toward, 61, 98, 103–106
Gantt Group, 17, 18, 229, 231, 247, 259
Gantt, Ralph, and secession movement in Local 28, 16–18, 259; and 1956 strike, 231, 232
Germans, in Kansas City, 41; in East St. Louis, 44
Giles, Steve, foreman, attitude toward union leaders, 192, 193
Gleffe, Herman (interview), company allegiance, 64
Godow, Henry, foreman (quoted), attitude toward worker, 91
Gold, Ben, 33
Gomez, Juan (interview), equal opportunities, 135, 136; union allegiance, 172
Goose Hill, 5
Gorman, Patrick E., secretary-treasurer of Amalgamated, 30, 34, 212; and House Un-American Activities Committee, 39, 40
Greeks in Kansas City, 42; in St. Louis, 44
Grelle, Ed., foreman (quoted), attitude toward foremen, 92
Grievances, comparative statistics, 206–208; percentage of cases settled in three plants, 208, 259
Grievance procedure, workers' attitude toward, 168, 200–209; union leaders' attitude toward, 201; attitude of stewards toward, 201; attitude of foremen, 201
Guadalupe Hill, Mexicans in, 42
Guzik, Bertha (quoted), suggestion system, 115

Haines, Clem (interview), attitude toward working conditions, 112, 113

# INDEX

Halliday, Pearl (quoted), attitude toward wages, 108; on union allegiance (interview), 171
Halusek, Andy, foreman, union endorsement (interview), 178, 179
Hamen, Joe, foreman (interview), attitude toward advancement, 124
Hanniford, Basil (quoted), on children following, 158
Harris, Della, union leader (quoted), 1956 strike, 233
Harris, Dolly (interview), strikes, 225
Harrison, George M., president Brotherhood of Railway Clerks, and Communism, 37, 40
Harrison, Roland (quoted), suggestion system, 115; (interview), attitude toward UPWA, 194, 195; strikes, 224, 225
Harwood, Charles (interview), company allegiance, 64; (quoted), suggestion system, 117
Hassett, Edward (quoted), attitude toward foreman, 90
Hawthorne plant, Chicago, study of, 251, 252
Hayes, Charles, director District One, 37
Heid, John, foreman (quoted), attitude toward workman, 91, 92
Helinski, Andy, foreman (quoted), attitude toward worker, 91; (interview), standards system, 151, 152
Helstein, Ralph, UPWA president, and Local 28, 17, 30; (quoted) 32, 34; views on merger breakup, 35; and Communism, 36, 37; letter to House Un-American Activities Committee, 38; and 1959 strike, 242, 245.
Hetzel, Joe (interview), company allegiance, 63; Standards System, 143
Hoffa, James, 39
Holmquist, Roger (interview), attitude toward foremen, 84, 85
Hook, Marvin, vice-president, AMC & BW, 212
Hormel, George A., and Company, and 1959 strike, 240
Housing, 48
House Un-American Activities Committee, investigates UPWA, 32, 36–39
Hubert, Tom, Local 78 leader (quoted), 22
Hunter Packing Company, 44
Hygrade Company, 4; and 1959 strike, 240

Illinois, University of, study of East St. Louis industrial climate, 46
Independent Brotherhood of Packinghouse Workers, 20; at East St. Louis, 23, 24
Independent Packinghouse Workers' Union, 20
Industrial relations case studies, 3

International Brotherhood of Swift Employees, 20
Interviewer, differences, 3; dual role, 7, 8; influence on interview, 8, 9, 126
Interviews, by author, 5, 6; influences affecting, 8, 9; criteria for judging, 9, 10
Irish in Kansas City, 41
Italians in Kansas City, 42; in East St. Louis, 44

Jackson, Porter (interview), attitude toward foremen, 88; (quoted), Standards System, 141, 142; on children following, 158
Jacobsen, Eugene, study, dual allegiance, 252
Japanese workers, study of, 249
Jefferson, Leroy (interview), pride of work, 101; attitude toward gang, 106
"Jester," Negro as, 131, 132
Jimerson, president of AMC, 212
Job, workers' attitude toward, 60, 61, 98–118, 162–164, 169; sex, race, and service variable, 99. See also Satisfaction, Pride of work
Johnson, Ronnie (interview), company allegiance, 69
Johnson, John, Negro (quoted), attitude toward UPWA, 198
Joint Unity Committee, 35
Jurkanin, John, president of Amalgamated Local 500, 31

Kahn and Tannenbaum, study, dual allegiance, 250, 251
Kahn, Robert (quoted), dual allegiance, 221
Kansas City, Greater, description, 41–43; interracial relations, 42, 47, 48; comparison with Chicago and East St. Louis, 48; neighborhoods, 41–43
Kansas City foremen, 86, company allegiance, 78, 79; attitude toward workers, 91–97; attitude toward wages, 108; attitude toward working conditions, 113; attitude toward suggestion system, 116, 118; attitude toward advancement, 124, 125; and Standards System, 150; union endorsement, 177, 178; attitude toward union, 177, 178; attitude toward union leaders, 190–193; attitude toward UPWA, 194; attitude toward stewards, 205
Kansas City Local 12. See Local 12
Kansas City Negro worker, 127, 129; and equal opportunity, 126; and children following, 154, 155, 158, 159; and attitude toward UPWA, 196, 198
Kansas City plant, 3, 5; history and description, 11, 12; characteristics of, 15, 16; and Negroes, 127; racial proportions, 127; Mexican workers in, 135, 136

## INDEX

Kansas City Workers, characteristics, 49–55; geographic origin, 51; turnover, 52, 53; absenteeism, 53; company allegiance, 62, 65–70; company disallegiance, 70, 71, 162; attitude toward job, 99, 163; attitude toward gang, 103, 104; attitude toward wages, 107–110; attitude toward working conditions, 112; attitude toward suggestion system, 116, 118; attitude toward advancement, 120; and Standards System, 138, 139, 143, 144; relation between output and attitudes, 146–148; attitude toward children following, 154–158; attitude toward union, 168, 169; union allegiance, 169, 170, 183, 215–217; and Employee Representation Plan, 180, 181; attitude toward union shop, 168, 182, 183; attitude toward union leaders, 168, 186, 190, 200–203; attitude toward UPWA, 10, 195, 196, 225; attitude toward grievance procedure, 200–203, 205, 209; attitude toward stewards, 201–205; union participation, 211–215; attitude toward strikes, 222, 225; dual allegiance, 254–260

Kasten, George (interview), attitude toward gang, 105; grievance procedure, 204

Katz, Daniel, study, dual allegiance, 250

Keane, Patrick, foreman (quoted), attitude toward worker, 91

Kiley, Ray, foreman (quoted), Negroes, 131

Kinnanon, Keith, foreman (quoted), attitude toward workers, 91

Kinsy, William, foreman (interview), union endorsement, 179

Kirkland, Paul, union leader (interview), Standards System, 149, 150

Kleine, Tony, president Local 78, 25

Klir, Jane (interview), Standards System, 144, 145

Korbet, Niles (quoted), attitude toward job, 100

Kornhauser, Arthur, et al., study, dual allegiance, 252

Kowalski, Evelyn (quoted), attitude toward job, 100

Kurowsky, Ted, union leader (interview), 1956 strike, 233, 234

Landez, Charles (interview), union allegiance, 173

Land, Jack (interview), union allegiance, 176

Lang, William (interview), attitude toward foremen, 85, 86

LaPoint, John, study, dual allegiance, 251

Larson, Anna (interview), company allegiance, 68; (quoted), on children following, 159, 161

Letto, Frank, foreman (quoted), attitude toward stewards, 205

Leydon, Thomas (quoted), suggestion system, 117; (interview), on children following, 157; attitude toward UPWA, 195

Lewis, John L., and communists, 35

Lighty, Virgil (interview), strikes, 224

Lithuanians in Kansas City, 42, 43; in East St. Louis, 44

Lloyd, T. J., president of Amalgamated, and House Un-American Activities Committee, 39, 40; and 1959 strike, 242, 245

Local 12 (NBPW), Independent, Kansas City, 4; history of, 19–22, raids by UPWA, 21, 22, 193, 259; membership, 22, 211; and Standards System, 139; attitude of workers toward Local 12, 168–170; attitude of foremen toward, 177, 178; and union shop, 183; attitude toward UPWA, 193, 198; workers' participation, 211–215; and 1959 strike, 246; and 1956 strike, 186

Local 12, leaders, 20; company allegiance, 74, 75, 77, 78; attitude toward working conditions, 113; attitude toward advancement, 122, and race relations, 127, 128; and Standards System, 149, 150; and children following, 159; workers' attitude toward, 168, 183, 186, 188, 190, 199, 200–203; attitude of foreman toward, 190–193 *passim;* attitude toward UPWA, 194; and 1956 strike, 228

Local 12, stewards; attitude of workers toward, 201–204; attitude toward foremen, 204, 205

Local 28 (UPWA), 4; attitude of workers toward; and Chicago cutback, 14; history, 16–19; secession movement, 16–19, 213; membership, 18, 211; aggressiveness and turnover, 53; race relations, 127, 128; and Standards System, 139; attitude of workers toward Local 28, 168–170; race variable and attitude toward, 175; workers' participation, 210–215; and 1956 strike, 189, 229–237; and 1959 strike, 189, 246, 247; second 1946 strike, 29; second 1948 strike, 29

Local 28 (UPWA) leaders, company allegiance, 74, 78; attitude toward Standards System, 149, 150; attitude toward children following, 160; workers' attitude toward, 186, 189, 190, 199; attitude of foremen toward, 190, 193; 1956 strike, and dual allegiance, 229–236

Local 28, stewards; attitude of workers toward, 200, 206

Local 78, Amalgamated Meat Cutters, East St. Louis, 4, 12; history, 22–25; mem-

bership, 25, 211; effect on company allegiance, 64, 65; race relations, 128; and standards system, 139; attitude of workers toward Local 78, 168–170; attitude of foremen toward, 177, 178; attitude toward UPWA, 193, 198; workers' participation, 211–215; strikes, 222; and 1956 strike, 237, 238; and 1959 strike, 246
Local 78, leaders, 12; company allegiance, 74, 77, 78; attitude of gang toward, 104; attitude toward working conditions, 113, 114; attitude toward suggestion system, 116–118; attitude toward Standards System, 149, 150; attitude toward children following, 159, 160; attitude of workers toward, 183, 186–188, 190, 199, 200–203; attitude toward union shop, 183; and union shop, 183; attitude of foremen toward, 190–193 passim; attitude toward UPWA, 194; and 1956 strike, 237, 238
Local 78, stewards; attitude of workers toward, 201–204; organization, 203; attitude toward foremen, 204, 205
Locals, comparison of, 25–29; characteristics of, 27, 28
Lopez, Fernando (quoted), equal opportunities, 136
*Local 78 News* (quoted), grievances, 205
Love, Art, Negro (interview), 129–131
Ludwig, Ross, foreman (interview), attitude toward union leaders, 191

McCarthy, George (quoted), on children following, 158
McComb, George (interview), company allegiance, 75, 76; (quoted), attitude toward foreman, 89, 90
Machinists' Union, study of, 252
Management, relations with union. *See* Union-management relations
Manzanilla, Juan (quoted), on children following, 156
March, Herb, 36
Martin, Charles (quoted), attitude toward job, 100; grievance procedure, 204
Martin, Mary (quoted), attitude toward UPWA, 195
Mayer, Albert J. et al., study, dual allegiance, 252
Mayer, Oscar, company, 4; and 1959 strike, 240
Mazey, Emil, 36
Mazey Report on Communism, 36
Meany, George, 33, 40; and Communism, 37
Meat packing division (AMC & BW), 34
Mendozo, Juanita, union leader (quoted), on children following, 159

Merger, attempts at, 29–35, 37, 259, 260
Merit ratings. *See* Employee merit ratings
Methodology, 3–5
Mexicans in Kansas City, 42
Mexican workers, and company allegiance, 66; company disallegiance, 71; discrimination against, 72; foremen attitude toward, 92, 93; attitude toward opportunities, 135, 136; attitude toward children following, 158
Miller, Glenn W., and Young, study, dual allegiance, 250; and Rosen study, dual allegiance, 250
Miller, Myrtle (interview), attitude toward wages, 108; (quoted), attitude toward children following, 156
Minority groups, attitude of foremen toward, 92–94
Monotony, workers' comments on, 100
Montgomery plant, 24
Monsanto Chemical Company, 45
Monsanto, Illinois, 45
Moore, Hall (interview), company allegiance, 63
Moore, Warren (interview), grievance procedure, 202
Moore, Sally (interview), strikes, 223
Morale, 12, 13
Moriarity, Hugh, foreman (quoted), attitude toward Negroes, 93, 94
Morrell & Company, 4, 44; and 1959 strike, 240
Morris, Nelson, and Company, 12
Motorola plant, Chicago, 252
Moulder, Morgan, U.S. congressman, and Communism in unions, 39
Murray, Philip, and Communism, 36

Nagler, Otto (quoted), 71
Nashville plant, 24
National Association for the Advancement of Colored People in Greater Kansas City, 42
National Brotherhood of Packinghouse Workers, representation in industry, 4; formation of, 20; failure to organize East St. Louis plant, 23; wins St. Louis plant, 24; characteristics of, 28; and Employee Representation Plan, 180; and 1956 strike, 228; and 1959 strike, 240, 242, 244
National City, Illinois, description of, 44
National Labor Relations Board, 20–23 *passim*, 29, 251
"National Retail and Packinghouse Committee to Save the Merger," 31
National Stockyards, 12, 43, 44, 47; Negro workers, 51
National Stockyards foremen and standards system, 150

Neace, Curtin (quoted), attitude toward gang, 105, 106; (interview), and children following, 155, 156; and union shop, 182; and union leaders, 187
Negroes, in Kansas City, 42, 43, 48, 49, 55; in East St. Louis, 44, 47–49, 55; in Chicago, 48, 49, 54, 55
Negroes. *See also* Bronzeville
Negro Union leaders. *See* Union leaders, Negro
Negro worker, and AFL, 19; in UPWA, 35; characteristics, 48–51, geographic origin, 51, education, 51, absenteeism, 53, company allegiance, 62, 66, 69 *passim,* 129; company disallegiance, 72; foremen attitude toward, 92–94; attitude toward job, 99; attitude toward working conditions, 112, 113; attitude toward advancement, 120, 121, 125; attitude toward equal opportunity, 126, 133–136, 260; discrimination against, 127, 128; status in Swift plants, 126–128; and supervisory positions, 129; Southern-born, 129; in "Jester" role, 131, 132; and standards system, 145; attitude toward children following, 154–158; comparison of attitude in three plants, 163, 164; attitude toward union leaders, 188; and dual allegiance, 255, 256; and service variable, 120. *See also* Race variable
Negro workers, female; education pattern, 48–50; attitude toward wages, 107–110; in Kansas City plant, 127, 129; in East St. Louis plant, 127–129; company allegiance, 129
Negro worker, male; education pattern, 48–51, 65; attitude toward wages, 107, 109, 110; in East St. Louis plant, 127, 128
Neighborhoods, effect on workers' attitude and behavior, 41–55; Negro, 41, 47

O'Brien, Jack, union leader (interview), 1956 strike, 232
Odaka, Kunio, study, dual allegiance, 249
Oliver, Marvin, Negro (quoted), attitude toward job, 100; (interview), race relations, 133–135; union allegiance, 176
Osborne, Mike, union leader (quoted), 1956 strike, 233
Output, relation to attitudes, 145–148

*Packinghouse Worker* (UPWA), 37 (quoted), 30, 33
Packinghouse Workers Organizing Committee, 19; and Communists, 35
Paone, Francis X., study, dual allegiance, 251
Participation behavior. *See* Union participation
Pay. *See* Wages

Poles in Kansas City, 41, 43; in East St. Louis, 44
Portland plant, 24
Powderly, John, president, Local 78, 23; (quoted), 25, 149
Pride of work, 100–102, 162, 260, 262. *See Also* Skills
Public Advisory Review Commission, 40

Race issue, views of UPWA and Amalgamated on, 32, 33; and attitude of Negroes toward UPWA, 196, 198. *See also* Attitude of foremen toward Negroes
Race relations in Greater Kansas City, 42, 47, 48; in East St. Louis, 47, 48; in Chicago, 47, 48; at Swift, 126–128, 259
Races, segregation of. *See* Segregation
Race variable, in Chicago, East St. Louis, and Kansas City, 48–51; effect on company allegiance, 67, 69; attitude toward foremen, 88; factor in foremen's merit ratings, 95; and attitude toward job, 99; and attitude toward wages, 107–110 *passim;* and attitude toward working conditions, 112, 113; and Standards System, 145; and children following, 154; and union allegiance, 174, 175; and union leaders, 190, 198; and union participation, 211, 212; and dual allegiance, 255. *See also* Negro worker, White worker
Ranson, Mary (interview), attitude toward UPWA, 195
Rath Company, and 1959 strike, 240
"Real Unity Committee," 16; and secession movement in Local 28, 16–19, 211, 213
Reeves, Jack (interview), attitude toward union leaders, 188, 189
Renault, Charles (interview), opinions on foremen, 82–83; (quoted), Employee Representation Plan, 181; (interview), strikes, 223; dual allegiance, 256
Research, 3; methods of, 5–10
Responsibility, foremen, sense of, 102, 103
Reece, Jim, foreman (interview), attitude toward advancement, 124, 125; attitude toward union leader, 192
Retail Clerks' International Association, 31
Reuther, Walter, and Communism, 36, 37, 40
Richardson, Martha (interview), attitude toward UPWA, 196
Riegel, John W., study, dual allegiance, 251
Riley, Walter (interview), pride of work, 101
Ritchie, Kile, foreman (quoted), 79; attitude toward workers, 92; (interview), rating workers, 95, 96; attitude toward union leaders, 191; (quoted), attitude toward stewards, 205

## INDEX

Roe, Dick (interview), union leaders, 186, 187
Roehe, Otto, foreman (quoted), attitude toward Negroes, 93
Ronson, May, attitude toward foreman, 87–88
Rose, Arnold, study, dual allegiance, 250
Rosen, Hjalmar and R. A. Hudson Rozen, study, dual allegiance, 252
Rosen, Ned and Miller, study, dual allegiance, 250
Rose, Tom, union leader (quoted), 1956 strike, 230
Rosedale, Mexicans in, 42
Rudolph, Joseph, steward (interview), attitude toward foremen, 205
Russians in Kansas City, 42

*St. Louis American,* 47
*St. Louis Argus,* 47
St. Louis Teamsters' Local, 688. *See* Teamsters' Local 688
Sandburg, George (quoted), 77
San Francisco plant, 24
Saposs, David (quoted), 36
Satisfaction with job, 60, 93, 98–103, 118, 152, 159, 164, 208, 237, 238, 260; with fellow workers, 103–106; with wages, 107–110; with working conditions, 111–114; with suggestion system, 114–118; and company related attitudes, 139; and Negro workers, 136, 198, 255; with Standards System, 147, 148, 419; interplant comparison, 162–164; with union, 170, 175, 178, 198, 199, 217, 260; with grievance procedure, 200, 201, 209; and dual allegiance, 255
Security League, 19
Segregation, in Greater Kansas City, 42; in Swift, 126–128
Seidman group study, 161; dual allegiance, 249, 250
Serbs in Kansas City, 42
Service variable, in Chicago, St. Louis, and Kansas City, 48–51; affecting company allegiance, 67, 70; factor in foremen's merit ratings, 95; and attitude toward job, 99; and attitude toward gang, 104; and attitude toward wages, 107; and attitude toward working conditions, 112; and attitude toward advancement, 120, 121; Negroes and company allegiance, 129; and Standards System, 145; and children following, 154; and union allegiance, 174, 175; and union leaders, 189, 190; and union participation, 211, 212; strikes, 223, 224
Sex variable, in Chicago, Kansas City, and St. Louis, 47–51; effect on company allegiance, 67; and attitude toward foremen, 87–89; factor in foremen's merit ratings, 95; and attitude toward job, 99; and attitude toward gang, 104, 105; and attitude toward wages, 107, 108; and attitude toward working conditions, 112; and standards system, 144, 145; and children following, 154; and union allegiance, 174, 175, 190; and union leaders, 189, 190; and union participation, 211, 212; and dual allegiance, 255. *See also* Negro workers, female; Workers, female; Workers, male
Sheppard, Harold L., et al., study, dual allegiance, 252
Skills, comparison, variables, affecting, 50, 51; and pride of work, 100, 101
Slavs in Kansas City, 41, 43
Slovenians in Kansas City, 42, 43
Soderstrom, Reuben, 37
"South End," 47
Spilker, Charles, manager of East St. Louis Chamber of Commerce (quoted), 46
Spreckels, Myra (interview), company allegiance, 68
Stagner, Ross, University of Illinois study, dual allegiance, 248, 249
Standards Dept., Negroes in, 128
Standard of living, workers' conception of, 107
Standards System (Swift's wage-incentive system), 71; cause of dissension, 104, 106; and attitude toward wages, 108, 109; attitude of workers toward, 137–148; attitude of union leaders, 149, 150; attitude of foremen toward, 150–152; workers' understanding and trust, 137, 138, 139, 145–152 *passim,* 260; individual vs. group application, 146–148; and unions, 139; and workers' satisfaction, 139; history of installation, 139; administration of, 140; factors affecting workers' attitude toward, 146–148
*The Star,* Kansas City (quoted), 10
Steelworkers, study of, 249
Stephens, A. T., 32; and Communism, 36, 37, 40
Stereotyping, 131, 132
Stewards, workers attitude toward, 168, 185, 200; Negro, 122, 128; attitude toward union leaders, 189; attitude toward grievance procedure, 201; attitude toward foremen, 204, 205; union participation, 213; and dual allegiance, 257, 259; and Standards System, 150
Stillman, Theodore (interview), company allegiance, 75–77
Strauss, Fred, union leader (quoted), 1956 strike, 231

## INDEX

Strawberry Hill, 5, 43
Strikes, workers' attitude toward, 168, 221–225, 246; and union allegiance, 169, 170; and attitude of workers toward union, 194; and dual allegiance, 221–247 passim, and service variable, 223, 224
Strike of 1921, 19
Strike of 1946, 20, 29
Strike of 1948, 7, 21, 24, 29, 169, 189, 222
Strike of 1956, 18, 186, 221, 222, 225, 229; issues, 226–228; and Local 28, 29, 229–237; and dual allegiance, 229–238
Strike of 1959, 29, 40, 189, 221, 222, 239–246; issues, 240–242
Studebaker workers, NLRB ruling on, 251
Studies, showing dual allegiance, 248–252
Suggestion system, 98, 99; attitude of workers toward, 114–118; attitude of foremen toward, 116–118
Supervision, workers' comments on, 100
Swedes in Kansas City, 41
Swift & Company for individual plant. See name of city, i.e. Chicago plant, etc.
Swift & Company, 3, 4; differences and similarities among plants, 15; court decision against, 19; and strike of 1956, 225–229, 236; and strike of 1959, 239–246
Swift Employees' Associations, 19, 23; at East St. Louis, 23, 24
Swift News, publicizes suggestions, 115

"T-test," 148
Taft-Hartley Act, 7, 10
Tagg, Richard, Swift negotiator (quoted), 1959 strike, 245
Tannenbaum and Kahn, study, dual allegiance, 250, 251
Teamsters, 39
Teamsters' Local 688, St. Louis, study of, 250
Tebbel, Jane (interview), attitude toward gang, 106
Thompson, Robert (interview), on children following, 158
"Trust," 137–139. See also "Understanding-trust"
Turnover, 51, 52, 55

UPWA. See United Packinghouse Workers
Un-American Activities Committee. See House Un-American Activities Committee
"Understanding-trust," 137–139, 145–152 passim
Union Allegiance, 167, 248, 259, 246; relationship of union attitudes and, 168–217 passim; and Local 12, and Local 78, and Local 28, 169, 184; of workers, 169–175, 215–217; variables affecting, 174, 175; of union leaders, 175, 176; and union shop, 181–184; and union participation, 210. See also, Dual allegiance
Union Endorsement of foremen, 176–179, 184
Union leaders, company allegiance, 74–78; attitude toward foremen, 89, 90; attitude toward working conditions, 113, 114; attitude toward suggestion system, 116, 117; attitude toward advancement, 122, 123; attitude toward Standards System, 149, 150; attitude toward children following, 159, 160; comparison of attitudes in three plants, 163, 164; attitude toward union, 175, 176, 217; attitude of workers toward, 168, 183, 185–190, 199, 222, 260; attitude toward union shop, 183; attitude toward union leaders, 189; attitude of stewards toward, 189; attitude of foremen toward, 190–193; attitude toward UPWA, 194, 198; attitude toward grievance procedure, 201; union participation, 213, dual allegiance, 257
Union leaders, left wing, 16, 17, 35, 36; company allegiance, 74, 75; attitude toward foremen, 89, 90; and Standards System, 149; and 1956 strike, 229–236 passim
Union leaders, Negro, attitude toward equal opportunity, 133–135
Union leaders, right wing, 16; company allegiance, 74; attitude toward foremen, 89; and 1956 strike, 229–236 passim
Union-management relations, 5
Union participation, 168, 169, 210–215, 260, 262; criteria, 210; and variables, 211, 212
Union shop, 18; workers' attitude toward, 168, 181–183; and 1956 strike, 226–228
Unions, history of, 11–40; attitude of worker toward, 168–217 passim; and seniority, 171, 172; and foremen, 172; and grievance, 172, 173; and wages, 172, 173; Employee Representation Plan and attitude toward, 180, 181; voting, 210–214; studies of, 248–252
United Auto Workers, studies of, 251, 252
United Packinghouse Workers, Executive Board, 17
United Packinghouse Workers (AFL-CIO), representation in industry, 4, 24; merger efforts, 4, 5, 29–35, 193, 198, 226, 245, 259, 260; attitude of workers toward, 7; and Chicago cutback, 13–15; and Armour, 14; and secession movement in Local 28, 6–8; raids on Local 12, 21, 22, 193, 259; strike of 1946, 20; strike of 1948, 21, 24; and East St. Louis, 23, 24; characteristics of, 28; cooperation during strike, 29, 30, 225, 226, 228, 242; and

## INDEX

House Un-American Activities Committee, 32, 35–40; differences with Amalgamated, 32, 34, 40; and Communism, 36–39; effect on company allegiance, 65, 66, 74, 75, 78, 79, 256; leaders' attitudes toward foremen, 89; and Negroes, 129; and Standards System, 139, 149; workers' attitude toward, 168; and union shop, 183; attitude of workers toward, 183–199, 260; attitude of union leaders toward, 194; attitude of foremen toward, 194; attitude of Negroes toward, 196–199; 1956 strike, 225–229; 1959 strike, 40, 240–246; 1948 strike, 169; and teamsters, 39
UPWA, 1950 Convention, Minneapolis, 36
UPWA, 1958 Convention, New York, 31, 32; and Communism, 36
UPWA Merger Committee (quoted), 31
Udell, Jim (quoted), attitude toward job, 100; suggestion system, 115
Urban League (Kansas City), 42

Valley District, 45
Variables, 3, 4; environmental, 47, 48; demographic, 49–55; affecting attitude toward job, 98, 99, 164; and union allegiance, 174, 175; and union participation, 211, 212
Variables. *See also* Age variable, Education variable, Race variable, Service variable, Sex variable
Voting, Union elections, 210–214

Wage and Hour Administration, 19
Wage Assignments, 51, 53, 54, 55
Wage-incentive system. *See* Standards System
Wages, attitude of workers toward, 61, 107–110; service variable and attitude toward, 107; sex variable and attitude toward, 107, 108; race variable and attitude toward, 107–110 *passim*
Wagner Act, 19, 29; and Employee Representation Plan, 180
Waller, James (interview), on children following, 156
Warren, Homer (quoted), strikes, 223
*Washington Post and Times Herald,* and House Un-American Activities Committee, 38, 39
Watertown plant, 24
Wells, Norma (interview), Standards System, 142, 143
Western Electric Engineers, study of, 250, 251
White, Ordway, union leader (interview), 1956 strike, 230

Wiggins, Larry, Negro (interview), 132; strikes, 225
Wilcox, Nora (interview), union allegiance, 173
Wilson and Company, 4, 11, 13, 20; and 1956 strike, 227; and 1959 strike, 240
Wolf, Kurt (interview), opinions of foremen, 84; (quoted), grievance procedure, 201
Women. *See* Workers, female; Negro workers, female
Woolley, Willie (quoted), dual allegiance, 172
Work, pride of. *See* Pride of work
Workers, personality structure of, 6; origins, 48, 51; differences in Chicago, East St. Louis and Kansas City, 49–55; comparative skills, 50; absenteeism, 53; wage assignments, 53, 54; company allegiance, 59–80; company disallegiance, 70–74; attitude toward foremen, 81–89; attitude of foremen toward, 90–97; attitude toward job, 60, 61, 98–118; attitude toward gang, 61, 98, 103–106; attitude toward children following, 60, 61, 99, 126, 153–164, 260; attitude toward standards, 60, 137–148; attitude toward equal opportunity, 60, 61; attitude toward suggestion system, 61, 98, 99, 114–118; and pride of work, 100–102; wages, 61, 107–110; conception of standard of living, 107; advancement, 60, 61, 119–136, 137; relation between output and attitudes, 145, 148; attitude toward white collar jobs, 161; ratings by foremen, 94–97; comparison of attitudes in three plants, 162–164, 215–217; participation behavior, 168, 169; attitude toward strikes, 168, 216, 221–225, 246, 260; attitude toward stewards, 168, 185, 200, 216; attitude toward grievances, 168, 200–209, 216; attitude toward union shop, 168, 216; attitude toward Employee Representation Plan, 168, 180, 181, 216, 217; attitude toward union, 168–217 *passim;* union allegiance of, 169–175, 184; attitude toward union leaders, 168, 183, 185–190, 216, 222; union participation, 210–215; attitude toward UPWA, 168, 193–199, 216; dual allegiance, 248–256
Workers, female, 49; company allegiance, 62, 67–70; attitude toward foremen, 87–89; attitude toward job, 99; attitude toward wages, 107–110; attitude toward working conditions, 112; and Standards System, 144, 145; attitude toward children following, 154, 156; attitude toward union, 169, 175; attitude toward union leaders, 190

# INDEX

Workers, male, 49; company allegiance, 62, 67; attitude toward wages, 107–110 *passim*

White workers, 48, 49; attitude toward advancement, 120–123, 125, 260; and attitude toward children following, 154; and attitude toward UPWA, 196, 198

Working conditions, workers' attitude toward, 60, 61, 98, 99, 111–114; definition, 111; foremen attitude toward, 113; union leaders' attitude toward, 113, 114

Young, James E., and Miller study, dual allegiance, 250